Breaching the Citadel

Breaching the Citadel

The India Papers I

Editors
URVASHI BUTALIA AND LAXMI MURTHY

ZUBAAN SERIES ON SEXUAL VIOLENCE AND IMPUNITY
IN SOUTH ASIA

International Development Research Centre
Centre de recherches pour le développement international

Zubaan
128 B Shahpur Jat, 1st floor
NEW DELHI 110 049
Email: contact@zubaanbooks.com
Website: www.zubaanbooks.com

First published by Zubaan 2018

This project was undertaken with financial support provided by the International Development Research Centre, Canada

10 9 8 7 6 5 4 3 2 1

ISBN 978-93-84757-78-6

Zubaan is an independent feminist publishing house based in New Delhi with a strong academic and general list. It was set up as an imprint of India's first feminist publishing house, Kali for Women, and carries forward Kali's tradition of publishing world quality books to high editorial and production standards. Zubaan means tongue, voice, language, speech in Hindustani. Zubaan publishes in the areas of the humanities, social sciences, as well as in fiction, general non-fiction, and books for children and young adults under its Young Zubaan imprint.

Printed and bound at Raj Press, R-3 Inderpuri, New Delhi 110 012

Contents

Zubaan Series on Sexual Violence and Impunity in South Asia

An Introduction

URVASHI BUTALIA, LAXMI MURTHY AND NAVSHARAN SINGH

The Sexual Violence and Impunity project (SVI) is a three-year research project, supported by the International Development Research Centre (IDRC), Canada, and coordinated by Zubaan. Led by a group of nine advisors from five countries (Bangladesh, India, Nepal, Pakistan, Sri Lanka), and supported by groups and individuals on the ground, the SVI project started with the objectives of developing and deepening understanding on sexual violence and impunity in South Asia through workshops, discussions, interviews and commissioned research papers on the prevalence of sexual violence, and the structures that provide impunity to perpetrators in all five countries.

The project began with some key questions and concerns. We noted that recent histories and contemporary political developments in South Asia had shown an exponential increase in sexual violence, particularly mass violence. And yet, even as such violence had increased across the region, so had the ever-deepening silence around it.

Why, for example, had the end of 25 years of violent conflict in Sri Lanka in May 2009 not resulted in an open and frank discussion about sexual violence as a weapon of war? Why had the International Crimes Tribunal (ICT) of Bangladesh, set up in 2009 to investigate and prosecute suspects for the genocide committed in 1971 by the Pakistan army and their local collaborators, paid such little attention to the question of mass rape, despite it being widely acknowledged that it had happened and many women having spoken out about it? Why did discussions on Kashmir in India or Swat in Pakistan, simply ignore the question of sexual violence? Why was caste violence, violence against sex workers and men and transgender persons barely spoken about?

Nor was silence the only issue here. Crucial to maintaining the silence was—and is—the active collusion of states in providing impunity to perpetrators, sometimes under the guise of protective laws and special powers to the armed forces, at others under the guise of nationalism. So heavily were the odds stacked against women that, until recently, very few had dared to speak out. Backed by culture, and strengthened by the state, and often with the active collusion of non-state actors, impunity then, remained largely unchallenged.

We asked ourselves if these conditions were specific to the South Asian region. Elsewhere in many parts of the world, we noted, rape was increasingly being discussed and accepted, not only as a weapon of war, but also as a crime against humanity and as an instrument of genocide. The 1998 Akeyesu judgment by the International Criminal Tribunal for Rwanda (ICTR) provided a clear definition of rape and delineated its elements as a crime against humanity and as an instrument of genocide. In the International Criminal Tribunal for the former Yugoslavia (ICTY) jurisprudence pioneered the approach that used acts of rape and other forms of sexual violence to include elements of other international crimes such as torture, enslavement, and persecution, which previously had not been litigated in the context of gender violence.

The Special Court for Sierra Leone (SCSL) brought into jurisprudence on violations of international humanitarian law a particular form of sexual violence prevalent in the conflict in Sierra Leone—forced marriages. In this case, forced marriage was distinguished from sexual slavery or sexual crimes and argued as a crime against humanity. Building on the progressive development of the case law for sexual and gender-based violence under ICTR, ICTY and SCSL, the Rome Statute of the International Criminal Court (ICC) includes rape and forms of sexual violence as part of the crimes of genocide, crimes against humanity, and war crimes, and specifically enumerates rape, forced prostitution, sexual slavery, forced pregnancy, enforced sterilization and prosecution on account of gender as specific crimes punishable under the statute.

The progressive thinking developed in the course of these trials brought sexual violence into the mainstream of international jurisprudence (something that was largely invisible until the 1990s) such that it became part of the collective knowledge to which women's movements worldwide have contributed enormously. In South Asia, a comprehensive and critical analysis of existing jurisprudence on sexual violence is a newly emerging area of scholarship, and a solid community of practice is still to emerge in this field. There are many dimensions of sexual violence—ranging from conceptual clarity on definitions of sexual violence, to legal, medical and forensic understandings of evidence gathering and monitoring and more—that remain inadequately explored.

South Asia has much to learn from advancements elsewhere. How do our countries expect a 'return' to peace (and we need to question the composition of such a peace) without addressing the question of the large-scale and calculated attack by perpetrators on women and the systematic violation of their right to bodily integrity and autonomy? How can this question be addressed without including rape and sexual violation squarely within definitions of crimes against humanity? What are the glaring silences of our domestic laws and policies? What do they have to say about the endemic sexual violence and rape driven by caste, ethnicity and religion? How can we think creatively about questions of reparation beyond the ways states in the region have done by ghettoizing women in rehabilitation camps where they remain stigmatized and marked as raped women, to be separated from others, as we saw in India following the partition of 1947 and post-1971 relief measures in Bangladesh?

As feminist activists and academics we were—and continue to be—concerned about the growing violence and the serious and continuing lack of accountability on the part of states and governments, the failure to address the impunity enjoyed by perpetrators, the absence of effective mechanisms to provide justice and reparations, and the virtual indifference to the psychological damage suffered by victims, survivors and their families and communities. We feel that our collective inability and unwillingness to address the profound impact of such violence is a serious impediment to peace and justice in our region.

Our discussions began in January 2012, when a group of women from South Asia came together in a meeting facilitated by a small IDRC grant, to begin the process of thinking about these issues. We were concerned not only at the legal silences around the question of sexual violence and impunity, but also at how deeply the 'normalization' of sexual violence and the acceptance of impunity, had taken root in our societies.

It became clear to us that women's movements across South Asia had made important contributions in bringing the issue of sexual violence and impunity to public attention. And yet, there were significant knowledge gaps, as we have pointed out earlier. However, an absence of adequate literature on the subject did not mean that there was nothing available. South Asia has a rich literary and scholarly tradition and indeed there is a fair amount of writing on sexual violence, and while impunity is not necessarily directly addressed in these writings, concern about it is implicit in most of them. We felt it was important to systematically understand the nature of impunity, and what legal, social and cultural norms states draw upon to enable and allow impunity for the perpetrators and to silence the demands for accountability. We thought, too, that it was important to document the lesser known ways in which women, and sometimes communities, create structures to deal with the trauma and dislocation caused by sexual violence. These stories had remained largely unknown. In much of caste violence in India for example, or in cases of feudal or tribal instances of retribution and punishment, the violation of women's bodies is an accepted way of establishing male superiority. And because these hierarchies of caste and tribe are so embedded even in the 'minds' of our secular, modern states, the victims/survivors often find solutions of their own, creating ways of ensuring some sense of justice.

It was out of these concerns that the SVI project grew. Over a period of time, we contacted scholars and researchers, conducted research, held several country meetings and a series of methodology workshops and, step by step, the project brought together a community of young researchers (we had consciously planned to stay away from established and overstretched scholars), more than 85 per cent of whom are, we are proud to say, under the age of 40. Our workshops focused on unpeeling the layers of impunity for sexual violence, on writing skills, on questions of ethics in researching subjects as sensitive as sexual violence, on the nature of evidence, on working with states and more.

During the time that the project has been under way, the region has witnessed many changes—in the public domain, a changed public discourse, as well as legal reform as a result of feminist and human rights' activism. These critical moments found resonance in the ongoing research—and indeed many of our researchers were centrally involved in working for these changes—and pointed to directions for future work.

The gang-rape and subsequent death of a young student in Delhi in December 2012 culminated in mass public anger, and generated public debate and feminist interventions. The testimonies of feminist activists to the Justice Verma Committee, constituted to recommend amendments to the criminal law for sexual assault against women, were an outcome of decades of intense engagement of the women's movement in India. The occasion provided a moment of deep reflection on the questions which activists were already grappling with. It also led to serious questioning within the movement: why, for example, did caste rape, or rape by the army, not result in the same kind of outrage, the same explosion of anger as the incident of 16 December 2012 had done? In the open discussions with the Verma Committee, feminist activists' testimonies did not remain confined to amendments in the law but demonstrated a remarkable understanding as they presented the continuum of violence against women from home to communities to the frontiers of the nation states where women's safety and bodily integrity were threatened in the name of protection of the borders.

In a small but significant step towards challenging impunity, on 6 September 2015, an army court martial awarded life sentences to six of its personnel found guilty in the 'fake encounter' case of April 2010 when the army killed three youths in the Machil sector of Kupwara district of Indian-administered Kashmir on the grounds that they were foreign militants. Even though the accused were not tried in a civil court, and the appeal process is ongoing at the time of writing, this conviction is significant since this is the first time army personnel in Kashmir have been handed life-terms on these charges.

Over in Sri Lanka, a significant judgment was the Jaffna High Court sentencing, on 7 October 2015, of four soldiers to 25 years rigorous imprisonment, compensation and reimbursement of legal fees for the 2010 gang-rape of a woman at a resettlement camp in Viswamadhu, Kilinochchi. Assigning culpability and ensuring strict punishment of the security personnel involved has been possible only with the sustained intervention of activists.

Undoubtedly, accountability has been a fraught issue across South Asia, especially when it comes to war crimes. December 2012 saw vehement protests in Bangladesh by the right-wing Jamaat-e-Islami supporters and their student wing, Bangladesh Islami Chhatra Shibir, demanding the disbanding of the ICT of Bangladesh set up three years earlier to investigate and prosecute suspects for the genocide committed in 1971 during the Bangladesh Liberation War by the Pakistani Army and their local collaborators, Razakars, Al-Badr and Al-Shams. The vigorous counter protests, of those pressing for accountability and an end to impunity culminated in the 'Shahbag movement'—a popular student movement for justice for war time crimes. The gazette notification recognition, on 12 October 2015, recognizing 41 Birangonas (war heroines) as freedom fighters for their contribution in the country's Liberation War in 1971 has been more than 40 years in the coming, but an official recognition that can be viewed as reparation for the stigma and suffering these women were made to face in addition to the sexual violence perpetrated on them.

In Sri Lanka, still staggering under the history of ethnic conflict and the Eelam war that ended in 2009, the report of the Office of the High Commissioner for Human Rights (OHCHR) released in September 2015 concluded that there were reasonable grounds to believe that war crimes and/or crimes against humanity had been committed with regard to a variety of abuses, including sexual violence and other forms of torture; unlawful killings by all sides; forced recruitment of adults and recruitment of children as fighters by the LTTE and enforced disappearances. The report recommended several legal, justice and security sector reforms and the establishment of an ad hoc hybrid justice mechanism integrating international judges, prosecutors, lawyers and investigators. In a move demonstrating the political will of the new regime to redress wartime human rights violations, a consensus resolution co-sponsored by Sri Lanka was passed on 1 October 2015 by the UN Human Rights Council encouraging the Government of Sri Lanka to implement its recommendations.

Following the end of Nepal's 10-year insurgency in 2006, while the Truth and Reconciliation Commission (TRC) made rape a crime for which amnesty cannot be granted, the 35-day statute of limitations for reporting of rape makes it virtually impossible for wartime rapes to go to court. Additionally, the TRC gave effective amnesty to those alleged to have been responsible for gross human rights violations and gave broad powers of reconciliation to the itself, with the result that victims will be forced to give up their right to justice as part of the reconciliation process with the commission empowered to undertake mediation between victims and perpetrators even in the case of rape.

Over the three-year period since this project began, there have been amendments in the criminal law in India and the definition of sexual assault has expanded: we have gained considerable grounds in our understanding on impunity for sexual violence and consequently are better able to speak about it and to fight for justice. It is noteworthy that during the targeted violence in Muzzafarnagar in India in 2013, seven Muslim women who were brutally gang-raped and sexually assaulted by men belonging to the other communities, filed writ petitions for protecting their right to life under Article 21. In a landmark judgment in March 2014, recognizing the rehabilitation needs of the survivors of targeted mass rape, the Supreme Court of India ordered that a compensation of ₹500,000 each for rehabilitation be paid to the women by the state government.

The Occupy Baluwatar movement of December 2012 in Nepal which some see as the ripple effects of the Delhi protests against sexual violence and demands for justice, had sexual violence and impunity at its centre. One of the major outcomes of the movement was the 27 November 2015 amendment broadening the definition of rape, bringing same-sex rape and marital rape into the ambit of law.

In Pakistan too, small steps forward were taken in the shape of a parliamentary panel approval in February 2015 of amendments in the anti-rape laws, supporting DNA profiling as evidence during the investigation and a prohibition on character assassination of rape victims during the trial.

The eight volumes (one each on Bangladesh, Nepal, Pakistan and Sri Lanka, two on India, and two standalone books on impunity and on an incident of mass rape in Kunan Poshpora in Indian-administered Kashmir) that comprise this series, are one of the many outcomes of this project. The knowledge built on the subject through workshops, discussion fora, testimonies and, interviews is part of our collective repository and we are committed to making it available to be used by activists, students and scholars. Of the 50 papers that were commissioned, nearly all came in. Along the way, we tragically lost two of our co-travellers, our advisor, Sharmila Rege and our young Sri Lankan researcher, Priya Thangarajah. Both Sharmila and Priya had been central to this project, bringing their considerable knowledge, their activism, their commitment to the work in hand. True to the feminist spirit of collectivity, their friends and colleagues rallied round to complete the work they had begun.

It is our hope that these volumes will begin the process of opening up the question of sexual violence and impunity in South Asia. The essays in these volumes, as well as the two standalone volumes address many of the issues we have raised above, and yet, significant gaps remain. We have not been able to adequately address questions of sexual violence and caste, the question of male and transgender sexual violence, or violence on queer communities. We need to gather more evidence about sexual violence on sex workers, on agricultural workers, in urban workspaces and more. We can only say with some satisfaction that through this collective endeavour, through putting our heads together, a fairly solid beginning has been made, layers have started to be uncovered and speech is beginning to replace silence. This systematic effort has allowed us to give this critical issue the focused attention that it deserves.

Creating a community of researchers and activists, building a common understanding resting on a shared history but not guided by national interests of the countries can make a significant move towards peace building in a region fractured by political, religious and ethnic divides. This series of books and other resources are being launched with the hope they will inspire the next generation of scholars and activists to build on this knowledge, and broaden and deepen it to end impunity for sexual violence.

The Last Song

TEMSULA AO

It seemed the little girl was born to sing. Her mother often recalled that when she was a baby, she would carry her piggyback to community singing events on festival days. As soon as the singers took up a tune and gradually when their collective voices began to swell in volume and harmony, her daughter would twist herself this way and that and start singing her own version of the song, mostly consisting of loud shrieks and screams. Though amusing at first, her daughter's antics irritated the spectators and the singers as well, and often, she had to withdraw from the gathering in embarrassment. What the mother considered unreasonable behaviour in a child barely a year old, was actually the first indication of the singing genius she had given birth to.

When Apenyo, as the little girl was called, could walk and talk a little, her mother would take her to church on Sundays because she could not be left alone at home. On other days she was left in the care of her grandmother when the mother went to the fields; but on this day there was no one to take care of her as everyone had gone to church. When the congregation sang together Apenyo would also join, though her little screams were not quite audible because of the group singing. But whenever there was a special number, trouble would begin. Apenyo would try to sing along, much to the embarrassment of the mother. After two or three such mortifying Sunday outings, the mother stopped going to church altogether until Apenyo became older and learnt how to behave.

At home too, Apenyo never kept quiet; she hummed or made up silly songs to sing by herself, which annoyed her mother at times but most often made her become pensive. She was by now convinced that her daughter had inherited her love of singing from her father who had died so unexpectedly away from home. The father, whose name was Zhamben, was a gifted singer both of traditional folk songs as well as Christian hymns at church. Naga traditional songs consist of polyphonic notes and harmonizing is the dominant feature of such community singing. Perhaps because of his experience and expertise in folk songs, Zhamben picked up the new tunes of hymns quite easily and soon became the lead male voice in the church choir. He was a schoolteacher in the village and at the time of his death was undergoing a teacher-training course in a town in Assam. He was suddenly taken ill and by the time the news reached the village, he was already dead. When his relatives were preparing to go and visit him, his friends from the training school brought his dead body home. Apenyo was only nine months old then. From that time on, it was a lonely struggle for the mother, trying to cultivate a field and bring up a small child on her own. With occasional help from her in-laws and her own relatives, the widow called Libeni was slowly building a future for her daughter and herself. Many of the relatives told her to get married again so that she and little Apenyo would have a man to protect and look after them. But Libeni would not listen and when they repeatedly told her to think about it seriously, she asked them never to bring up the subject again. So mother and daughter lived alone and survived mainly on what was grown in the field.

At the village school Apenyo did well and became the star pupil. When she was old enough to help her mother in spreading the thread on the loom, she would sit nearby and watch her weave the colourful shawls, which would be sold to bring in additional income. Libeni had the reputation of being one of the best weavers in the village and her shawls were in great demand.

By and by Apenyo too learned the art from her mother and became an excellent weaver like her. In the meantime, her love for singing too was growing. People soon realized that not only did she love to sing but also that Apenyo had an exquisite singing voice. She was inducted into the church choir where she soon became the lead soprano. Every time the choir sang it was her voice that made even the commonest song sound heavenly. Along with her singing voice, her beauty also blossomed as Apenyo approached her eighteenth birthday. Her natural beauty seemed to be enhanced by her enchanting voice, which earned her the nickname of 'singing beauty' in the village. Libeni's joy knew no bounds. She was happy that all those years of loneliness and hardship were well rewarded by God through her beautiful and talented daughter.

One particular year, the villagers were in an especially expectant mood because there was a big event coming up in the village church in about six months: the dedication of the new church building. Every member of the church had contributed towards the building fund by donating in cash and kind and it had taken them nearly three years to complete the new structure of tin roof and wooden frames to replace the old one of bamboo and thatch. In every household the womenfolk were planning new clothes for the family, brand new shawls for the men and new skirts or *lungis* for the women. The whole village was being spruced up for the occasion as some eminent pastors from neighbouring villages were being invited for the dedication service. Pigs earmarked for the feast were given special food to fatten them up. The service was planned for the first week of December, which would ensure that harvesting of the fields would be over and the special celebration would not interfere with the normal Christmas celebrations of the church. The villagers began the preparations with great enthusiasm, often joking among themselves that this year they would have a double Christmas!

These were, however, troubled times for the Nagas. The Independence movement was gaining momentum by the day and even the remotest villages were getting involved, if not directly in terms of their members joining the underground army, then certainly by paying 'taxes' to the underground 'government'. This particular village was no different. They had been compelled to pay their dues every year, the amount calculated on the number of households in the village. Curiously enough, the collections would be made just before the Christmas holidays, perhaps because travel for the collections was easier through the winter forests or perhaps because they too wanted to celebrate Christmas! In any case, the villagers were prepared for the annual visit from their brethren of the forests and the transaction was carried out without a hitch.

But this year, it was not as simple as in previous years. A recent raid of an underground hideout yielded records of all such collections of the area and the government forces were determined to 'teach' all those villages the consequences of 'supporting' the rebel cause by paying the 'taxes'. Unknown to the villagers, a sinister plan was being hatched by the forces to demonstrate to the entire Naga people what happens when you 'betray' your own government. It was decided that the army would go to this particular village on the day when they were dedicating the new church building and arrest all the leaders for their 'crime' of paying taxes to the underground forces.

In the meanwhile, the villagers, caught up in the hectic activities prior to the appointed day, a Sunday, were happily busy in tidying up their own households, especially the ones where the guests would be lodged. The dedication Sunday dawned bright and cool, it was December after all, and every villager, attired in his or her best, assembled in front of the new church, which was on the same site as the old one. The villagers were undecided about what to do with the old one still standing near the new one. They had postponed any decision until after the dedication. That morning the choir was standing together in the front porch of the new church to lead the congregation in the singing before the formal inauguration, after which they would enter the new building. Apenyo, the lead singer, was standing in the middle of the front row, looking resplendent in her new lungi and shawl. She was going to perform solo on the occasion after the group song of the choir. As the pastor led the congregation in the invocatory prayer, a hush fell on the crowd as though in great expectation: the choir would sing their first number after the prayer. As the song the crowd was waiting to hear began, there was the sound of gunfire in the distance, it was an ominous sound which meant that the army would certainly disrupt the festivities. But the choir sang on unfazed, though uneasy shuffles could be heard from among the crowd. The pastor too began to look worried; he turned to a deacon and seemed to be consulting with him about something. Just as the singing subsided, another sound reverberated throughout the length and breadth of the village. A frightened Dobashi, with fear and trembling in his voice, was telling the people to stay where they were and not to attempt to run away or fight. There was a stunned silence and the congregation froze in their places, unable to believe that their dedication Sunday was going to be consecrated by the arrogant Indian army.

Very soon the approaching soldiers surrounded the crowd, and the pastor was commanded to come forward and identify himself along with the *gaonburas*. But before they could do anything, Apenyo burst into her solo number, and not to be outdone by the bravery and foolishness of this young girl, and not wishing to leave her thus exposed, the entire choir burst into song. The soldiers were incensed; it was an act of open defiance and proper retaliation had to be made. They pushed and shoved the pastor and the gaonburas, prodding them with the butts of their guns towards the waiting jeeps below the steps of the church. Some of the villagers tried to argue with the soldiers and they too were kicked and assaulted. There was a feeble attempt by the accompanying Dobashi to restore some semblance of order but no one was listening to him and the crowd, by now overcome by fear and anger, began to disperse in every direction. Some members of the choir left their singing and were seen trying to run away to safety. Only Apenyo stood her ground. She sang on, oblivious of the situation, as if an unseen presence was guiding her. Her mother, standing with the congregation, saw her daughter singing her heart out as if to withstand the might of the guns with her voice raised to God in heaven. She called out to her to stop but Apenyo did not seem to hear or see anything. In desperation, Libeni rushed forward to pull her daughter away but the leader of the army was quicker. He grabbed Apenyo by the hair and dragged her away from the crowd towards the old church building. All this while, the girl was heard singing the chorus of her song over and over again.

There was chaos everywhere. Villagers trying to flee the scene were either shot at or kicked and clubbed by the soldiers who seemed to be everywhere. The pastor and the gaonburas were tied up securely for transportation to army headquarters and whatever fate awaited them there. More people were seen running away desperately, some seeking security in the old church and some even entered the new one hoping that at least the house of God would offer them safety from the soldiers. Libeni was now frantic. Calling out her daughter's name loudly, she began to search for her in the direction where she was last seen being dragged away by the leader. When she came upon the scene at last, what she saw turned her stomach: the young captain was raping Apenyo while a few other soldiers were watching the act and seemed to be waiting for their turn. The mother, crazed by what she was witnessing, rushed forward with an animal-like growl as if to haul the man off her daughter's body but a soldier grabbed her and pinned her down on the ground. He too began to unzip his trousers and when Libeni realized what would follow next, she spat on the soldier's face and tried to twist herself free from his grasp. But this only further aroused him; he bashed her head on the ground several times, knocking her unconscious and raped her limp body, using the woman's new lungi afterwards, which he had flung aside, to wipe himself. The small band of soldiers then took their turn, even though by the time the fourth one mounted, the woman was already dead. Apenyo, though terribly bruised and dazed by what was happening to her, was still alive, though barely so. Some of the villagers who had entered the old church saw what happened to mother and daughter and after the soldiers were seen going out towards the village square, came out to help them. As they were trying to lift the limp bodies, the captain happened to look back and seeing that there were witnesses to their despicable act, turned to his soldiers and ordered them to open fire on the people who were now lifting up the bodies of the two women. Amid screams and yells the bodies were dropped as the helpless villagers once again tried to seek shelter inside the church.

Returning towards the scene of their recent orgy, the captain saw the grotesque figures of the two women, both dead. He shouted an order to his men to dump them on the porch of the old church. He then ordered them to take positions around the church and at his signal they emptied their guns into the building. The cries of the wounded and the dying inside the church proved that even the house of God could not provide them security and save them from the bullets of the crazed soldiers. In the distance too, similar atrocities were taking place. But the savagery was not over yet. Seeing that it would be a waste of time and bullets to kill off all the witnesses inside the church, the order was given to set it on fire. Yelling at the top of his voice, the captain now appeared to have gone mad. He snatched the box of matches from his adjutant and set to work. But his hands were shaking; he thought that he could still hear the tune the young girl was humming as he was ramming himself into her virgin body, while all throughout the girl's unseeing eyes were fixed on his face. He slumped down on the ground and the soldiers made as if to move away, but with renewed anger he once again gave the order and the old church soon burst into flames, reducing the dead and the dying to an unrecognizable black mass. The new church too, standing not so far from the old one, caught the blaze and was badly damaged. Elsewhere in the village, the granaries were the first to go up in flames. The wind carried burning chunks from these structures and scattered them amidst the clusters of houses, which too burnt to the ground.

By the time the marauding soldiers left the village with their prisoners, it was dark and, to compound their misery, it rained the whole night. It was impossible to ascertain how many men and women were missing apart from the pastor and the four gaonburas. Mercifully, the visiting pastors were left alone when it became known that they did not belong to this village. But they were ordered to leave immediately and threatened in no uncertain terms that if they carried the news of what had happened here, their own villages would suffer the same fate. The search for the still missing persons began only the next morning. They found out that among the missing persons were Apenyo and her mother. When a general tally was taken, it was discovered that many villagers sustained bullet wounds as well as injuries from severe beatings. Also, six members of the choir were not accounted for. An old woman whose house was quite close to the church site told the search party that she had seen some people running towards the old church.

When the villagers arrived at the burnt-out site of the old church building, their worst suspicions were confirmed. Among the rain-drenched ashes of the old church they found masses of human bones washed clean by the night's rain. And on what was once the porch of the old church, they found a separate mass and through a twist of fate, a piece of Apenyo's new shawl, still intact beneath the pile of charred bones. Mother and daughter lay together in that pile. The villagers gathered all the bones of the six choir members and put them in a common coffin but those of the mother and daughter, they put in a separate one. After a sombre and songless funeral service, the question arose about where to bury them. Though the whole village had embraced Christianity long ago, some of the old superstitions and traditions had not been totally abandoned. The deaths of these unfortunate people were considered to be from unnatural causes and according to tradition they could not be buried in the village graveyard, Christianity or no Christianity. Some younger ones protested, 'How can you say that? They were members of our church and sang in the choir.' The old ones countered this by saying, 'So what, we are still Nagas aren't we? And for us some things never change.' The debate went on for some time until a sort of compromise was reached: they would be buried just outside the boundary of the graveyard to show that their fellow villagers had not abandoned their remains to a remote forest site. But there was a stipulation: no headstones would be erected for them.

Today, these gravesites are two tiny grassy knolls on the perimeter of the village graveyard and if one is not familiar with the history of the village, particularly about what happened on that dreadful Sunday thirty odd years ago, one can easily miss these two mounds trying to stay above ground level. The earth may one day swallow them up or rip them open to reveal the charred bones. No one knows what will happen to these graves without headstones or even to those with elaborately decorated concrete structures inside the hallowed ground of the proper graveyard, housing masses of bones of those who died 'natural' deaths. But the story of what happened to the ones beneath the grassy knolls without the headstones, especially of the young girl whose last song died with her last breath, lived on in the souls of those who survived the darkest day of the village.

And what about the captain and his band of rapists who thought that they had burnt all the evidence of their crime? No one knows for sure. But the underground network, which seems able to ferret out the deadliest of secrets, especially about perpetrators of exceptional cruelty on innocent villagers, managed not only to piece together the events of that black Sunday, but also to ascertain the identity of the captain. After several years of often frustrated intelligence gathering, he was traced to a military hospital in a big city where he was being kept in a maximum-security cell of an insane asylum.

***

P.S. It is a cold night in December and in a remote village, an old storyteller is sitting by the hearth-fire with a group of students who have come home for the winter holidays. They love visiting her to listen to her stories, but tonight Granny is not her usual chirpy self; she looks much older and seems to be agitated over something. One of the boys asks her whether she is not feeling well and tells her that if so, they can come back another night. But instead of answering the question, the old woman starts talking and tells them that on certain nights a peculiar wind blows through the village, which seems to start from the region of the graveyard and which sounds like a hymn. She also tells them that tonight is that kind of a night. At first the youngsters are skeptical and tell her that they cannot hear anything and that such things are not possible, but the old woman rebukes them by saying that they are not paying attention to what is happening around them. She tells them that youngsters of today have forgotten how to listen to the voice of the earth and the wind. They feel chastened and make a show of straining their ears to listen more attentively and to their utter surprise, they hear the beginnings of a low hum in the distance. They listen for some time and tell her, almost in triumph, that they can hear only an eerie sound. 'No,' the storyteller almost shouts, 'listen carefully. Tonight is the anniversary of that dreadful Sunday.' There is a death-like silence in the room and some of them begin to look uneasy because they too had heard vague rumours of army atrocities that took place in the village on a Sunday long before they were born. Storyteller and audience strain to listen more attentively and suddenly a strange thing happens: as the wind whirls past the house, it increases in volume and for the briefest of moments, seems to hover above the house. Then it resumes whirling as thought hurrying away to other regions beyond human habitation. The young people are stunned because they hear the new element in the volume and a certain uncanny lilt lingers on in the wake of its departure. The old woman jumps up from her seat and, looking at each one in turn, asks, 'You heard it, didn't you? Didn't I tell you? It was Apenyo's last song', and she hums a tune softly, almost to herself. The youngsters cannot deny that they heard the note but are puzzled because they don't know what she is talking about. As the old woman stands apart humming the tune, they look at her with wonder. There is a peculiar glow on her face and she seems to have changed into a new self, more alive and animated than earlier. After a while a young girl timidly approaches her and asks, 'Grandmother, what are you talking about? Whose last song?'

The old storyteller whips around and surveys the group as though seeing them for the first time. She then heaves a deep sigh and with infinite sadness in her voice, spreads her arms wide and whispers, 'You have not heard about that song? You do not know about Apenyo? Then come and listen carefully....'

Thus, on a cold December night in a remote village, an old storyteller gathers the young of the land around the leaping flames of a hearth and squats on the bare earth among them to pass on the story of that Black Sunday when a young and beautiful singer sang her last song even as one more Naga village began weeping for her ravaged and ruined children.

Breaching the Citadel

An Introduction

URVASHI BUTALIA AND LAXMI MURTHY

Early in 2012 a group of South Asian feminists met in Delhi to begin discussing the possibility of putting together a research project on sexual violence and impunity in the region. Their concern and interest in the subject were guided by several questions: all were agreed that the South Asian region had, in recent years, seen a noticeable increase in sexual violence, particularly the collective violence of wars and political conflicts. Alongside this increase—which was evident also in the more hidden but widely known violence that took place within the guarded space of the home and the neighbourhood—was another phenomenon, the growing lack of accountability for perpetrators. What was it that time and again, allowed perpetrators of sexual violence to get away, and which, despite so much research and activism, repeatedly brought blame, opprobrium, culpability, to the victim and survivor?

Over the next few months, as ideas were being discussed, and areas specified for the research, a number of events unfolded in India that lent greater urgency to the project. In cities across the country, in workplaces, in public spaces, and in situations of political and sectarian strife, incident upon incident of sexual assault and violence began to come to light. In December of the same year, Delhi, and many other parts of India, exploded into massive protests after the gang-rape of a young medical student, Jyoti Singh Pandey, by a group of six men (one of them a juvenile) who abducted her and her male friend, brutalized both inside a bus, and then threw them, half naked, onto the road, to die. Jyoti's friend survived, but she succumbed to her grievous injuries after several harrowing days in hospital.

The protests around Jyoti Singh Pandey's assault marked, in some ways, a turning point in India, not only for the women's movement, but for civil society in general. As such explosive moments often do, this one too created multiple and complex reactions. The protests—that focused on what is usually seen as a 'women's issue' and, importantly, involved people from all classes and backgrounds—brought a sense of solidarity and built hope that change was possible, in an environment that seemed to be becoming increasingly hostile. The involvement of young people and large numbers of men, as well as families, brought hope that sexual violence was at last being seen as something more than just a 'women's issue'. The protests also brought a sense of urgency and new energy to the ongoing struggle for women's rights. But equally, they surfaced many uncomfortable questions, particularly for activists in the women's movement. What was it, they asked, about this particular incident of sexual violation that resonated so much with people across class, caste, location, region? Did the reaction, the protests, the sense of rage and solidarity with the victim/survivor, have anything to do with her perceived mainstream 'normalcy'? A young, middle class, urban, professional woman, aspiring to join the world of medicine, out with a friend for a 'harmless' activity such as seeing a film, and heading home at a 'reasonable' hour—were these the things that held meaning for those who came out to protest? Or was it just that people had had enough? Would there have been so much sympathy if the victim/survivor had been, say, a sex worker, a Dalit or a poor woman? Why had cases of terrible sexual violence in the past—assaults on poor women, caste rape, the sexual violation of sex workers and transgender persons, rape by the armed forces—not resulted in similar outrage?

The generality of these questions was given sharper focus by Dalit feminists across the country who pointed to the long history of the sexual violation of Dalit women's bodies and asked why anger and outrage of the kind so evident in the protests about the violation of Jyoti Singh Pandey, had been conspicuous by its absence in such instances. Why had the media remained silent? Was it because the mockery of their bodies, and their violation, was so routine and naturalised that it did not merit anger or outrage? (V.Geetha: 2016: 16)

If caste rape has become so naturalised and normalised that it is hardly commented upon or noticed—a fact that makes for ongoing impunity for the perpetrators—there are other situations that lead to similarly disturbing and complicated consequences. In the Naga areas in Northeast India, as Dolly Kikon points out in a hard-hitting essay (Kikon: 2016) the army's sustained presence over several decades and the valorization of Naga men as resisters of state power and heroes in the community, has led to a widespread perception that the only kind of sexual violence that exists is what Naga women experience at the hands of the army. The sexual violation of Naga women by their own men is hardly addressed. While the perpetrator who can be identified as 'the enemy' can be named, the one who is your own, and who belongs within your community, has the collusion and silence of the community to uphold his impunity.

Such questions were not being asked only inside closed feminist circles. In Srinagar, in Indian-administered Kashmir for example, a group of five young women, students and lawyers, watched the protests in Delhi with interest and growing discomfort. Aware of the many allegations of sexual assault against the army (who have held sway in the area under the Armed Forces (Special Powers)

Act, that allowed them extra legal authority and impunity) they wondered why there has been less public outrage when the army engaged in such acts. Why was it, for example, that the women of the villages of Kunan and Poshpora in Kupwara district, who alleged mass rape at the hands of the army in 1991, had never really seen justice? Was it because the armed forces were seen to be protecting and defending the nation and therefore were beyond question? Or was it that sexual violence was considered to be merely collateral damage in the cause of duty and therefore did not deserve attention? These questions also helped the young women to turn the spotlight on themselves: what did they, as young Kashmiri women, know of their own history? If the army had enjoyed impunity in cases of sexual violence, so, in many ways, had militant factions who were also complicit in using women's bodies and against whom no one dared speak out. Was this silence not part of the construction of impunity for perpetrators?

In the years to come, these questions would come to acquire more urgency and would lead to feminist activists reflecting deeply on their own practices and confronting their own biases. The tragedy is that it took the sexual violation and death of a young woman, to bring such questions to the fore.

A SENSE OF URGENCY

Sexual violation, whether individual or collective, has been one of the subterranean (and sometimes not so subterranean) narratives of modern India. Beginning with the moment of Independence, when the country was also divided into two, the rape and abduction of women took place on a large scale (estimates put the figures for both countries at roughly 100,000) and women's bodies often became the battleground on which men fought their wars. Heated debates inside the Constituent Assembly on the subject of 'our' women and 'their' women led to the setting in place of the Central Recovery Operation, a process enabled by law that remained in place for nearly seven years, to 'recover' abducted and raped women and to 'restore' them to their 'homelands'. It was feminist scholars and activists who uncovered this history, revealing how the narrative of the nation was so deeply intertwined with the stories of the violation of women's bodies, and how profound the silence was around these stories, for when you are in the process of making the 'nation', how can you allow that narrative to be disrupted by stories of sexual violation? (Menon and Bhasin 1998; Butalia 1998)

In post-independence India, the question of the nation was supposedly 'settled'—or so the state would have us believe. But the narrative of sexual violence did not go away. Whenever the 'peripheries' erupted into anti-state violence, the sexual violation of women, and indeed of some men—the Northeastern states and Kashmir provide ample evidence of this—cut across the contesting 'truths', whether of the state and its institutions such as the army, or of non-state actors. Whenever protest and resistance movements from within the so-called 'mainstream' of the nation-state took root and grew, similar stories emerged, whether in peasant movements, or in trade unions, or within the left. No matter that ideologies set political actors at different ends of the spectrum, there seemed to be a disturbing similarity in the way sexual violence was viewed as a non-serious issue, and in the manner in which states, non-state actors, political parties, heads of institutions, viewed the question of sexual violence and impunity.

It is not surprising therefore that one of the earliest and long-standing struggles of the feminist movement of the seventies was around the issue of violence against women, in particular sexual violence. Activists took up case after case of sexual violence. In Maharashtra, the rape of Mathura, a young tribal woman by two policemen, and their subsequent acquittal by the Supreme Court, became a cause to mobilize across the country. Four lawyers wrote an open letter to the Chief Justice of India protesting the acquittal and this letter became the galvanizing force for a nationwide movement on the issue of sexual violence. In Hyderabad the case of Rameeza Bee, a Muslim woman, and her rickshaw puller husband, led to a public furore outside the police station where Rameeza Bee was raped and her husband killed. In Baghpat, Haryana, the rape, stripping, and parading, by policemen, of Maya Tyagi, a woman travelling with her husband to attend a wedding, caused outrage in north India. In Sangamner, Patiala, Malur, there were incidents of police and landlord rape. In Guwahati, women protested the rape of women by the army in Kamrup. In the Santhal Parganas the Central Reserve Police Force (CRPF) colluded with upper caste landlords to attack and rape tribal women, and to target Dalits who chose to stand with the Santhals in their bid to address longstanding issues of land ownership. In Rajasthan, a group of Gujar (higher caste) men raped a Dalit woman, Bhanwari Devi, from Bhateri village, who worked with a government programme called the Women's Development Programme. In Imphal, Manipur, personnel of the Assam Rifles forcibly picked up a young woman, Thangjam Manorama, whom they suspected of being a member of a people's army, and the next morning, her sexually violated and mutilated body was found abandoned. In Chhattisgarh, Soni Sori, a tribal schoolteacher was arrested, ostensibly for being in sympathy and collusion with the Maoist movement in that state. In custody, she was subjected to torture and sexual assault. And this list does not even touch the tip of the iceberg.

Everywhere, incident after incident, it became clear that the perpetrators were more than confident that they would get away. Sometimes the lack of accountability and the impunity they enjoyed had to do with the reluctance of the victims and survivors to report the crime. The perception of sexual violence—that it is almost always the fault of the victim/survivor, or that it is not a 'serious' crime—resulted in victims/survivors holding back from speaking out, for how do you get the harm that has been done to you taken seriously, when that harm itself is barely recognized as such?

Disturbing in themselves, these questions raise more questions regarding societal perceptions not only of sexual violence against women but also with regard to women's status and place in society. A brief look at the clichés and language-use that shape our perceptions of women who are raped and the men who rape them may provide some answers. How often have we heard, in India, that the victim/survivor of rape is like a 'zinda laash' or a living corpse? If that is where society locates the victim/survivor, the difficulty of speech is self-evident. The cliché of rape as a 'fate worse than death' for women, valorizes, virginity even as it simultaneously reduces her worth—or lack of it—to the condition of the hymen, goes hand in hand with another trope: that the 'woman who gets raped is the woman who asks for it'. As a result, not only is the rape survivor rendered worthless, but this internally conflicted victim-temptress combine recoils on the survivor, depriving her of both value and voice and frees perpetrators from responsibility for the crime.

Equally, the fear of making themselves vulnerable to external pressure also contributed to victims/survivors holding back. In public discourse, for example, there exists a clear hierarchy of violence in which sexual violence occupies perhaps the lowest rung, so if it occurs as part of other kinds of violence—say that of sectarian strife, or caste-based attacks or army intervention in conflict areas—it is seen as 'collateral damage' and often set aside. In the 'larger picture' there is little or no place for it.

However, victims/survivors' reluctance to speak out was not the only factor that led to perpetrators of sexual violence enjoying widespread impunity. Even when women did speak out, and when they chose to take the battle into the arena of the courtroom, perhaps the only place where they could even begin to entertain the hope of justice, their experience did not inspire confidence. The justice system itself, despite years of law reform on paper, more often than not, fails the victim/survivor of sexual violence. It is, first of all, filled with the weight of prejudice about the survivor—the prejudice of years of erroneous knowledge. Victims/survivors are seen as essentially lying subjects; to be credible, or to be seen as credible, they must conform to the idea of the helpless innocent victim. Any deviation from this can go against them. If desire enters the picture at all in the form of a woman who may have previously had sex or may have expressed a desire to do so, condemnation swiftly follows. If medical experts find that the victim's body establishes through the double violation of the ignominious two-finger test that she has experienced sex before, then the body is further assumed to be complicit. There remains, as Pratiksha Baxi points out, a gap between the letter of the law and spoken law as it functions on the ground. In her words: 'More than thirty years after the Open Letter protesting against the Mathura judgment, this precedent of injustice still echoes in our courtrooms. The cacophony of cross-examinations that divide the body into sexual parts, calibrate duration, map ejaculation, chart marks of resistance, and choreograph postures resounds in our courtrooms. The judicial gavel is not always raised to regulate these ways of talking to rape survivors.' (Baxi 2014: 342)

Over the years it also became clear to activists that the figure of the perpetrator of sexual violence could not be so easily defined. He did not conform to a particular class or description. While some of the early protests (Mathura, Rameeza Bee, Maya Tyagi, or in the Santhal Parganas or Kamrup) focused on the police, or other arms of the state such as security forces or the army, and landlords, the question of who the perpetrator of sexual violence was, and why men committed acts of sexual violence became much more complex. While moments such as the Partition had shown how men of differing religious persuasions saw sexual violence as a way of attacking men of the 'other' religion through the violation of their 'property' in the shape of the bodies of 'their' women, other histories revealed different truths. In battles between landlords and peasants, or landless workers—often Dalits—any form of resistance was met with brutal violence, but as far as Dalit women were concerned, their sexual violation was seen not as reprisal but as a matter of right and entitlement. A report on the gang-rape of Dalit women in Bhojpur, Bihar points out that: '[the] violence of dominance against Dalits as a crude sociological reality is an integral part of a broader cultural psyche of Hindu society. The present case of gang-rape of six Dalit women is yet another example where sexual violence was caused without any assertion of rights. Here it is important to understand that as a matter of historical reality, rape against Dalit women is not caused for the purpose of psycho-sexual pleasure; rather sexual violence is used as a time-tested weapon of collective humiliation and collective psychological subjugation of Dalits. The public glorification of the rape of more than 200 Dalit women between the ages of 6–70 years committed by the Savarna Liberation Army in July 1992 can be cited as perfect example to that.' (Delhi Solidarity Group: 2014: 3) The low caste female body had no rights at all, an assumption that even the law endorsed by obliterating sexual violence from instances of the repression of resistance movements. In the Khairlanji massacre for example (Khairlanji is a small village in Maharashtra where in September of 2006 four members of a Dalit family were brutally beaten, the two women raped, and all four murdered, by higher caste villagers), police and panchayat collusion was an open secret, their impunity a given. And yet, an important piece of legislation, the Prevention of Atrocities Act, 1989, that recognizes historical discrimination and hurt, allowed the one remaining member of the family to file a case in court.

The sessions court judgment, when it came, however, absented the question of sexual assault.

In cases where the armed forces were accused of rape, and especially in locations where they enjoyed immunity under the Armed Forces Special Powers Act, the question of how the sexual violation of women (and indeed also of men) could ever be seen as having taken place in the course of duty, was never raised. Under which jurisdiction did army courts hear cases of sexual violence by their forces? The fact that these cases were never taken before the law of the land (notwithstanding the fact that the law of the land leaves much to be desired) reveals the intention of ensuring impunity for their members by the armed forces.

The police, the army, landlords: the list does not end there. In 2013 a self-styled godman, Asaram Bapu, who commands a huge following all over India, and has enormous wealth, and later his son, Narayan Sai, were accused of rape by three women, one—a sixteen-year old—accusing the father, and two sisters speaking out against the son. The speaking out came reluctantly, and at a huge cost for the survivors and their families, and indeed for those who had known of and tolerated the crime (repeated with many other women) and had remained silent. Thus, too, is impunity created. And yet, the silence and complicity of the witnesses was not necessarily wilful collusion, but perhaps a finely judged decision about the difficulty of tackling power that is built on claims of divinity and wealth. And for those who did eventually speak out, this fear has been borne out, for many of the witnesses have been brutally attacked and one killed. It is widely known that the attacks were carried out at the behest of the perpetrators, or their followers. Meanwhile, at the time of writing, both father and son remain in custody and the case is ongoing. Indeed, so sure are the perpetrators of their power that the son had the temerity to ask for bail to be able to stand for elections in a recent state election.

The combination of religion and politics, he well knows, can be a formidable one and can buy you permanent impunity.

Power, however, is not the only element here. Asaram Bapu, Narayan Sai and the numbers of other 'godmen', enjoy a kind of immunity by virtue of the large followings they collect, and whose members are vocal—and often violent—in their refusal to believe that their gurus can ever be guilty of the crimes they are accused of and turn their opprobrium always on the victim.

In the early nineties, Digambar Jain Muni, the powerful spiritual head of the influential Jain community in India, was exposed by a doctor, a woman gynaecologist, who reportedly performed abortions twice on a woman disciple the guru assaulted. Once exposed, many other accusations came out of the Muni's long history of sexual violence against women, but he was unrepentant and, predictably, tried to turn the blame on the woman, accusing her of 'having relations with many men'. Although the disciple did not file a police case, preferring to keep things 'within the community', she did speak of what had been done to her at a public meeting. Likewise, Asaram Bapu's 'god-like' status apparently helped provide impunity, since there was a belief that a holy man was incapable of committing such a crime. Arguments by the army, the police, soldiers, insurgents, fathers, brothers, priests and principals, sound remarkably similar. However, in a welcome development, on April 25, 2018, Asaram Bapu was sentenced to life-imprisonment by a special SC/ST court designated to try cases filed under the Scheduled Castes and Tribes (Prevention of Atrocities) Act, 1989. This was the second conviction of a powerful religious leader after the conviction of Gurmeet Ram Rahim, self-styled 'messenger of god' of the Dera Sacha Sauda in Haryana. Ram Rahim was sentenced in August 2017 by a special court to twenty years imprisonment on two consecutive counts of rape. His devotees' violent outrage over the conviction led to the death of thirty-one persons, attacks on the media and immense damage to property.

A similar kind of immunity attaches to politicians and even to self-righteous mobs. In a recent and tragic incident of the abduction, repeated rape and murder of an eight-year old child in Kathua in Kashmir, local politicians belonging to the right wing Bharatiya Janata Party, participated in public processions in defence of the perpetrators, hailing them as heroes and these processions drew substantial crowds. The crucial question of how any society can condone such violence, and particularly on a child, remained unanswered.

The history of sexual violence is long and varied. If the state tolerates, encourages, sometimes actively colludes in the perpetration of sexual violence, there are other actors too who inhabit other realms of power, whether simply patriarchal power, or familial authority, or indeed institutional power such as that of the armed forces, or the insurgents, or religious heads and so on. For the victims and survivors—not only women but also men, transgender persons, queer people—impunity begins, as V. Geetha points out, with the refusal to recognize what is being done to them as a crime, and with the refusal to acknowledge their pain and suffering. The fact that nowhere in the world is the recognition of sexual violence as a crime free from questions about the character or history of the victims/survivors is revealing, for it is this that lies at the heart of the impunity of the perpetrators. If the crime is not recognized as being serious, if it is not given a name and the serious attention it deserves, if the very nature of recognizing the seriousness of the crime depends on the character of its victim, then the battle is lost before it even begins. V. Geetha eloquently describes how the search for justice by victims and survivors of sexual violence demands a shared humanity, a call for a recognition of the suffering of the victim/survivor, a call that understands and acknowledges that harm has been done, and redress is necessary. Addressing state impunity, she says, the recognition of suffering, 'challenges and illuminates the contours and details of State impunity. Further, it positions impunity as not merely a legal or political conundrum, but as a resolute refusal on the part of State personnel to be part of shared humanity. For, apart from setting itself above the law and the realm of justice, State impunity refuses to either recognize or take responsibility for the hurt it causes, and actually relishes its authority to be that way. This relish is most evident in the State's elaborate and completely fantastic justifications of wrong-doing. Paradoxically, this move to fabricate reasons for its actions is indicative of the State's illegality, of the fact that it has lost its sovereign character and remains set in authority chiefly on account of its enormous power to both cause hurt and disclaim responsibility for acts that result in suffering.' (V. Geetha: 2016: xxvii)

Impunity, thus, is rather like a mesh in which the different threads are so entangled that it is difficult to separate the one from the other. Institutional strength, combined with patriarchal privilege, the perception that rape is what women deserve and indeed ask for, to which are added the vulnerability of those on the margins, the desire, on the part of the victims and survivors to maintain silence or to keep redress within the community, the fear of the violation that law represents—each thread weaves into the other. Over the years, as our knowledge of the interlinkages that create and strengthen structures of impunity has grown, so have our strategies to deal with it. The essays in this volume traverse a diverse terrain and address various aspects of the experience of sexual violence and assault for the victims/survivors, and the ways in which the search for justice has proceeded. They are historical, and contemporary, and address the experiences of political activists, minority women, sex workers, refugees, ordinary women; they focus on state collusion in impunity for perpetrators, on the experiences of minority women in situations of sectarian strife, on the media, on forensics and they make a beginning in addressing the psycho-social making of perpetrators. There are, it is important to point out, some key gaps: although our volume does focus on other forms of marginalization, it absents the question of caste and there is little on the experiences of transgender people and of queerness; agricultural workers and labour in general. These are crucial areas in which we failed to find researchers willing to write in the time that we had. It is our hope that these will become the focus of research for us in the years to come.

THE MANY FACES OF IMPUNITY

We begin with a historical moment in the early forties, the Tebhaga movement (a movement launched by peasants in undivided Bengal in 1946 to demand a fair share of the produce). Kavita Panjabi traces the involvement, in the movement, of Ila Mitra, an activist and leader and a member of the Communist Party. In her essay 'Between Honour and Justice: Rendering the Law Ineffective', Panjabi incisively analyses the conundrum between disclosure, necessitated by the justice system, and silence that is demanded by the community and family.

She points out that where 'honour' prevails, the law can only fail since 'honour' and justice seem to be juxtaposed as an either-or option for the majority of women who have experienced sexual violence. The 'safeguarding' of women's 'honour' thus becomes one of the surest grounds of impunity for men who violate women sexually, she says, to create a 'black hole of justice'. Panjabi goes on to examine the ways in which the codes of 'honour' form a template within the tensions inherent in the emergent post-colonial democracy interact with the compulsions of a progressive left party, from 1949-51, in the case of the iconic Ila Mitra, a member of the communist party active in the Tebhaga peasant movement launched in undivided Bengal in 1946 to demand a fair share from landlords. In a brutal suppression of the movement, Santhal adivasis were killed, beaten and detained by the police of the then East Pakistan. Arrested and tortured in police custody, Ila Mitra's stark testimony in court, of sexual torture and graphic descriptions of her ordeal, represented an unprecedented challenge to taboos of 'honour' and silence about sexual violence. These frank testimonies notwithstanding, some humiliations, such as being mocked and paraded almost nude in front of the adivasi prisoners, is a violation that even Ila Mitra could not reveal. Panjabi, in examining the layers of Ila Mitra's court testimony, urges us to consider the interplay of a violated woman's own need to speak out and the utilitarian compulsions of a party that would 'benefit' from her revelations of brutal sexual torture. How must her words be read against the backdrop of a seemingly common agenda, but with a hint of moral compulsion from a political party she was deeply invested in? And how did she read her own words, more than four decades later? Her discomfort with her disclosure is a poignant reminder of the contradictions and complications inherent in the breaking of silence, and the meaning that the voicing of sexual violence takes in different contexts and time periods. Indeed, the power of articulation might sometimes be turned against the survivor, as Ila Mitra's own resistance, breakdown, struggle and mainstream negotiation with shifting notions of 'honour' testify. In a poignant telling of Ila Mitra's own erasure of the memory of her testimony in court, Panjabi draws attention to the trauma of recalling, retelling and thus reliving sexual torture and the accompanying loss of dignity. She cautions, 'The political gains of such public testimonies can only become more meaningful when they also address the personal costs to the victims.'

The tactic of labelling the struggle for justice for Ila Mitra as one inciting 'communal tensions', has echoes till date in the manner in which institutions of the state entrench impunity by their very framing of the discourse of resistance. In the case of Ila Mitra, the newly-formed Pakistani and Indian states colluded to divert attention and deny her justice.

If Ila Mitra in 1950 found herself at what Panjabi describes as "the crossroads of the state's strategic deployment of regressive patriarchal codes of 'honour' and vendetta by the state, and the Communist Party's apparently progressive refusal of such sedimentations of patriarchal ideologies", Rajashri Dasgupta examines these very anxieties in contemporary West Bengal, a state that saw the ravages of partition three times over—during the Partition of Bengal in the early twentieth century, in 1947 at the time of the formation of East Pakistan and then during the formation of Bangladesh in 1971. 'The Circle of Violence' reminds us that neither sexual violence nor impunity are linear in an ever-changing political landscape. She presents a searing account of the three-decade rule of the Left Front government which came to power on the platform of land reform, and democratic de-centralization, but failed when it came to justice for women victims/survivors of sexual violence. In a continuation of the use of violence to suppress the Tebhaga movement, Dasgupta traces the history of the use of force by the Congress government at the Centre to tackle the Naxalite movement which had emerged in response to abysmal poverty and deprivation. Yet, the Left's approach to tackling violence against women, specifically sexual violence, did not inspire any confidence that the state would hold perpetrators accountable. The 1990 gang-rape of three women health workers in Bantala, on the outskirts of Kolkata, showed up patriarchal thinking in a government and political formation assumed to be progressive. The Chief Minister's shocking utterance that, "[s]uch things happen," attempting to normalise the abnormal was revealing in its lack of understanding of the structural causes of violence against women. Slowly but surely, the masculinist use of force by the cadre and deployment of state arms like the police to control dissent were a cynical reminder that the ideology of state power more often than not, trumps political ideology, however progressive it purports to be.

The fierce opposition to the government's land acquisition for industries and the setting of 'special economic zones' renowned elsewhere for their exploitation of labour, was accompanied by a pattern of sexual violence against women. Singur, Lalgarh and Nandigram, from sites of industry became known for the resistance led by women. Dasgupta describes the irony of 'industrial resurgence' being ushered into the Left's red bastion through the barrel of the gun—and even sexual violence—for the 'larger good'. In the backdrop of the Left Front's increasing lack of political imagination in dealing with global phenomena like liberalization and privatization, Dasgupta goes on to examine whether the Trinamul Congress (TMC) led by a woman chief minister, taking over the state government in 2011 on the exhilarating slogan of *paribartan* or change, made any difference in state accountability to crimes against women. She promised good governance and accountability to people fed up of decades of rhetoric and misrule. Yet, what she doled out was not justice, but sops for victims, silencing the opposition through co-option; declaring complainants to be liars, or plain denial. Resistance to state rule and lack of accountability for perpetrators of sexual violence against women inflamed Kamduni, in much the same way as Bantala had risen against Left Front rule. The struggle against impunity comes full circle: '*Bantala theke Kamduni, saab shasaker ek dhani*' (from Bantala to Kamduni, every government sings the same tune).

In dark times there are also moments of light. The testimony of Suzette Jordan, who did not allow the gang-rape she experienced in 2012 to define her as the 'Park Street victim', offers a glimmer of hope of how women might interrogate notions of honour, and reject the assumption that rape is a 'fate worse than death'. Her assertion that "nothing is more precious than life" is particularly poignant in light of the fact that she succumbed to illness in March 2015, eight months before a sessions court found all the three accused guilty of gang-rape. Even though she did not live to see this victory, Jordan, a single mother of two, unapologetic about her love for dancing and going to the pub for a drink, had boldly pushed the definition of the 'pure' victim, challenging victim blaming every step of the way.

Lesser citizens

The construction of the victim subject and the notion of the 'authentic victim' who is impoverished, powerless and helpless has long been the subject of feminist discourse in India.[1] It can perhaps be argued that the depth of the silence around sexual violence is directly proportional to the deviation from the norm of who is a victim deserving of sympathy. In her essay for this volume, Bani Gill in 'Behind the Silence: Sexual Violence Against Afghan and Burmese Refugee Women in Delhi' explores these silences among refugee women in India: silence in the middle of an angry outburst, silence when the topic of sexualized violence was broached, silence when violence inflicted by members of their own refugee community was discussed, and silence as resistance to discussing or explaining their ambiguous legal status. In listening to these silences, she foregrounds what Ratna Kapur calls the 'peripheral subject' in order to force a deeper analysis of the standard victim of sexual violence. The refugee woman in India occupies a space characterized by uncertainty and fluidity, swaying between legality and illegality within an ambiguous legal regime. And in this amorphous space, sexual violence is tackled with silence. India houses one of the largest refugee populations—Tibetans, Bangladeshis, Sri Lankans, Burmese, Afghans—fleeing from neighbouring countries, but is not party to international conventions governing refugees, relying instead on ad hoc executive orders and piecemeal legislation. Gill spotlights the trauma of women refugees fleeing from a bad situation at home to another in an alien land that might even be worse: "For many Afghan and Chin women the threat of or trauma of sexual and gender based violence constituted a critical factor in their decision to flee those contexts. However, their location in India as an ethnic, gendered 'other' renders them susceptible to new conditions of dislocation and violent hostility, the redressal of which is difficult for a host of reasons." She also touches upon the sensitive topic of violence within the refugee communities, with men's dislocation and sense of alienation being articulated as violence on women. The nuanced understanding of the category of 'refugee women' as someone 'not from here' seems to echo the location of women who have experienced sexual violence—occupying a limbo between reality and hope of redress.

Law as a site of struggle has long been understood as a contentious space, and as Valerie Kerruish (1991) articulates, jurisprudence as an ideology not only functions within an iniquitous social dynamic, but also helps create and maintain it. This is most apparent in the case of sex workers, who hover in the grey areas of criminality, illegality or semi-legality. Seen through a societal moral lens that permeates the legal machinery, Meena Seshu and Laxmi Murthy argue that the violence of stigma and discrimination—also reflected in the law criminalizing sex work—forms a backdrop within which sexual violence against sex workers must be understood. Going beyond the notion of prostitution as inherently violent, the essay attempts to understand the gendered ways in which sex workers—female, male and transgender—experience violence and how they find ways to resist it. Evidence shows that female sex workers tend to 'normalize' sexual violence, perhaps due to the view—which they have themselves internalized–that 'sex workers cannot be raped since their job is to provide sex'.

Interestingly, male and transgender sex workers who described experiences of gang-rape most often did not use the term, perhaps due to a perception that men cannot be raped or gang-raped, or maybe due to the humiliation, shame and stigma associated with rape. This selective articulation of sexual violence by male and transgender sex workers demands further exploration of the complexities of gender-based sexual violence.

Testimonies of sex workers show evidence of extensive abuse of power by law enforcement personnel who exploit the ambiguity of laws that criminalize sex work or certain aspects of it, as well as public order laws. Where sex work is illegal, the criminalization of sex work and sex workers by extension legitimizes acts of violence, since criminals are not seen as deserving of human rights, and this goes on to create impunity for police violence.

The impunity enjoyed by policemen provides licence to clients, family members, intimate partners and the general public to perpetrate violence on sex workers with little fear of consequences. The intersection of the complex terrains of labour and sexuality in the understanding of sex work provides an opportunity to understand a complex notion: sexual extortion. The extortion of sex by the police, though it meets standard definitions of rape i.e. coerced sex or sex under threat of further harm, was regarded not so much as 'sexual violence' but as 'economic violence'. Such grounded realities open up spaces to explore notions of consent which might involve 'choosing' an option that could reduce future violence or loss of income. Being on the fringes of society, their work stigmatized and criminalized in most countries, sex workers unless collectivized, were rarely able to access their rights or entitlements as citizens.

Who is entitled to the rights enshrined in the Constitution of India? It would seem that the 'ideal subject' who is eligible to access rights has a narrow definition. From Neha Dixit's reports from ground zero of the battle which played out on women's bodies in Muzaffarnagar, Uttar Pradesh in 2013, it would appear that Muslim women are lesser citizens of India. While independent India has witnessed communal conflict and ethnic pogroms on a horrifyingly regular basis, what makes this episode noteworthy is that it came just months after the upheavals following the gang-rape and subsequent death of a student in Delhi in December 2012. The Criminal Law Amendment Act of 2013 had introduced Section 376(2)(g) into the Indian Penal Code to deal with rape committed during communal or sectarian violence as a form of aggravated rape. In conjunction with Section 114-A of the Indian Evidence Act whereby the burden of proof is shifted to the accused considering the coercive circumstances in which the rape is committed, the amendment theoretically provides some opportunities for redressal. Yet, the Muslim women who reported having been raped by dominant caste Hindu men, had a hard time even registering First Information Reports, leave aside taking the cases to court. The women's bodies are prominent sites for this assertion of power. The assertion of the collective identity of the community, transformed into what Veena Das calls, "the desire to humiliate the men of other nations and communities through the violent appropriation of 'their' women" (Das 2007) continues to have the same visage through the decades, from Partition onward. The fact that the medical examination was delayed, from anywhere between three to six weeks after the rape, once more spotlights the feminist demand to consider other forms of evidence to establish rape, especially in situations that are communally charged.

Delayed medical examinations, indifferent collecting of medical evidence, an overemphasis on injuries, confusion about what to record: if this is how health professionals respond to victims/survivors of sexual assault, then justice will continue to remain an elusive, if not impossible, goal, and impunity a given. CEHAT's systematic research in Mumbai hospitals shows that there are serious lacunae in the responses of medical professionals in terms of forensic practices. The overemphasis on whether or not the victim/survivor has injuries on her body harks back to the solidified belief that sexual assault can only be credible if the victim shows signs of having fought back, rendering invisible the terrible trauma and fear that victims are often caught in. Similarly, the invasion of the victim/survivor's body through violative practices like the two finger test to check the elasticity of the vaginal opening, or the focus on the status of the hymen are all common medical practices. The tragic omission of any sense of the survivor's mental condition or the trauma she has faced, are not even seen as gaps in medical practice. The work of CEHAT, a Mumbai-based organization working in the field of health, traces the gaps in the health system's response to sexual assault in India and the writers argue for the need to have a uniform and gender sensitive health care response to victims of sexual assault and violence. They discuss the pioneering health care programme put in place in Mumbai as a collaborative venture between the Brihanmumbai Municipal Corporation and CEHAT, presenting challenges in dealing with the mindset of health professionals, as well as attempts being made to bring in knowledge and practice change in the health system. Case briefs and case analyses allow them to reflect on the possible benefits to survivors of such a programme, and to present a case for putting in place protocols and procedures that are gender sensitive and that can help to operationalize the right to health care, including psycho-social care, for survivors.

The challenges for the health systems and professionals in conflict zones such as restricted mobility, state complicity, attacks on hospitals and professionals, and a politicized environment are also examined in order to understand the need for uniform procedures and protocols and the training of providers to ensure justice and care/healing for victims of sexual violence in conflict.

Unpacking Impunity

Drawing from both her practice as a psychotherapist and as a social researcher, Shobna Sonpar suggests the adoption of an integrated, multi-factorial framework in order to understand sexual violence as a complex interplay of individual, group and socio-cultural factors. Several of the essays in this volume describe and analyse the macro environment that provides the 'cultural scaffolding' that legitimises sexual violence as well as the nuances of the legal impunity that permeates the law enforcement machinery, in both states of exception and 'ordinary' times. Sonpar's analysis of how sociocultural norms are powerfully pushed through group behaviour—very different from how those same individuals act alone—is extremely useful to understand gang-rape especially in a charged situation of communal and caste conflict, where the system too legitimises the violence. Articulating the category of 'moral impunity', she points towards research that shows how '...group processes compromise moral accountability. They reset individual moral radar through de-individuation, that is, the loss of a person's sense of individual identity and personal responsibility. De-individuation leads to diffusion of responsibility as perpetrators feel personally anonymous as identities merge with the group.'

She touches upon a subject that is less documented: sexual violence against men by female combatants, for example in Abu Ghraib. The notion of 'combat socialization' as well as the pressures on female combatants to masculinise themselves goes some way towards explaining this phenomenon, and also strengthens the perspective that sexual violence is less about unbridled sexuality than it is about an exercise of aggressive power.

To the oft-asked bewildered question 'how could he/they do that?' in the face of unimaginably brutal acts of sexual violence, Sonpar draws upon research that explores the 'moral radar' which can get switched off, particularly in acts of group perpetration of sexual violence. '....regulatory self-sanctions can be selectively disengaged for inhumane conduct by converting harmful acts to moral ones through linkage to worthy purpose, obscuring personal causal agency by diffusion and displacement of responsibility, misrepresenting or disregarding the injurious effects on victims and vilifying the recipients of abuse by blaming and dehumanizing them.'

Sonpar draws our attention to the tension between legal and moral accountability and suggests that when there is broad social tolerance or condoning of ideas supportive of sexual violence, and sociocultural biases permeate civil and state institutions, there is resistance towards passing relevant legislation (for instance, against marital rape) and the implementation of anti-rape laws.

The social construction of impunity is starkly on display in the media. Building consensus about 'legitimate' forms of violations, invalidating certain forms of violations or certain kinds of victims, the media is implicated in strengthening impunity. Divya Arya, brings to bear her own experience as a journalist in electronic media in a country where half the population of over a billion people watches television. Analysing the process of news production from the stage of selection, newsgathering and presentation, she traces shifts in the media reporting sexual violence in the period following the gang-rape and subsequent death of a student in a moving bus in Delhi. Rape, she suggests, is different from other violent crimes, since the inherent sexual component puts it in an altogether separate category for the news media. For the news audience too, sex crimes have the unique ability to touch upon their deep-seated beliefs about gender roles. With the cycle of news being 24 hours for the print media, and even less for the electronic and online media, the ability to analyse in-depth, on a broader spectrum, the social, political and economic bases of sexual violence, creates its own compulsions. With senior editors terming coverage of rape 'fashionable' it is little wonder that the coverage of sexual violence is sporadic and peaks at times of sensational cases that "shock the nation". This lack of consistency is not new, as senior journalists Ammu Joseph and Kalpana Sharma (2006) note in the coverage of what came to be known as the 'Mathura Case' in the early 1980s: 'Notwithstanding the extensive coverage provided to the issue at the height of the campaign, little notice was taken of the new rape law when it was finally passed nearly four years later—only one paper commented on it in an edit.'

Arya through her interviews with media practitioners presents evidence of what is generally believed to be bias in news reporting: the notion in the newsroom of 'real' rape and 'real' victims, whose stories were more likely to be presented sympathetically by the media—usually rape by strangers, outside the house, and rape on minors. Arya points to another factor—the practicalities of coverage when resources are limited—that tends to skew coverage of sexual violence in favour of metropolises, leaving atrocities in villages and small towns to vie for space. In a saturated news universe, mere coverage of a crime does not garner much impact now, says Arya. She goes on to analyse what she refers to as 'campaign journalism' i.e. sustained coverage over a period of time, which can stand out and builds pressure on government, police, judiciary and the general public.

We end this volume with a set of four interviews, with activists and lawyers who have worked on sexual violence, and with victims/survivors of sexual violence. As with all other essays in this volume, while these interviews record situations in which women have confronted terrible violence, they also provide reasons for hope. Farah Naqvi, an activist and one of the authors of the pathbreaking report, 'The Survivors Speak' on the violence in Gujarat in 2002, focuses on that moment, detailing both the immediate and long-term needs of survivors and the challenges for activists who seek to intervene. She makes a passionate plea to both recognize the seriousness of the crime of sexual violation and rape but not to think of it as the 'worst thing that can happen to a woman', and suggests we focus instead on understanding and implementing a reparative process that is sensitive to the needs of survivors. Suzette Jordan and Christine Marrewa Karwoski, both victims/survivors of sexual violence and assault, make a fierce claim to their identities and their names, refusing to hide, refusing to allow themselves to be targeted and blamed for a crime they did not commit. They underscore the importance of truth telling—yes, I like to drink and dance, says one, yes, I kissed him, says another—and of bodily integrity and choice. Vrinda Grover, a feminist human rights lawyer and activist, speaks of both the importance of law as a path to justice but also of its limits for survivors, pointing to its cumbersome processes, its alienating language, while at the same time flagging people's faith in it. She draws on her many years of experience to illustrate the serious and often conflicting dilemmas victims and survivors face when choosing the legal path to justice and marks the challenges this poses for the lawyer supporting them in their battles.

THE BATTLE HAS BEGUN

Taken together, the essays add to our understanding of exactly how impunity is strengthened and how victims and survivors of sexual violence live with the trauma of such violation, but also how they have, individually and collectively, fought back. They have made hard fought gains that are threatened at every step, but that nonetheless add to the inch-by-inch progress of the battle for change. In the aftermath of the December 16, 2012 case, young women from Srinagar in Indian-administered Kashmir, for example began to ask themselves some questions about rape in their backyard. They did not stop there, however but went on to explore what had happened in relation to the search for justice of the survivors of Kunan and Poshpora. With the help of other women—a total of 50 who agreed to be part of the search for justice—they succeeded in reopening the case (which, they discovered, had never actually been closed) and later wrote a book entitled *Do You Remember Kunan Poshpora?* which has today—a quarter century after the event—become an important instrument in the survivors' search for justice.

Activists have also continued to create knowledge in order to make it a powerful tool for justice. In October of 2012, for example, two months before the Delhi gang-rape case, Dalit activists and mediawatch groups, concerned about the rising rates of rape of Dalit women in the state of Haryana, created a map of the state which was entitled '30 Days in a Rape State'. The map contained locations and basic information on the rape of 19 girls who had been raped during that month. (WSS: 2012: 2) An examination of these cases laid bare the ways in which caste and patriarchy, as well as violence against women were so enmeshed in the state of Haryana (and elsewhere) where Dalit assertion was creating fear among the upper castes who hit back with ever growing violence towards women.

Over the three-and-a-half year period that this project ran there were amendments in the criminal law in India and the definition of sexual assault was expanded. Some ground has been gained in our understanding of the structures that contribute to strengthening impunity for sexual violence. This understanding will help in being able to better speak about it and to fight for justice. Further, recent trends show that increasing numbers of women, often supported by their families, are coming out to speak about sexual violence. Following the targeted violence in Muzaffarnagar, Uttar Pradesh in 2013, seven Muslim women who were brutally gang-raped and sexually assaulted by men belonging to the other community, filed writ petitions for protecting their right to life under Article 21.

In an extensive interview, lawyer Vrinda Grover speaks about this, referring to the Muzaffarnagar rapes:

> I think here you can now see that the discourse that emerged post the 2012 gang-rape actually is beginning to have its [effect]...you can hear it in very different spaces. When those families [of the rape survivors] came—again they came forward only because there was a social activist who brought them forward but they had already lodged their FIRs—and they came with their husbands and they sat in the office and they told me about what had happened with their husbands sitting there which, to my mind is very different from what one saw in 1984 where the [Sikh] community completely hushed up [rape] and one just heard stray comments about what had happened....[With Muzaffarnagar] there was no shame and stigma attached either in talking about it, nor were the men saying, 'Oh my god! What has happened to the woman?'... So, it's not as though there has been a complete shift but one can see the glimmers of some changes, both in the women and in the families...Again, in the Muzaffarnagar cases for the first time a new provision was introduced in the law which recognized rape during communal or sectarian violence.

In a landmark judgment in March 2015, recognizing the rehabilitation needs of the survivors of targeted mass rape, the Supreme Court of India ordered that a compensation of INR 500,000 each for rehabilitation be paid to the women by the state government. In another significant move, in 2017 the Supreme Court convicted all the accused (barring a juvenile and one person who died while in prison) in the December 2012 gang-rape case. All were given the death penalty. While large sections of feminists do not uphold the death penalty—and they were not in favour of it in this case too—the judgment showed that courts are now perhaps more willing to recognize the seriousness of the crime of rape.

An equally important judgment was in the Mumbai High Court in what is known as the 'Bilkis Bano case'. Bilkis Bano lost almost her entire family and her small child to the anti-Muslim pogrom in Gujarat in 2002. In addition, she faced sexual assault and rape from the perpetrators. The filing of the case and the naming of the perpetrators—whom she was able to identify—meant that Bilkis Bano came under a great deal of pressure to withdraw the case, something she was able to surmount by appealing to the courts (who were sympathetic) to have the case moved to Mumbai. The judgment in the case indicted the police who falsified evidence, the doctors who colluded with them, and the actual perpetrators who carried out the attack. The importance of this judgment cannot be overstated for it establishes, perhaps for the first time in India, the principle of justice for the victims of mass rape, and it brings into the ambit of accountability not only the perpetrators but also those who colluded and collaborated with them.

But if these judgments provided reason for hope, there remains much to be concerned about. In recent months, the rape and murder of an eight-year-old girl in Kathua, the suspicious death of the father of a young woman from Banaskantha in Uttar Pradesh who alleged rape by an MP of the ruling Bhartiya Janata Party, the growing numbers of sexual crimes against Dalit women (sexual crimes rank second in the number of crimes against Dalits) and the continuing violence on the transgender community, particularly trans women, are all cause for concern. In the words of Salma Khan, a trans woman who runs a support group called Kinnar Maa Trust in Mumbai: 'The Indian Constitution does not discriminate, but its keepers certainly do. Of the transgender people registered with us, at least one in four has been a victim of rape, gang-rape or serious sexual violence. And of these only 10 per cent were successful in getting complaints registered with the police. Most of them were deterred with the same question: you're neither female nor male, how can you be raped?' The Indian state is still unwilling to accept marital rape as a crime and a violation of a woman's autonomy and bodily integrity. It is hard to escape the conclusion that once a woman enters marriage with a man, the State stands firmly behind the man in endorsing any violence he exercises towards his wife as legitimate. Her rights do not exist, his impunity has state sanction.

The battle is far from over for, as V.Geetha tells us, 'There exists an immense tolerance for sexual violence against women in the social and cultural worlds we inhabit...' The state's reluctance to prosecute or take seriously sexual crimes draws on this tolerance. '...[T]he social meanings invested in the violated woman's body on the one hand and her so called 'character' on the other precede and frame understanding and prove decisive in determining what she deserves: justice or the horrific violence she was subject to. In itself, sexual violence is not seen as problematic.' (Geetha: 2016: 1)

Clearly, there is much that remains to be done, but perhaps we can take heart from the fact that the battle has, on many fronts, at least begun.

NOTE

1. See, for example, Ratna Kapur in *Erotic Justice: Law and the New Politics of Postcolonialism* (2005). London: Glasshouse Press.

REFERENCES

Baxi, Pratiksha. 2014. *Public Secrets of Law: Rape Trials in India*. New Delhi: Oxford University Press.

Butalia, Urvashi. 1998. *The Other Side of Silence: Voices from the Partition of India*. New Delhi: Viking Penguin Books.

Changoiwala, Puja. 2018. 'India: No Country for Transgender Women'. https://www.scmp.com/week-asia/society/article/2154077/india-no-country-transgender-women

Das, Veena. 2007. *Life and Words: Violence and the Descent into the Ordinary*. Berkeley: University of California Press.

Delhi Solidarity Group. 2014. *Oppression of Dalit Women in Bihar: Emerging Political Challenges on Caste and Communal Issues*. Delhi Solidarity Group.

Geetha, V. 2016. *Undoing Impunity: Speech After Sexual Violence*. New Delhi: Zubaan.

Kapur, Ratna. 2005. *Erotic Justice: Law and the New Politics of Postcolonialism*. London: Glasshouse Press.

Kerruish, Valerie. 1991. *Jurisprudence as Ideology*. London: Routledge.

Joseph, Ammu, and Kalpana Sharma. 2006. *Whose News? The Media and Women's Issues*. New Delhi: Sage Publications.

Kikon, Dolly. 2016. 'Memories of Rape: The Banality of Violence and Impunity in Naga Society' in U. Chakravarti (ed.), *Fault Lines of History: The India Papers Volume II* (Zubaan Series on Sexual Violence and Impunity in South Asia), New Delhi: Zubaan.

Menon, Ritu, and Kamla Bhasin. 1998. *Borders & Boundaries: Women in India's Partition*. New Delhi: Kali for Women.

Women Against Sexual Violence and State Oppression. 2012. '30 Days in a Rape State.' Women Against Sexual Violence and State Oppression.

1

Between 'Honour' and Justice

Rendering the Law Ineffective

KAVITA PANJABI

I

A critical paradox marks a sexually violated woman's search for justice in South Asia. The processes of legal redress necessitate disclosure, yet the force of community 'honour' compels her into silence. 'Honour' thus propels women into a chasm between the judiciary's demand for revelation and the community's imperative towards concealment. When the pressures of her family or community drive a woman into silence, it is unlikely for such knowledge or evidence to reach the courts of law; and absence of detailed knowledge of a crime virtually renders the law inoperative. Where such 'honour' prevails, the law can only fail. 'Honour' and justice thus seem to be experienced as an antithetical either/or option by a majority of sexually violated women right across the global South. The 'safeguarding' of women's 'honour' becomes one of the surest grounds of impunity for men who violate women sexually.

That the dynamics of 'honour' open up a readymade ground of impunity, and that this makes violation of 'honour' the most strategically advantageous choice for oppression, has clearly not been lost on modern masculinist political institutions at war with each other. Exploited by modern regimes of power ranging from political parties to the state, 'honour' has been renewed as a secure ground of impunity for men, preventing women's access to justice even in situations of sexual violence so grim and so pervasive that they put all medieval exploitations of honour to shame. This has been evident especially in conflict-ridden areas from Gujarat to Kashmir to the Northeast, from Sindh to Chattogram, and from Nepal to Sri Lanka. Yet this resurgence of 'honour' in the realms of gendered political strategy is not exclusive to South Asia alone. As Jean Franco has shown in her recent incisive study of cruelty as integral to modernity, *Cruel Modernity* (2013), it is also pervasive in other contexts right across the world where kinship systems are strong, as amongst the indigenous peoples of Peru and Guatemala. Franco observes that '[h]onor underscores the gap between individual behavior and legality and indicates a place where the law is ineffectual' (ibid.: 89).

In fact, this readymade ground of impunity marks a black hole of justice, and constitutes one of the most brutal grounds of modernity. It also signals a harsh fact, 'the truth that humans greatly outdo the animal in acts of bestiality that we then describe as "bestial"' (Franco 2013: 83). Of course, this is not new or even exclusive to modernity alone, but it does make it imperative to identify the 'manholes' in modern democratic thought and practice that still allow for the perpetuation of such impunity and 'bestiality'. It also calls for a pulling apart of both the symbolic notions of community 'honour' vested in a woman's chastity, as well as the internalizations of community 'honour' that continue to hold sway over our subjectivities.

The stalemate that 'honour' underscores for women seems to be an indication of an unaddressed lack of fit between the norms of older kinship systems and modern judicial processes, or even of the conflict between residual patriarchal feudal values and contemporary democratic ones. For the 'shame' that women experience upon being sexually abused or raped derives from both the external social pressures of patriarchal communities, and a continued subjective internalization of taboos of individual and community 'honour'. These imperatives bring upon women a sense of 'shame' which pre-empts disclosure right across the world to this day. What such censorship in the name of 'honour' indicates then is that the force of older forms of feudal, patriarchal culture still reigns, powerfully sedimented, in the constitution of contemporary democratic identities. As patriarchy and democracy are founded on mutually antithetical principles of domination and autonomy, modern democracy thus flounders on the grounds of such 'honour' in the complex layering of our politicized social as well as intimate personal subjectivities.

What is imperative for ensuring the judicial guarantees of democracy then is not just the institution of democratic laws but also a challenging, at a deep societal level, of such forces of patriarchy that overdetermine legal processes. Required simultaneously is a transformation of subjectivity that involves a dismantling of these constructions of 'honour' and 'shame' sedimented in the interiors of our very being. Forging a critical historical understanding of how 'honour' has been used as a strategic weapon by the democratic state and even by progressive political parties (and not just by dictatorships or fascist and totalitarian governments, as well as conservative parties and groups that we associate with reactionary gendered ideologies and then distance as 'medieval') may help us to comprehend the ways in which our political edifices of 'modernity'—the state and political parties—are actually premised on and guarantee impunity to the very feudal patriarchal practices against which they officially define themselves.

This study is an attempt to examine the ways in which the codes of 'honour' structure the confrontation between the institutions of an emergent secular, democratic South Asian state and a progressive left party, at the intersection of the forces of religion, ethnicity, class and gender. Covering the period from 1949 to 1951, it examines the case of Ila Mitra, the legendary leader of the Tebhaga peasant movement that had been launched right across undivided Bengal in 1946.[1]

II

In 1951, the Rajshahi court of East Pakistan witnessed an exceptional case of the overcoming of taboos of individual and community 'honour'. India and Pakistan had established themselves as 'modern', democratic nation-states less than four years previously in 1947, and both had been marked by the violence of the contesting forces of the nation-state and the armed revolution of the Left since 1948. Independence, for large numbers of poor peasants, had meant little more than a transfer of power from the British government to the new states of India and Pakistan. The betrayal of the promises of independence for peasants and workers, which underlay the Left's slogan 'Yeh azaadi jhooti hai,'[2] led the Communist Party (CP) to launch a programme of armed revolution in 1948 under the leadership of B.T. Ranadive. The Tebhaga peasants' movement, which had begun with an anti-feudal and anti-imperialist thrust, developed a militant anti-state dimension after independence and partition. At the same time, the newly formed states of India and Pakistan resorted to blatant violence in their determination to contain the groundswell of peasant movements. The Tebhaga movement too intensified the tactics of armed struggle. Among the revolutionaries arrested and tortured by the East Pakistani state was Ila Mitra, an upper-caste

Hindu woman from the Indian city of Calcutta. A CP activist of the Tebhaga movement, Ila Mitra became a leader of the adivasi Santal tribes of Rajshahi district in what is now Bangladesh. She was married to Ramen Mitra, veteran communist leader of Tebhaga and the son of a zamindar of Rajshahi. Ila was arrested on 7 January 1950 for leading the Santals in the murder of two police officers when the latter attacked the Tebhaga stronghold of Santals in Nachol village. The subsequent torment that she was subjected to, her staunch resistance in the face of it, the testimony she delivered in the Rajshahi court of this devastating torture in custody and her renewed commitment to left politics in West Bengal, India, after recovery from a nervous breakdown have become legendary on both sides of the border.[3]

The testimony, the likes of which had never been heard before in South Asia—and maybe not in any other court in the world either—was a radically explicit disclosure of gruesome sexual torture by the state of a kind that had never been perpetrated before, not even by the colonial state as far as the available evidence goes. Narratives of Ila Mitra, disseminated in historical and biographical accounts, essays, pamphlets, fiction, poetry and songs, comprise images of a woman's body repeatedly brutalized and torn into in the war waged by a newly emergent nation-state against its tribal peasants and communists. In their narration of her resistance and steadfast refusal to betray the Santals and the communists, these accounts, albeit somewhat hagiographical, are simultaneously some of the most inspiring narratives related to the Tebhaga movement.[4] There are many extraordinary facets of this history: that over 60 Santals succumbed to savage police torture rather than betraying their leader Ila Mitra's identity; and that she had the strength to survive brutal sexual torture, deliver a radically explicit testimony of her torture in the Rajshahi court, and actually recover from her breakdown and renew her commitment to active politics. Equally extraordinary is the fact that half a century later, when 71-year-old Ila Mitra returned to Bangladesh from India for the 50th anniversary celebrations of Tebhaga in 1996, over 100,000 Santal men and women turned up in festive attire from across Bangladesh to offer a rousing welcome to a leader whom none of them had ever set eyes on before.

Yet, there are several questions still hovering below the surface of this 'heroic' history that have never been asked. What were the reasons for the state subjecting her to severe sexual torture *after* she had been arrested and was no longer a threat? What enabled her to overcome the taboos of 'honour' and deliver such an explicit testimony of sexual torture in court, and what was the role of her political party (the CP) vis-à-vis Ila in this extraordinary history? What was the nature of the psychological trauma Ila Mitra suffered as the 'object' of such brutal politico-sexual abuse by the state on the one hand, and as the consequent 'agent' of the CP's retaliation on the other? What were the reasons for the complete impunity of the state and its players, such that no one was ever called to task for such a brutal crime? What were the strategies by which norms of state accountability were elided to secure such impunity? What challenges does her history raise for feminist politics in the subcontinent? I will address the first three questions in this section of my inquiry, the next two in the section III, and the last one in the final section of this essay.

* * *

The army had razed to the ground virtually all the villages of Tebhaga activists in the area, followed by a mass exodus of Santals to India. Thus, the revolt had been crushed. The threat of the CP as well as the Santals had virtually been extinguished. The Hindu woman who had transgressed all norms to actively lead a militant Left tribal movement against a Muslim-dominated state too had been arrested, and her ability to jeopardize the state had also been contained. The crisis was over. After this, what could be the reasons for the police to torture Ila Mitra? There were no concrete threats or fears that can explain the brutality with which Ila was abused through the weeks that followed her arrest. The reasons for this, as I have argued earlier, seem to lie in the realms of anxiety and hatred that formed the subconscious of the new nation and defined it. Thus, sexual violence became a privileged mode for inscribing the boundaries of the nation-state, both within and without. Ila Mitra's body became the ground for the newly emergent nation-state's confrontation with multiple forces, communist, Santal and Hindu, all of which extended across the borders of the nation and were perceived simultaneously as an internal as well as an external threat to its 'integrity' (Panjabi 2010: 54).

There is another critical question in this case—the Santal men were beaten to death, so why was Ila Mitra too not beaten to death? Why was the upper-caste Hindu woman kept alive and tortured sexually? One reason for her being kept alive could, of course, be that given her Hindu identity and Indian origin, the newly emergent Pakistani state may not have wanted to risk antagonizing the Indian state, or set off another spate of communal riots in the two Bengals. The choice of torturing Ila Mitra instead reveals two facets of the state. One is its investment in patriarchal modes of vendetta, evident in its deployment of savage sexual violence as a weapon to show down the under-caste, left and Hindu forces all in one fell swoop by demolishing the 'honour' of all these communities, which would traditionally be perceived to be vested in the 'honour' of any one of their women, and thus so much more in their leader herself. The other is the confidence of the state in securing its own impunity, even in repeated acts of sexual violence, an impunity that it could not have secured in the case of the finality of a killing.

The testimony that Ila Mitra delivered in the Rajshahi district court in the first week of November 1950 is as follows:

> I was arrested at Rohanpur on 7.1.50 and taken to Nachol. When I reached there I was beaten up by the police, and then I was taken to a cell. The SI [sub-inspector] threatened to strip me naked unless I confessed everything about my role in the murder. Since I had nothing to confess, they took away all my clothes and I was kept locked up in the cell completely nude. I wasn't given any food, not even a drop of water. That evening, in the presence of the SI, the constables started hitting me on the head with the butts of their guns. My nose started bleeding. After this, my clothes were returned to me and late at night, around 12, I was taken, probably to the SI's quarters, but I wasn't very sure of that. There they continued torturing me in many different, inhuman, ways in the attempt to extract a confession. My legs were placed between two sticks and pressed hard. Those standing around me were saying that I was being given the Pakistani injection. While this torture continued, I was gagged with a handkerchief. When they failed to get me to say anything, they also began pulling my hair out. After that torture the constables had to carry me back to my cell as I couldn't stand up any more. Inside the cell the SI ordered the constables to bring four boiled eggs and declared, 'She'll speak now.' After that four to five constables forced me to lie on the ground, flat on my back, and one constable forced a warm boiled egg inside my vagina. I felt as if I was being burnt. I lost my consciousness after this. When I regained consciousness on 9.1.50 morning, that same SI and some constables came into my cell and started kicking me on my stomach with their boots. Then a nail was driven into my right heel. At this time, in my state of half consciousness, I could hear the SI saying that, 'We're coming back at night and unless you confess, the constables will rape you one by one.' Late at night the SI and the constables came back and uttered the same threat again. When I refused to say anything, three or four constables held

me down forcibly, and one constable really started raping me. Soon after this I lost my consciousness again. When I regained consciousness on 10.1.50 morning, I discovered that I was bleeding profusely all over. All my clothes were completely drenched in blood. In that very state I was taken to Nawabganj from Nachol, and at the Nawabganj police station the constables welcomed me with hard blows on my face. I was in a completely bed-ridden state then. So the court inspector and some constables carried me into a cell. I was still bleeding and had a very high temperature. It was most probably a doctor from the Nawabganj government hospital who checked my temperature and found it to be 105 degrees. When he heard about my bleeding, he assured me that I'd be treated with the help of a female nurse. I was also given some medicines and a couple of blankets. On 11.1.50 a nurse from the government hospital came to check me up. I don't know what kind of report she submitted about me, but after she left, my blood-smeared clothes were changed for a fresh sari. This entire period I spent in a cell in the Nawabganj police station, under the treatment of one doctor. I was running a very high temperature, experiencing a lot of bleeding, and also losing consciousness from time to time. On 16.1.50 evening a stretcher was brought to my cell, and I was told that I had to go somewhere else for treatment. When I said that I could hardly move, I was hit with a stick and forced to get on the stretcher. I was then taken to a different house, where too I confessed nothing, but the constables forced me to sign on a sheet of white paper. At this point I was running a very high fever and was only half conscious. Since my condition was steadily deteriorating, I was shifted to the government hospital in Nawabganj the next day. But my condition became more critical, and on 21.1.50 I was brought to the Central Jail in Rajshahi and admitted to the district hospital. At no point of time had I said anything to the police, and I have nothing more to say than whatever I've said in this statement.[5]

Nothing about the Nachol incident, or this testimony, appeared in any newspaper 'due to extraordinary control over the press' (Umar 2004: 143). Communist activists distributed Bangla and English versions of this court deposition through the workers of the Students Federation (ibid.: 143), and it was thus picked up by the Indian press too. But even less is known about the treatment meted out to Ila Mitra after that, in the Rajshahi central jail. Badruddin Umar writes:

> The transfer of Ila Mitra and the Santal prisoners to the Rajshahi central jail coincided with large-scale communal violence in East and West Bengal. The jail authorities and the police tried to create communal excitement inside and even outside the jail. The wife of the police officer who was killed on 5 January by the Santals would come to the jail gate at Rajshahi everyday, abuse the Santals and Ila Mitra everyday in bad language and describe the incident in a distorted manner. This created a great deal of tension among the prisoners, and some of them, along with the prison guards, tried to instigate prisoners against the Hindu detainees, including the political prisoners. The wife of the dead police officer, Tafizuddin, also did the same thing. Sometimes Ila Mitra also would be taken to the jail gate almost naked and they would tell the prisoners to have a look at the 'queen'. (Ibid.: 142–43)

Some humiliations run so deep that they defy articulation. Thousands of pages of popular literature on Ila Mitra remain silent on this spectacle of humiliation, as did Ila Mitra herself in all the hours she spent talking to me across three years. Such are the blatant humiliations that formed the underbelly of 'secular democracies' in the subcontinent.

It was only after the Hindu prisoners had been on hunger strike for eight days, from 2 February onwards, that the district magistrate visited them on 10 February, Tafizuddin's wife's visits stopped, and the communal activities of the police and the jail authorities were stemmed (Umar 2004: 143). It is evident from the description above that in addition to communal politics, there was a clear anti-adivasi dimension too, represented not only in the daily abuse of the Santals but also in the reference to Ila Mitra as the 'queen'. At first instance this might seem to refer to class politics, for Ramen Mitra, son of a wealthy zamindar of Nachol and Ila Mitra's husband, was referred to as Raja Babu, and she, by extension as Rani Ma, the significations of 'king' and 'queen' in these epithets hearkening back to feudal usage. However, the fact that the Santals chose to refer to them thus *after* both of them had declassed themselves and lived with the Santals in their homes in the direst of conditions for years, infused these references with the love and respect extended by the Santals to their communist leaders, replacing the earlier class or feudal significations. The snide usage of 'queen' for Ila Mitra thus points to the underlying anti-communist and anti-adivasi anxieties of the establishment, as much as it plays itself out in the triumph of the prison establishment at the public humiliation of such a 'queen' of adivasis and communists.

As I have argued earlier, the repeated torture of Ila Mitra thus carries valence at multiple symbolic levels, all condensed into the figure of one woman. Assertion of any one of these identities, Santal, communist, Hindu or woman, would jeopardize the homogeneity of a patriarchal Muslim majority state, and Ila represented all combined in one, either by political affiliation or by origin. The power of this figure was also different from the earlier symbolic linkages of woman with nation and oppositional community, because she was not just the enemy without. In her converged all the multiple threats to the new nation, and she stood for the condensation of all the enemy forces within too that had to be purged to ensure the homogeneity, integrity and stability of the nation. The relentless, repetitive nature of the torture she was subjected to is an index of the intensity of the obsessive fear, the 'primitive' challenge to middle-class certainty, the threat of class warfare as well as the paranoid fear of the communal other (Panjabi 2010: 55).

In such a situation, Ila Mitra's articulations and determined resistance were extraordinary in that they signified a 'breaking of boundaries' that unsettled established constraints of gender and sexuality. Yet, what was it that had driven Mitra to reject the codifications of 'honour' that underlay the state's violation of her body, sexuality and dignity?

It was clearly advantageous for the CP to have Ila Mitra testify to the inhuman torture by the state. The political imperative to have Ila Mitra deliver a candid testimony clearly overshadowed all the sexual taboos of the CP as it urged her to put political commitment before all else. Whether Ila Mitra too had indeed experienced the sexual violations as violations of 'honour', we will never know now, but her sense of dignity and privacy had clearly been violated in the act. However, this is, not unexpectedly, a much-elided concern in heroic narrative of Ila Mitra in official Left historiography. Badruddin Umar (2004: 141) structures his account thus:

> At the Rajshahi central jail, Ila Mitra was kept in a solitary cell and a case was instituted against her and all the Santal prisoners.... Ila Mitra was considering what she would state in her deposition before the court, because it was a really delicate and difficult matter to state in detail of what actually happened to her, and the kind of torture that the police inflicted on her [at] Nachol and then at the Nawabgunj and Rajshahi jails. At that time she unexpectedly received a secret letter from Manorama Basu of Barisal and Bhanu Devi of Khulna, both of whom were detained at the Rajshahi central jail at the time. They urged her to state everything that had happened to her and asked her not to feel shy. The letter was helpful to Ila Mitra who finally rose above all inhibitions and stated in

> very clear language the inhuman torture and outrage on her honour that was committed by the brute policemen of the … government of Pakistan.

Despite the relative sensitivity of the approach, this version too toes an official masculinist line in its interpretation that the letter was 'helpful' to Ila Mitra. That it was certainly 'helpful' to the party is evident in the fact that Ila Mitra did ultimately deliver the explicit and powerfully indicting testimony. What the cost of this second round of violation of personal dignity—the first one consisting in the actual endurance of such sexual torture, the second in having to narrate it in a public court—might have been for her was never considered.

Ila Mitra's own version, narrated haltingly, painfully, had a different thrust. She indicated that the letter the CP women had sent her carried a barely veiled threat of exclusion; she had to deliver the testimony on threat of banishment from the CP. Manorama and Bhanu had clearly privileged the political gains that the CP would derive from such explicit testimony over the loss of dignity it would mean for an already traumatized woman comrade. Yet, it was the time of the armed revolution; the party diktat was inviolable. There was a deep tension between Ila's subjectivity and the CP's political strategy, discernible even 50 years after the event. Unease and silences continued to punctuate her political confidence when I met her in 1996. Ila Mitra's narrative, while predominantly one about the sacrifice of the Santals, her own political commitment and struggle for survival, was nevertheless also underlined by silences and distortions of memory that signal ambiguities revealing the impact of both state violence and the repressive frameworks of the CP. Delivering her testimony, in a public court, of sexual violence done unto her by the East Pakistani authorities after her arrest, had not been easy. In her own words, she was 'after all … a Hindu wife', indicating that a certain degree of privacy regarding sexual matters was integral to her being. Ironically, party notions of appropriate political subjectivity in that historical moment had eroded the CP's sexually conservative stance and opened up the space for an explicit public discourse on sexuality. Later when I met her in 1997, Ila di's disquiet with her own testimony and its sexual explicitness that made for uneasy reading seemed to have undergone yet another shift. Her changed sense of herself, from the radical leadership of those days to that of a member of the legisative assembly,[6] now seemed to be inflected with the more conservative contemporary party notions of 'proper' political subjectivity, underlining the fact that once the crisis was over, the vocabulary for expressions of sexual experience had been purged out of its political discourse.[7]

So what do we understand from these shifting sands of 'honour' that take on contradictory valences in times of peace and crisis for revolutionaries and for the state? How do even the most progressive of political parties deploy 'honour' for strategic purposes? 'Honour' does not have a steady, unchanging signification. Do its mutations and strategic transformations then offer us any way of understanding how we may also transform the notions of 'honour' for women in ways that may be meaningful to us, in ways that it may not remain the ground of impunity that it is today?

One of the most disturbing experiences during three years of conversations with Ila di was witnessing a woman as tough as her completely at a loss as to how to share her testimony with me. First she tried to narrate it herself, but faltered in her very first line. Then she handed me Maleka Begum's biography of her to read, as it carried the testimony in full. And finally she decided to read it out to me herself from the book, in an attempt to sidestep both the trauma of recalling it afresh from memory, as well as the impersonality of just handing it to me to read. Thus she forged the human connection with me of narrating her testimony herself, even if only by reading it out. What was almost equally disturbing was learning from her biographer Maleka Begum that Ila di had lost all memory of the testimony she had delivered in court. Why had Ila di lost her memory of this testimony? Once back in Calcutta three years after her initial arrest, she had suffered a complete nervous breakdown. Yet, when she recovered a few years later, she remembered the details of the rest of the struggle in full detail. Why did she draw a blank vis-à-vis the contents of her own testimony? Was it the experience of the unbearable nature of the torture itself that could be lived with only by blocking it out of memory, or was it the trauma of a complete loss of dignity while narrating it in court that had forced her to block it out? Or both? Her question to Maleka Begum, who carried a copy of the testimony to her more than 40 years later, was, 'Did I really say all this in court?' Ila di never really asked, 'Did I really endure all this—how?' Or maybe she did, but never talked about it. In recent years, truth commissions in Latin America have recognized the toll it takes on victims of severe sexual torture to recall, retell and thus relive all over again the terrifying indignity of such violations. The political gains of such public testimonies can only become more meaningful when they also address the personal costs to the victims.

III

What were the reasons for the complete impunity of the state and its players, such that no one was ever called to task for such a brutal crime? What were the strategies by which norms of state accountability were elided to secure such impunity?

No one was ever tried, far less convicted, for the heinous torture of Ila Mitra or the murder of over 24 Santals. The reason why all the violators enjoyed impunity, it is evident, relates to the state's anxiety to control the adivasi, communist and Hindu forces. While the nature of such statist anxieties may vary across India and Pakistan, and across time, it is important to analyse the precise strategies by which all norms of state accountability were elided, for they may reveal the patterns of discourse set in place in the founding years of these two nation-states that continued to shape their mirroring sectarian, elitist, communal and patriarchal politics.

The Government of East Pakistan had clearly taken up a de facto position favouring landowners. Its official report titled 'Precis of the Case of Srimati Ila Mitra, a Convict in the Nachole Murder Case' (Government of East Pakistan 1955) begins thus:

> Mrs Ila Mitra and her husband Ramen Mitra alias Habu of Nawabgunj P.S. [Police Station] of Rajshahi district were communist workers.... They used to *incite the Santals of the locality against the levy system*. Hundreds of volunteers were enrolled and trained in the area by Ramen Mitra and his wife Ila Mitra. (Ibid., emphasis added)

There is no word about the disinheritance of the Santals or the exorbitant agricultural levy and cut-throat interests these peasants had to pay the feudal landowners, not to mention the latter's sexual exploitation of landless peasant women such that they could lay sexual claim to any peasant bride on the night of her wedding. The levy system was the chief mode by which the landowners exploited the peasantry, and the indication is that the government perceived it as its duty to ensure that its sanctity was maintained. This is further reinforced in the document just quoted, which cites Nachol P.S. Officer-in-Charge Moulvi Tafizuddin Molla's initiative to prevent Santals from removing paddy belonging to the landowner Akshaya Pandit as a law-keeping move.

There are clear discrepancies between the government version and that of the Left regarding what followed, with the former stating that the Santals arrived, surrounded the police and tricked them into laying down their arms, and the latter asserting that it was in retaliation against the opening of fire by the police and the killing of one peasant, and so on. However, it is agreed that the Santals turned on the police and killed the sub-inspector and three of his men. Ila Mitra was arrested (accompanied by the Santals, of whom this document makes no mention at this point) at Rohanpur station before she could board the train to flee across the border. The précis records that a case was started 'under Section 148, 333, 379 and 302', which was followed by a preliminary enquiry in the lower court by a senior district magistrate, who in turn 'committed the accused persons to the Sessions Court of Rajshahi for trial' (Government of East Bengal 1955). Here, Ila Mitra delivered her statement in court; the text of the statement was then included in this précis.

What was especially significant about this case was that it took on international dimensions; there ensued a crossfire between the Indian and Pakistani governments. The ways in which the cross-border dynamics of communalism were framed by East Pakistan to elide issues of sexual torture by the state, as well as the way in which the confrontation was resolved, are instructive for comprehending the strategies by which the states colluded in securing impunity against crimes of sexual violence.

It is telling that the précis refers to the reports in the Indian press—in the Calcutta and then the Bombay papers—as 'Indian propaganda', reinforcing the government's bias against Ila Mitra even in its documentation, but also displacing newspaper demands for justice for a violated woman to the level of a confrontation between the two states. The précis further files the response to the reports in the Calcutta press under the subheading 'Government of East Bengal Press Note to Counteract Indian Propaganda'. This press note, it further states, also formed the basis for the reply sent by the Government of East Pakistan to an official query made by the Government of India.

The press note, issued by the Director of Publicity, East Bengal, on 3 February 1951, deploys precisely the same binary of silence versus disclosure with which this paper began, to 'prove' Ila Mitra's allegations to be 'altogether false'. It first cites her silence as proof that there had been no 'ill-treatment':

> She was found to be physically fit at the time of her arrival at Nawabganj under police escort and production before the Magistrate there to whom she made no complaint, nor did she complain of any ill-treatment at a later stage when she was again produced before a Magistrate to whom she made a confession which was judicially recorded. (Government of East Bengal 1953)

And then it frames her disclosure of the sexual violations as a 'not uncommon strategy of alleging "police torture" to attract sympathy': 'Government are satisfied that her allegation are [*sic*] without substance and that, while retracting her confession in course of her trial, she has adopted the not uncommon strategy of alleging "police torture" to attract sympathy and support from different quarters' (ibid.).

The fact that the initial silence may have been due to severe trauma, or a complex experience of a violation of 'honour', or a sense of profound violation of dignity, or all of these is strategically elided, as is the fact that Ila Mitra's testimony clearly asserts that she was compelled, under force, to sign the earlier confession, which carried no complaint of sexual violence. Similarly, the fact that the disclosure, which was made at a later date, and after further violations in Rajshahi, could be because she had had some time to think things over, or might have been spurred by anger at further subjection to torture and humiliation, is not a consideration, as it was in the interests of the state to write it off as a false charge. The underlying implication of course is that such an explicit account of sexual violation from a woman of Ila Mitra's background, combined with the 'inconsistency' of her behaviour, could only have been a matter of political strategy.

Questionable here is the very mode that the Director of Publicity adopted to assess the veracity of a sexually brutalized woman's silence and disclosure.[8] Words carry meaning depending on the uses made of them in different realms of human life. Silence, for example, signifies completely different realities in the contexts of a robber or a rapist, and a woman who has been sexually brutalized. There exist in the world multiple communities of meaning, some of which may also be incommensurable, that comprise different discursive systems, such as the feminist, the patriarchal, the judicial, the religious, the scientific, and so on, that are marked by different investments, needs, desires, beliefs or goals. They produce their own meanings and rules of circulation, what Lyotard refers to as 'phrase regimens'. Basically, what was at work in the case of Ila Mitra, even if she had been allowed to defend herself, was the politics of incompatible 'phrase regimens', or idioms, of gendered experience and patriarchal judicial discourse. Lyotard defines the situation of a differend thus:

> I would like to call a differend the case where the plaintiff is divested of the means to argue and becomes for that reason a victim. If the addressor, the addressee, and the sense of the testimony are neutralized, everything takes place as if there were no damages. A case of differend between two parties takes place when the regulation of the conflict that opposes them is done in the idiom of one of the parties while the wrong suffered by the other is not signified in that idiom. (Lyotard 1992: 12)

Since the regulation of the conflict is done in the dominant patriarchal, judgemental genre of discourse, the sexual violations suffered by women do not find place in that idiom, and the harm done to women cannot be presented in the idiom of such judgement. In the case of sexual violations, the problem is that what women experience is not given a place in judicial discourse. However, it is not that it *cannot* be represented, but that it is *deliberately* not represented; it is marginalized out of the idiom of the judiciary.

This leads to an important definition of injustice, which involves using language rules from one 'phrase regimen' and applying them to another. To live ethically thus, also involves becoming alert precisely to such forms of injustice; it involves paying attention to experiences and perspectives in their specificity and not just within frames of abstract conceptuality. The government reports in Ila Mitra's case deliberately played on the contrary politics of two different idioms: it strategically elided the significations of her gendered idiom and privileged the patriarchal judicial idiom. But this crossfire signals the importance of bridging the multiple idioms of diversity and giving recognition to different communities of meaning. It points to the need to build bridges between the feminist idiom and the juridical one by opening up juridical discourse to represent gendered perspectives and feminist claims at the basic level of language and its multiple significations.

The other 'game' that comes to light in the documents of the time is of the government securing impunity for itself by charging those seeking justice for Ila Mitra with inciting communal tensions. Thus, gender violence was given short shrift via the bogey of communalism. In a letter written on 28 December 1950 by N.M. Khan, chief secretary, Government of East Bengal, to Muhammad Ali, secretary general, Government of Pakistan in Karachi, about a story on Ila Mitra carried in the *Blitz* dated 23 September 1950, the former asserts:

> We feel that the attention of the Government of India should be invited to this matter and they be requested to take action against the 'Blitz' for publication of news which is bound to

> have adverse effect on communal relations. The article offends against the provisions of clause 7(c) of the Delhi agreement.

Why is it that there was an agreement already in place by 1950 between the two nations regarding incitement of communal tensions, but none in place even today, 65 years later, against making women's bodies the ground for cross-border politics? Why is it that a young 14-year-old Bangladeshi girl, Fellani Khatun, shot by Indian Border Security Force (BSF) guards while climbing the barbed-wire fence back into her country, was left hanging there for four hours till she died pleading for water? This happened on 7 January 2011. The BSF guard was let off scot-free in a closed BSF trial in 2013, and has not been convicted to date. Clearly Fellani was left to die a slow death, her body perched on the barbed-wire fence between India and Bangladesh, as a threat to Bangladeshis, and as an indicator of Indian supremacy in the subcontinent.

It is a hard fact of the politics of states in the Indian subcontinent that states and their representatives continue to enjoy impunity when they wage violence against women, but any hint of a charge of communal violence has to be addressed as the utmost priority. It seems from the précis that the Government of India remained dissatisfied with the responses sent to it by the Pakistani government, and sent repeated demands for further enquiries to be made in Ila Mitra's case. Yet it is interesting to see how the case was resolved between the two countries. When the Government of India again enquired about the 'serious illness of Mrs. Ila Mitra in Jail', the press note issued by the Government of East Bengal on 12.4.54 in this connection (and also included in the précis) stated:

> Due to her ill health her sentence has been suspended for a period of 6 months which means that for that period *she is an entirely free person*. Government have helped her to take admission in the Medical College Hospital and have also

> arranged for those costly medicines which are not available in the hospital.
>
> She has also taken out a Pakistani passport which would enable her to *travel abroad for the purpose of treatment* if she so desired. *No restriction has been placed on her movements* and there is nothing more the Government can do. (Government of East Bengal: 1953; emphases added)

When the Indian government's demands for enquiries into Ila Mitra's case finally gave way to one about her 'serious illness', the thrust of the East Pakistani response was clearly that India could have her back. For other than reassuring the Indian government that she was being treated at the Dhaka medical hospital and even being supplied 'costly medicines' by the state, the central point that this note makes emphatically is that, for the period of the next six months, she was an 'entirely free person', with 'no restriction' on her movements, actually suggesting that she could go to India, 'travel abroad if she so desired'. This note is evidence of the East Pakistani government's virtually handing back to India the woman it had subjected to sexual torture in custody, after having countercharged the Indian government with spreading propaganda, and its press with attempting to incite communal violence, to deflect attention from its own crime. It was virtually an act of buying silence, buying impunity. Ila Mitra came back to India for treatment, stayed on and obtained Indian citizenship. The Indian government eventually dropped all its charges against the East Pakistani government after Ila Mitra returned. Ila was invited back to Bangladesh later, with full honours as a state guest, by Sheikh Mujibur Rahman, and then again on the 50th anniversary of the Tebhaga movement, but she died without ever receiving justice. The Indian and Pakistani states had colluded successfully in ensuring the impunity of the latter.

IV

There is a central paradox in the social structuring of 'honour'. 'Honour' relates to a social code of behaviour, in which human beings are assigned worth and stature by a society based on its moral codes. Yet simultaneously, it also derives from the formative personal bonds that establish one's personal dignity and character, and is understood to be rooted in one's conscience. 'Honour' is thus structured upon the judgement of a community, but its integral component, dignity, is rooted in the assessments of individual conscience. This conflation of social and personal values rests on an assumption of an integral agreement between the moral judgement of a society and the conscience of an individual—and unquestioning acceptance of this assumed conformity is the basis of this second dimension of confusion.

What happens when the moral codes of a society are built on the proprietorship of women's bodies, irrespective of their personal dignity, their identities as thinking beings, and in complete denial of the conscience at work in every individual woman? What is actually an irresoluble conflict between the moral codes of patriarchal societies and the dignity, self-worth and conscience of individual women as human beings, is suppressed in the privileging of normative social structures of 'honour'. Codes of 'honour' are thus also effective in concealing the conflict between socially constructed morality and women's experience of such morality as being destructive of their dignity and well-being. What is to be done when 'honour', which is supposed to be a guarantor of dignity and worth, is itself in irresoluble conflict with both?

It is evident then that the significance of 'honour' in terms of dignity, worthiness and nobility is completely antithetical to its significance in relation to female chastity and 'respectability' as well as other forms of male sexual dominance and control of women's sexuality. 'Honour' thus pre-empts women's agency, makes the law ineffective and guarantees men impunity; it is damaging to a violated woman's sense of self, and in fact, that of every woman who is compelled to live by the codes of dress, decorum and behaviour dictated by such 'honour'. It camouflages the deep conflict between social morality and women's interests and well-being.

What complicates matters further are several layers of confusion and repression that impede women's agency. One is at the level of confusion—the deep distress of having one's intimacy violated is simultaneously experienced as social 'shame' that impels one into concealment of the crime, rather than as anger that could propel one into demanding justice. The personal experience of injury is overlaid by the public construction of it as 'shame'. Often such personal distress, or even severe trauma, and outrage are repressed under the burden of shame, or even dislocated by it, leading to deep psychological disturbances and breakdowns. Such confusions and repressions, experienced by women at profoundly subjective realms of being, often obfuscate their vision of the crime done unto them; and such subsumption of the intimate injury of a violated self into socially constructed structures/notions of disgrace and humiliation succeeds in robbing women of agency. 'Honour', far from being a matter of pride that reinforces self-worth and dignity, is thus experienced by violated women as a complete loss of both; it is experienced as that which is destructive of self, which forecloses agency.

In fact, what is even more insidious about this patriarchal sense of 'honour' in its intersection with caste, community or political party identities, is that it actually sanctions crimes against women across community, caste and other rivalries or hierarchies, and this sanction in turn becomes a guarantor of impunity. This has become more than evident across the last six and a half decades of 'modern' India, right from the sexual violations of women across communities during the partition to the gang-rape of Bhanwari

Devi by upper-caste men, the daily violations followed by murders of dalit women, the ritualized gang-rapes and butchery in broad daylight of Muslim women in Gujarat in 1992, the recent rampant sexual violence against women in Muzzafarnagar, the gang-rapes of women in Nandigram by Communist Part of India (Marxist) (CPI-M) workers and the current rapes and also public exhortations to rape of CPI-M women by members of the Trinamool Congress. In Gujarat, the gang-rapes took place in broad daylight; in Bengal today, the exhortations to rape are voiced proudly in broad daylight and with full media coverage. The exhorters enjoy impunity and walk free as honourable members of the ruling party. Somewhere along the line, the sense of victory in rivalry, implicated in most medieval, including Mughal, notions of honour, has been emptied of the equally honourable (albeit patriarchal) respect for women's dignity and integrity.

It is indeed telling that the terms 'honour' and 'honourable' in their most widespread positive usages pertain to men—to a man of honour, or to an honourable man; rarely is a woman referred to as a woman of honour, or as an honourable woman. For women, it is the discourse of the 'loss of honour' that is the most pervasive, and ironically so in cases of sexual violation where the actual loss of honour should be of the male violator. The dishonourable action is that of the man, yet the dishonour is transferred onto the woman who in turn is socialized, as is all of society, into experiencing this injustice paradoxically as 'shame'.

Given the significant levels of sophistication and sensitivity in contemporary reflections on sexual violence, the ground is already well laid for us to deconstruct notions of 'honour' and theorize the impunity it guarantees men; in fact, much work has already been done on this (cf. Sangari 2008). Yet honour is much more than a mere code of behaviour; it is a notion that involves the very structuring of our intimate selves. The most difficult challenge lies in the realization that 'honour' comprises such a cherished aspect of our subjectivities that not only is it inadequate to merely deconstruct it, but it cannot be ejected from our subjectivities overnight. 'Honour' is so deeply implicated within our very selves as women too, that even if we do not comply with all its codes, it still remains a treasured value in profound ways. To be an 'honourable' woman is still vital to the sense of self-worth. 'Honour' is integral to the structuring of our selves, and is as real a condition of intimate being as is love, but the problem is that it is also posited at the interface of self and society, of woman and patriarchy. Centuries of sedimentation and internalization of a privileged sense of 'honour' have ensured that either option—of reimagining 'honour' or even reimagining a self without 'honour'—is an insurmountable task.

Can we re-evaluate honour and thereby restructure our selves? The question then is how we can identify what it is at the core of what we call 'honour' that we value, that is crucial to a human being's sense of self, and salvage this from all the patriarchal machinations that have made it a 'bestial' trap, for women of course, but also for men compelled to act by its dictates. Or do we need to eject it as a value from our subjectivities as we have the notions of chastity and virginity? If we were to consider other values, such as those of self-respect, human dignity and worthiness, in its place, then which of these in our languages has not already been co-opted by sexualized, patriarchal notions of honour? Notions of a woman's *laaj* (modesty) or *izzat* (honour) have already been recognized as clichéd patriarchal traps; *maryada* (rectitude) is too heavily implicated in the image of *maryadapurushottam* Rama (Rama as the ideal follower of rules amongst men) and in the epic hero's insistence on Sita's undergoing the chastity test of fire; and the idea of *imaan* (the basic mark of a person's identity, stemming from the Arabic *amana*, and relating to the safeguarding of a sacred trust), is also overdetermined by norms of chastity in the case of women.

Merely dwelling upon the significations of language that represent honour, or even deconstructing these concepts, is clearly not going to get us anywhere. The point is that even as we have begun to understand language through the prisms of the histories in which its meaning has been structured, so we can reinvest it with renewed meaning only through the creation of new histories in which the older patriarchal meanings are refused. Such renewals of meaning require not only progressive communities of consensus, but also close attention to how we structure our sexual experiences in the psyche.

A deep sense of the violation of personal dignity and intimacy continued to haunt Ila Mitra throughout her life. She had found herself at the crossroads of the state's strategic deployment of regressive patriarchal codes of 'honour' and vendetta by the state, and the CP's apparently progressive refusal of such sedimentations of patriarchal ideologies. Self-respect of women was given short shrift, as was personal dignity, in the crossfire between the nascent, elitist state and the resisting CP that had nevertheless adventitiously compelled Ila Mitra to deliver a candid testimony of intimate violations of self. When the movement died out, however, so did the glory of her resistance, leaving her unable to cope with the loss of dignity, the humiliation, and the devastation of a violated self.

This sense of humiliation is perhaps a central pivot for launching a new stage of political transformation in the fields of 'honour'. For, as Gopal Guru cautions us, the experience of social humiliation is too easily reduced to a psychological feeling of hurt. Humiliation is a systemic strategy for perpetuating domination. The challenge lies in dismantling the structures of humiliation, in figuring out ways to 'negotiate the *experience* of humiliation with the claim to *reason*' (Guru 2012). One way, Guru suggests, is to counterpose humiliation with self-respect. In fact, responding to the question of why he needs to 'invoke the moral category of self-respect and the opposite humiliation when the Indian constitution has provided for the protection of self respect … and terms like equality, justice and freedom have already taken care of setting people free from possible humiliation', he asserts : 'The question that needs attention is: do these terms accommodate the essence of self-respect?' (Guru 2009: xi). Guru's *Humiliation: Claims and Contexts* is a landmark volume comprising reflections on humiliation and self-respect in the context of untouchability by a range of thoughtful scholars. What this self-respect, or *atmasamman*, would constitute from the standpoint of women in terms of dignity, a sense of self freed from systemic sexual control, and experiential significations not overruled by patriarchal interests, would require another such body of sustained, collective thinking.

Certainly there was a sense of another kind of 'honour', a certain dignity and self-valuation, in Ila Mitra's act of delivering a radical, sexually explicit testimony in court propelled by the CP. This was an honour that, even as it undermined her psychological and ontological well-being, did nevertheless reinforce her political sense of being. Ila Mitra drew upon her identity as a revolutionary to resist shame and charge the state with injustice, but it is clear from her unease with the sexual politics of the CP that this rational political identity may not have been enough to rebuild herself after her breakdown. Ideological solidarities are motivating, but there is more to the make-up of personhood, and Ila's life is testimony to the importance of historical commitments as well as *ontological* rootings of choice. It is significant that four years after her arrest and torture, when she returned to India in 1954, she was still in a state of nervous breakdown. The psychological trauma clearly ran deep, and the critical question is what was it that finally enabled her to heal to a point where she could actually enter the field of political activism again and even stand for elections and become a member of the West Bengal Legislative Assembly. It is well known that several left poets, singers and writers would visit her regularly, offer solidarity, and try to revive her spirits by sharing their songs, poems, writings—and she did acknowledge their contribution gratefully. However, each time when she was asked what it was that had enabled her to heal to a point where she could become a dynamic political activist again, her response had been *otiterjed*, the persistence of the past. She would recall poignantly her experiences of bonding, both humorous and tragic, with the Santals. I have shown elsewhere that this was no ordinary commitment to a past of revolutionary ideals, however sincere that can be; it was a commitment to a Santal past, of the hopes and ideals of a tribe repeatedly devastated through history. This commitment was born out of a deep ontological identification with her Santal comrades, with whom she had lived, fought, risked her life and been tortured—and if she had seen them choosing to be killed before her very eyes rather than betraying and thus committing her, their leader, to any danger, then she too had chosen to continue to be tortured for their sake rather than give up on her active struggle for their rights.[9] This ontological bonding was of a kind that has rarely found a place in our political culture, and it is this that sustained her into recovery and enabled her to restructure herself, to regain a sense of self-worth in living up to atiterjed, the claims of their shared history.

Ila Mitra's history has profound implications for us also in relation to the ways in which we build our movements and our solidarities—they cannot be structured on shared ideologies or locations within caste, class and patriarchal systems alone, as the cultures of even the most progressive of left parties usually are. Human bonding, rooted in a shared ownership of history, forged through mutual affective relations such as the Santals shared with Ila Mitra and she with them, is what ultimately gives human beings the courage to resist cultures of impunity in ways that may make them victorious in the long vision of history, even if the immediate battles might be lost.

NOTES

1. Cf. my article 'Otiter Jed or Times of Revolution: Ila Mitra, the Santals and the Tebhaga Movement' (Panjabi 2010) for a detailed account of the history of Ila Mitra and the Santals. Some of the material used in the next section, especially by way of introducing Ila Mitra and her history, is drawn from there. I indicate page numbers when I quote specific arguments I have made in that paper. Also see 'Women's Subjectivity and the "Political" in Oral Narratives of the Tebhaga Movement: Alienation in a Politics of Liberation' (Panjabi 2012) for an analysis of women's activism in the Tebhaga movement, in relation to which the history of Ila Mitra may be understood better.
2. 'This freedom is a farce.'
3. See Kamal (1996) and Umar (2004) for a historical account of Ila Mitra's role in the Nachol revolt, and Begum (1987) for a biographical account of her life. See *Aparajeya* (1996), *Samaj Chetana* (1997) and *Chalar Pathe* (1997) (Mitra 1996, 1997) for testimonial essays by Ila Mitra.
4. See *Samaj Chetana* (1996), *Tebhaga Sangram* (1997) and the books by Das (1996), Dutta (1985) and Isma (1996) for heroic and hagiographical accounts and poems dedicated to Ila Mitra. Maleka Begum's biographical narrative, *Ila Mitra* (1987), a documentation of Mitra's activism and letters as well as of poems and fiction centring around her, takes on hagiographical dimensions too in its framing of her resistance as sacrifice, and in referring to her home in Kolkata as a pilgrimage centre for Bangladeshis. The same is characteristic of innumerable essays and pamphlets on Ila. For a fictional account, see Selina Hossain's (1989) novel. A postage stamp was issued by the Government of Bangladesh during Ila Mitra's visit on the fiftieth anniversary celebrations of Tebhaga.
5. Translation of the testimony read out to me by Ila Mitra from Maleka Begum's biography of her. Cf. also Umar (2004: 141–42) and Government of East Bengal (1955). I am deeply grateful to

Wilhelm van Schendel for sending me copies of the documents cited here from the National Archives of Bangladesh.

6. Ila Mitra was elected on a CPI ticket from the Maniktala constituency in 1962, 1967, 1969 and 1972.
7. Cf. Panjabi (2012) for an earlier version of this argument, and, for a more detailed working out of it, see Chapter 6, '"Premer Jomir Khonje—In Search of the Terrain of Love": Alienation in a Politics of Violence', in my book *Unclaimed Harvest: An Oral History of the Tebhaga Women's Movement*, Zubaan (2017).
8. This press note decrees the 'allegations' by Ila Mitra to be false on the basis of the enquiry made 'personally' by a district magistrate. Neither the text of the district magistrate's report, nor that of the judgement in the Ila Mitra case in which all the accused were convicted, was available to me. Hence, I do not have access to the precise language in which the judiciary may have 'proven' Ila Mitra's allegations to be false, if at all her testimony featured in the proceedings of the case. The press note quoted here has also been included in the official government précis of the case cited earlier.
9. Cf. Panjabi (2010). A longer version of this essay is presented in Chapter 5 of *Unsung Harvest: An Oral History of the Tebhaga Women's Movement*, Zubaan (2017).

REFERENCES

Begum, Maleka. 1987. *Ila Mitra*. Dhaka: Gyan Prakashani.

Das, Ajit Kumar. ed. 1996. *Nachole Ila Mitra*. Nababganj: Tebhaga Krishak Andolaner Ponchash Bachhor Purti Udjapan Committee.

Dutta, Shekhar. 1985. *Tebhaga Andolan*. Dhaka: Bangla Akademi.

Franco, Jean. 2013. *Cruel Modernity*. Durham: Duke University Press.

Government of East Bengal. 1953. Director of Publicity, 'Press Note', 3 February 1951. National Archives of Bangladesh, Home (Political) (C.R.) B. Proceedings 222–24, February.

————. 1955. 'Precis of the Case of Srimati Ila Mitra, a Convict in the Nachole Murder Case', 11.5.54. National Archives of Bangladesh, Home (Political) (C.R.) B. Proceedings 532–37, March.

Guru, Gopal. 2009. *Humiliation: Claims and Context*. New Delhi: Oxford University Press.

————. 2012. 'Humiliation Condemned to Remain "Hurt"—Notes from a Talk by Gopal Guru: Parth Pratim Shil & Ankita Pandey'. Kafila, 31 May. http://kafila.org/2012/05/31/humiliation-condemned-to-remain-hurt-notes-from-a-talk-by-gopal-guru-parth-pratim-shil-ankita-pandey/ (accessed 17 June 2016).

Hossain, Selina. 1989. *Kaanta Taare Projapati*. Dhaka: Jatiya Sahitya Prakashani.

Isma, Shahidul. 1996. 'Ranima Ashchhen'. *Samvaad* (Dhaka), Sunday, 29 Kartik, 1403.

Kamal, Mesbah. 1996. 'Post-Partition Peasant Movements in East Bengal: A Case Study on Nachole Uprising', Chapter 6, Unpublished Ph.D. thesis, Department of History, Dhaka University.

Lyotard, Jean Francois. 1992. *The Differend: Phrases in Dispute* (translated by Georges van den Abeele). Minneapolis: University of Minnesota Press.

Mitra, Ila. 1996. 'Amar Jeebane Swadhinatar Swad', in Mahasveta Devi (ed.), *Aparajeya*. Calcutta: National Publishers (reprinted in *Chalar Pathe*, August 1997, pp. 41–43).

————. 1997. 'Ila Mitrer Nachol Baktita'. Lecture delivered by Ila Mitra on the occasion of the 50th anniversary celebrations in Nachol, Bangladesh, November 1996. *Samaj Chetana*, January–February, pp. 12–13.

Panjabi, Kavita. 2010. 'Otiter Jed or Times of Revolution: Ila Mitra, the Santals and Tebhaga Movement', *Economic and Political Weekly*, 14(33): 53–59.

————. 2012. 'Women's Subjectivity and the "Political" in Oral Narratives of the Tebhaga Movement: Alienation in a Politics of Liberation', in Kavita Panjabi and Paromita Chakravarti (eds), *Women Contesting Culture: Changing Frames of Gender Politics in India*, pp. 304–23. Kolkata: Stree.

————. 2017. Unclaimed Harvest: An Oral History of the Tebhaga Women's Movement. New Delhi: Zubaan.

Sangari, Kumkum. 2008. 'Gendered Violence, National Boundaries and Culture', in Radhika Coomaraswamy and Nimanthi Perera-Rajasingham (eds), *Constellations of Violence: Feminist Interventions in South Asia*, pp. 1–33. New Delhi: Women Unlimited.

Umar, Badruddin. 2004. *The Emergence of Bangladesh: Class Struggles in East Pakistan, 1947–58*. Karachi: Oxford University Press.

2

The Circle of Violence

RAJASHRI DASGUPTA

> Such things [gang-rape and murder] happen ... anti-socials are the same everywhere.
>
> (Jyoti Basu, Chief Minister of West Bengal from 1977–2000)

It was one of the darkest chapters in Kolkata's history. On 30 May 1990, three women health officials were dragged out of their car and chased by a frenzied mob on the eastern fringes of the city. The women were gang-raped, one was murdered; the driver lost his life trying to save his passengers. The women were so brutally battered that doctors at the emergency ward of the hospital had initially supposed all the three women to be dead.

There was shock and disbelief in Kolkata, the capital of West Bengal. The city saw an outpouring of angry protests and demonstrations that refused to die down; never had such a heinous crime ever been committed on women in the city or in its vicinity. Protesters demanded punishment for the guilty whatever the political affiliation of the perpetrators. Overnight, Bantala, 10 kilometres east of the city centre and until then a little-known area, grabbed the limelight and became infamously associated in the public mind with sexual brutality. Young girl students (now adults) remember the atmosphere of panic in their neighbourhoods, how parents were in the grip of such fear that they refused to allow them out alone after sunset, escorted them home, and curtailed their social activities.

The ruling Left Front (LF) state government in West Bengal, led by the Communist Party of India (Marxist) (CPM), failed to grasp the enormity of the Bantala incident. It made an attempt to downplay the incident, and failed to rise above political considerations as narrow party politics took precedence over human lives. All that the Marxist chief minister Jyoti Basu could comment in response to the incident as people demanded accountability was that anti-socials 'behave the same way everywhere', and that it did not mean that law and order was 'that bad' in Bengal. 'Such things happen [*erokom to hoye thake*],' Basu told the media, further stoking public anger (cited in Menon 2010). The health minister's remark was equally offensive: he wondered aloud what the 'women' (his own officials!) were doing there in the evening as the area 'was known to be a den of anti-social elements'. The then state information minister, Buddhadeb Bhattacharjee (who later became chief minister), vouchsafed that 'such incidents are exceptions rather than the norm [in Bengal]' (Bhattacharjee 2011). People's expectations of a high standard of public morality from a Marxist government were dashed in Bantala; the administration failed to respond boldly and missed the opportunity to initiate a widespread campaign for women's safety.

Behind the public anger following the incident was a deep anguish among people searching for answers: why didn't local people intervene to stop the madness of the mob? Kolkata is a city where women are respectfully addressed as *ma* (mother) or affectionately as *didimoni* (sister); a city where women may be seen moving about without fear even after dark; a city steeped in left culture, a city of endless causes and processions, of poignant poetry espousing the values of humanity, and of nameless, unsung heroes ever ready with a helping hand—what went wrong that fateful evening? Kolkata's pride in its social conscience was ground to dust by that single incident in Bantala.

In a powerful editorial in the journal *Mainstream Weekly* ('Bantala and After' 1990), the editor Nikhil Chakravarty voiced the people's concern when he wrote, 'Bantala stands as our danger signal of social degeneration.... degeneration of not only the perpetrators of the crime, but those of us who do not spend sleepless nights over how to combat what it stands for.' The Murari Mohan Dutta Commission, set up by the state government to inquire into the incident, asked the state government to determine whether the perpetrators had political patronage. If this was investigated, the findings were never made public. Ultimately, a few of the accused were sentenced to life imprisonment and others to 10 years in prison; but even this failed to quell the outrage. What festers in the public memory is the political patriarch's terse comment: *such things happen.*

The lack of sensitivity and state accountability on the part of the LF government in the Bantala incident can hardly be said to have been an exception during its unbroken 34 years of rule (1977–2011) in Bengal. The LF, led by the Marxists, failed to rectify its mistakes by setting exemplary norms and standards to address issues of sexual violence in the state. Instead, in the highly volatile politics of Bengal, political parties tend to politicize incidents of rape and sexual violence; the focus is not so much on achieving justice for the victims as on protecting perpetrators so that political parties may safeguard their image.

The Trinamul Congress (TMC) took over the reins of government from the LF in 2011, having won the elections on the basis of a campaign centred on the riveting slogan of *paribartan* (change). This essay will explore whether the shift in regimes meant a significant difference in state accountability for crimes against women. There were high expectations that the first woman chief minister of Bengal, Mamata Banerjee, would succeed in setting strict protocols to deal with perpetrators of sexual violence irrespective of their political affiliation. From the quick response of Banerjee's administration to the sensational gang-rape and murder of a student in Kamduni village in 2013, it might be thought that the administration had succeeded in instilling greater confidence among people in general, and women in particular, and that this would lead to a fall in the crime graph against women.

What is the experience of women who have faced sexual violence in Bengal, how has the violence impacted their lives, and what has been the social and economic cost to them and their families? This essay will try to probe and understand whether there has been greater state accountability for the safety and well-being of women in Bengal over the decades, be it under the Marxists or a woman leader of the TMC. Are the medical and police investigations, the legal processes, sensitive to the trauma of victims? Can women enjoy human rights when the rights of other social categories of society are in jeopardy?

'ABANDONING THE MOVEMENT TO GOVERN'

The parliamentarian Marxists ruled Bengal unchallenged for 34 years with overwhelming popular support, setting the world record for continuous rule by a single political party. It was the land reform movement of 1977 that had endeared the LF to the rural masses. The party followed this up with the devolution of power to the panchayats, making West Bengal one of the few Indian states to insist on regular elections to democratize and strengthen local government in villages. In the early 1990s, the implementation of reservation of one-third of the seats for women (mandated by the

73rd and 74th amendments to the Constitution) enabled women's active involvement and participation in the panchayat system.

For many decades, the geopolitics of the eastern state of West Bengal has intrigued and attracted activists and scholars alike (Bagchi and Dasgupta 2003; Chatterji 2007; Sengupta 2006). The trauma of the Partition, with East Pakistan being carved out from greater Bengal in 1947 at independence, displacing millions of people, has continued to linger in the social, cultural and political psyche of generations of Bengalis. Once again, in 1971, when East Pakistan broke away from Pakistan to form the new country of Bangladesh, Bengal relived the 'Partition experience' of impoverished refugees crossing the 4,500-kilometre porous border in droves. It was this large, displaced refugee population that was to form a resolute social and political base for the the Left and democratic movements in the state of West Bengal in the future. Moreover, the state occupies a strategic location, sharing international borders with Bhutan and Nepal that give it proximity to China, and serving as the 'link' between mainland India and the seven north-eastern states of the country. This location makes deltaic Bengal, with its population of 91 million people, an important political hub.

The rise of the LF's popularity was also closely linked to the authoritarian rule of the Congress Party at the centre. The prime minister, Indira Gandhi, had declared internal Emergency in 1975, curtailing fundamental rights throughout the country. Thousands of activists and political opposition leaders were jailed, and the Indian media encountered state censorship for the first time in independent India; left activists were murdered in fake police 'encounters' and prisoners were tortured. In 1977, when the Emergency was lifted and Indira Gandhi was forced to hold national elections, the Congress Party suffered an ignominious defeat, including in Bengal.

Political observers like the Marxist economist and columnist Ashok Mitra and cultural historian Sumanta Banerjee argue that violence as a political strategy emerged in Bengal during the rule of the Congress chief minister Siddhartha Shankar Ray, the chief architect of the Emergency, who used the state machinery to kill hundreds of left workers (both CPM and Naxalites) and imprison them during the 1970s (personal communication, Ashok Mitra and Sumanta Banerjee). The LF won the state assembly elections in 1977 on the single promise of releasing political prisoners and restoring democratic rights. With such impeccable credentials, how could Marxist leaders then be dismissive about Bantala? The slogan 'women's rights are human rights' took on greater significance in the charged atmosphere of the early 1990s (ibid.).

Since the 1990s, there has been a marked change in the fortunes of the LF as it gradually lost ideological focus and control under the onslaught of the policy of economic liberalization. The LF failed to understand the need for change and for the modification of its policies; it started to rely more on retaining power at any cost and on controlling people by the force of the numbers of its cadres rather than by the force of its ideology, says political scientist Partha Chatterjee (interview with author). Marxist economist Prabhat Patnaik (2014) calls it the 'abandonment of the movement by an exclusive preoccupation with the governing option', which he argues happens to all bourgeois parties; this is relevant to the left too, which would become 'indistinguishable' from other political parties (ibid.). In the 2014 Lok Sabha polls, the LF suffered its worst setback in its history: it won only 2 seats out of the 594 parliamentary seats. Earlier, in the 2011 Bengal state assembly elections, it had been ignominiously reduced to 34 out of 294 seats, paving the way for the victorious takeover by its political arch-rival the TMC, a breakaway party of the Indian National Congress set up in 1998 by its leader, Mamata Banerjee.

'MORO, NAMARO'

Notwithstanding its claims of commitment to democratic rights and Marxist ideology, the LF began to behave like any powerful state, becoming arrogant and intolerant of political dissent. The cadre-based party became increasingly authoritarian; there were complaints of terror attacks and murders by armed CPM cadres known as *harmad*s. Homes of political rivals were burnt down, and people were forced to flee from their villages. Lakshman Seth, among others, was a strongman of the CPM and known for his strong-arm tactics and high-handedness, exhorting cadres to die, or kill (*moro, namaro*) (Datta 2007). After allegations of corruption and violence were heaped on him, he was expelled from the party (Sengupta and Phadikar 2014). The systematic and determined subjugation of dissent and the opposition that had been set in motion by the Congress Party was being perfected by the ruling CPM.

The increasing politicization of the police force and its tendency to serve the interests of the ruling party were brought home in July 1993 when 12 protesters were shot dead in the heart of the city, and more than 200 Congress members were injured. Police fired on protesters led by the then Youth Congress leader Mamata Banerjee when they blockaded the Writers' Building, the state secretariat in Kolkata, demanding that voters' identity cards be the only document required for voting in order to stop 'scientific rigging' of elections by the left. The LF declined to institute any judicial probe, and no police officer was held guilty for the deaths in the police firing.[1]

A gang-rape in Dhantolla in 2003 again revealed how political interests converged with police apathy. It required the direct intervention of the chief minister Buddhadeb Bhattacharjee himself for the first information report (FIR) of the rapes to be filed and medical examination of the women to be conducted several days after the incident. Six women were gang-raped in two busloads of passengers in a marriage party in Dhantolla, while one bus driver lost his life and many were injured and robbed. The violence was the result of a bitter turf war between two rival factions led by senior CPM leaders. The electronic media aggressively tracked the crime and brought the horror of the incident directly and vividly into homes; the role the print media had played during Bantala was taken over now by the TV channels. The State Women's Commission's report on the incident was scathing; it boldly focused on the political–criminal nexus and dereliction of duty by senior policemen.

The rot had set into the system even earlier, with crimes being committed by the 'protectors' themselves. Between 1982 and 1992, there were at least 42 cases of custodial rape; women were sexually assaulted by policemen, including a foreign tourist and a college teacher.[2] Activists Mira Roy and Soma Marik made the significant observation that though the CPM had aggressively nurtured the police as a political constituency over the years, this did not mean that the police had imbibed left leanings! (Roy and Marik 2007).

The Bantala incident in 1990 was not 'an exception', as the CPM leadership made it out to be; several incidents of sexual violence followed in quick succession in Dhantolla, Birati and Phulbagan police station. The CPM-led LF abandoned the opportunity to make history and establish new moral and administrative standards for state accountability. Instead, Bantala became a benchmark of state impunity and continues to symbolize sexual brutality in a degenerate society.

'NOT OVER OUR DEAD BODIES WILL WE GIVE OUR LAND'

The policy of economic liberalization shifted the focus of investment from the public sector to private capital, both Indian and foreign, and to industry from agriculture. Many public sector units were privatized and sold to Indian business houses, which began to play an increasingly important role. The LF government too felt that attracting corporate houses to the state was vital to revive industrial growth in Bengal. To woo investors, it provided concessions including subsidized land and sales tax waivers, as in the case of Tata's Nano automobile project in Singur. In 2002, when the central government embarked on promoting special economic zones (SEZs) and giving control of natural raw materials (coal, bauxite, iron ore and so on) at almost free or low prices, the LF identified land in Nandigram for an SEZ for a chemical hub with foreign aid from the Salim group in Malaysia. Thus, in a fertile, deltaic state with a high density of population, there was a bid to acquire agricultural land for industrialization.

This proved to be the nemesis of LF rule. From 2006 onward, land acquisition gathered momentum. Rural people's deep anxiety about being dispossessed of their land and livelihood was met by force; even women were not spared. If Bantala or Dhantolla were signs of how sexual crimes could be addressed by the state in normal times, the social movements against forcible land acquisition in Singur and Nandigram and adivasis' quest for dignity and development in Lalgarh were met with brutal state terror. Women agitators at the forefront of the movements were repeatedly targeted, assaulted, abused and gang-raped to silence protests. Yet they held on, saying, 'Not over our dead bodies will we give our land.'

It is not a coincidence that during this period of escalating violence in Bengal over forcible land acquisition and violation of adivasi rights, among other issues, the rate of sexual crimes also rocketed in the society at large, making West Bengal one of the most unsafe states for women. Over the next few years, as state accountability floundered with the society in turmoil, Bengal recorded the second highest incidence of sexual crimes in India.

From 1,731 rape incidents in 2006, sexual violence peaked at 2,363 rapes in 2011, with Bengal ranking second only to Madhya Pradesh in five consecutive years as the state with the highest incidence of rape.

'WE WILL BE REDUCED TO BEGGARS IF WE GIVE UP OUR LAND'

In 2006, Singur, located 45 kilometres away from Kolkata in Hooghly district, posed the toughest challenge to the LF's 34-year-old rule. Instead of persuading the farmers about the importance of industrialization in the state, the LF used brute force and intimidation to acquire 997 acres of fertile agricultural land for the Tata small car factory. The hypocrisy was even starker because in other states, CPM-led organizations were at the forefront of several democratic rights movements, including against land acquisition. Local women joined the struggle in their hundreds, creating iconic posters like 'Tata *babu*, ta ta, bye bye,' and blocked Tata officials from entering the factory site. 'We will be reduced to beggars if we give up our land,' was the common concern heard from the women.[3]

Terror continued to stalk Singur. It looked like a battleground, with the state government deploying huge contingents of police, and later armed police. Marches, demonstrations, public hearings, peaceful hunger strikes and *bandh*s (general strikes) were organized both in Singur and in Kolkata, joined by human rights and women's rights organizations, trade unions and intellectuals. The police blocked all roads and railway stations to stop activists and supporters from entering the villages; 'outsiders' joining the local agitation were branded 'Maoists' to discredit the movement and create a fear psychosis. Once again, this illustrated the influence wielded by the ruling party over the security forces to safeguard its political interests. It is ironical that 'industrial resurgence' was being ushered into the CPM's red bastion at any cost, through the barrel of the gun—and even sexual violence—for the 'larger good'.

When the state government failed to break the resistance, members of the CPM used sexual violence to target a young protester at the forefront of the movement. Tapasi Mallick, 16 years old, was raped and burnt to death in Singur at the peak of the movement. Though the CPM first tried to pass off Tapasi's murder as suicide, the Central Bureau of Investigation (CBI) exposed the involvement of senior CPM members. The zonal committee secretary, Suhrid Dutta, and another party supporter were sentenced to life imprisonment, but were later released by the high court on bail.

'WHAT HAS THIS THING CALLED RAJNITI DONE FOR US?'

> Even if I die I will not give up my land.... My family has been traditional CPM supporters. But this is not about politics, it's about my land. We are uneducated, who will give us jobs? If we do, we will end up washing Salim's feet.

These words were spoken by Anuradha Khera of Sonachura village, 36 years old and a mother of two children, as she voiced the fears of people in Nandigram. Anuradha was referring to the Salim Group, the Malaysian company that was to set up a chemical hub in Nandigram, Medinipur district, on agricultural land.[4] Many say this was the downfall of the LF in Bengal politics. The bitter experience of Singur and memories of land grab in nearby regions had created a climate of fear among farmers, who united across party lines to offer resistance. Even when the chief minister Buddhadeb Bhattacharjee declared that land would not be taken over, people had lost faith and were unwilling to believe him. Women were among the most articulate protesters and joined the struggle in large numbers. The LF senior minister Benoy Konar's infamous comment that CPM women supporters would 'show their backsides' to protesting activists like Medha Patkar in Nandigram demonstrated the level of vulgarity the ruling party could descend to in order to blunt dissent (Gupta 2007; Patkar 2007). The state resorted to sexual violence once again to repress the movement and create fear.

On 14 March 2007, when a large contingent of police prepared to enter Nandigram, the Bhoomi Ucched Pratirodh Committee, formed to resist land acquisition in the area, immediately appealed to the women to form a human shield. Anuradha and other women later told a fact-finding team (of which this author was part), 'Some of us stood guard from daybreak to stave off any attacks on our land. We didn't think they would attack us' (Sanhati 2007). But this did not deter the police from firing on the peaceful protesters, leaving 14 people dead, two women among them; men and women were seriously injured in the firing or were bayoneted. Several women were raped and many more were sexually assaulted. Anuradha was shot in the knee, and her husband was seriously injured in the firing.

Koely Manna,[5] 36 years old, a mother of four children from Kalicharanpur who was gang-raped by policemen, said: 'Tell Buddhadeb [the chief minster] to return my honour … all my years of hard work, dreams … feeding my children…. There is so much terror, no one can sleep or eat.… what is this thing called *rajniti* [politics]? What has this rajniti done for us?' (Sanhati 2007).

Radha Rani Ari,[6] 45 years old, of Gokulnagar village, was gang-raped twice within a year during the agitation. On the fateful day of 14 March, she was badly beaten by the police. 'I prayed for forgiveness with folded hands … they used abusive language … said "whores, what honour do you have?" [*khanki toder abar ijjat*] … one put the gun through my vagina … I shouted out in pain' (Sanhati 2007).

Months later, the fact-finding team on another visit found that peace was yet to return to Nandigram; there was a silence as if of the graveyard as villagers rushed indoors at sunset. Many claimed they felt safer remaining in relief camps. Those who returned to their homes lived in constant fear. Women said the harmads had threatened, 'Tell your men to leave the house. Light up your lamps at night, keep the door open and wait for us to come' (Sanhati 2007).

'ARE WE NOT CITIZENS OF THIS COUNTRY?'

By now, the LF was increasingly losing touch with its own people. On 2 November 2008, after an alleged Maoist bid on Buddhadeb Bhattacharjee's life in Junglemahal, the forested region bordering three districts of western Bengal, the area exploded with violence. The police went on a rampage against unarmed adivasis living in the region, suspecting them of being Maoists. This was followed by armed operations by joint central and state forces in June 2009. These operations were marked by atrocities, including the killing of activists and common people, indiscriminate beatings and detentions, rapes, looting and ransacking of houses.

Junglemahal had not been left untouched by the turmoil in Singur or Nandigram, but it was not the direct target of big corporations in search of mineral wealth, as in other forested regions of the country. The adivasis here were steeped in poverty, exploitation and lack of development due to the nexus between corrupt forest officials and political functionaries, contractors, and timber and *tendu* leaf (a highly valued leaf used to wrap tobacco in the manufacture beedis, or indigenous cigarettes) merchants. The repressed anger, accumulated over years of negligence and police high-handedness, repeated humiliation and violation of their community's way of living, was mobilized into an uprising that spread across Junglemahal. And it was women who rose in numbers against state violence, having borne the brunt of police attacks even in normal times during their daily chores of fetching water or collecting firewood and leaves in the forests.

It was a unique mass democratic movement led by the People's Committee against Police Atrocities (PCPA) that sought justice and dignity for the deprived adivasis. The PCPA challenged the state, demanding to know whether it had the right to administer a people whose need for well-being and humanity it had never recognized. In every village unit of the PCPA, 50 per cent of the representatives were women. The men were forced to flee the villages to evade arrests, and women were left to fend for the household, the children, the sick and the elderly—and at the same time continue the fight for dignity.

On 30 June 2010 at 5 am, the joint armed forces raided the adjoining Sonamukhi village backed by local CPM harmads. For eight hours they ransacked the village in search of Maoists. The men had earlier fled the village, and, finding the women alone, the joint forces gang-raped seven women,[7] while others were sexually molested, abused, beaten, dragged by their hair and kicked. The men spoke in Hindi, said the women, and threatened them that the next time the women should be naked so that it would be easier to rape them; all the time, the harmads stood by and watched. The forces jumped on a 70-year-old woman when she tried to protest, and then left her to die of her injuries.

According to the editor of *Khoj* Krishna Bandopadhyay, who visited Lalgarh many times during the movement, medical facilities near the village turned away the women saying that they 'did not treat Maoists'. Even the sub-divisional officer (SDO), despite his assurances of visiting the village, did not do so. According to Kirity Roy, director of MASUM, (human rights organization Banglar Manabadhikar Suraksha Mancha) who met villagers in Lalgarh on 20 July, the women made written complaints to the SDO about rape by the joint forces, but were afraid to file complaints with the police. They were admitted to the Jhargram sub-divisional hospital and examined for rape on the insistence of the SDO. When the superintendent of the hospital asked the women to file a police complaint, he was transferred within an hour's notice.

Over the next few days, thousands of women marched with the injured to Jhargram's block development officer demanding medical treatment for the raped women and others injured in the attack. They were met with police barricades, lathi charges and arrests. The women raised only one question: You have raped us, humiliated us and killed us. Now tell us, where do we get medical treatment?

Jyostna Mahato of the now-defunct Nari Ijjat Bachao Committee, Junglemahal, said at a public meeting in Kolkata in December 2010,

> We care about our self esteem.... is this what you call Maoism? Even when women are raped and people murdered, nobody raises a voice? Is every adivasi a Maoist? Are we not citizens of the country? We will fight for our land and our self-respect ... till the government learns to respect us. (Quoted in Bandopadhyay 2012)

THE AFTERMATH OF THE VIOLENCE

The State Women's Commission, then headed by Professor Jasodhara Bagchi, well-known feminist and activist in her own right, came under severe criticism for its 'indifferent role' during the Singur and Nandigram movements. Feminists and activists in the country were disappointed and felt that Bagchi had been 'soft' on the state government's oppressive role, being 'close' to the ruling party and under pressure to toe the line of the administration, a charge that Bagchi vigorously refuted:

> I will say this that in six and a half years in the women's commission, I have never faced any direct interference from the state, I would have resigned on the spot.... on several occasions we [the Commission] have written critically about the state, which people may not have noticed.[8]

Human rights institutions like the State Women's Commission and the State Human Rights Commission are viewed by human rights activists with suspicion as instruments of the state. 'To gain credibility and earn the confidence of the people, they should be willing to challenge the government and hold it to task. HRIs [human rights institutions] have to function without fear or favour of the state,' said Supreme Court lawyer Vrinda Grover (personal communication). The situation is complicated, since the commissions are constituted by the government and are dependent on it for funding, making an 'independent role' nearly impossible where state impunity is concerned. 'To steer clear of pressure both from civil society and the government is very difficult,' said Bharati Mutsudi, former member of the State Women's Commission, West Bengal,[9] during left rule (personal communication).

In the Nandigram and Lalgarh movements, a large number of women were raped and sexually assaulted. Fact-finding teams and the People's Tribunal have verified several of these incidents. Intervention was limited to fact-finding and street protests; women's rights groups and civil rights organizations did not file criminal complaints, or did not succeed in forcing the state to investigate and follow up. 'We failed to drive relentlessly for litigation in rape cases though we know how to demonstrate with great fervour,' say activists. In individual cases, activists have succeeded to some degree in forcing rape cases to trial and standing in support of the survivor; but in cases of community-based mass sexual violence like in Nandigram and Lalgarh, it has been almost impossible. The remoteness of the area and the widespread terror are among several factors that work as deterrents. From convincing and building faith in women to file complaints, to providing emotional and psychosocial support, witness protection, and resources, rape trials demand continuous political engagement. One reason, perhaps, why legal justice remains so elusive in Bengal.[10]

In the face of the agitations and delays, the Tatas set up their car unit in Gujarat. Tragically, both in Singur and in Nandigram, the communities today still remain bitterly divided and suspicious; women strive to bring about a semblance of normalcy with their chores and by making amends with their neighbours. In Singur, the resentment is between those who enjoy the compensation money from sale of land; a section of farmers who are unable to cultivate their land made barren by lumps of concrete and semi-permanent structures; and those who have lost hope of ever getting back their land acquired for the car factory, a promise Mamata Banerjee made repeatedly before the elections.

In 2007, the Calcutta High Court said the firing in Nandigram was 'wholly unconstitutional' and 'unjustified', acting on a petition filed by the Association for the Protection of Democratic Rights and others (Patkar et al. 2007). It ordered a CBI inquiry and asked the state government to a pay compensation of Rs 500,000 each to the relatives of those killed, Rs 200,000 each to victims of rape,[11] and Rs 100,000 each to those injured. After a long legal dispute, the high court order was upheld by the Supreme Court in 2011. Reports of irregularities and cases of delayed payment of compensation continue to be heard. The LF state government argued that the police had fired in 'self-defence'; there was no criminal prosecution of those responsible for the tragedy. And no woman was raped in Nandigram, since there was not a single complaint filed.

The Women against Sexual Violence and State Repression (WSS) team found that women who had once been the face of the movement in Nandigram, and who aided in the defeat of the LF and the victory of the TMC, have now been marginalized in the political space and continue to suffer from their severe injuries. Tapasi Das, who almost lost her thigh to a bullet wound, lives in perpetual pain with nobody to care about her treatment. Women leaders say they are now confined to their homes, and continue to face social stigma and patriarchal oppression. They have to pay heavier dowries to get their daughters married, and some have been thrown out of their marital homes as 'punishment'.

The peaceful movement for adivasi rights lies in tatters in Lalgarh. The Maoist takeover, an intransigent LF state government, the onslaught by joint armed forces and the sell-out by the TMC have crushed the aspiration of the forest people for basic human and democratic rights. Despite the change in political leadership in Bengal in 2011, and the TMC's electoral promises, according to reports, rape FIRs have not yet been filed in Lalgarh. On the contrary, the police have filed false cases against the rape victims accusing them of being Maoist sympathizers, forcing them to flee their villages.

On 13 October 2011, when an adivasi woman complained of rape by jawans in Belpahari village in Junglemahal, Mamata Banerjee, the new chief minister, said, 'Such complaints are fabricated every time the police move to nab criminals' (Bandopadhyay 2012). The fiery leader of the downtrodden of the Singur, Nandigram and Lalgarh struggles had now donned the garb of the ruler, and thus state impunity came full circle in West Bengal.

THE PROMISE OF PARIBARTAN

> In 30 days the rape trial will be completed.
>
> ('Calcutta High Court to Monitor Kamduni Probe' 2013)

7 June 2014: Kamduni had changed rapidly since that fateful day exactly a year earlier. Every month villagers gathered around a

garlanded photograph, the curling smoke from incense sticks blurring the image of a young girl in a blue sari. With their morning chores over, women gathered hurriedly in large numbers; children played in front of the photograph, and the old forwent their siesta and made their way to the front of the village primary school. Life in Kamduni had changed since 7 June 2013, when Suthi Ghosh, a 20-year-old college student from the village, was gang-raped and murdered.

Every seventh of the month, the villagers of Kamduni in Barasat district gathered to renew their pledge to seek justice for Suthi, whose mangled body was found dumped in the fish ponds bordering the sides of the desolate village road. The nondescript village of daily wage earners and unskilled labourers, about 25 kilometres from Kolkata's business centre, had shot into the limelight overnight. Suthi, the first in a family of wage earners to attend college, had struggled to change her destiny. If her struggle had inspired people not only in Kamduni but also in other parts of West Bengal, the brutality with which her young life was snuffed out shocked people's conscience.

There were gasps of disbelief as well as accolades for the beleaguered state government when, within a few days, the accused were arrested. Chief Minister Mamata Banerjee immediately declared that charge-sheets would be filed against them within 15 days and the case completed within a month, promising, 'We will plead for death sentence for the men,' as Kamduni villagers chanted '*phansi chai, phansi chai*' (we demand that [the criminals] be hanged) ('CM Promises, Kamduni Seethes' 2013). Never in the history of Bengal had the state responded so promptly and promised quick justice for incidents of sexual violence and murder.

In this section, I ask whether Mamata Banerjee lived up to her promise in handling the situation in Kamduni. The legal process, with the prompt arrest of the accused, quick charge-sheeting and trial, was supposed to instil a sense of justice among the aggrieved. Has the TMC government effected a significant difference in state accountability when it comes to crimes against women? As a woman leader, Banerjee's style of functioning and leadership was expected to instil greater confidence among people in general and women in particular. Do violence-affected families and communities like those in Kamduni feel that justice is now possible in Bengal?

'MA MATI MANUSH'

The most significant beneficiary of the powerful people's movements in Singur, Nandigram and Lalgarh was Mamata Banerjee. She wrested power from the ruling LF in 2011 to become the first woman chief minister of the state (Gupta 2012).[12] Unlike other women leaders in South Asia, Mamata Banerjee is unmarried, a self-made leader who rose through the ranks without the backing of a powerful political mentor or the emotional appeal of a deceased kin.

The defeat of the once-invincible LF government in 2011 was one of the most dramatic upheavals that West Bengal state has witnessed in recent years. Banerjee shrewdly usurped the rhetoric and slogans of the left, claiming solidarity with the CPM's traditional vote bank, the peasants and the downtrodden, making the Marxists look like elites in cahoots with the big industries. 'The CPI(M) has emerged as the new zamindars of Bengal who are selling off their properties to Tata and Salim,' Banerjee would thunder at every public meeting (Sarkar 2007). Her emotive slogan, '*Ma Mati Manush*' (mother, land, mankind) found a deep resonance among the people of the state and held out hope of 'paribartan'.

Banerjee first moved centre stage in 1993 as a youth leader (she was then with the Congress Party) when she stormed the Writers'

Building, the state administrative secretariat, with a raped hearing- and speech-impaired girl, claiming that the rapist had not been arrested because he was a CPM supporter. She stubbornly sat outside the LF chief minister Jyoti Basu's office (Basu refused to meet her) for three hours before she was dragged away by the police.

As part of the opposition, at every public meeting across the country, she focused on the gang-rape and murder of Tapasi Mallick in Singur, and dragged to the stage the tortured and raped victims of Nandigram to expose the 'real face of the Reds'. If she projected herself as the leader in the Singur agitation, in Nandigram she consolidated her image, while in Lalgarh she promised the withdrawal of the joint armed forces and the release of political prisoners if she was elected chief minister. People craved governance—and, most importantly, accountability—having reeled for decades under the high-handedness and arrogance of LF misrule.

Once Banerjee came to power, riding on the single-point agenda of 'anti-CPM' besides her own personal popularity, however, she had nothing to offer the people, no programme nor any policy. The TMC today suffers from centralized command, dominated by Banerjee, in sharp contrast to the cadre-based CPM. One major trend that emerged was Banerjee's approach of openly appropriating activists from several movements as well as victims and their families, by bestowing official posts or doling out compensation and raining awards on intellectuals and artists. This was the new government's way of neutralizing dissent.[13] Among the few notables who refused an award was the poet Sankha Ghosh.

'WHAT MORE DO YOU WANT?'

'So what are you folks still agitated about now?' members of the ruling TMC had asked human rights activists. 'Our chief minister has taken immediate action. *Akhon aar ki chao* [what more do you want]?' (as told to us by Swapna, an activist in Kamduni).

Suthi's murder opened up a floodgate of protests in Kamduni and elsewhere in Kolkata. Kamduni villagers did not slacken their vigilance in seeking justice for Suthi, and linked it to the safety of women in the village. The villagers were apprehensive that Suthi's rape and murder would spread fear among families and impede the education of young girls and the mobility of women in the village. During the memorial meetings, villagers repeatedly demanded lights for the village streets and public transport along the four-kilometre-long desolate road connecting the village to the highway so that villagers might move around freely without fear. To strengthen their movement, a few months later, the villagers formed an organization, the Pratibadi Manch (Protest Forum).[14]

Kamduni became a household name symbolizing resistance against the state. Kamduni villagers never missed an opportunity to voice their demands from every platform, whether in the media or in demonstrations in Kolkata or elsewhere in the state. Violence against women, which had so far been perceived as 'a women's problem' and of concern only to women's groups and feminists, for the first time became a talking point in all conversations cutting across different social groups. For many in the state, it was not the murder of Suthi but the decision of the villagers, especially the young women in Kamduni, to protest boldly and stand up to state coercion that caught their imagination.

Various organizations, activists and intellectuals penned songs and poems in admiration of Kamduni's resistance. Inspired by Kamduni's courage, regular reports of rape and sexual crime poured in from other parts of the state, as organizations formed broader alliances to challenge systemic and structural impunity and steeled themselves to take their protests forward. This sustained struggle, the formation of new protest groups with men equally involved in 'women's issues', instilled a deep unease in the state administration.

'CHUP! YOU ARE MAOISTS!'

17 June 2013: The chief minister visited Kamduni, 25 kilometres from the state administrative headquarters, 10 days after the crime was committed and after prolonged agitation and protests. Her visit was greeted with optimism. Villagers were certain that Didi (elder sister), as she is popularly called, would address the problem of women's safety. Young Moushumi Koyal of Kamduni said, 'We felt confident the chief minister's presence would signal [to] the perpetrators that she was serious about arresting and punishing them and would also signal the police to act swiftly' (interview with author).

When the women heard that Mamata Banerjee was visiting their village, they rushed out of their homes eagerly, urging her to ensure their safety, highlighting the unsafe condition of the roads and lack of street lights. At the forefront of the crowd were Tumpa and Moushumi Koyal, two neighbours. The villagers were taken aback when the chief minister reacted angrily, targeting the two young women: '*Chup, chup, chup* [Keep quiet]. Shut up. I have heard enough. You are all CPM and Maoists!' When Tumpa insisted that she should listen to their problems (*apni kotha shunun*), the chief minister shot back, addressing the villagers, 'See? She is a Maoist!' The villagers were stunned (Moushumi Koyal, interview with author).

The chief minister's visit did not provide the salve the villagers were yearning for. Her terse response to their pleas and her branding their women 'Maoists' left them seething, angry and hurt. Kamduni, a wounded community following Suthi's death, was seeking comfort from Mamata Banerjee, assurances of safety from their chief minister. 'We believed that as a woman Didi would be most sensitive to our needs, and understand and respond to our fears about our children's security and our own,' said 23-year-old Tumpa Koyal (interview with author). The villagers' collective memory of Mamata Banerjee was of a firebrand leader; her reputation was of one who had fought for women facing violence, whether in Nandigram or Singur. No wonder that at the local government panchayat elections in Kamduni, the TMC had bagged 11 of the 12 seats riding on her popularity. 'Has Didi changed so much that she cannot understand our insecurities? How does seeking her help make us Maoists?' asked Tumpa in bewilderment (ibid.).

To silence protests and mitigate uncomfortable situations, the state has invariably resorted to various tactics. In the age-old strategy of labelling political opponents as 'dreaded Maoists', the unstated argument is that if you are a Maoist you have no legal rights, whether to ask questions or to protest. By branding villagers as Maoists, Mamata Banerjee tried to evade their legitimate demands. On another occasion, when women activists of Maitree, a network of women's rights groups, protested in Kolkata against the Kamduni incident, several were arrested on the pretext that they were Maoists. A woman student was similarly branded by Mamata Banerjee for asking her 'Maoist questions' during a TV programme about a rape incident in the city. In a public meeting, Shiladitya, a farmer, faced arrest for asking the chief minister a 'Maoist question' on high fertilizer prices.

'JUSTICE? WILL THERE BE JUSTICE IN MY LIFETIME?'

The simmering resentment and frustration in Kamduni can be understood only from the perspective of the villagers and Suthi's family, and not from the rigid, legal point of view of the state.

More than two years had passed (at the time of writing) since Suthi's rape-murder; the trial dragged on in the so-called fast-track court in Kolkata as her family awaited justice. This was in sharp contrast to the conviction in the gang-rape and murder of the medical intern in December 2012 in Delhi, within nine months of trial. Even the perpetrators in the gang-rape of the young photojournalist in Shakti Mills in Mumbai in July 2013 (less than a month after Suthi's death) had been convicted within eight months.

The judicial system holds out promise of redress and accountability, but for the common people it remains an opaque, protracted and losing battle in the search for justice. Every time news of convictions in rape trials reached the village, Suthi's mother felt frustrated with the slow pace of her daughter's trial and expressed doubt whether the perpetrators would ever be punished at all, said another villager. 'Justice? Will I in my lifetime see justice for my child?' Suthi's mother wept.

The criminal justice system is seen, as in the Kamduni case, increasingly to value symbolism over substance. The police investigation of Suthi's murder was haphazard right from the start, despite the 'keen interest' shown by the chief minster herself. The FIR was full of gaps, DNA tests were not conducted on the corpse to establish evidence of semen and so on; the charge-sheet was so faulty, in fact, that the district judge punched gaping holes in it and demanded a revised one. Also, the main witness, Suthi's uncle, had died in hospital following a lathi charge during a demonstration; he was the only witness to have seen Suthi alive walking back to the village before she was attacked.

The final blow was struck when the case was shifted to Kolkata from the Barasat District Court. Villagers found it difficult to travel the distance to the city to appear as witnesses; they were burdened by the loss of daily wages and travel expenses. After the initial trial dates, the author found that it was difficult for members of Suthi's family or of the Pratibadi Manch to be present in the trial court. As a result of the delaying strategy the state has resorted to time and again, it had become exhausting to maintain the momentum of the protests and appearances at the city court, and the large number of supporters had dwindled. Fearing 'interference', a group of villagers from Kamduni went to meet the president of India in Delhi to plead for a CBI probe and appealed to the high court for a fresh CBI investigation. Even before the trial began full steam, villagers had lost faith in the state police investigation and the criminal justice system.

Immediately after Suthi was gang-raped and murdered, Mamata Banerjee had thunderously demanded a death sentence for the guilty. But the question remains, has this proved to be a deterrent and brought down the number of rape cases in West Bengal? There were six instances of rape in June 2013 following Suthi's murder; so the chief minister's threat did not sow fear among rapists in the following month. Take any random month, September and October 2013 for instance, during which there were 31 and 23 incidents of rape, respectively, in the state.[15] Activists say that,

> [r]ape survivors would have benefited instead if the chief minister was serious about setting up a systemic victim support programme to help them through the entire procedure from filing FIR in police stations, to medical examination, police investigation to court room trial, the entire gamut of phases a rape victim has to go through (interview with author).

Instead, politicians from the Bharatiya Janata Party (BJP) to the TMC lay emphasis on populist strategies like demands for the death penalty and demonizing individual perpetrators, instead of setting up institutional reforms that would redress and prevent sexual violence.

'HIGH STAKES IN KAMDUNI, IT'S A TEST CASE'

The spirited demand for justice in Kamduni was the first flare-up in a rural community since the TMC came to power in June 2011. This also meant the stakes were high in Kamduni for the new state government to prove its credentials; as a result, Kamduni came to be regarded as a test case. It is also infamous for showing how the state resorts to every possible means to bring a people's movement for justice under its control for narrow political gains. For the new government, it was important to suppress the Kamduni protests, to signal to other groups not to overstep the *lakshman rekha* (an imaginary boundary that should not be transgressed) and mount a challenge to the state.

The legal symbolism has consequences, because it inspires faith in the feel-good agendas that elected leaders have promised to achieve. 'When they predictably fail, popular disillusionment deepens' (Samuelson 2014). This was true of Kamduni too. The TMC government realized the mood in Kamduni and ordered the arrests and the trial. When these proved to be inadequate fig leaves, it employed devious new tactics to break the spirit of the community seeking justice for Suthi. The spontaneous movement by villagers turned into a takeover battle by the ruling party. From giving out sops in the form of compensation and jobs to Suthi's family, to veiled and open threats to Pratibadi Manch members, muzzling protests in the village, creating division among villagers by setting up rival protest platforms, spreading rumours and instilling suspicion among the villagers, the ruling party left no stone unturned in trying to break the solidarity of the villagers and hijack the protests.

For the TMC, it was important to silence Kamduni. These cynical manoeuvres were engineered to safeguard the battered image of a state government unable to curb crimes against women, rather than effectively carrying out its administrative and constitutional duties to deliver justice. Within three years of TMC rule, the rising graph of violence against women and the spate of protests in the state demonstrated that all was not well in West Bengal. For the second year on the trot, the state recorded the highest number of crimes against women:[16] a total of 30,942 cases of crimes against women were registered in the state in 2012, which accounted for 12.67 per cent of the total crimes against women in the country.[17] 'The state government could not afford to let the Kamduni protest roll out of hand,' said *Khoj* editor Krishna Bandopadhyay (personal communication). 'There are high stakes involved in Kamduni—it's a test case for the new state government.'

Not content with branding the villagers Maoists, the TMC leadership resorted to another devious move to sow seeds of suspicion in order to break the spirit of the movement. It created a rift between Suthi's family and the rest of the village, forcing the family ultimately to leave Kamduni because of social isolation and shame. During her visit to Kamduni, when the chief minister had offered compensation to Suthi's family, her distraught father, a daily wage earner, had cried out, 'We are not beggars, what I want for my daughter is justice' (Moushumi Koyal, interview with author). However, later the Ghosh family succumbed to pressure and accepted Rs 100,000 from the Chief Minister's Fund as compensation for Suthi's death. They were also assured employment for the three members of the family. But the pitiful compensation that was rightfully theirs was made out to be a largesse given by a benevolent state. At every opportunity, the state food minister (Kamduni fell in his constituency) would hold Suthi's brothers in a close embrace before the rolling TV cameras to demonstrate his 'closeness' to the family. During a national TV interview,[18] the chief minister claimed, 'The family is totally with us, we have given them total support.'

'Given that Suthi's father is abysmally poor and unskilled, the compensation money is hardly a fortune, and his employment rumoured in the local panchayat office is not an issue with the villagers,' explained the primary school teacher Pradip Mukherjee (interview with author). What aggrieved the villagers was that the entire move had been made 'slyly' without taking them into confidence. 'Why didn't they [Suthi's family] tell us about it? We are protesting together and under so much pressure for keeping Suthi's memory alive and demanding justice,' said Moushumi Koyal, secretary of the Manch (ibid.).

'IT'S DIDI WHO LIT THE FIRE … IT WILL KEEP BURNING'

The unkindest cut was a signed letter sent by Suthi Ghosh's family to the Pratibadi Manch on 29 September 2013, in which they accused the Manch members and a section of the media of 'taking lakhs of rupees', of 'tarnishing the image of the humanitarian chief minister' who had stood by them and promised 'ultimate punishment to the guilty'. As a result, four members of the Ghosh family declared they had resigned from the Manch. The letter, ostensibly written by the Ghosh family, reads like a political pamphlet, an endorsement of the chief minister's image and actions with a focus on her benevolence. But the effect of the letter on the villagers was electrifying; the Ghosh family found themselves socially boycotted by the villagers and had to leave Kamduni hurriedly. The extended Ghosh clan (Kamduni is roughly divided into four caste groups) found themselves equally isolated from the rest of the village. 'It's never been the same,' said Suthi's elderly aunt, wiping her tears. 'Everyone now walks away and stops talking when they see us. People are angry that Suthi's family did not inform them that they were accepting the CM's offer. Believe me, I too did not know of it, though I live under the same roof.'

Suddenly, Kamduni became the centre of attention. From the CPM[19] and the Aam Admi Party to the BJP, political parties feverishly wooed the villagers to join them. To further its divide-and-rule tactics, the TMC tried to take over the movement when it set up a rival Manch in the village. On 7 February 2014, when this author revisited Kamduni, she spotted Suthi's two brothers standing quietly in a corner, not making eye contact with anybody. No neighbour approached them to ask about their well-being; they stood alone despite the fact that it was their sister's memorial service. The silencing of the Ghosh family by the state could not have been more cynical.

At the memorial stone erected in Suthi's memory at the crossing of the village road and the Barasat highway, the local TMC leaders paid rich homage to the leadership of the chief minister and to her kindness. Suthi's name was not once mentioned; the young girl had been forgotten in the growing darkness of the evening and the profusion of political oratory. The ruthlessness of these political manoeuvres by a woman who ironically rose to popularity and power on the issue of sexual violence could not be more cynical. An old woman standing beside me, and looking intently at Suthi's photograph, murmured to herself, 'Fire. It's Didi who lit the fire. We expected her to be with us in our sorrow. Instead she left us even more wounded. This fire will burn.' Kamduni has never been the same again.

THE CULTURE OF IMPUNITY

'It's all stage-managed! A conspiracy!' 'Rape? It's all concocted ... a conspiracy to malign the administration!'[20] The angry response of the chief minister of West Bengal as she dismissed the gang-rape on Park Street at the heart of Kolkata in February 2012 shocked the people of her state. A few days later, when an impoverished seamstress in Katwa, Burdwan district, was dragged out of a train and raped in front of her daughter, the chief minister again claimed that the crime had been 'stage-managed' (*shajano ghotona*) to discredit her government ('Mamata Does It Again in Rape Case' 2012).

Conspiracy theories are a significant feature of Bengal's polarized politics, and have now spilled over into the issue of rape and violence against women. By branding complaints of rape as 'conspiracies' and accusing victims of 'concocting' the crime, the tenor of impunity has been set by none other than the chief minister herself. In less than a year after Banerjee formed the West Bengal government in June 2011, safeguarding the image of her administration had become more important than the due process of law. She quickly acquired the nickname 'Shajano [concocted] Banerjee' for her all-too-predictable response.

When complaints of rape are perceived by the leader of the state as conspiratorial attacks on her governance, it signals that the administration does not view sexual violence as a serious crime that demands immediate and severe punitive measures. For the rape victim, this adds insult to her injury; already traumatized by violence, confronted by a callous police force and insensitive medical professionals, she has to face public humiliation because of being branded by the head of state—a woman herself—as a liar. It is a betrayal of the victim's rights and a gross demonstration of state impunity when the victim is condemned even before the police investigation is over and the judicial trial has begun.

'THE POLITICAL PARTY HAS REPLACED OTHER SOCIAL INSTITUTIONS'

It is not surprising that when the top leadership of the state treats women with little respect, degeneration sets into the polity as well. The culture of impunity has become increasingly malignant in the context of Bengal's political divide. Fostered by senior members of the ruling party, set rolling by the LF and mastered by the TMC, it has taken an alarming direction as powerful leaders go unpunished for their crimes, hate speech and misogynist comments.

'There is a difference in the sophistication of left techniques of wielding power which was careful to conceal its partisanship in a cloak of bureaucratic procedure and the brazen partisanship of Trinamul methods which shows no respect for any procedure,' says social scientist Partha Chatterjee (ibid.). As a result, people now fear that that there is no one to appeal to against TMC oppression—'the police and administration are powerless, the courts are too expensive and slow,' the left has vanished.[21] Only the BJP as the party in power in Delhi could come to the rescue of the people. In an unprecedented turn of events in the state, for the first time in its history, the BJP, the right-wing Hindu party, won a parliamentary seat in 2014; equally ominous is the swelling of its ranks with many members from the CPM, who have been unable to withstand the attacks by TMC goons with the Marxists failing to provide protection to their cadres.

In Bengal, political affiliations, mobilization and political organizations have become the essential identity overshadowing all other identities; people's aggressive allegiance to a specific political party blinds them and dominates their lives to such an extent as to fracture all social cohesion, a situation that pervades both private and public life. In several states, while women have borne the brunt of targeted caste and communal violence against the 'other', in Bengal, it is not uncommon for women to face sexual brutality based on their own or their family's 'political identity', or as a means of establishing the domination of the political affiliation of the perpetrator or the ruling party.

One of the fundamental changes that took place in West Bengal following the left's coming to power in 1977 was that earlier institutions of social control, such as the zamindar's *baithakkhana* (parlour), caste council and religious institutions, either vanished or lost legitimacy, says Partha Chatterjee. 'Instead, the local party office became the most powerful social institution, taking over other institutions such as the club or school or even temple administration. Only in Muslim-dominated areas did religious institutions retain some of their authority.' As a result, not only political issues but even social disputes involving family quarrels, marriage, education, sports and public entertainment began to be controlled by local party leaders through the party office or the panchayat. 'The situation has remained the same after the Trinamul came to power, with Trinamul local leaders replacing CPM local leaders,' says Chatterjee.[22]

In fact, the omnipresence of the political party in recent years has superseded even the local administration, this has been made possible with the rapid criminalization of politics and with ideology taking a back seat. This was once again demonstrated in the case of a Santhal village, where a a tribal council ordered a 20-year-old woman to be gang-raped in January 2014 for being in a relationship with a Muslim man, but at the instigation of the local political leader. In the last few decades, the 'Party' has increasingly acquired the status of the basic social institution in Bengal superseding all other institutions, including the police and the administration. In recent years, the lack of accountability of the ruling party, the TMC, has become even more brazen, smothering all public protests. This has been made simpler by the abject, demoralized existence of the opposition, the CPM, which has been unable to reorganize itself.

'I WILL LET MY BOYS LOOSE TO RAPE THE WOMEN!'

Bengali movie stars, roped into politics by the TMC to add glamour and status to the party,[23] who play daredevil lovers or romantic heroes on the big screen, morph into real-life villains as they speak insultingly of the women in the state. Tapas Pal, chubby-faced hero of thousands of female fans and now a TMC member of Parliament (MP), physically threatened and gesticulated obscenely at the opposition CPM at a public meeting in his constituency: 'I am a goonda … I can pull the trigger myself … I will shoot you guys if you [CPM] insult the mothers and daughters of TMC workers.… I will let loose my boys in your homes and they will commit rape' ('Tapas Pal Rape Remarks and Aftermath' 2014). What is even more alarming is that every time Pal shouted the word 'kill' or 'rape', he was heartily greeted by whistling, clapping and hooting from his audience. Following a hue and cry, the chief minister let Pal off with an 'unconditional apology' as he promptly admitted himself into a hospital.

Earlier, during the March 2014 Lok Sabha election campaign, young matinee idol and TMC candidate Dev remarked casually when asked about his experience in joining politics, '*Are yaar*, it [politics] is like getting raped. You either scream or enjoy it' ('Dev's Rape Analogy Draws Widespread Criticism' 2014). Dev got away with a meek apology, was feted a month later by the chief minister with a top film award, and was specially chosen to promote business in Singapore.

Recently, both the BJP and the TMC resorted to the use of the issue of rape in their game of one-upmanship when, in June 2014, Mamata Banerjee in a retaliatory mood sent a TMC team to investigate a rape incident in Madhya Pradesh, after a BJP-led central team visited Bengal 'to take stock' of violence-prone areas. 'If there is any violence or rape in any BJP-ruled state we will send the TMC central team. This is not one-sided or fair. This is tit for tat,' said Banerjee ('MP Government Bristles at TMC's Tit for Tat' 2014). It was not concern for the women victims but the agenda of embarrassing political opponents that propelled this heightened activity among the political parties.

Tapas Pal shares his fame with TMC colleagues known for their penchant for hate speech and life threats. Manirul Islam, TMC member of the legislative assembly (MLA), threatened his political rival, a Congress leader: 'It will not take a minute to behead you.' He boasted that he had 'trampled to death' three men ('Trinamool MLA Threatens to Behead Congress Leader' 2013). Anubrata Mandal, another TMC leader, exhorted his supporters to burn down the houses of his political rivals, threatened to cut off their hands, and hurled bombs at the police and administration ('Rape Threat, Filmi Style' 2014).

The incidents involving Islam and Mandal as well as Pal were caught on camera and have been broadcast widely and repeatedly by news channels and social media. Despite this, there have been no police investigations, charge-sheets against the accused, or arrests for inciting violence and rape. When protests refused to die down following Pal's comments, Mamata Banerjee could only retort, 'What do you want me to do? Kill him?' ('Mamata on Tapas Pai's "Rape" Threat'2014).

When members of the political class can murder or threaten to kill political opponents, assault ordinary citizens, and incite the mob to rape women, it contributes to the exacerbation of state impunity. In the absence of political accountability and in the face of systemic violations of the law, the dilemma is even more acute for women; they can hardly hope to achieve justice against sexual violence.

An avowed admirer of Rabindranath Tagore, the chief minister quotes the Nobel laureate at every opportunity to 'save the culture' of Bengal, but does not hesitate to use abusive language to attack her political opponents. For instance she has gone on record, saying, 'If you have the right to shove a bamboo up the rear of those who are doing honest politics, then I too have th right to speak ('Twice-Wielded, Bamboo Is Official Weapon' 2014]). Today at every public rally, when Banerjee assures her supporters that she will 'not allow anyone to do wrong' in the state, she is greeted with intense applause. But truth can become principle only when it is universal; as the leader of the state, the chief minister must allow the law to take its course even if senior members of her own party have transgressed.

'WHERE IS MAMATA GETTING MONEY? FROM WHICH BHATTAR?'

If the TMC's misogynist attitude towards women has evoked immense revulsion and protests in the state, CPM leaders have made history by using controversial language especially while targeting Mamata Banerjee. The tone was set, in this case too, by the CPM leadership when chief minister Jyoti Basu used unparliamentary language: he called Banerjee a '420' (cheat). The late CPM state secretary Anil Biswas had dubbed her '*jomero aruchi*' (one whom even the devil would not touch).[24] From stopping short of implying that Mamata was prostituting herself, to ridiculing her single status, comments made by a few expose what constitutes a 'bad woman' in their worldview. These leaders with their professed Marxist beliefs demonstrated openly their disdain towards women political opponents in particular, and their bias against women in general.

Recently, when the TMC state government declared a compensation policy for rape victims, CPM MLA Anisur Rehman shocked even his party comrades when he said, 'I would like to ask Didimoni [Mamata] what *her* fee will be if someone gets Rs 20,000 after being raped' ('If You Are Raped What Will Be Your Fee' 2012). The West Bengal Human Rights Commission condemned Rahman's derogatory comments and asked the director general of police to file a report.

Even while in power, CPM leaders did not miss an opportunity to insult Mamata Banerjee. In a shocking incident in April 2011, Anil Basu, a seven-time MP, stooped low enough to ask, 'Where is she getting the money from? From which *bhattar* [slang for illicit male partner] did she get Rs 24 crore to fund the TMC's poll expenses?' ('CPIM Leader Anil Basu Abusing Mamata Banerjee' 2011). The sex workers of Sonagachi burnt Basu's effigy in protest against the insult.

The former CPM chief minister Buddhadeb Bhattacharjee was furious: 'I have told the party to caution him [Anil Basu] so we don't have to hear such language in future. He did not spare a thought for decency ... such remarks go against Communist culture. It's an unpardonable offence' ('Budhadeb Censures CPI [M] Leader for Abusing Mamata' 2011). Basu was later suspended from the party for three months, not for his unpardonable, offensive, sexist comments but for corruption.

Though Bhattacharjee argued that it would be wrong to assume that 'bad language' was the culture of the party, another senior CPM leader, Sushanta Ghosh, baited Mamata Banerjee: 'Those who are unmarried and do not apply *sindur* [vermillion] are scared of red' (Tapadar 2011). Along the same lines, another minister, the late Subhas Chakraborty, had ridiculed the TMC leader's 'Ma-Mati-Manush' slogan saying: 'She is an infertile woman; what does she know about Ma?' ('Offensive Remarks on Mamata' 2011). Bhattacharjee may have been correct about communist culture, but his party men continued to commit indefensible offences.

In an interview in 2007,[25] the political theorist Noam Chomsky argued for moral universalism, the philosophy of the existence of a universal ethic. Certain behaviours are simply wrong regardless of the circumstances, Chomsky says. 'If something's right for me, it's right for you; if it's wrong for you, it's wrong for me.' The CPM refused to abide by this basic moral truism and disregarded the writing on the wall. The TMC is repeating history. Ethics was—and is—what is missing in today's politics.

HER WORDS, HER STRUGGLE

Nothing is more precious than life![26]

'I am so grateful to be alive,' said Suzette Jordan, wrapping her arms protectively around herself, her face mirroring both relief and shock in equal measure. This reality once again hit Suzette when she went to Kamduni to meet Suthi's mother after the brutal incident of Suthi's rape and murder on 7 June 2013. Initially, Suzette, herself a victim of gang-rape, was reluctant to go, apprehensive about reliving her ordeal and facing the bereaved family. Instead, it proved to be a cathartic experience for Suzette, helping her to get a fresh perspective on her situation. She exclaimed:

> I could have been that mangled body dumped on the roadside like her! I was petrified with fear at the mere thought of what Suthi must have endured! At least I had survived, she had not. I got lucky. Believe me, nothing is more precious than life!

Suzette had been gang-raped, beaten and stripped. A year and a half before Suthi was murdered, a man had held a gun inside her mouth, choking her. 'I could not breathe,' said Suzette, 'I thought I was already dead!' It was hard to ignore the agitation of her expressive hands with their jangling bangles and bracelets. The men were screaming, laughing and abusing her at the same time, she recalled, each egging the other on. The more she resisted, the more violent the men became. They clawed her face and body, beat her with their fists and pinned her down by her long curly hair. Finally, the men threw her out of the moving car on the road, her face and nose bloody, her body bruised, her hair falling out in clumps. It was 3:30 am in the early hours of the morning.

On 5 February 2012, Suzette's life changed overnight—Suzette Jordan, a 37-year-old, fun-loving, endearingly trusting woman who laughed easily, mother of two schoolgoing children, who started dancing the moment she heard the first beats of music, who loved to dress up and go out with friends in the evenings. That evening, Suzette and her friends went to a well-known bar in Park Street, the entertainment district at the heart of Kolkata. They had a few beers, thoroughly enjoying themselves, and Suzette was not willing to call it a day. Suzette had gone through a rough professional phase recently, losing money from a business she had set up with her sister.

Earlier, she had taken up odd jobs working at a sales counter, as a receptionist at a health club, then as a call centre executive, juggling work with the running of her family as a single mother. In 2011, in a bold move, she and her sister started their own call centre, but by January 2012 they had been cheated and lost massive sums of money. They were forced to shut down. 'I was despondent, and the evening proved to be a welcome distraction from my financial worries,' recalled Suzette. After her friends left, she stayed on. 'I have gone out dancing with friends before and since we live in different parts of the city, I have generally travelled back home alone.' For Suzette, Kolkata felt rightfully hers; she had grown up there and lived in the city, and she was confident despite the late nights and commuting alone.

Suzette met a 'pleasant-looking guy' in the bar, exchanged pleasantries and drinks, and when he offered to drop her home, she declined politely at first. But then she gave in to his insistence that he escort her to the taxi stand. An unsuspecting Suzette entered his car and, before she could get her bearings, four men had climbed in. The doors auto-locked as she tried to get out. As she described the ordeal of the next few hours in that car in a torrent of agonized words, I tried to assure her that she did not have to relive the horror and the pain of that night. But she said, 'Let me speak. I feel lighter.'

'MY FATHER FEARED I WOULD FACE PUBLIC HUMILIATION IF I COMPLAINED'

Suzette staggered home in the early morning, bruised and battered. Her family was shocked, but they stood by her, especially her 75-year-old grandmother who was 'like the rock of Gibraltar'. Suzette's elder daughter, 15 years old, bathed her, consoled and comforted her like a baby as she wept in pain and humiliation. 'My daughter is a beautiful, compassionate child,' said Suzette softly. Her grandmother, on hearing the news, had rushed to her side, and in the following months proved to be the family anchor, providing both moral courage and food for the family. The feisty old lady ('She had been a headmistress and was nicknamed Hitler,' laughed Suzette) was insistent that Suzette should report the violence to the police. 'No Suzzie!' she said. 'You are not going to remain silent. Not you, my baby.' Her uncle went with her to the police station to file the criminal complaint, and her aunt reported the incident to a Bengali daily when the police refused to cooperate. It was her father who drew back, extremely reluctant and cautioning her about the social backlash, stigma and humiliation she would face if she went public with her rape. He was afraid the police would dwell on the fact that she had been a single mother for 11 years. 'I don't want people to call you names,' Suzette's father had pleaded.

Suzette's father's fear was not baseless. Overnight, Suzette came to be branded as the 'Park Street Rape Victim'. Political leaders called her a liar, others branded her a prostitute, and the typical cynical response was that 'she had asked for it.'

For years, women's organizations have spent their funds and energies on holding training workshops to sensitize the police on gender issues; but let alone being sensitized, the police do not even follow the minimum protocol for treating the complainant with sensitivity and helping her to register a rape complaint. Political parties of all hues have been stridently vocal and vociferous on the populist issue of the death penalty for rapists; yet they have never worked for radical systemic changes that would be women-centric, making the environment safer and the task of reporting rape less daunting for survivors of sexual violence.

On the evening of 9 February, when Suzette finally gathered the courage to file a criminal complaint of rape at the Park Street *thana* (station), the police questioned her for almost five hours till the wee hours of the morning. They interrogated her in her uncle's presence, humiliating her with derisive comments and sneering innuendos.

'Are you sure you were raped? Really! Raped?' was the response of the policemen, with incredulous expressions, looking pointedly at her jeans. There was no woman constable present at the thana. '*Kya* position *tha*? [In what position?]' she was asked casually, as her uncle, shocked and angry, protested, 'Can't you see her state? Her bruises? She was raped at gunpoint!' The policeman rolled her name, Jordan, over and over on his tongue as though she was an alien; she could hear laughter from an inside room as the men repeated her name and sniggered at the word 'rape'. 'I was actually feeling bad for my uncle as he had to witness my humiliation. The policemen treated me like a slut,' said Suzette.

It was worse when she stated that she had been drinking beer at the bar down the street the evening she was assaulted. The policemen kept focusing on the words 'beer', 'drink' and 'nightclub'. 'Your favourite drink, eh?' asked another. (On 14 February when she was again at the thana: 'Beer?!' one policeman said loudly to another, 'Hey what do you think of having a beer … a beer this evening with me? It's Valentine's Day.') At 1:30 am on 10 February, Suzette and her uncle finally made their way home, exhausted and smarting from the experience. 'I thought I would be treated with compassion after the ordeal I had gone through. Instead I was made to feel guilty. I wanted to scream!'

The hallmark of rape trials in the country is the insistence on looking for marks of resistance as evidence of the woman's testimony. Suzette's aunt had taken her immediately for a medical examination and treatment at a well-known government hospital. Later on 14 February, in the Medical College Hospital, Suzette felt once again humiliated like on her earlier visit to the hospital. 'The departments treat victims with little regard for compassion and sensitivity,' said Suzette. The callousness with which she was tersely ordered to strip, the doctor exploiting her vulnerability so that he could stare at her breasts, and then told laconically, 'Since you are so fair the bruises still show,' made Suzette realize that her trauma was not over the night she was gang-raped. She understood that it would continue at the hands of people in those very institutions that were, ironically, established to help victims of violence.

Aspersions were cast on Suzette's character, and there was a constant insinuation that she was habituated to having sex. 'Why will I not have sex? I was in relationships, they meant something special to me; I may have a chance of a good marriage,' exclaimed Suzette. 'Just because my husband and I separated years ago does not mean I am dead, life doesn't stop there. I am young. Having sex is made out to be such a taboo!' Overnight, neighbours and landlords changed their attitude and behaviour towards her, as if Suzette was some kind of a pariah. Gates and doors were rudely shut in her face, as neighbours looked at her oddly, commented about her daughters and her mother, and said rudely to her face: 'Where has she come from? Just look at her!'

Another rape survivor narrated a similar experience to this author:

> I don't know which was worse, the gang-rape, or the attitude of the neighbours and so-called friends after the incident. From looking at me with pity to viewing me as a kind of curiosity

> object to passing moral judgement about my behaviour, they were in fact inflicting more violence on me. (Agarwala 2008)

'WE SUFFER FROM FOOT-IN-MOUTH DISEASE'

At the time of writing, the 'fast-track' trial court was yet to give its verdict,[27] though court proceedings had started in March 2013. 'Dragging myself to court every day to give my statement was a nightmare,' said Suzette. When family members or women activists accompanied her, the day was bearable. The relatives of the accused, who were all from well-to-do families, were present in court in their numbers; they would follow Suzette with their stares, try to make eye contact, or break into lewd Hindi songs whenever she passed. Even while deposing in the courtroom, the accused were on the stand less than two feet away from her. 'It was scary. Traumatic. I felt they only had to reach out to touch me. I could almost hear their breathing and feel their eyes on me,' said Suzette.

One person Suzette spoke of with admiration and deep respect was Kolkata's then joint commissioner of police (crime), Damayanti Sen. She was diligent, thorough and efficient, and had been successful in arresting three of the five accused;[28] she immediately confirmed that there was 'truth' in the gang-rape, said Suzette:

> She was very stern while questioning me … very, very firm, but patient and kind. She was doing her job, trying to probe and find out whether there were any inconsistencies in my statement. But not once did she humiliate me … not once. For her, it was her job: to keep the city safe. She made sure to get to the bottom of the matter.

Inexplicably, Mamata Banerjee immediately stepped in, insulted Sen publicly when she told the media that Suzette had been gang-raped (contradicting the chief minister's earlier comment that the incident had been fabricated), and was unceremoniously and promptly transferred to a police training institute, considered a punishment posting. As public criticism mounted, the chief minister exclaimed in exasperation: 'Are all women being raped in the state? They blame me for everything … as if it was I who went to rape … if only I were a man!' ('Mamata's Bizarre Defence for Increased Crims in State' 2013). This incredible outburst prompted one of the TMC's senior leaders to comment sarcastically, on condition of anonymity: 'Ah yes, do you know of the new disease in Bengal? We now suffer from foot-in-mouth disease … have you heard of it, eh?'

'WHY IS EVERYONE MAKING POLITICS OF MY RAPE?'

> Why is everyone making politics of my rape? I have been beaten, humiliated and raped. Is this what I deserve instead of protection and assurance from the political leaders? I pleaded with Didi of Ma, Mati and Manush, she is the mother of the state, I appealed to her to help me. But she is silent and did not even respond.… why am I cast away like a piece of wood? I did not lie about my rape … why would I?

Suzette Jordan was reacting in anguish and bewilderment to Mamata Banerjee's comment that her complaint of rape was concocted. As if on cue, Suzette Jordan's rape complaint was promptly dismissed by a senior minister as 'stage managed'. On television, the state transport and sports minister, Madan Mitra,[29] shrewdly employed a mix of insinuation and morality to discredit her complaint, raise doubts about the crime and cast aspersions on Suzette's personal life. Mitra asked dramatically during the panel discussion: 'I believe the woman has two children at home?

Isn't she separated from her husband? Then why did she go to a nightclub and drink?' (Mohan 2013).

Implicit in the minister's comment was the insinuation that single mothers should not drink and go to nightclubs; explicit was the idea that women should not be having fun; if they did, then they were asking for trouble. Linked to his perception about single mothers and women having fun, Madan Mitra's bias was coloured by the fact that the victim was an Anglo-Indian, a shrinking minority in the city. Why would he otherwise ask rhetorical questions; what connection did the complainant's personal life have with the crime committed against her?

Reinforcing the bias, another TMC leader, Kakoli Ghosh Dastidar, referred to the crime as one of a 'negotiation' gone awry, implying that it was a sex worker–client relationship, not an incident of rape. 'As it is, women anyway hesitate to file complaints fearing social stigma,' pointed out Mira Roy, activist, in an interview with this author. 'Instead of encouraging victims to speak up and fight back, political leaders are heaping more insult on the victims.' As Suzette put it:

> Every time I hear people comment that my situation was the result of a deal gone bad between a woman and a client, it actually makes me feel sick, to think how cheap these people are, how cheap their thinking is. It does not show who I am, but it definitely shows what they are made up of.

'I AM NOT A PERSON TO GIVE UP ... AT LEAST, NOT THAT EASILY'

Suzette was determined to see her case through to the end and attended every court date, many times alone, without a friend, activist or family member accompanying her. 'I want justice. I have not done any wrong. Those who violated me and gave me so much pain must be punished. I believe in the court; I believe in God, he will not abandon me.' There were organizations like Swayam ('Anuradha was there for me any time and saw me through my worst period') and lawyers who stood by her steadfastly, and sought to reach out to her with legal advice and solidarity. But there were times when she would prefer to go it alone. 'I am not the person to give up … or at least not that easily!' Her hearty laugh shook her entire body.

It was not easy for Suzette. There were long periods of despair and frustration while Suzette's case was being investigated; the trial and questioning dragged on in the 'fast-track' court; there were abusive phone calls and threats and she would scream back into a silent phone. Strangers would stop her father on the road and say threateningly, 'Tell your daughter to stop behaving like a mad woman, tell her to behave.' She became paranoid if her children were even 10 minutes late returning from school, screaming at them in fright; she would wake up at night in a sweat, suffering nightmares and even contemplating suicide.

Each time, Suzette bounced back with renewed energy and courage. 'My two little babies are my life. How could I leave them?' Trying to find employment, to earn enough to run her family was also difficult. Suzette sought peace in writing poetry, and found love in a charming young man. 'Yes I am very happy and excited,' she messaged, 'It's been ages; all this happiness was long overdue from the big man above.' At the end she messaged me, 'I am still trying to heal myself. The only way you can heal yourself is when you fight your fight and you get justice for it.'

In a most tragic and unexpected turn of events, Suzette died on 13 March 2015 of multiple organ failure from meningoencephalitis at a hospital in Kolkata. Friends and family members were shocked. So were people across the country, even those who had never met her but were familiar with her fight against the system and felt connected with her.[30] Her daughter says[31] that she taught them 'to work hard just to be able enough to fight this world. She taught us that no work makes you big or small, and no job defines you.' She was a rebel who believed in being real. People on social media raised a toast to her courage and spirit in fighting for justice. Discussions and articles on her highlighted how Suzette's struggles and small victories once again demonstrate how the country has failed to create functional support systems for victims of rape and sexual assault.

Suzette's case dragged on in the fast-track court. The investigating officer gave her testimony, the last to depose before the arguments from both sides were heard, while everyone awaited the judgement. It took nearly four years from the time Suzette began her fight for justice, and she was not among the crowds to celebrate the verdict. But women across the country will celebrate her life for her spirit that dares them to win.

'HE HISSED THAT HE WOULD FINISH OFF MY FAMILY'

Similarly distressing experiences with an apathetic police force, insensitive medical institutions and intimidating court proceedings are narrated repeatedly by women who have survived sexual violence. In a bizarre sequence of events in 2013, 16-year-old Shamim, a minor, failed repeated attempts to file an FIR of rape in Karayathana, Park Circus, in the heart of Kolkata. In protest—and in frustration—Aminul Islam, a social worker in Shamim's neighbourhood, burned himself to death in front of the Park Circus thana when the police thwarted his efforts to help Shamim, and instead accused him of theft! Even after Aminul Islam's dying statement was recorded, the police refused to act on his complaint. Finally, when the rape FIR was filed following public protests and the case went to trial, the accused was acquitted for 'lack of evidence'. Once set free, the accused again attempted several times to rape and harass Shamim. In a vindictive move, the accused filed false cases of rape against Aminul Islam's friends for helping Shamim. In a vicious act of revenge, the accused and his friends gang-raped Shamim's aunt for her unstinting support to her niece throughout her ordeal.

Who was this man against whom the police refused to file complaints? How was he so powerful as to be able to repeatedly harass Shamim, abuse her family members and Aminul's friends? What was the basis of his power, the source of his impunity to repeatedly violate laws and norms? Why did the rape case, despite numerous witnesses, fail to prosecute the accused? Shamsul,[32] a history-sheeter, is a powerful promoter-builder in the Park Circus area. Recent investigation shows there are at least three more complaints of rape against Shamsul in different thanas.

Numerous witnesses, including a young neighbour and Shamim's aunt Afisa Begum, testified in court as to how Shamsul would hound and sexually assault the young girl. 'Shamsul is a terror, he would not leave my niece alone. He would harass young girls, who are silent out of fear,' said 40-year-old Afisa (interview with author). An outspoken, bold woman, she had brought up Shamim and her siblings as her own children when her sister was out on work as a domestic. Shamim, gaunt, her face pinched with fear months after the acquittal, described how she was hounded by Shamsul. 'He would look for any *mouka* [opportunity] to molest me, any dark corner or when I went to work. He and his friends would chase me on his motorbike through the narrow lanes,' said Shamim, clutching her hands nervously. Shamsul took full advantage of her vulnerable situation. He knew she would be forced to seek work or go out to shop for the family; and whenever she raised an alarm, he would speed off and return to assault her at the next opportunity.

In court, however, Shamim failed to testify that Shamsul had raped her repeatedly. 'I was terribly afraid, *bahut daar giyatha*,' said Shamim looking away, reluctant to speak about her experience (interview with author, 2014). Every time we met her, she was running a fever and was fidgety and nervous about looking people in the eye. According to her, Shamsul's wife came to her home while the case hearing was on, and abused and threatened Shamim's family if she testified against her husband in court.

'The final day in court was the worst day in my life,' recounted Shamim in a whisper, looking down at her hands. Just before she entered the courtroom to give her testimony, Shamsul's father stood at the door glaring at her, his eyes never leaving her face. 'He hissed that he would finish off my family if I dared say anything against his son. *Hum dekhlenge.* I completely lost my nerve!' In the courtroom, apart from the judge and the lawyers of both sides, in the witness stand, Shamim faced Shamsul, who 'glared malevolently' at her. 'I knew he would harm my family, he would never leave us alone. I was so nervous I didn't know what to say when I was being questioned. I was completely terrified, tongue-tied.' The cross-questioning had confused her, and the language of questioning was also confusing; though Shamim spoke Hindi, it was a specific dialect. Shamim threw back her head, closing her eyes as if to shut out the nightmare. Shamsul's very presence in the courtroom overwhelmed the young Shamim into silence, and Shamsul was acquitted unconditionally.

What was the source of Shamsul's power, his strength of impunity? Wading through a mix of tales and facts, the legend of Shamsul that emerges is that he grew up in a slum as a motor mechanic to become one of the biggest construction goods suppliers in Park Circus. Locals point out his three-storeyed house amidst a bustling, crowded *bustee* (slum). After a stint in jail for theft, young Shamsul was picked up by a local policeman who groomed him to be a police informer. As he sharpened his skills at snooping, he simultaneously cultivated the art of proximity and association with senior police officers and local politicians, and his muscle and money power grew in leaps and bounds. 'Shamsul is close to police officers in different thanas, and that's why he moves around freely with arrogance even when there are criminal complaints against him,' said Afisa Begum (interview with author, 2014). This was a view held by many in the area where Shamsul operated. Afisa was picked up at gunpoint one evening in June 2014 and gang-raped, allegedly by Shamsul's henchmen. '*Yaad rakhna*! [Don't forget!]' they snarled as they threw her out of the moving car. Afisa is not one to forget—she promptly filed a police complaint for rape and is gearing up for a fight.

One of Aminul's closest friends, who has been with the family throughout the ordeal and has, along with other friends, organized protests and marches in the neighbourhood against the role of the police and Shamsul, was slapped with false cases of rape to intimidate him. It was found, according to media reports, that poor girls were lured by Shamsul's men to file false rape complaints in lieu of favours. One was promised a tiny one-room place in the bustee, says activist Swapna, who has been a pillar of support for Aminul's family .

'Aminul's family and friends are devastated that Shamim did not "speak up" despite an airtight case against Shamsul; if she had, Shamsul would have been convicted and Aminul's life would have achieved justice,' says Swapna (interview with author, 2014). Shamsul continues to haunt the area, harass people while they continue to seek and hope for justice for Aminul's death. The State Human Rights Commission had ordered Rs 500,000 as compensation to the family, but the state government is yet to respond. 'Why did my son have to die?' asks Aminul's mother, her once-beautiful face lined with sorrow. 'He readily helped people, he never turned away any one disappointed. I have never asked for anything in life, I only demand *insanyaat*, humanity justice for my son.'

'I FEEL MORE HEALED AFTER I REVEALED MYSELF'

For Shamim, despite the support of her family, Aminul's friends and women's groups, her fight was against the most powerful person in her neighbourhood. Shamsul's monetary and muscle power proved to be even more intimidating in the absence of witness protection. Shamim's stay in a government short-stay home for 'protection' when Shamsul repeatedly tried to assault her, proved to be a disaster. The loneliness of being away from her family, the bullying by older inmates and the poor quality of the food provided led Shamim to plead in court that she preferred to be back in her own home.

'BANTALA THEKE KAMDUNI, SAAB SHASAKER EKDHANI'

Protests took over the state. This was nothing new for Kolkata, known as a city of causes; marches and demonstrations occurred routinely in the city during the last few years of LF rule. It was more sporadic then; it is angrier now under the TMC government. What has been significant is the participation of rape survivors and their families, issue-based alliances and innovative protests. Moreover, the protests against rape and sexual assault, until now the concern of women's groups alone, have become a 'public issue', widely discussed at street corners and protested by various sections of society. Suthi Ghosh's gang-rape and murder in June 2013 in Kamduni set loose people's pent-up anger against the four-year-old TMC state government.

In an unprecedented show of solidarity on 21 June, two weeks after Suthi's murder, more than 10,000 people took to the streets. This rally of several groups, organizations and individuals was an agenda-based alliance. First, it was called by intellectuals like the poet Sankha Ghosh, the economist Ashok Mitra and others, and not by any political party. Second, it was for the first time that the city witnessed an outpouring from such a wide cross-section of society,[33] about an issue generally left to women's groups and feminists to battle: the safety and security of women. Prominent banners that read 'Don't Play Politics with Rape' and 'Bantala *theke* Kamduni, *Saab Shasaker Ekdhani*' (from Bantala to Kamduni, every government sings the same tune) revealed how rape had become a political tool and called attention to the LF and TMC governments' similar treatment of sexual violence.

Third, the rally was an outpouring of indignation against the constant bogey of 'Maoists' raised by Mamata Banerjee to gag dissent. For the people of Bengal, when the rallying cry of *azaadi* (freedom) was raised, a word usually associated with the Kashmir movement, the slogan '*Hum Chahte Hai Azaadi*' (we want freedom) took on a larger significance as a cry for dignity. It meant freedom of women from violence, the freedom to speak up, to question, and the freedom to protest. Basically, azaadi or freedom from fear.[34] Says Partha Chatterjee, who walked in the rally:

> The public reaction to Kamduni was not primarily a protest against sexual violence *per se*. It was a protest against the complete submission of the police to the unfair demands of political leaders and support for the courage of the women of Kamduni who decided to protest. (Interview with author, 10 December 2014)

The coming together of thousands of angry protesters across the social and political spectrum was reminiscent of the protests of November 2007 on the issue of Nandigram, against the absence of state accountability on the part of the ruling LF. Bike-riding and armed *harmadbahini*, supporters of the CPM, had forcibly recaptured Nandigram, spreading terror in the region. Earlier that year in March in Nandigram, 14 people had been shot dead in police firing, many women raped and many more injured when they resisted the acquisition of their lands. More than 60,000 people walked in angry protest against the LF's terror tactics.

In a radical departure, for the first time in Bengal, rape survivors actively and openly participated in the protests and marches, some without a scarf, their faces uncovered, unashamed to reveal their identity in public. Suzette led from the front in a demonstration protesting Suthi's murder. Her face uncovered, shouting 'Halla Bol!' with raised fist, she marched down the streets of the city, finding the experience 'most liberating'. To protest police inaction in her case, Shamim was in the front row of a procession holding the lead banner, walking with hundreds of local men and women from her community in her neighbourhood. She had her face covered with a black dupatta, but for the first time in her life she had the 'courage to walk on the streets'.[35]

This courage was not limited to women from Kolkata city. Tearing apart the social stigma around rape, women from Sutia village, North 24 Parganas district, participated in large numbers, among them women who had been gang-raped, trafficked and sexually assaulted during LF rule in the 2000s. Then there were relatives, neighbours and friends of women who had been raped and murdered, from Kamduni and Gede, a village about 140 kilometres away from the city in Nadia district.

Over the last decade, the state has also witnessed vigorous mobilization initiated by men on violence against women. It was a schoolteacher, 40-year-old Barun Biswas in Nadia district, who took the initiative to organize the women who had suffered, and along with some men set up the Pratibadi Manch against the criminal gang who terrorized the population. The perpetrators enjoyed the patronage of the ruling party, while the police looked the other way. According to media reports, 33 women had been gang-raped and 12 murders committed in the area. In a public awareness meeting, Biswas told his people: 'if we lack the courage to take on the rapists, we deserve more punishment than they do'. On 5 July 2012, Biswas was shot dead for his 'arrogance'; but the women in Sutia have not been intimidated into giving up their fight for justice.

Protests thereafter became even more novel. Members of the United Students Democratic Front went to the Writers' Building with an earthen pot full of the mouth-watering Bengali sweet, *rosogolla*. They presented the jar to the security for Mamata Banerjee's 'high performance' in crimes against women. The police, however, were not amused, and the rosogolla bearers were promptly locked up in the thana.

In August 2014, several victims of human rights violations set up a platform, Akranta Amra (We the Victims); this included the Jadavpur University professor earlier arrested for circulating cartoons of the chief minister, and Shiladitya Chowdhury, the farmer whose query about rising fertilizer price was labelled a 'Maoist question' by the chief minister and who was then arrested under her orders.

CONCLUSION

There remains much to be achieved on the report card of state accountability in Bengal. Unfortunately, regardless of which political party has come to power, sexual violence and misogyny have pervaded the political discourse, but not as a human rights challenge to bring about justice for women. It is bizarre that the two political opponents, the TMC and the CPM, so bitterly apart in political ideology, are similar in their actions and attitudes to sexual violence and violation of democratic procedures. The tradition of valorization of impunity in Bengal was established by the Congress government and picked up by the LF with the politicization of the police force; its cadres mastered the techniques of appropriating social institutions with criminals entering politics. The TMC has taken this process to a logical conclusion, eroding administrative and legal institutions and procedures with the leader playing the role of the investigator, judge and jury. In this diminishing democratic space, it has become increasingly difficult for women to obtain justice for sexual crimes when the social fabric itself is at risk.

Despite this, women continue to dare. Suzette's case has a critical bearing on the efforts of feminists and activists to deepen their understanding of 'bad woman, bad victim'. Suzette could fit the archetype 'bad woman'; she received social flak despite the fact that she was the victim of sexual violence. First, she broke the accepted social codes: she was out at night in Kolkata's version of Sin City, drinking, having fun, dancing, and then engaging with strangers. She was perceived as 'tempting fate', persistently taking 'risks'. She was not behaving in the manner that society would expect from a mother of two children, least of all a single mother. Unwittingly, she was asserting her right to pleasure, to loiter, the right to be anywhere, anytime, with or without reason.

The way sexual crimes are projected (also in the media) affects how we understand them. Moreover, victims of sexual assault are not equal in the public perception. The public response to the crime is intrinsically related to what a 'victim' or a 'good woman' should be like, and to the class and social category to which she belongs. The public sympathy and outrage were understandable in the cases of both Suthi and Shamim, since they belong to deprived families. Suthi of Kamduni was murdered because of her yearning for higher education and determination to change her destiny; Shamim, a child labourer, was repeatedly violated in her endeavour to supplement the family income. Suzette never hid the fact that her purpose was neither; she unashamedly stated that she was out for fun. While the right to mobility for women for the purpose of education and work are today socially acceptable to some extent, the right to leisure (considered a 'bourgeois trait') remains a 'morally questionable' issue even among a section of radicals and feminists. It is this critical space that feminists would need to establish for women to move around freely without fear, without any explanation, without societal judgement.

Second, Suzette broke new ground even after her rape. Unrepentant, she refused to comply with the idea of shame; sick of being branded as the 'Park Street Rape Victim' and of hiding behind a shield of anonymity, she came out in public.

> I was initially scared to death … but I had to overcome it, and it was exhilarating. I feel more healed after I revealed myself. If this incident had not happened to me then I would have introduced myself to you as Suzette Jordan, very proudly. I am not ashamed of something somebody else did to me. Why should I go through life with that tag of the Park Street Rape Victim?

Third, despite her ordeal before and after the violence, Suzette was most grateful to be alive and living life on her own terms. She went back to her trinkets, lipsticks, friends and dancing. This is contrary to what society expects of rape victims, condemning them to living like a *zindaa laash* (living corpse). Suzette not only came out but grabbed every opportunity to speak out and describe her ordeal and what it meant to survivors of rape. From talking to judges about her experience at the hands of the police and during the trial proceedings, to participating in TV talk shows and discussing safety with schoolchildren, Suzette engaged head-on with the issue of violence against women. Her public presence gave confidence to women, taking the stigma off rape victims in particular. 'Because I am educated, I was able to have the opportunity to voice my feelings and experience,' says Suzette.[36]

The voices of protest in Bengal, albeit fragmented, few and far between today, increasingly bring hope that people will refuse to be silenced by state impunity. The hope lies in young people forming new alliances and new formations of protests. Though individuals alone do not bring about change in society, but are supported by the groundswell generated by many grassroots movements, individuals do stand out for the role they play, consciously or unwittingly, by questioning the system. Suzette Jordan is disturbing to society because she, like Bhanwari Devi[37] before her, both challenged the discourse of victimhood.[38]

NOTES

1. Twenty-one years later, in 2014, a commission headed by Justice S. Chatterjee dubbed the firing as 'unjustified, unconstitutional and without provocation'. The commission observed that the police had overreacted to please their political bosses. 'It was worse than the Jallianwala Bagh massacre,' stated the report. See '1993 Kolkata Police Firing Worse than Jallianwala Bagh, Says Commission' (2014).
2. Statistics compiled by Nari Nirjatan Pratirodh Manch, Ahalaya and Association for the Protection of Democratic Rights based on media reports, published in the leaflet, *Gato dash bachare Paschim Banglai police hepajate darshaner ghatana matra ekti?* (In West Bengal, only one custodial rape during the last 10 years?).
3. Interview with activist Anuradha Talwar, president of Paschim Banga Khet Mazdoor Samiti, who was active in the Singur agitation of 2008.
4. Information on Singur, Nandigram and Lalgarh is based on the following sources. Nandigram: *Interim Report of an Independent Citizens' Team from Kolkata on the Current State of Affairs in Nandigram* (Sanhati 2007) (I was part of this fact-finding team and conducted personal interviews during my visits to the area over a period of time); *Nandigram: What Really Happened? Report of the*

People's Tribunal (2007); press statement issued by a seven-member team from Women against Sexual Violence and State Repression (WSS) that visited Nandigram on 10 March 2015 (WSS 2015b); reports on Nandigram, Lalgarh and Singur by WSS (2015a, 2015c, 2015d).

Singur: www.sanhati.com; and interviews with activist Anuradha Talwar, president of Paschim Banga Khet Mazdoor Samiti, who was active in the Singur agitation of 2008.

Lalgarh: www. sanhati. com; and interviews with Krishna Bandopadhya (editor of *Khoj*), Nisha Biswas (activist) and Rungta Munsi (human rights lawyer), all of whom visited Lalgarh several times during the movement. Also see *War and Peace in Junglemahal: People, State and Maoists* (B. Roy 2012); and *Letters from Lalgarh* (Sanhati 2013).

5. Not her real name, in compliance with the law prohibiting disclosure of the identity of a victim of rape.
6. Radha Rani went public with her rape.
7. According to MASUM, a human rights organization, based on the statement of seven women, four women were raped while three were sexually assaulted.
8. Interview given by Jasodhara Bagchi in February 2013 as part of the Zubaan Poster Women archives to record the oral histories of women.
9. Dola Sen, the Indian National Trinamool Trade Union Congress president, on taking charge as vice-president of the Women's Commission said, 'We shall follow the Mamata Model. We are here to help the chief minister' (Chakraborty 2014).
10. On 10 March 2015, a seven-member women's team from WSS visited Nandigram. There was no concrete information on the status of the cases filed by the rape survivors. It is not certain that cases of rape were filed at all. Supriya Jana and Basanti Kar were among the women killed. Seventeen women had been raped, while many others had been molested and severely injured.

    A three-member WSS team visited Lalgarh on 11 October 2015. On 12 May 2015, six leaders of the Lalgarh movement had been sentenced to life imprisonment. The families of those jailed were living in severe hardship; they had received little support in the absence of their menfolk. The lack of irrigation in the villages and rampages by wild elephants had aggravated the economic situation. Many faced severe food shortage, while young women continued to suffer mental trauma. It is a source of inspiration that, even in the face of these adversities, the children were determined to continue their studies, and the women were keen to encourage and support their children. There continued to be a striking presence of armed forces, and the temporary camps had become permament. The TMC maintains that there is peace in the region, but it is obvious that this peace is maintained by the use of armed forces.

The WSS team visited Singur on 27 February 2016. 'If you can't break them, buy them' is the principle followed by the TMC in the region. Land was yet to be returned to the unwilling farmers who had refused to give their land to the Tatas. But the movement had died down; Mamata Banerjee had been quick to silence any discontent by handing out a monthly dole. In May 2012, a monthly compensation of Rs 1,000 (since increased to Rs 2,000) and later 16 kilos of rice at Rs 2 per kilo were being distributed to the 'unwilling farmers'. Since then, 3,569 beneficiaries from among the sharecroppers and agricultural labourers have been receiving a monthly dole that has reached a total of more than Rs 100 crore (Rs 1 billion).

11. According to the WSS report, only 3 of the 16 rape survivors have received compensation (WSS 2015a).
12. In *Didi*, Monobina Gupta (2012) traces Banerjee's rise in the state's politics.
13. Bancharam Manna, the fiery activist and face of the Singur movement, is now a submissive TMC member of the legislative assembly (MLA). Rizwanur Rehman, who married his student, a rich girl from a Hindu family, was found dead on the railway tracks one day. Following an unprecedented public hue and cry, his mother was inducted into the Railway Committee (when Banerjee was union railway minister). Rehman's brother became a TMC

MLA. Feroza Begum who had lost her son in the 14 March 2007 firing in Nandigram also became a TMC MLA.

14. Since this paper was written, on 30 January 2016, the additional district and sessions judge sentenced three accused to death and three to life imprisonment for the gang-rape and murder of Suthi. Ansar Ali, Saiful Ali and Amin Ali were sentenced to death for gang-rape and murder, while the other three—Emanul Islam, Bhola Naskar and Aminur Islam—were handed life terms for gang-rape. Two other accused in the case were acquitted and one died in custody.

    Though the protests in Kamduni have now petered out, Kamduni continues to symbolize the spirit of resistance of common villagers against government and police high-handedness. Local villagers have mobilized for larger struggles under Akranto Amra (We Are Under Attack), a social platform for protesters against injustice in Bengal.
15. Compiled by Swayam, a non-governmental women's rights organization, based on media reports.
16. State Crime Records Bureau, West Bengal, 'Crime against Women (including Kolkata) for the Year 2008', http://scrbwb.gov.in/User/Crimeagainstwomen.html (accessed 5 August 2016).
17. The state director general of police contested the data, claiming that rape had come down 'considerably', while the bulk of the crimes came under Section 498A of the Indian Penal Code.
18. Broadcast on 9 March 2014 on Times Now.
19. In April 2015, the primary school headmaster Pradip Mukherjee fought the municipality elections with the backing of the LF.
20. These remarks by the chief minister were widely reported in the press. See, for example, 'Crime to Conviction in Case Like No Other' (2015).
21. Partha Chatterjee, email interview, 10 December 2014.
22. Ibid.
23. Mamata Banerjee's fetish for celebrities was reflected once again when she packed the State Women's Commission with Tollywood personalities.

24. Gupta (2012) systematically traces the abuse heaped on Banerjee.
25. Chomsky's quote is referred to in several places. See, e.g., Wendy Connick, *Opposing Viewpoints vs Moral Relativism*, http://www.tailoredcontent.com/library/metaethics.php (accessed 28 June 2016).
26. The quoted statements in this part of the chapter are primarily from formal interviews that I conducted with Suzette Jordan in 2012, as well as various informal interactions with her from 2012 onwards.
27. On 12 December 2015, Additonal Sessions Judge Chiranjib Bhattacharya sentenced three accused (Ruman Khan, Naser Khan and Sumit Bajaj) to 10 years of rigorous imprisonment and Rs 100,000 fine each the day after they were convicted of gang-rape. The verdict came nearly four years after Suzette was gang-raped in February 2012. The accused were found guilty under Sections 376(2)(g) (gang-rape), 120B (criminal conspiracy), 323 (voluntarily causing hurt) and 506 (criminal intimidation) of the Indian Penal Code. Forty-five witnesses were examined during the trial. Two accused are still absconding. See 'Park Street Gangrape Verdict' (2015).
28. The main accused is yet to be arrested.
29. Madan Mitra was arrested in December 2014 in connection with the multi-crore Saradha chit funds scandal investigated by the CBI. He has been refused bail.
30. Before this draft was submitted, in February 2015, I had emailed Suzette requesting her to cross-check the section on her for factual errors. She laughed over the phone at bits of description, angry about the case all over again, happy at Madan Mitra's arrest: 'The man above never misses a thing,' she commented. That was the last time I spoke to her. On 8 March, before leaving the country, I texted to apologize for not being able to meet her as promised and wished her solidarity on Women's Day. I didn't receive a reply, which was nothing unusual, only to hear later from Urvashi Butalia that she had passed away.

31. In a moving tribute titled 'My Mother Suzette Jordan' by Rhea Jordan, published in the *Ladies Finger*, 16 March 2015.
32. Shamsul is not the real name of the accused, though there is no law barring him from being named. This initiates a debate as to whether the accused should be named before he is convicted. Does it go against natural justice? After all, an accused is innocent till proven guilty. In many instances there is stigmatization and social boycott even when the accused is absolved of the charges. In the early years of the women's movement, there was a conscious move to name and shame the accused, since police and the courts did not respond to the complaints. This situation still continues. Major injustices have occurred when the accused have been named, for example, in the Azamgarh arrests following a police shootout in Delhi accusing the boys of being Indian Mujaheedins; today it is very difficult for boys from Azamghar to get accommodation, to get admission to colleges, or even to get married.
33. The rally was attended by activists from the human rights and women's movements, students, youth, working men and women, the old and the young, cultural performers, intellectuals and scholars.
34. Since 2011, with 'paribartan', any protest or even whiff of dissent has been dismissed as a conspiracy by Mamata Banerjee, with the dissenters dubbed by her as 'Maoists'.
35. This was in sharp contrast to the experience of Radha Rani Ari of Nandigram. Radha Rani told the WSS team that she had once been in demand for political campaigns to describe her sexual torture. 'My body was like a property to get votes.' Feeling abandoned later, she contemplated suicide several times.
36. In the case of Shamim, despite the unconditional support from her family, friends and activists, the young girl from a humble background found it difficult to overcome her fear of Shamsul.
37. Bhanwari Devi, a Dalit social worker, was campaigning against child marriage as part of a government programme in Rajasthan. Enraged, upper-caste men of her village gang-raped her to teach her a lesson. She refused to hide her face in public and allowed

the media to use her name. 'It's not my shame. Those who did this crime should be ashamed,' she said.

38. This essay has been possible as a result of living for decades in Kolkata, being part of the autonomous women's movement since its inception in the early 1980s in the city, heated discussions on politics and feminism with fellow activists and friends and also through my interactions with people as a journalist. It is impossible to thank each and every one who has contributed to my understanding of sexual violence, state impunity and politics, which in many ways has helped in the writing of this piece. To all the women who have enriched my life, my salaam.

    Both Urvashi Butalia and Laxmi Murthy have been my fellow travellers. This time too, they showed untiring patience and humour in seeing this 'baby' through. Basanti Chakravorty, my friend, was ever ready to read the manuscript, and I value her comments. The comfort of Sushil always being there made this possible.

REFERENCES

'1993 Kolkata Police Firing Worse than Jallianwala Bagh, Says Commission'. 2014. *Indian Express*, 30 December. http://indianexpress.com/article/india/west-bengal/1993-kolkata-police-firing-worse-than-jallianwala-bagh-commission/ (accessed 6 August 2016).

'Are All Women in West Bengal Getting Raped? Mamata's Bizarre Defence for Increased Crime in State'. 2013. *India Today*, 23 June. http://indiatoday.intoday.in/story/are-all-women-in-bengal-getting-raped-mamatas-bizzare-excuse-for-increased-crime-in-state/1/284945.html (accessed 7 August 2016).

'Bantala and After'. 1990. *Mainstream Weekly*, 14 July.

'Budhadeb Censures CPI (M) Leader for Abusing Mamata'. 2011. *Hindu*, 23 April. http://www.thehindu.com/news/national/other-states/buddhadeb-censures-cpim-leader-for-abusing-mamata/article1761239.ece (accessed 5 August 2016).

'Calcutta High Court to Monitor Kamduni Probe'. 2013. IndiaTV, 4 July. http://www.indiatvnews.com/news/india/calcutta-high-court-to-monitor-kamduni-probe-24602.html (accessed 6 August 2016).

'CM Promises, Kamduni Seethes'. 2013. *Telegraph*, 18 June. http://www.telegraphindia.com/1130618/jsp/calcutta/story_17019898.jsp#.V6WXBOCx_Dc (accessed 6 August 2016).

'Crime to Conviction in Case Like No Other'. 2015. *Telegraph*, 11 December. http://www.telegraphindia.com/1151211/jsp/calcutta/story_57828.jsp#.V6W8nuCx_Dc (accessed 6 August 2016).

'Dev's Rape Analogy Draws Widespread Criticism'. 2014. *Indian Express*, 25 March. http://indianexpress.com/article/cities/kolkata/devs-rape-analogy-draws-widespread-criticism/ (accessed 6 August 2016).

'If You Are Raped What Will Be Your Fee: CPI-M Leader to Mamata'. 2012. ZeeNews, 28 December. http://zeenews.india.com/news/west-bengal/if-you-are-raped-what-will-be-your-fee-cpi-m-leader-to-mamata_819322.html (accessed 6 August 2016).

'Mamata Does It Again in Rape Case'. 2012. *Telegraph*, 29 February. http://www.telegraphindia.com/1120229/jsp/frontpage/story_15193555.jsp#.V6W8BuCx_Dc (accessed 6 August 2016).

'MP Government Bristles at TMC's Tit for Tat'. 2014. *Times of India*, 19 June.

'Offensive Remarks on Mamata; CM Steps In'. 2011. *Telegraph*, 24 April. http://www.telegraphindia.com/1110424/jsp/frontpage/story_13895599.jsp (accessed 6 August 2016).

'Park Street Gangrape Verdict: Court Sentences Three Convicts to 10 Years Jail'. 2015. *Indian Express*, 12 December. http://indianexpress.com/article/india/india-others/park-street-gangrape-case-court-sentences-three-convicts-to-10-years-jail/ (accessed 6 August 2016).

'Tapas Pal Rape Remarks and Aftermath'. 2014. *Indian Express*, 1 July. http://indianexpress.com/article/india/politics/tapas-paul-rape-remarks-all-you-need-to-know/ (accessed 6 August 2016).

'Trinamool MLA Threatens to Behead Congress Leader'. 2013. *Hindu*, 22 July. http://www.thehindu.com/todays-paper/tp-national/trinamool-mla-threatens-to-behead-congress-leader/article4939950.ece (accessed 6 August 2016).

'Twice-Wielded, Bamboo Is Official Weapon'. 2014. *Telegraph*, 14 December. http://www.telegraphindia.com/1141214/jsp/frontpage/story_3616.jsp#.V6XFF-Cx_Dc (accessed 6 August 2016).

'What Do You Want, Should I Kill Him? Mamata on Tapas Pal's 'Rape' Threat' 2014. *Times of India*, 1 July. http://timesofindia.indiatimes.com/india/What-do-you-want-should-I-kill-him-Mamata-on-Tapas-Pals-rape-threat/articleshow/37590187.cms (accessed 6 August 2016).

Agarwala, Susama. 2008. 'I am Not a Victim', in Swati Bhattacharjee (ed.), *A Unique Crime: Understanding Rape in India*. Kolkata: Ganchil.

Bagchi, Jasodhara, and Subharanjan Dasgupta. 2003. *The Trauma and the Triumph: Gender and Partition*. Kolkata: Stree.

Bandopadhyay, Krishna. 2012. 'Women's Power vs State Power', in Biswajit Roy (ed.), *War and Peace in Junglemahal: People, State and Maoists*. Kolkata: Setu Prakashani.

Bhattacharjee, Buddhadeb. 2011. Letter to the Editor, 'Bantala and After', *Mainstream Weekly*, 49(19).

Chakraborty, Ajanta. 2014. 'Dola Sen Appointed as Vice-chairperson of Bengal Women's Commission', *Times of India*, 4 July. http://timesofindia.indiatimes.com/city/kolkata/Dola-Sen-appointed-as-vice-chairperson-of-Bengal-womens-commission/articleshow/37783635.cms (accessed 6 August 2016).

Chatterji, Joya. 2007. *The Spoils of Partition: Bengal and India, 1947–67*. New York: Cambridge University Press.

Chattopadhyay, Suhrid Sankar. 'Rape Threat, Filmi Style'. 2014. *Frontline*, 25 July. http://www.frontline.in/the-nation/rape-threat-filmi-style/article6189572.ece (accessed 6 August 2016).

Datta, Debojit. 2007. 'They Kill People Like Birds', *Tehelka*, 24 November. http://archive.tehelka.com/story_main36.asp?filename=Ne241107They_kill.asp (accessed 5 August 2016).

Gupta, Monobina. 2007. 'Monobina Gupta on Nandigram and the CPM Whitewash', Kafila, 14 March. https://kafila.org/2007/03/14/monobina-gupta-on-nandigram-and-the-cpm-whitewash/ (accessed 4 August 2016).

———. 2012. *Didi: A Political Biography*. New Delhi: Harper Collins.

Menon, Ramdas. 2010. 'The Legacy of Jytoi "Candlelight" Basu', *New Indian Express*, 28 January. http://www.newindianexpress.com/opinion/article411750.ece (accessed 7 August 2016).

Mohan, Shriya. 2013. 'How Do You Survive Being Named "The Park Street Victim"?' https://in.news.yahoo.com/how-do-you-survive-being-named-%E2%80%98the-park-street-rape-victim%E2%80%99--054758334.html (accessed 7 August 2016).

Nandigram: What Really Happened? Report of the People's Tribunal. 2007. Delhi: Daanish Books.

NDTV. 'CPIM Leader Anil Basu Abusing Mamata Banerjee'. YouTube Video, 2:42. Apr 2011. https://www.youtube.com/watch?v=6xwWuXMvdpE (accessed 6 August 2016).

Patkar, Medha. 2007. 'Medha Patkar on Civil War in Nandigram', Kafila, 15 March. https://kafila.org/2007/03/15/medha-patkar-on-civil-war-in-nandigram/ (accessed 4 August 2016).

Patkar, Medha, Sandeep Pandey and Pranab Bannerji. 2007. 'Nandigram: Kolkata High Court Upholds Human Justice', CNS, November. http://www.citizen-news.org/2007/11/nandigram-kolkata-high-court-upholds.html (accessed 6 August 2016).

Patnaik, Prabhat. 2014. 'The Governing Option', *Telegraph*, 20 August. http://www.telegraphindia.com/1140820/jsp/opinion/story_18725609.jsp#.V6U73uCx_Dc (accessed 5 August 2016).

Roy, Biswajit. ed. 2012. *War and Peace in Junglemahal: People State and Maoists*. Kolkata: Setu Prakshani.

Roy, Mira, and Soma Marik. eds. 2007. *Women under the Left Front Rule: Expectations Betrayed*. Vadodara: Documentation and Study Centre for Action.

Samuelson, Robert. 2014. 'Why We Can't (or Won't) Govern', *Hindu*, 18 November (from the *Washington Post*).

Sanhati. 2007. *Interim Report of an Independent Citizens' Team from Kolkata on the Current State of Affairs in Nandigram*, 30 November. http://sanhati.com/news/537/ (accessed 6 August 2016).

————. 2013. *Letters from Lalgarh: The Complete Collection of Letters from the Peoples' Committee against Police Atrocities*. Kolkata: Setu Prakashani.

Sarkar, Arindam. 2007. 'Mamata Dares Budha on SEZ', *Hindustan Times*, 5 February. http://www.hindustantimes.com/india/mamata-dares-budha-on-sez/story-a8DpaKj9VQo9r44wzviehO.html (accessed 6 August 2016).

Sengupta, Anindya, and Anshuman Phadikar. 2014. 'Expelled Seth a Selling Point in Election Season', *Telegraph*, 16 April.

Sengupta, S. 2006. *Curzon's Partition of Bengal and Aftermath*. Kolkata: Naya Udyog.

Tapadar, Pradipta. 2011. 'Personal Abuse and Attacks Mar Bengal Poll Campaign'. https://uk.news.yahoo.com/personal-abuse-attacks-mar-bengal-poll-campaign-100443993.html (accessed 6 August 2016).

WSS (Women against Sexual Violence and State Repression). 2015a. 'West Bengal: WSS Statement on the Condition of Women in Nandigram', 15 March. http://sanhati.com/articles/13092/ (accessed 6 August 2016).

————. 2015b. 'WSS Press Statement', 14 March. http://sanhati.com/excerpted/13110/#2 (accessed 6 August 2016).

————. 2015c. 'WSS Report on Lalgarh Visit', 3 December. http://sanhati.com/excerpted/15599/ (accessed 6 August 2016).

————. 2015d. 'WSS Report on Singur Visit', 14 April. http://sanhati.com/excerpted/16861/ (accessed 6 August 2016).

3

Behind the Silence

Sexual Violence against Afghan and Burmese Refugee Women in Delhi

BANI GILL

> Sexual and gender based violence can occur at every stage of the refugee cycle: during flight, while in the country of asylum and during repatriation. (UNHCR, 2006)

INTRODUCTION

Refugee narratives of forced flight, asylum seeking, repatriation, resettlement and reintegration frequently report the experience of sexual and gender-based violence (Giles and Hyndman 2004; Hyndman 2000; Indra 1999). For refugee women in particular, the search for a 'safe' space is marred by marginalization, discrimination and security risks. Gender is an important variable in understanding the cause of flight as well as the specific experience of displacement (Freedman 2007). As Binder and Tosic (2005) have shown, sexual violence against refugee women tends to be very high within the country of origin during the period of flight as well as in the host or receiving country. This essay seeks to document sexual violence perpetrated against refugee women by host or receiving societies, with specific reference to Afghan and Burmese Chin refugee women in Delhi.[1] Beginning with a description of India's multipronged approach towards refugees, this essay will address the varied forms of sexual and gender-based violence faced by the figure of the *refugee woman* in India by raising the question of resettlement and impunity in this context.

Statistics on refugees the world over are unreliable and vague. Freedman (2007) estimates that there are about 21 million people of concern to the UNHCR, but it is nearly impossible to determine how many among them are women. The same situation persists in India, where gendered statistics on refugees are difficult to come by, and data assessing the scale and impact of sexual violence against refugee women is even more ambiguous. The lack of accurate statistics, data or mainstream reporting relating to sexual violence against refugee women in particular is reflective of these limitations, and of a silencing of gender in India's asylum process. The economic, legal and social clandestinity that permeates the everyday life of refugee women in Delhi is also crucial to understanding this silence.

The 'silence' referenced in the title of the essay is then an attempt to address the important question of what is, or rather what isn't, being addressed and discussed in the public domain. To understand why refugee issues may assume centre stage when it comes to the assessment of diplomatic ties or electoral politics—for instance, India's policy towards Tibetan refugees or the vitriolic rhetoric against Bangladeshi 'illegal immigrants'—and why this momentum in public space is lost or restrained when it comes to the issue of sexual violence.[2] At the same time, it is not enough to merely state that these issues are being silenced without reflecting on the politics of silence in terms of context and meaning attributed by 'survivor' and 'perpetrator' both. As Singh and Hoenig (2014: xxxi) remind us, 'Silence as a reaction to violence can be a signifier of an array of social phenomena. It may betray endorsement or guilt on the part of the perpetrator; it can be an expression of paralysis or dignity on the part of the survivor'.

Silence formed an integral part of my own fieldwork, both as a form of communication and subversion. My interviews with refugee women and survivors of sexual violence were riddled with long gaps and silences—silence in the middle of an angry outburst, silence when the topic of sexualized violence was broached, silence when violence inflicted by members of their own refugee community was discussed, and silence as resistance to discussing or explaining their ambiguous legal status. Many women were hesitant about recorded interviews or of revealing sensitive information that may adversely affect their current status in India or that of family members left behind. For the present respondent group, silence reflected a fear of confiding thoughts to an 'Outsider', a sense of isolation in the host country, as also a very real silence due to the absence of a mutually understandable language combined with an eagerness to discuss other 'more important' issues—such as resettlement to a third country. The varied forms of silence and narrative recorded in this paper bring to focus the multiple forms of violence prevalent against refugee women, where impunity is generated by the very ambiguity of their legal status. A discussion and explanation of this ambiguous legal status requires an investigation into refugee policy in India, to which we now turn.

INDIA'S REFUGEE POLICY

Despite housing one of the world's largest refugee populations, India is not party to the 1951 Convention relating to the Status of Refugees or the 1967 Protocol, the two international conventions regulating refugee and asylum processes. These conventions are key legal documents defining who is a refugee, their rights and the legal obligations of states, and yet India has abstained from both.[3] There is no regional or national legislation to guide the treatment of refugees in India either. Instead, the Registration of Foreigners Act of 1939, the Foreigners Act of 1946 and the Foreigners Order of 1948 are the primary documents that regulate the status of foreigners as well as refugees and asylum seekers.[4] These Acts, remnants of a colonial legacy, define a foreigner as any person who is not a citizen of India, and treat foreigners, migrants, asylum seekers and refugees all on the same plane. This generic categorization means that refugee movements in India are regulated by contradictions and inaccuracies.

Over the years—especially since landmark events such as the partition of 1947, the Tibetan crisis of 1959, the Bangladesh Liberation War in 1971 and the Sri Lankan civil war, all of which led to massive migratory waves—the Indian state has devised special legislative measures and ad hoc executive decisions to distinguish refugees from foreigners and to respond to various refugee-related crises. Today, India follows a multipronged strategy when dealing with refugee inflows. Three broad categories of refugees may be identified. Category I includes those fleeing neighbouring South Asian countries, protection for whom is decided upon by the Government of India. The majority of these are Tibetan and Sri Lankan refugees, of which the latter are mostly housed in government run camps that the UNHCR has only recently been allowed access to. Category II refugees are mandate refugees acknowledged only by the UNHCR and subsequently protected under the principle of non-refoulement.[5] UNHCR's mandate includes more than 22,000 refugees and asylum seekers who are living independently mainly within New Delhi.[6] Category III constitutes of those fleeing persecution who have entered India and assimilated into the local community without formal recognition by the government or the UNHCR, for example, Chin refugees from Burma living in the state of Mizoram

(Sengupta 2014; SAHRDC 1997). A fourth category may be added of the 'stateless', for instance the Rohingya communities in India.[7] This essay deals mostly with Category II refugees, who fall under the mandate of the UNHCR.

The office of the UNHCR in India is empowered to issue refugee certificates to those who fulfil the criteria of the 1951 Convention, creating a de facto system of refugee protection in the country. Even though India is not a party to the 1951 Convention, it has, since 1995, been a member of the executive committee of the UNHCR (Sengupta 2014). Currently, the UNHCR does not have a branch office agreement with the Government of India and works under the umbrella of the UNDP in India. The website of the UNHCR lists one main office located in New Delhi, the site of the present research, and only a field office listed in Chennai where limited repatriation assistance is provided to Sri Lankan Tamil refugees recognized by the Indian government. Mandate refugees or asylum seekers located elsewhere in the country may not have access to UNHCR assistance and are, consequently, constantly shadowed by illegality. One may well cite the paradoxical example of Burmese refugees in Mizoram who live as illegal immigrants there, whereas they may well be recognized as legal refugees if they were to have the resources to go to Delhi to seek UNHCR protection.

The UNHCR in Delhi registers new asylum seekers, conducts Refugee Status Determination (RSD) operations and provides them with documentation protecting them from non-refoulement.[8] The RSD process in particular is considered to be the cornerstone of refugee policy in countries like India, which are not signatories to the 1951 Refugee Convention. But despite RSD operations being deemed 'a core UNHCR refugee protection function', these procedures have come to be criticized for failing to implement basic standards of procedural fairness (Kagan 2006). Credibility assessment of asylum claims is a significant step for deciding who should be offered humanitarian assistance as refugee and yet, as Kagan (2003) points out, credibility assessment is based in large part on the personal judgement of the officer in question and has the potential of being influenced by cultural misunderstanding. In India in particular, due to lack of knowledge and awareness of refugee issues and legal protocol, asylum seekers are unable to present their claims effectively. They are, thus, faced with the arduous task of convincing decision makers of the credibility of their asylum and protection claims, while decision makers are faced with an almost positivist hunt for the 'truth' of asylum claims. Credibility is, of course, not one of the explicit criteria for refugee protection in international law. Even the UNHCR's own *Resettlement Handbook* (2011: article 199) states that 'untrue statements by themselves are not a reason for refusal of refugee status' and claimants must ultimately prove that their fear of persecution is well founded on account of race/religion/nationality/social group or political opinion. However, since applicants are rarely able to corroborate their claims with specific independent evidence, establishing the facts in refugee cases usually depends on the credibility of applicant testimonies (Kagan 2003). This process of distinguishing 'real' refugees from 'fake' presents a situation whereby asylum seekers are forced to package their story in such a way that it fits the criteria laid out by the 1951 Convention, as that of a 'victim' bereft of agency, vulnerable, and in dire need of protection and assistance

In India, while the biggest refugee groups—the Tibetans and the Sri Lankans—are regulated and monitored by the government, mandate refugees from non-neighbouring countries and Burma are under the care of the UNHCR. As of July 2013, this latter group consists of over 24,000 urban refugees and asylum seekers (Table 1). The Afghan and Burmese form the largest community within these, and are the respondent group for this essay.

TABLE 1: MAIN REFUGEE POPULATIONS REGISTERED BY THE UNHCR (JANUARY 2013)

POPULATION	ASYLUM SEEKERS	REFUGEES	TOTAL
Afghan	958	10,046	11,004
Myanmar	2,627	9,507	12,134
Somalian	19	715	734
Other	199	514	713
Total	3,803	20,782	24,585

Source: JIPS, UNHCR and Feinstein International Center (2013).

METHODOLOGY

While in terms of numbers the Tibetans and Sri Lankans constitute the largest bulk of refugees, the Afghan and Burmese communities represent the largest mandate refugee community in India, recognized and assisted by the UNHCR. Consequently, this essay is based on ethnographic research, narrative and semi-structured interviews and focus group discussions conducted with twelve Afghan and ten Chin women over a period of six months from January to June 2014.[9] Although the respondents are recognized refugees whose claims had been legitimated by the UNHCR, through the course of my fieldwork I also met and interacted with asylum seekers as well as those whose claims had been either rejected or were being re-appealed. Both refugees and asylum seekers, while open to informal interactions, were hesitant about recorded interviews and were cautious in revealing their thoughts and experiences of violence. Names of all respondents have thus been changed.

Interviews were also conducted with the UNHCR office in Delhi, community-based organizations such as the Women Rights and Welfare Association Burma (WRWAB) and the Refugee Community Development Project (RCDP), as well as with national and international NGOs such as the Chin Human Rights Organization (CHRO) and the Chin Refugee Committee (CRC). Field visits were made to initiatives run by the UNHCR implementing partners in locations such as Vikaspuri and Wazirabad in Delhi where the Chin and Afghan communities live in large numbers. The interview process was also facilitated through the active cooperation of organizations like Aman Trust, Delhi, and Ara Legal Initiative.[10]

Urban refugee communities in Delhi are mostly located on the outskirts of the city. Chin community members are clustered around specific neighbourhoods of west Delhi such as Janakpuri and Vikaspuri, sites of industrial compounds and factory units where many of them are employed. The Afghan refugee community is in a sense more dispersed, and located in north Delhi (such as in Wazirabad), as also in areas of south Delhi, for instance, Lajpat Nagar and Saket. While south Delhi is no doubt more expensive as a living quarter, it is attractive to refugee communities because of the presence of organizations like the RCDP as well as big hospitals such as Max Healthcare where a lot of Afghans come for medical purposes. These provide a source of employment for Afghan refugees who work as translators.

While I use the term 'refugee women' to enumerate on the experiences of both Afghan and Chin women, this conflation is not to suggest a uniformity of experience. Both Afghan and Chin refugee communities have had a relatively long history of exodus and refuge in India, but the political context of their flight has been quite different. Minority Chin refugees from Burma seek asylum to escape the severe human rights abuses inflicted by the military regime there, which includes the policy of Burmanization and discrimination against ethnic minorities. 'Women in particular leave the country due to gender-based violence, including rape, harassment, forced marriages to military officials or border trafficking (Kumari 2012: 3). In Afghanistan, the last few decades of war and conflict have wreaked havoc upon the lives of Afghan women (and men), forcing an exodus of millions of people seeking refuge across the globe. More recently, in the Taliban-dominated political landscape of Afghanistan, women's bodies have taken centre stage as the sites of interethnic and interreligious conflicts, as well as religious conservatism (Hans 2004). The difference in the personal and political histories of both these communities is reflected in the way they have organized themselves in Delhi. Chin refugees are represented by national and international NGOs like the CHRO and CRC, which deal exclusively with their concerns and which I was able to access with relative ease. The issue of sexual violence against women of their community is a rallying point for these organizations providing support in terms of both advocacy and intervention in cases of gender-based violence. That there is visibility and discussion around these issues can also be seen by the regular reports published by organizations such as the Pann Nu Foundation (2013), the Chin Refugee Committee (2011), The Other Media (2010) and the Jesuit Refugee Service (2013).

It was relatively harder to make contact with Afghan refugee women. The RCDP initially facilitated the interviews, but going through these institutional structures ran the risk of raising expectations as I was frequently misunderstood to be a UNHCR representative. The interviews were consequently dominated by the theme of resettlement—of convincing those perceived as being 'higher authorities' of the urgent need for resettlement—rather than an engaged collaborative research process. I then opted for a different approach through the Ara Legal Trust, making myself more visible in refugee communities and spaces, frequenting restaurants and places of worship, and striking up informal conversations. In this way, I was able to engage more extensively and informally with the community. Often, I was invited to people's homes and the interviews were not regulated by space-time constraints.

The sensitive nature of the research process meant that often women were apprehensive and reticent about speaking freely, especially if there were men present. Recounting experiences of abuse and violence may have a destabilizing psychological impact and the process of narrativization is not necessarily cathartic. To ensure a sensitive, respectful encounter with the interviewees, the research methods chosen were open, allowing for great flexibility and spontaneous adjustments. At the same time, it must be acknowledged that the 'voice' that has emerged here is as much infused by my own subject position as a middle-class, Indian, woman researcher. In the words of Stuart Hall (1990: 222), 'We all write and speak from a particular place and time, from a history and a culture which is specific.' Issues of gender, class, age, race, nationality and legal status constantly shape and impinge upon social interactions, and power relations must be accordingly acknowledged in a research setting.

Unequal power relations also raise the question of ethics in research, especially when faced with a marginalized respondent group that has limited recourse to legal redressal. In my fieldwork and interviews, I was constantly mistaken as a UNHCR representative, someone who may be able to reassess their socio-economic protection needs and provide assistance or push their case for resettlement. The reactions ranged from outright hostility towards the figure of the voyeuristic researcher asking uncomfortable questions about sexual violence, to curiosity and a misplaced sense of deference to a perceived authority figure. Despite clarifying my limited mandate time and again, people milled around me hoping to get assistance at an institutional or personal level. This presented a grave dilemma. On the one hand, I was a visible outsider documenting narratives of everyday violence and oppression, and yet there was little in the way of long-term assistance forthcoming, especially regarding the continued demand of resettlement. Through the course of my fieldwork,

I also felt increasingly voyeuristic about asking questions relating to sexual violence. I thus opted to make extensive use of secondary material—reports and previous testimonies of violence recorded by academics, activists and NGOs—in an effort to be sensitive to the 'silence' spoken of earlier, to not appear probing or voyeuristic of these deeply troubling experiences for the purpose of my own research.

Translators were used and hired for the interviewing process where necessary. While they no doubt facilitated the research process, it must also be acknowledged that their presence, particularly as translators, formed a crucial part of the process of knowledge production. As Simon (1996: 138) points out:

> Translators must constantly make decisions about the cultural meanings which language carries, and evaluate the degree to which the two different worlds they inhabit are 'the same'... in fact, the process of meaning transfer has less to do with finding the cultural inscription of a term than in reconstructing its value.

In the process of this translation, crucial nuances of language may have been overlooked. At other times, the presence of a translator may have restricted responses, particularly when talking of sexual violence or discussing the issue of violence within refugee communities.

SEXUAL VIOLENCE AND REFUGEE WOMEN

The narratives of refugee women in Delhi reveal trajectories of violence and displacement, and a rising political consciousness of their status as 'others/outsiders' in India, prompting the demand for resettlement. For many Afghan and Chin women the threat of or trauma of sexual and gender-based violence constituted a critical factor in their decision to flee those contexts. However, their location in India as an ethnic, gendered 'other' renders them susceptible to new conditions of dislocation and violent hostility, the redressal of which is difficult for a host of reasons. A report of the UNHCR (2013: 12) explicitly states that:

> Sexual gender based violence (SGBV) is a significant threat for all women in New Delhi, and refugee women in particular.... Indian women may be more likely to report this harassment to the police and access advice through national systems e.g. the women's helpline. Because of language barriers and a lack of confidence in reporting procedures, refugee women were not accessing the Indian social welfare of the criminal justice system.

To echo Giles and Hyndman (2004: 4) then: 'Sites of war and peace are ultimately linked; both can be sites of violence.' The intersectionality of ethnicity, gender and legal status produces multiple forms of discrimination and violence faced by refugee women. Myriad and subtle forms of systemic and cultural violence, discrimination and inequality—such as limited livelihood options, restricted access to health and education, social isolation and adverse community attitudes—reinforce more overt forms of violence (Kumari 2011).

> I left Burma in 2008, after my husband who was arrested for political activities died in prison. I crossed the border into Mizoram where I stayed for about a month. I did not want to leave Mizoram, since being close to the border meant I may hear information about my son who had disappeared a few years earlier. But in Mizoram, the local population is hostile to us as illegal immigrants and there is constant threat of deportation. In Delhi, I went to the UNHCR office and became a refugee. (Ms M)

Ms M is one amongst thousands of Burmese refugees who typically seek asylum across the border in Mizoram in India's North-Eastern state of Mizoram. The reaction to Chins in Mizoram is complex; on the one hand, they share a common intertwined history and have similar ethnic and linguistic roots; and on the other, the Chin people have been the target of anti-foreigner campaigns in the region and are identified as 'economic migrants' (Chin Seeking Refuge 2011). Lacking a legal status, they are vulnerable to arrest, detention and deportation as foreigners. Only a small percentage are able to make the journey to Delhi where they can apply for refugee status for protection against deportation. Technically, refugees get residence permits by the Foreigner Regional Registration Office and have a refugee status certificate renewable every eighteen months. The UNHCR has now started giving refugees a 'smart card'—and identity card with a microchip—that is valid for three to five years.

Finding affordable accommodation in Delhi is an arduous task, made harder still by the fact that these paper certificates or the 'smart card' are often the only identity papers possessed by refugees (UNHCR 2013). Living spaces occupied by refugees are often relegated to the outskirts of the city. Most of the Chin refugee population stays in areas of west Delhi, living in one-room houses, with shared kitchen and toilet facilities. Such cramped living quarters suggest that refugee women are forced to stay in close proximity with local men who allegedly harass them, particularly as they wait in line for the toilets. Many times it is the landlords who make unwarranted advances towards the women, exorbitantly raising rents first and then proposing sexual favours to pay them off. Mrs P calls the landlords 'gangsters'—she lives alone in Delhi with her daughters and has had to change houses five times in the last seven years for this reason. Ms L, speaks of her own traumatic experience in 2012, when her landlord forcefully entered the house and sexually assaulted her. Too scared to alert the authorities then, she has kept the details of her assault hidden from her husband till date for fear that she will be stigmatized and he will leave her.

The physical space of the 'home' for Chin refugees is constantly marked by the threat of violence, not only by locals and Indian men, but also by male members of their own refugee community. Studies have documented how, among refugee men, the collapse of traditional structures of patriarchy and the pressures of hegemonic masculinity creates conditions where men confront the erosion of their once-domineering male identity through violent means (Kaapanda and Fenn 2000). In most patriarchal societies, men are socialized from a young age to take on the role of protector and provider, to conform to the role of a breadwinner in order to exercise symbolic control over the private space of the home. However, the experience of persecution, war and forced migration creates a destabilizing effect on men and masculinities, which manifests in different forms of violence in the domestic space. In addition, widespread unemployment, conditions of poverty, overcrowded living spaces and an increase in alcoholism were widely reported to be the factors that contribute to rising domestic violence against refugee women. In the context of Burmese refugees, the Women's League of Burma (WLB) runs a safe house for refugee women in Delhi and provides them with food, security and counselling.

Domestic violence or intimate partner violence occurs the world over, often with complete impunity, and remains underreported in a vast majority of contexts. For refugee women, the lack of a definite legal status combined with the fear of social ostracism further inhibits their agency to engage in legal processes in a foreign country (ibid.). Even though refugee women, both Chin as well as Afghan, made references to the beatings and verbal assault perpetrated by husbands and other male authority figures in their homes, violence within the domestic space was never explicitly brought up in the interviews. Conversation centred more on the invasive outsider gaze and the fear of rape and sexual assault by 'local' men. This selective reporting is again reflective of a silencing of issues of sexual violence due to fear of social stigmatization, 'dishonour' or reprisal at the hands of male authority figures. In a particularly revealing moment, an interview I was conducting with a Chin woman was abruptly terminated by my male translator (himself a Chin refugee) when the issue of domestic violence came up. On asking why, he said this information was not useful for me because she was discussing 'private matters between husband and wife'.

Violence perpetrated with impunity by neighbours and landlords stems in part from extreme financial hardship of refugee women who are unable to move to a somewhat safer location away from the perpetrator(s). The findings of an urban profiling report conducted between January and June 2013 by the UNHCR, the Joint IDP Profiling Service (JIPS) and the Feinstein International Center (TUFTS University) reveal that both Burmese and Afghan refugees face varying degrees of housing insecurity due to restricted access to accommodation, discrimination by landlords and evictions. Refugees from Burma (and Somalia) 'reported facing the most discrimination and harassment—in the neighbourhood, by landlords, at work, in school, and by local authorities—and had the worst relations to the local communities, though they were 'counterbalancing this by strong intra community support networks' (JIPS, UNHCR and Feinstein International Center 2013: 6).[11] This came out strongly in my own research where the Chin respondents reported unfriendly relations with local neighbours, yet continued to live there because of the presence of other Chins and because of relatively lower rents.

Incidents of molestation, harassment and violence on the streets were reported in almost every interview conducted with Chin women. Cases of sexual assault are allegedly treated indifferently by the police due to the inability to identify the perpetrator.

When the culprit is apprehended, he is soon let off either on bail or by bribing the police officials concerned, and comes back to live in the same locality as the survivors. A report on urban refugees published by the UNHCR (2013: 2) also recognizes that 'sexual gender-based violence is prevalent in New Delhi and refugee women are victimized because they look different'. During the course of my fieldwork, Delhi was unanimously described as being unsafe for Chin refugee women because of their perceived 'difference'—'our physical features are different', 'we are from a different culture' and because 'we have a different legal status as refugees'. The act of 'becoming' a refugee implies recognition of this difference and an increase in vulnerability—not least of all due to language barriers—which limits active reporting of such crimes. There also exists the fear that retaliatory action may be taken against Chin refugees by the local Indian community should cases be reported and filed.

Although India has, since 2012, allowed mandate refugees the right to apply for long-term visas that would provide them with the legal right to work (UNHCR 2013), a majority of refugees continue to work in the informal sector where job opportunities are limited, low paying, labour intensive and exploitative. The UNHCR provides a minimal subsistence allowance for those recognized as most 'vulnerable', but in many cases this has to be accompanied by another monetary source to make ends meet.[12] Both inflation and low wages in Delhi compel women to take risks for jobs. Those with skills and professional qualifications have a difficult time getting them recognized by Indian institutions. Chin refugees work long hours in irregular factories such as manufacturing or as domestic workers where conditions of employment are fraught with abuse; there are serious risks involved even in the travel to and from work, especially at night (ibid.).[13] Even though reports of discrimination and sexual harassment in the workplace are rampant, most abuse is perpetrated with impunity either because it is unreported—since women fear losing their jobs and meagre sources of income—or owing to a lack of law enforcement (CRC 2011).

Kaapanda and Fenn (2000: 26) use the term 'dislocation' to describe 'a psycho-social transition whereby the individual's identity and sense of self are disrupted, causing trauma but also forcing the individual to seek out a new identity in order to adapt to a new social context'. Dislocation and displacement due to war and conflict represents transition in its most violent and bewildering form, specially for women. For instance, as they point out, many female refugees find themselves to be the new heads of their household, not out of choice necessarily, but due to the fact that they have lost the male head of the family. This involves adopting not only new familial roles, but also new social and economic responsibilities, new values and ways of thinking, new lifestyles and occupations. In Afghanistan, as in most cultures worldwide, traditional roles are performed on a gendered basis, where men are responsible for going out and financing the family, and the women takes care of domestic chores and familial needs. Most Afghans refugees to Delhi come by air, and their immediate point of entry into India is through the capital city of Delhi, where they are confronted with the challenges of urbanism right away. For Afghan refugee women—especially those unaccompanied by males—this presents an entirely new set of negotiations in the public space compounded by an unfamiliarity with the local language. Financial constraints and limitations encourage Afghan refugee women to find sources of paid employment. Many of them engage in activities centred on the domestic sphere—selling home-cooked meals in markets or tailoring and stitching at home. A younger generation of women, inspired in part by Bollywood music and culture, are more inclined to learn Hindi, which opens up more avenues of employment. A number of the young Afghan refugee women interviewed for this essay make their living as translators for Afghan medical tourists in Delhi.

The lack of quality health services in Afghanistan has prompted many Afghans who can afford it to go overseas for treatment. India has, through the years, emerged as a favoured destination for such medical tourism as a cheaper and closer alternative to countries of the West. Institutions such as Max Super Specialty Hospital and Indraprastha Apollo Hospital in Delhi have dedicated desks and translation services specifically for Afghans. In addition, freelance *tarjumans* (Dari–English–Hindi translators) have come up across the length and breadth of the city, who act as guides and facilitators for Afghan medical tourists. Many young Afghan women are also hired by *tarjumans*, but the risk of harassment and exploitation in this informal, unorganized sector is rife since there are no laws or guidelines regulating hours of work or job content. Being a female Afghan interpreter in India, on the one hand, provides for a higher source of income and financial stability, but on the other, it increases vulnerability by making them more 'visible' in public spaces, especially at night. Afghan men who come for medical treatment reportedly make lewd passes and demand sexual favours from their female guides and translators. Refusal to do so may result in immediate termination of their services and wages withheld. There is an incommensurate demand-and-supply pattern for these jobs: translators can be easily replaced by other refugees desperate to earn a living, especially women who have no male relatives/partners for support.

The transition from a culturally conservative society like Taliban-dominated Afghanistan, which prohibits women from taking on paid employment or even travelling without a male companion, to a host society like India that, at least on paper, accords women the democratic freedom of movement, speech and expression suggests that dislocation may also be an empowering experience. However, for many Afghan women refugees, especially those from women-headed households or single women, their new-found economic agency also makes them the target of verbal abuse and stigmatization from other Afghans who may continue to hold conservative views regarding a woman's role and place in society. Interviews with Hameeza and Parzana were particularly revealing in this regard.

Hameeza and Parzana are sisters who fled Afghanistan following threats by the Taliban against the latter, who had worked as a TV presenter. The women, along with their other siblings and mother have been living in India since 2008. Both spoke Hindi and were employed as freelance translators to make ends meet. They lived in the bustling expanse of Khirkee Extension in south Delhi, close to Max Hospital, where a number of Afghan families have settled. Although economically self-sufficient, they reported feeling stigmatized by both fellow-Afghans and locals who are suspicious about the type of work and the long hours they have to put in. The young women of the house—aged between 14 and 22—feel threatened by the presence of men each time they step out, even if it is to just go to the neighbourhood market, because they are followed and subjected to whistles, catcalls and lewd Bollywood numbers. The false sense of freedom accorded in the democratic right to mobility—and indeed a number of women interviewed felt that India was a less conservative society, and they valued the option of traversing the street in the clothing of their choice—is compromised by a patriarchal, sexist male gaze. Harassment by locals and Afghan men alike, combined with the pressures of poverty on the one hand and community shaming on the other, has led Hameeza to remark that, 'We live in this place of freedom, but personally I feel I am in jail.' After a particularly traumatic incident in 2013, when a mob of ten to twelve men tried to forcibly enter their house in the middle of the night, they called one of the UNHCR's implementing partners, the Social Legal Information Centre (SLIC) for legal help.[14] Once the police arrived, they allegedly asked for a bribe to even record a complaint. The family has since then been repeatedly requesting help from the UNHCR, but a meeting with them only came six months after the incident. As Parzana said, 'What is the point of responding so late? Is the UNHCR waiting for us to be dishonoured before they will act? Our honour and security was the reason we left our home country… and even here we are worried about our security.'

Similar cases of harassment were reported by other Afghan refugee women as well, who find it difficult to rent accommodation because landlords are wary of 'renting houses to Muslims' and specifically to women-only households. Zubeida's family, for instance, consisting of her three daughters and two sons, live under the constant shadow of eviction should there be even a slight delay in paying rent. During a field visit to Wazirabad, I noticed that her two-room house, despite the oppressive heat, was barricaded and shut in every way possible. Not even a window remained open. This, she told me, is to ward off threats by the local boys who make their life very difficult. 'They look at us with a bad eye,' says her daughter Nabila, 'even going to tuition or to the market becomes difficult…. It's because we don't have a father and our brothers are young. People target single women like us.' Like Hameeza's family, Zubeida and her sisters too were attacked by local boys and men who forcibly entered their house in 2011. Quick thinking by their neighbours prevented a full-fledged assault, and even though the police showed up at their door right away, the accused were let off after being merely reprimanded. The perpetrators still live across the street from their house, and even though the SLIC and police authorities have been apprised of their situation, little in the way of concrete action has been forthcoming. Interviews with the UNHCR reveal that they conducted regular sensitization workshops with police officials on the issue of sexual and gender-based violence, and even though Zubeida did not feel the police or the SLIC were hostile to their case per se, it was also clear that she had no faith or hope of support in the UNHCR.

More disturbing then—and this is perhaps where the question of impunity comes in again—is the perceived indifference, apathy or nonchalance on the part of authorities, the UNHCR and the implementing partners to look into these cases. Consider another testimony documented by the CHRO regarding Mrs C's young daughter who was sexually assaulted on the landing just outside the door of her home in August 2013 by a local Indian youth:

> I rushed to the Women Protection Clinic [part of the UNHCR] to seek urgent help. But the security guards at the gate told me I wouldn't be able to see anyone and refused to let me inside. I was desperate, so I rushed to the emergency department of the DDU Hospital [Deen Dayak Upadhyay, an Indian government hospital tied with the UNHCR] to get some help for my daughter.... But to my shock, the doctor just scolded me. He accused me of lying and said no-one would do such things to a small child. The doctor just ordered us to leave the room without conducting a proper examination. The next day I went to SLIC to report the case. The staff from SLIC did not believe me at first.... But after the medical examination, the doctor confirmed that my daughter had been sexually assaulted. After that the staff at SLIC just told me I should be taking better care of my daughter and didn't offer me any proper advice.... I expected the UNHCR implementing partners to understand our problem and provide us appropriate assistance and guide us on what we can do for my daughter's suffering. But all of them, including the doctor, were just blaming me for what had happened instead of helping us. (as reported in Zahau and Fleming 2014)[15]

Complaints against the bureaucratic and apathetic proceedings of UNHCR and its implementing partners were rife in the interviews conducted. A number of the refugees interviewed—men as well as women—spoke out against the perceived 'high handedness' of the

UNHCR. It was reported that often their complaints of violence and assault were simply dismissed or not actively followed up. In cases where a formal police complaint was lodged, the economic burden of making numerous trips to the police station or to courts of law was seen as being incommensurate to the delay in successful prosecution of cases. A combination of these factors—financial hardships, language barriers, lack of physical security, racist and xenophobic attitudes of host communities—has led these refugees to reject integration as a durable solution on account of their perceived difference which renders them more susceptible to violence. Resettlement then is seen as the only effective form of redress.

RESETTLEMENT AND SEXUAL VIOLENCE

> We can't go back to Burma, and we don't want to live in Delhi. We want resettlement. (Mrs P)
>
> Resettlement will never solve a refugee problem. It is essential that a political solution is found for their plight to end. (Antonio Guterras, United Nations High Commissioner for Refugees, as quoted in Kak Ramachandran 2013)

The UNHCR has traditionally presented three durable solutions for protracted refugee situations: repatriation to the country of origin; local integration in first countries of asylum; and resettlement in third countries. In the interviews conducted with Chin and Afghan refugee women, the first two options were ruled out by members of both communities because of conditions prevalent in their home countries and because of the poor living conditions under the constant the shadow of illegality in India. Sexual violence against women was cited as a major reason for resettlement application to a 'Western' country—identified largely as USA, Canada or Australia. But resettlement is a process that relies heavily on the will of resettlement countries and comes with its own challenges of assimilation and integration in receiving societies. It is for these reasons that 'of the 10.5 million refugees of concern of UNHCR around the world, only about 1 per cent are submitted by the agency for resettlement'.[16] In the context of Afghan and Burmese refugees in India as well, the UNHCR has made it clear that resettlement is not a right; in 2013, only 3 per cent of the total refugee caseload was granted resettlement.[17]

The UNHCR South Asia Global Appeal 2014–2015 (p.3) states: 'For those refugees whose protection needs cannot be met in India, UNHCR will facilitate resettlement'. A threat to protection—defined in terms of specific international needs or where the physical and legal security of a refugee may be at stake—is thus recognized as pertinent grounds for resettlement (UNHCR 2012). While no state is under any legal obligation to receive refugees, it is important to note that even the 'option' of resettlement is only applicable to those identified as the most vulnerable within a larger group of refugees. Effective identification is thus dependent upon an effective appraisal of *protection needs*. This language of protectionism—apart from successfully disguising the autonomy of resettlement countries to select individual refugee caseloads, which may be dependent more upon integration potential than security risks of applicants—is itself problematic. In defining the refugee as a stateless subject, existing outside of the binary logic of citizenship (Haddad 2003), the figure of the refugee is constructed as being continually transient due to fear and thus in a constant 'need' of protection, assistance and training. Stripped of individual agency or contextual history, the refugee is imagined as a romanticized receiver of the benevolence and goodwill of state actors and aid providers (Baines 2004; Hyndman 2000; Ong 2003, as cited by McKinnon 2008). A gap is created right away between refugee experts making policy and assessing protection needs on behalf of an essentialized refugee population that is only identified as receivers rather than contributors (Baines 2004, Harrell-Bond 2002). Where protection needs are identified and provided by institutions and service agencies, the 'voice' of refugees in charting their own futures and survival strategies runs the risk of getting compromised.

Indeed, in using the term 'refugee experience' or focusing on the 'refugee woman', this essay itself runs the risk of essentializing women's experience independent of their class, religion, ethnicity, age, etc. A discussion on resettlement and sexual and gender-based violence faced by refugee women becomes important in this regard to deconstruct the language of protectionism and to understand that refugees and women themselves 'exercise a very particular type of agency in re-appropriating and mobilizing these representations for their own benefit' (Freedman 2007: 116). The axis of protectionism, which assumes refugees to be agency-less victims in 'need' of protection, may potentially also represent a space of subversion when it comes to articulating resettlement needs. As explained before, in RSD processes, asylum seekers need to actively represent themselves as 'victims'—through the active packaging of their stories in terminology specified by the convention itself—to be recognized as mandate refugees. This logic applies in resettlement cases too. For instance, the UNHCR is mandated to identify 'women who have protection problems particular to their gender' (UNHCR 2011: 263) and has initiated a 'Women at Risk' programme to expedite the resettlement of refugee women who may be single head of households, unaccompanied or accompanied by other family member to one of seven developed countries sponsoring the programme. This language of protection means that refugee women may actively use their narratives of sexual violence as a pragmatic strategy for improving their own situation (Ratner 2005, as cited by Freedman 2007: 116) or for relocation to a perceived safer context. Representation of victimhood may thus be structured and manicured for the sake of survival. This is not to suggest that these accounts of violence are false or fabricated per se; my interest here is to direct attention away from a normative framework to understand how and why the language of protection becomes conflated with the pursuit of protection by both refugees and the UNHCR.

An overriding concern with resettlement or a safe sanctuary that protects women's bodies from physical and sexual harm runs the risk of diverting attention from the question of women's rights, and making these rights accessible an imperative agenda. The terms of the debate in this context may have to be redefined—engendering protection must necessarily take on the protection of women's rights in addition to their physical bodies, equity as well as security (Hans 2003). As Snyder (2010: 153) writes, 'Action plans for protection should include culturally appropriate reporting systems regarding gender-based violence, as well as long term support through legal, psychosocial and reproductive health services.' It is further imperative that the language of protection be replaced by a language of rights, failing which institutions concerned with 'protection' run the risk of imitating a normative patriarchal gaze emphasizing the female body as the very source of tension.

Interviews with CHRO officials revealed that there was a rising perception that the UNHCR had stopped taking the allegations of sexual harassment against Chin refugee women seriously. Not only was it allegedly guilty of disbelieving these reports, but it is also accused of denying that such attacks or instances of violence are occurring at all. Further, the UNHCR has also been accused of victim blaming by the Chin community. For instance, a 2013 UN report on urban refugees in Delhi (p.12) states that: 'Sexual gender based violence (SGBV) is a significant threat for all women in New Delhi, and refugee women in particular. Because Myanmarese women look delicate and dress in modern clothes, they are often targeted, especially when they are coming home from work at night.' In light of such statements, the UNHCR was seen as contributing to a climate of impunity by almost legitimizing the violence 'because... (they) dress in modern clothes'. CHRO activists reported that in light of such apathetic statements, they themselves discourage women from speaking out or lodging formal complaints against sexual violence. For the redressal they seek is not punishment of perpetrators in India, but rather resettlement to a third country altogether.

The denial of sexual violence or of victim blaming has extremely problematic connotations as it effectively shuts the space for dialogue or redressal, de-politicizes women's experiences and reinforces a climate of impunity in the face of gender inequality. The demand for resettlement as outlined earlier is predicated upon the (lack of) protection for a woman's body, and yet resettlement to a third country in no way guarantees protection or respect for their rights. As Pittaway and Bartolomei (2001: 27) point out:

> Refugee women, like many migrant workers, are frequently treated as second-class citizens in their countries of destination. Racist state policies of host countries in the West and the Asia-Pacific, particularly on labour and immigration, result in the exploitation of refugee and migrant women. They are discriminated against in terms of wages, job security, working conditions, job-related training, and the right to unionize. They are also subjected to physical and sexual abuse.

However, this is not to suggest that the diverse complexity of experiences of women refugees can be reduced to one of loss, disruption or vulnerability alone. As Kumari (2012: 12) demonstrates in her work relating to Burmese refugee women in India, the female refugee experience also provides 'opportunities for activism, independence, building social interconnectedness in a new location and inculcating a sense of ethnic consciousness and belonging'.

CONCLUDING REMARKS

India, with its democratic aspirations, arguably offers a 'safe' refuge for scores of refugees escaping conditions of war, conflict and violence. For many of the Chin and Afghan refugees interviewed, their location in Delhi was positioned against those they had left behind and those others who had successfully managed to make their way to more prosperous countries of the West. The demand for resettlement on grounds of sexual violence faced in India is an extension of the protection axis put forth by the UNHCR. The logic of this protection claim demands a structured narrative of violence, to resist the 'culture of denial and victim blaming' that the UNHCR and other local organizations faced with the task of protection are accused of promoting (Karen News 2014). Chin and Afghan refugees enjoy a modicum of refuge in Delhi, but a policy of local integration as the primary durable solution has been deemed unacceptable for both communities. The increasing vulnerability of refugee women and girls combined with the lack of adequate law enforcement has added to the mistrust between refugees and the UNHCR. Refugees from both communities view themselves as outsiders, as refugees in transit, occupying the fringes in their home countries and in India, united in their language of resettlement.

A significant step in addressing sexual violence and a culture of impunity came in the form of a judgement in November 2013, which resulted in the successful prosecution of an Indian man accused of sexually assaulting a Chin refugee woman. This was a landmark case as the perpetrator was sentenced to ten years in prison and fined Rs 60,000. The New Delhi government was also required to pay reparations to the woman under the New Delhi Victims Compensation Scheme, which entitles a rape survivor to a minimum compensation of Rs 300,000. Despite the 200-odd cases of assault documented by the CHRO in the last couple of years, this has been the only successful prosecution. Nevertheless, this case has set an important precedent for justice for refugee women survivors of rape.

According to Frances Tomlinson (2010 as cited by Kumari 2012; 11), 'the label "refugee woman" is inherently multiple, indicating not only gender and placement in a category replete with political overtones, but also a position as "not from here", and thus able to be placed in some minority, ethnic or cultural group'. While there is no uniform 'refugee experience', refugee women from diverse communities face a similar set of challenges particularly because of their identity as gendered minority/'other'. At the same time, these narratives inform us that combating impunity is more than a legal process and consists of defining 'protection' in terms of the rights of women, refugee women in particular, of acknowledging the multiple forms of violence experienced by refugee women in their everyday lives and visibilizing their struggles. This was echoed in Pareeza's statement; when asked what her reasons were for participating in this study, which offers little in the way of immediate 'solutions' to her current plight, she said, 'All we want is for people to listen to us, to hear us... From the piles of documents that the UNHCR has, to look at us and to see us.'

NOTES

1. In 1989, the State Law and Order Protection Council (SLORC) in Burma, which later became the State Peace and Development Council (SPDC), renamed the country Myanmar. However, this paper makes use of the pre-SLORC moniker Burma, as many opposition parties do not agree with the political renaming that came about as a result of the 1988 military coup. For a detailed understanding of the politics behind the renaming, please see Dittmer (2008).

2. For more information and an annotated bibliography on Tibetan refugees in India, please see Artiles (2011).
3. Article 1A(2) of the 1951 Convention states that:

    > The term 'refugee' shall apply to any person who:
    > owing to a well-founded fear of being persecuted for reasons of race, religion, nationality, membership of a particular social group or political opinion, is outside the country of his nationality and is unable, or owing to such fear, is unwilling to avail himself of the protection of that country.

    For more information on India's criticism of the 1951 Convention and the 1967 Protocol relating to the Status of Refugees, please see Chimni (2008), Sen (2015) and Weiner (1993).
4. For a more detailed discussion on the legal implications of these documents, please see Acharya (2004).
5. The Principle of Non-Refoulement is a crucial part of customary international law, to which every state is obligated, regardless of being a signatory to the 1951 Convention or its 1967 Protocol. It may also be noted that the Foreigners Act allows the government to refoule foreigners—who could also be asylum seekers—under the present law in clear violation of customary international law.
6. By the end of 2012, the UNHCR (2013) reported the following composition of refugees in New Delhi: 7,289 Hindu and Sikh Afghans, 2,344 ethnic Afghans, 6,680 Chins from Myanmar, 991 others from Myanmar, 739 Somalis, 113 Iraqis, 60 Palestinians (mostly from Iraq) and 275 other nationalities, Iranians and people from other African countries.
7. According to the UNHCR:

    > Nationality is a legal bond between a state and an individual, and statelessness refers to the condition of an individual who is not considered as a national by any state. Although stateless people may sometimes also be refugees, the two categories are distinct and both groups are of

concern to UNHCR. Statelessness occurs for a variety of reasons including discrimination against minority groups in nationality legislation, failure to include all residents in the body of citizens when a state becomes independent (state succession) and conflicts of laws between states.

For more information, please see http://unhcr.org.ua/en/who-we-help/stateless-people/241-searching-for-citizenship (accessed 22 April 2015).

8. UNHCR India works with five implementing partners to execute its mandate: Bosco, New Delhi; the Socio Legal Information Centre (SLIC), New Delhi; the Gandhi National Memorial Society (GNMS), Pune; the Confederation of Voluntary Associations (COVA), Hyderabad; and the Development and Justice initiative (DAJI). These help refugees access additional rights and services, including formal employment and tertiary education. As of 2012, the Government of India has started issuing long-term visas to refugees recognized by UNHCR.
9. Afghans in India comprise a mix of those who come for business, students, medical tourists as well as refugees and asylum seekers. Hindu and Sikh Afghans form the bulk of this population, who began to move to India soon after the 1979 Soviet invasion of Afghanistan. More recently, the rise of the Taliban since the early 1990s has caused a massive exodus of people. The respondents of this paper were mostly Muslim Afghans who came to India between 2008 and 2013.

   Chin refugees originate from the Chin state in Burma and identify with ethnically and linguistically different sub-tribes such as the Matu, Hakha, Falam, Zomi, Lushai, Mizo, Zo, Asho Lai and Khumi. Statistically speaking, the bulk of the Burmese refugee population in Delhi consists of Chins, although there are refugee communities here amongst the Kachins, Burmans, Rakhine, Arakanese and Kukis as well. The participants of this paper were mostly Chin refugees.

10. Ara Legal Initiative is India's first refugee law centre providing legal aid to UNHCR mandate refugees. For more information about their work, please see http://www.aralegal.in/ (accessed 22 April 2015).
11. According to the same report, Afghan refugee households, in contrast, experienced less discrimination and far fewer perceived their neighbourhood as unsafe. At the same time, they reported having less intra community networks.
12. The UNHCR limits the Subsistence Allowance (SA) to refugees assessed to be in need—like, single-women-headed households and widows—for three months at a time, with the exception of unaccompanied and separated children who get SA until they turn 18. It says:

    > The monthly subsistence allowances were set at 3,100 INR (=US$ 55) for the principal applicant and 950 INR (=US$ 17) for dependents at the time of this report. The common monthly rental amount in the refugee neighborhoods was about 2,500–3,000 INR for a studio apartment that was usually shared by a three to five people. In South Delhi, where the Afghans live, a two room apartment could cost 12,000 INR (=US$ 215) per month. (UNHCR 2013: 15)

13. Working hours are often long and unregulated, lasting ten to twelve hours a day, and sometimes the pay was reported to be as low as Rs 70 per day, a figure less than the minimum wage. There is no job security and employers are reportedly free to sack employees as and when they want to.
14. The SLIC is a non-profit legal aid and educational organization, registered under the Registration of Societies Act, 1860, Indian Public Trust Act, 1950, and the Foreign Contributions (Regulation) Act, 1976. An implementing partner of the UNHCR, the SLIC is responsible for providing legal services and general assistance to refugees living in Delhi. It is supposed to renew refugee certificates, assist refugees in obtaining residential permits from the Foreigners

Regional Registration Office, and provides mediation services as well as assistance when problems arise within the refugee community or between refugees and the local community in filing reports with the police.

15. https://www.opendemocracy.net/rosalinn-zahau-rachel-fleming/%E2%80%9C-constant-state-of-fear%E2%80%9D-chin-refugee-women-and-children-in-new-delhi
16. For more information about resettlement procedures please see the *UNHCR Resettlement Handbook* (UNHCR 2011).
17. The UNHCR has noted a steady decline in the rates of resettlement for Burmese refugees since 2009 due to a global recession, prompting a policy of integration in India (The Other Media 2010). Similarly, Afghan refugees in India are encouraged to voluntarily repatriate with the active assistance of the UNHCR or to integrate with local societies. However, for a majority of Muslim Afghans as well as Chin refugees, the immediate demand is for resettlement.

REFERENCES

Acharya, B. 2004. 'The Law, Policy and Practice of Refugee Protection in India'. Url: https://notacoda.files.wordpress.com/2014/08/acharya-the-law-policy-and-practice-of-refugee-protection-in-india.pdf (accessed 30 April 2015).

Artiles, C. 2011. 'Tibetan Refugees' Rights and Services in India',Minority Rights, *Human Rights and Human Welfare.*

Baines, E. K. 2004. *Vulnerable Bodies: Gender, the UN, and the Global Refugee Crisis.* Aldershot: Ashgate.

Binder, S. and J. Tosic. 2005. 'Refugees as a Particular Form of Transnational Migrations and Social Transformations: Socio Anthropological and Gender Aspects', *Current Sociology,* 53(4): 607–24.

Chimni, B.S. 2008. 'Status of Refugees in India: Strategic Ambiguity', in Ranabir Samaddar (ed.), *Refugees and the State: Practices of*

Asylum and Care in India, 1947–2000, pp. 444–45. New Delhi: Sage Publications.

Chin Refugee Committee (CRC). 2011. *Lives of Chin Refugees in Delhi: Case Studies*. New Delhi: CRC.

Chin Seeking Refuge. 2011. 'Seeking Refuge: The Chin People in Mizoram State, India', December. http://media.virbcdn.com/files/b3/FileItem-222256-SeekingRefugeTheChinPeopleinMizoramState India1211pdf22912.pdf (accessed 30 April 2015).

Dittmer, L. 2008. 'Burma vs Myanmar: What's in a Name?' *Asian Survey*, 48(6): 885–88.

Freedman, J. 2007. *Gendering the International Asylum and Refugee Debate*. UK: Palgrave Macmillan.

Giles, W. and Hyndman, J (eds). 2004. *Sites of Violence: Gender and Conflict Zones*. Berkeley: University of California Press.

Haddad, E. 2003. 'The Refugee: The Individual between Sovereigns', *Global Society: Journal of Interdisciplinary International Relations*,17(3): 297–323.

Hall, S. 1990. 'Cultural Identity and Diaspora', in J. Rutherford (ed.), *Identity: Community, Culture, Difference*, pp. 222-237 London: Lawrence and Wishart

Hans, A. 2003. 'Refugee Women and Children: Need for Protection and Care', in Ranabir Samaddar (ed.), *Refugees and the State: Practices of Asylum and Care in India, 19472000*, pp. 355–95. New Delhi: Sage Publications,.

———. 2004. 'Escaping Conflict: Afghan Women in Transit', in W. Giles and J. Hyndman (eds), *Sites of Violence: Gender and Conflict Zones*, pp. 232-249 Berkeley: University of California Press.

Harrell-Bond, B. 2002. 'Can Humanitarian Work with Refugees Be Humane?' *Human Rights Quarterly*, 24 51–85.

Human Rights Law Network (HRLN). 2007. *Report of Refugee Populations in Delhi*. New Delhi: HRLN.

Hyndman, J. 2000. *Managing Displacement: Refugees and the Politics of Humanitariaism*. Minneapolis: University of Minnesota Press.

Indra, D. (ed.). 1999. *Engendering Forced Migration: Theory and Practice*. New York: Berghahn Books.

Jesuit Refugee Service. 2013. 'Chin Refugees in Delhi: Realities and Challenges'. https://jrssa.org/assets/Publications/File/ChinRefugeesDelhi.pdf (accessed 30 April 2016).

Joint IDP Profiling Service (JIPS), UNHCR, Feinstein International Center. 2013. Urban Profiling of Refugee Situations in Delhi. Refugees from Myanmar, Afghanistan and Somalia and their Indian neighbours: A Comparative Study. http://fic.tufts.edu/publication-item/urban-profiling-of-refugee-situations-in-dehli (accessed 22 April 2015).

Kaapanda, M. and S. Fenn. 2000. 'Dislocated Subjects: The Story of Refugee Women', *Refugee Watch*, June. http://www.mcrg.ac.in/dislocated%20subjects%20refugee%20women.pdf (accessed 30 April 2015).

Kagan, M. 2006. 'The Beleaguered Gatekeeper: Protection Challenges Posed by UNHCR Refugee Status Determination', *International Journal of Refugee Law*, 18(1): 1–29.

Kagan, Michael. 2003. 'Is Truth in the Eye of the Beholder? Objective Credibility Assessment in Refugee Status Determination', *Scholarly Works*, Paper 633. http://scholars.law.unlv.edu/facpub/633

Kak Ramachandran, S. 2013. 'India's Refugee Policy Is an Example for the Rest of the World to Follow', *Hindu*, 4 January. http://www.thehindu.com/opinion/interview/indias-refugee-policy-is-an-example-for-the-rest-of-the-world-to-follow/article4269430.ece (accessed 30 April 2015).

Karen News. 2014. 'From One Hell to Another: Chin Refugees Fleeing Persecution in Burma- Victims of Sex Attacks in India', 20 April. http://karennews.org/2014/04/from-one-hell-to-another-chin-refugees-fleeing-persecution-in-burma-victims-of-sex-attacks-in-india.html (accessed 22 April 2015).

Kumari, S. 2011. 'Burmese Refugee Women in India: Victims and Agent of Empowerment', *Peace Print, South Asian Journal of Peacebuilding*, Vol. 4, No.1: Summer 2012.

McKinnon, S. 2008. 'Unsettling Resettlement: Problematizing "Lost Boys of Sudan" Resettlement and Identity', *Western Journal of Communication*, 72(4): 397-414. Url:http://www.academia.edu/312224/Unsettling_Resettlement_Problematizing_Lost_Boys_of_Sudan_Resettlement_and_Identity (accessed 30 April 2015).

Ong, A. 2003. *Buddha is Hiding: Refugees, Citizenship, the New America.* Berkeley: University of California Press.

Pann Nu Foundation. 2013. *'Doke Kha Bon': Unheard Plight of Chin Refugee Women in Delhi.* New Delhi: Pann Nu Foundation and Burma Centre.

Pittaway, E. and Bartolomei, L. 2001. 'Refugees, Race and Gender: The Multiple Discrimination against Refugee Women', *Refuge*, 19(6): 21–32. http://pi.library.yorku.ca/ojs/index.php/refuge/article/viewFile/21236/19907

Ratner, H. (2005), *Refugee Women and Stories of Sexual Violence: Agents in their Victimisation?*, Unpublished manuscript, Copenhagen: Institute for Antropology.

South Asia Human Rights Documentation Centre (SAHRDC). 1997. 'Refugee Protection in India'.

Sen, S. 2015. 'Understanding India's Refusal to Accede to the 1951 Refugee Convention', *Refugee Review: Re-conceptualizing Refugees and Forced Migration in the 21st Century*, 2(1): 131–138.

Sengupta, I. 2014. 'UNHCR's Role in Refugee Protection in India'. Infochange Agenda, October. http://infochangeindia.org/agenda/migration-a-displacement/unhcrs-role-in-refugee-protection-in-india.html (Accessed 18 April 2016).

Simon, S. 1996. *Gender in Translation: Cultural Identity and the Politics of Transmission*. London: Routledge.

Singh, N. and P. Hoenig (eds). 2014. *Landscapes of Fear: Understanding Impunity in India*. New Delhi: Zubaan.

Snyder, Elizabeth. 2010. 'Engendering Protection: The Case of Women Refugees', *Journal of the Motherhood Initiative*, 1(1): 145–56.

The Other Media. 2010. *Battling to Survive: A Study of Burmese Asylum Seekers and Refugees in Delhi*. New Delhi: The Other Media.

Tomlinson,F. 2008. 'Marking Difference and Negotiating Belonging: Refugee Women, Volunteering and Employment", 17(3),278-296.

UNHCR. 2006. 'The State of the World's Refugees 2006: Human Displacement in the New Millennium'. http://www.unhcr.org/4a4dc1a89.html (accessed 30 April 2015).

————. 2011. *UNHCR Resettlement Handbook*. Geneva: UNHCR. http://www.unhcr.org/46f7c0ee2.pdf (accessed 30 April 2015). UNHCR. 2013. Refugee resettlement: 2012 and beyond. Research Paper No. 253http://www.unhcr.org/510bd3979.html (accessed 18 April 2016)

————. 2013. 'Destination Delhi: A Review of the Implementation of UNHCR's Urban Refugee Policy in India's Capital City'. Policy Development and Evaluation Service (PDES), July. http://www.unhcr.org/51f66e7d9.pdf (accessed 30 April 2015).

————. 2014–15. 'South Asia: UNHCR 2014–2015 Global Appeal'. http://www.unhcr.org/528a0a310.pdf (accessed 24 April 2015).

Weiner, M. 1993. 'Rejected Peoples and Unwanted Migrants in South Asia', *Economic and Political Weekly*, 28(34): 1737–46.

Zahau, R and R. Fleming. 2014. '"A Constant State of Fear": Chin Refugee Women and Children in New Delhi', OpenDemocracy, 25 March. https://www.opendemocracy.net/rosalinn-zahau-rachel-fleming/%E2%80%9C-constant-state-of-fear%E2%80%9D-chin-refugee-women-and-children-in-new-delhi (accessed 18 April 2016).

4

Getting Away With It

Impunity for Violence against Sex Workers

MEENA SARASWATHI SESHU AND LAXMI MURTHY

Sex work, defined as the provision of sexual services by adults in exchange for money, poses severe challenges to patriarchy.[1] This subversion of patriarchal norms draws the ire of both state and society, which have sought to regulate, manage or abolish sex work altogether. Sex workers view sex work as 'work', and, like workers in any other kind of work, negotiate possible discrimination, exploitation, bad working conditions and risk of violence that could be part of their everyday lives. However, when sex work is viewed as inherently violent, it assumes that all women in sex work are kidnapped, purchased, fraudulently contracted through organized crime syndicates or procured through love and befriending tactics. This view assumes that all individuals in sex work are coerced into it, and that paid sex with multiple partners is itself a form of violence as it amounts to the 'marketing of sexual exploitation', especially of women (Barry 1979). To end such victimization and exploitation of sex workers, it is believed, sex work itself must be abolished. Such a view aligns itself with the dominant anti-trafficking perspective that holds that the majority of women are trafficked into prostitution, and that consent to sell sexual services is a 'false contract' that allows men access to the female body (Pateman 1988). The issue, encompassing as it does the fraught areas of sexuality, consent, notions of 'work', labour rights and livelihoods, continues to be contentiously debated among feminists.[2] As Jyoti Sanghera (1997) points out, 'On account of its moral and ethical underpinnings due to its association with a realm of life which is considered private, intimate and emotional, the issue is ridden with controversy and disagreements.' The issue is further complicated by the increasingly visible presence of male and trans*[3] sex workers who do not fit neatly into the template of 'exploitation of women'.

The societal and state response to sex work has largely been a legal one, an approach imbued with notions of vice and victimhood, with the state as the saviour. However, as Valerie Kerruish (1991) argues, jurisprudence as an ideology not only operates within an unjust social dynamic, but also helps create it. Thus, the approach of criminalizing the manifestations of sex work such as soliciting, pimping, brothel keeping and trafficking, which also criminalizes sex workers, is based on an ideology of moralistic patriarchy. These laws act as instruments through which sex workers are harassed and their human rights regularly violated by law enforcement agencies, health authorities and non-paying clients. In countries where sex work—or any manifestation of it—is illegal, sex workers feel there is little they can do to address the violations perpetrated against them.

Interestingly, although sex workers—particularly women—are considered to be victims, they are also viewed as wanton and liberated sexual beings, but morally weak and debauched because they earn what is considered non-productive income from sex. The 'whore' stigma emphasizes the 'evil' influence of such 'debased' women on the 'good' moral character of society, deeming them 'deviant' women who transgress the norms of 'acceptable' social behaviour. The concept of the deviant sex worker has always governed public opinion, policy and law, and the stigma around sex work has served not only to drive violence, but is a form of violence in itself. Sex workers have therefore been policed, coerced and raided, to be rescued, reformed and rehabilitated by a society that would like to order and control them, and regulate or abolish prostitution. In a scenario where sex workers themselves are considered a vice to be eliminated, it is little wonder that the violence they experience is masked.

INVISIBLE VIOLENCE

Gender-based violence has been internationally recognized as a human rights issue and a public health concern.[4] It is understood to mean forms of violence rooted in gender inequality and power differentials, and thus there is a growing recognition that some men and trans* individuals in vulnerable situations—such as in state custody—as well as those who challenge gender norms, can also be subjected to gender-based violence, including sexual violence. However, gender-based violence is framed, in both popular discourse and academia, as violence against women, and mainstream representations of 'sex workers' are largely of women, but discussions around violence against women rarely include female sex workers. Moreover, a discussion on violence against female, male and trans sex workers is missing from the global discourse on gender-based violence.[5] This is despite the fact that the literature (Sluggett 2013) indicates that there is a high prevalence of violence in the sex industry.

There are two possible explanations for this significant gap. The first factor, as mentioned above, is the widespread view that prostitution is violence per se, and 'sex work' is a misnomer. The violence that sex workers experience is thus regarded as part and parcel of the 'institution' of sex work.

The other significant development globally has been the discourse around the HIV pandemic, and the identification of sex workers as vectors of transmission and therefore a site for control and regulation. Since the 1980s, a steadily increasing body of evidence has linked the violence that sex workers experience to HIV risk, since unprotected sex is the norm in incidents of sexual violence where the ability of sex workers to negotiate condom use is reduced or non-existent, in addition to injuries common during violent sexual acts (Baral et al. 2012; Decker, McCauley et al. 2010; Decker, Wirtz et al. 2013; Deering et al. 2013). Much writing that took as its base a public health perspective viewed violence against sex workers mainly in terms of higher risk for HIV and other sexually transmitted infections. A great deal of this research was premised on the notion of sex workers as vectors of disease. This assumption has since been proved inaccurate, with the growing recognition that sex workers are only links in the much broader network of sexual transmission of HIV, thus complicating the debate (Csete and Seshu 2002; Seshu 2003; WHO 2012).

This essay frames violence against sex workers as a human rights violation, and also seeks to understand the structural causes of impunity and lack of accountability of those who perpetrate such violence. We will cite primary data from qualitative research carried out in Yangon (Myanmar), Kathmandu (Nepal), Colombo (Sri Lanka) and Jakarta (Indonesia)[6] (only examples from Kathmandu, Yangon and Colombo will be quoted due to similarities in cultural contexts and legal regimes). The study was conducted with the active participation of sex workers at every stage—in research design, training of researchers, data collection, validation of findings and analysis. A methodological limitation in the study is the non-measurement of the severity, extent and regularity of violence. However, it is undeniable that multiple and overlapping forms of violence, including rape, gang-rape, arbitrary detention, beatings, humiliation and public shaming were an overarching experience across all gender categories, in work settings and in public life. Besides presenting an understanding of violence in the work sphere, we also attempt to present the myriad ways in which sex workers resist violence, counter stigma and build networks of solidarity to access their right to livelihood and a life of dignity.

LAW ENFORCERS AS PERPETRATORS

Sex workers who participated in the study reported violence and discrimination in the family, and from intimate partners, neighbours, the general public and health care personnel. However, the most common perpetrators of violence against sex workers across all countries and gender categories were police personnel and clients, both paying and non-paying.[7] In many countries, sex workers are the primary means through which the police meet arrest quotas, extort money and extract information. The illegal or ambiguous status of sex work commonly acts as a deterrent to reporting violence by client procurers,[8] owners, managers of establishments, clients or the general public, allowing perpetrators to act with impunity (Beattie et al. 2010).

Police were the most common perpetrators of physical, sexual, economic and emotional violence, usually using more than one type of violence at one time.

> The way they treat us is the worst! After doing everything [that is, sex], they harass us, assault us, without giving money they say, 'fucking *ponnaya*',[9] you give your ass and ask for money from us!' By hitting and harassing us, they do whatever they want. They kill us without killing us. (Male sex worker in Colombo)

Sex workers experienced physical and emotional violence by police while at work, including beating, kicking, in one instance shooting by rubber bullets, yelling, name calling, verbal abuse, spitting, and threats of arrest, public exposure and death threats. These were aggravated during raids that were undertaken to 'cleanse the city', 'arrest vagrants' or 'maintain law and order'. Study participants had experienced violent police raids, justified by the law that criminalizes various aspects of sex work, including the prohibition on brothels, soliciting on streets and living off the earnings of a sex worker. The ambiguity between laws to combat human trafficking and those pertaining to sex work often led to situations where anti-trafficking strategies, including raids on establishments, led to the violation of the rights of sex workers.

During raids of massage parlours, lodges or bars, sex workers were dragged, pulled by their hair, bodily lifted, slapped, beaten, hit with rods, mauled and groped, stripped and publicly humiliated by policemen conducting the raids.

> They knocked on the door and abused us saying *randi bhalu* [whore]. Then they took us to the toilet and stripped us.... The clients had already run away. They kicked us with their boots and hit us with sticks. I sprained my leg. They also took Rs. 4000. (Female sex worker working at a discotheque in Kathmandu)

Interestingly, while a greater proportion of female sex workers were raided, more trans* than female sex workers reported severe physical violence by police during raids. Using sexist abuse was a common strategy to humiliate sex workers, especially those who were gender-transgressive.

> With a long bamboo long stick [*bhata*] they beat me. Some of them slapped me hard on my face. Then they called me hijra, *chakka*. One kicked me on my chest saying that you are

> moving around like a girl [with breasts]. Neither do you have *dudh* [breasts] nor you have anything, nor you have a hole [vagina]. (Trans* sex worker in Kathmandu)

Sex workers in the study also reported that police used the possession of condoms (as evidence of doing sex work) as an excuse to stop and search sex workers in public places as well as detain and harass them in police custody. Female sex workers reported being arrested for not having a valid government-issued identity card, being without a male companion or not possessing a marriage certificate, indicating that as single women in public spaces, they were suspected of being sex workers. A few trans* sex workers and male sex workers who were less masculine in their presentation were also targeted by police for possessing condoms.

Sexual violence by the police was rampant, with sex workers reporting having been raped or gang-raped by the police, including being forced to have sex with police under the threat of arrest: 'I was unable to go to the toilet for two weeks after police gang-raped and physically abused me,' said a female sex worker in Kathmandu. While female sex workers more commonly reported it, a significant number of trans* and male sex workers also reported having been raped and gang-raped. For male and trans* sex workers, who are generally the 'receptive' partners and not the penetrative partners, the experience of violation was similar to that of female sex workers.

> They took me down to the police station … they didn't arrest me officially, they kept me overnight and I had to please six of them. They didn't pay me, they said they'll let me off. But they didn't put me in the cell. They took me to another room and then came in one by one and told me to do this and that. I did whatever they wanted.… [Another time] a cop in uniform took me right into their quarters through the back entrance … asked me to remove my clothes and wanted to do it in my

> backside. I said no, not without a condom. He said there was no time for all that, the other cops would be here soon. (Trans* sex worker in Colombo)

Violence by police in custodial situations was widely reported in Nepal, Myanmar and Sri Lanka. The police used violence in police vehicles, at police stations, in prisons and in 'rehabilitation centres'. It was not uncommon for formal charges not to be registered and arbitrary detentions for unspecified durations to take place instead. In line with the popular notion that sex workers cannot be raped since they render sexual services for money, the police, in complete contravention of the law, often used rape in lieu of fines.

> They kept me in the station. I told them that I did not have money. They kept me there for 20 days. Three police asked me to have sex. They abused me for 20 days. After that they said my money was paid by having sex and they released me. (Female sex worker in Kathmandu)

> When they arrest us, they take hold of us by our hair and throw us into the jeep and kick us.... We were behind bars without water. They have asked me to crawl under a chair [and] hit my bones.... They have even had sex with me inside the police station.... They have sex with us and then present us in court. They use the filthiest language possible: *veesi* [whore], *gona* [cow]. (Female sex worker in Colombo)

In custody, sex workers faced beating, kicking, torture such as electric shocks, combined with sexual violence of different types. Female sex workers faced rape and other forms of sexual violence under threat of imprisonment. Stripping, especially of trans* sex workers, was common, and trans* sex workers additionally faced humiliation and forced gender performances. Male sex workers faced gang-rape and high levels of physical violence, including torture.

Where most or all aspects of sex work were criminalized, sex workers across gender categories who were convicted were sent to prison, and female sex workers to detention centres. Violence in prison was brutal, with several sex workers reporting 'torture'-like situations. Denial of basic facilities and violence in prison were common, with several being denied sufficient food, water to bathe or a place to sleep because of the hierarchy of prisoners, in which sex workers came at the bottom. Forcible testing for HIV in custody without the outcome being disclosed was another human rights violation to which detained sex workers were subjected.

Violence within state institutions (prisons, detention or rehabilitation centres, police stations) added to this sense of shame as it defined sex workers as deviants. It added state legitimacy to violence against sex workers and underlined the fact that they had little redress and access to justice. The law, as well as legal practices shaped by the dominant social and moral discourse, allows the state and its functionaries to get away with violence against those who are considered less than equal citizens since their method of earning a living is itself declared illegal.

Regardless of legal context, there is evidence of extensive abuse of power by policemen who exploit the ambiguity of laws that criminalize sex work or certain aspects of it, as well as public order laws, in the form of threats of violence, use of official weapons, arrest, and disclosure of their sex worker identity to perpetrate predominantly sexual and economic violence against sex workers. In many instances across all country sites, their official position is what gives these policemen the impunity to rape sex workers or not pay for sex.

SEXUAL EXTORTION

Sex workers interviewed said that police regularly extorted sex, and they submitted in order to not get arrested or to be released from custody. Sex workers described this sort of police extortion as 'fuck and steal'. Not submitting could lead to more violence and arrest. While this form of abuse meets international definitions of rape, that is, coerced sex or sex under threat of further harm (including where sex is provided to avoid arrest, given the high rate of violence reported in custodial settings), sex workers did not perceive it as sexual violence, but more as 'economic' violence, that is, not being paid for a service rendered. This perhaps is linked to their perception of consent, and their choosing the option which entailed less violence, less loss of income or both. Other studies have also found that such acts are often described as 'free services' or services in exchange for release, a characterization that does not explicitly acknowledge the inherent power imbalance between the police and sex workers (Decker et al. 2013).

> When they [police] catch us from restaurants, the owners give them money to release us. But if we are caught when we are doing sex work, the owners do not do anything. In that situation, police used to ask us either we have to give them fuck or we have to give them money. We choose one of the options to get release from them. (Female sex worker working in a dance bar in Kathmandu)

The police also routinely extorted money from sex workers, which was perceived as a form of economic violence. Several sex workers working in establishments such as massage parlours, karaoke bars and night clubs reported paying off police (individually or through owners and managers) to prevent raids from taking place in their establishments.

> I always say to the police 'you think gays are like an ATM machine.' That's true. If a gay is walking down the street the police threatens to arrest him, if arrested he would be put in jail and then sent to court—meanwhile he could also get

> physically and verbally abused. So they would rather exchange 1000 Kyat instead of going through all that abuse. (Trans* sex worker in Yangon)

Male sex workers reported paying off the police not just to prevent being arrested, but also as blackmail money to prevent police divulging either their sex worker status or that they had sex with other men. Several trans* sex workers reported being subjected to acts of public shaming by police that were transphobic and homophobic, which included being forced to engage in gender performances such as dancing in a feminine manner or being forced to cut their hair (a marker of their femininity). In a few instances, once a sex worker became 'known' locally by the police, they faced police harassment even when not engaged in sex work. Police violence is a reflection of the social stigma that attaches to sex workers, and it further fuels such stigma. Indeed, impunity for violence by the police is a driver of violence by other members of the community.

LICENCE TO RAPE

Violence by clients and non-paying clients was reported by sex workers across all gender categories. A majority reported that they had been raped, gang-raped and forced by these men to perform oral and anal sex, and to have objects inserted into the vagina and anus. Physical violence, including beating, kicking, slapping, biting, hitting with belts and other objects, was also widespread.

Client violence took place across all work settings and in cars, guesthouses and clients' own homes in the case of outcall sex workers. Though male and trans* sex workers did report incidents of sexual violence by clients, female sex workers were more likely to face sexual violence from clients such as rape, forced oral sex, coercive sex while menstruating, being forced to have sex without a condom, attempted anal sex in spite of resistance, squeezing of breasts, forcible insertion of objects including sticks, eggs, bottles, sharp objects and electrical vibrators into the anus and vagina, forcible insertion of penis into the mouth, and being forced to service more clients than agreed. This was often accompanied by physical violence such as being beaten, slapped, kicked, punched or burnt with cigarettes as well as emotional abuse, name calling and humiliation.

> A single person took me, he came in a red car and he put me into the car. So I got in. Then he got two more into the rear seat. So I said, 'what are you doing?'… He took me and went. All three stayed with me by force. They took me to an abandoned place, in the dark. I don't even know where. So what could I do? I stayed with all three. They hit me…. I could not even scream, as they threatened to kill me. Then I was scared, no? I value my life. So I just stayed, even as I got beaten. (Male sex worker in Colombo)

Sexual and economic violence were again intertwined in several cases, with study participants in all countries across gender categories reporting being coerced into situations with more clients than what was agreed on, or more or different sexual acts than agreed. Several of these cases were not just a 'deal gone wrong' but instances of gang-rape, even though not all participants in the study (especially the male sex workers) used this terminology.

A critical outcome of violence was also loss of income as they had to stop work for injuries to heal, and incurred further costs if they sought treatment—for medical expenses, hospitalization, emergency contraception (for females) or tests. Visible injuries, especially on the face, also prevented a few sex workers from going back to work. In the case of trans* sex workers, acts of humiliation that they were forced to undergo (such as shaving of their hair) also meant they could not go back to work. For many sex workers whose daily meals depended on the income they earned each day, being unable to work was a serious setback and threatened their livelihood and well-being or those of their families, in case they supported dependents.

Violence by clients was more likely to go unreported due to the environment of criminality associated with sex work. Within a legal framework that illegalizes several aspects of sex work, the view that sex workers 'ask for it' since they are doing something immoral or even illegal, determines the response to violence related to work. In the widely prevalent abolitionist perspective, improving working conditions, decreasing risk and increasing negotiating power are therefore not seen as part of the strategy to reduce violence against sex workers. Moreover, the complete impunity with which police and other security personnel perpetrate violence against sex workers encourages a lack of accountability for such violence and discourages reporting it, or seeking medical help. Client violence, however, was effectively countered by organized collectives of sex workers or those attached to non-governmental organizations (NGOs). Violent clients were identified by word of mouth, and they were refused sexual services.

Over the years, sex workers have learnt how to identify signs of violent clients and share information about potentially dangerous clients.[10] Greater experience in the sex industry sharpens their ability to recognize risk, reduce vulnerability and determine how better to organize their work. An ability to profile clients, good negotiation skills, tricks for getting a client to use a condom and skills to manage conflict situations all help prevent situations from escalating into violence. Being mobile (able to move from one place to another with ease) has enabled sex workers (particularly male and trans*) to change their work sites to less risky ones. Often, older sex workers transmit this knowledge and skill to newer entrants to the business. Collectivization has also helped to build community networks in order to formalize safe work practices (Beyrer et al. 2015). For there is no doubt that hazards at work are mainly due to the stigmatization and criminalization of sex work.

BRUTAL SILENCE

Why was there such a silence around violence when physical injuries were sometimes so severe they needed medical attention, and in several cases caused permanent disability and required surgery? Yet, the rate of seeking treatment even for broken limbs, cuts and wounds, as well as anal and vaginal tears and other genital swellings and wounds, was relatively low. Sex workers said that they had experienced further emotional and psychological abuse, discriminatory behaviour and denial of treatment, particularly if they were living with HIV.

The use of multiple types of violence during sexual assault, including beating or the threat of physical violence or death, verbal abuse and economic violence (threatening not to pay or robbing the worker) had a debilitating effect and reduced the ability of sex workers to negotiate condom use. Sexual violence, and gang-rape in particular, heightened the risk of HIV infections because there were multiple perpetrators, no condoms and often genital damage, anal and vaginal tearing and bleeding.

Since the police routinely search or arrest sex workers simply for possessing condoms, this often discourages them from keeping condoms. And this, in turn, decreases their ability to successfully negotiate condom use with clients. The chronic sexual violence in custody and in prison reported by several sex workers posed different risks, being settings in which condoms were not provided or used.

Experiences of acute and recurring violence, social stigma and the stress of living on the margins had a direct impact on mental health. As a female sex worker in Kathmandu said: '[Police] behaviour makes us feel sad. We become hopeless, feel pain, feel frustrated.... The police and everybody always abuse us and hate us and we are mentally tortured.'

Emotional violence in particular had a long-lasting impact on the sex workers, and some sex workers, especially trans*, experienced emotional and psychological violence as more debilitating than even physical violence. Analyst Carl Jung has called shame a 'soul-eating' emotion, which thrives in the dark, causing trauma to fester. Emotional violence that was rooted in the stigma attached to being a sex worker, such as name calling or verbal abuse, discrimination, being treated badly in health care settings and in the community, or being socially excluded from family and community events, led to distress, and threatened self-esteem and emotional well-being. In a few cases this was life-threatening, and triggered suicide attempts. For male sex workers, being raped was perceived as a loss of manhood and was particularly destabilizing. Marginalization because of discrimination within the gay community for engaging in sex work also contributed to alienation and the inability to seek help for injuries resulting from violence, especially sexual violence. In the words of a male sex worker from Kathmandu: 'I was gang-raped.... At that time blood was flowing from my anus. In the hospital, the doctors did not behave well. Then I wanted to commit suicide and went with a rope to hang myself in the jungle.'

Sex workers living with HIV and those who were drug users faced additional emotional violence and discrimination due to the stigma attached to HIV and drug use. The disclosure of a sex worker's HIV status by medical professionals without the sex worker's consent had disastrous consequences for the life of the sex worker and induced mental stress. Because the consequences were so drastic, sex workers opted not to reveal their HIV status even to doctors, thereby exposing themselves to infection and increasing the risk of transmission to others in such situations.

MULTIPLE INJUSTICES

Non-disclosure about the violence they experience can be seen as an outcome of deep social stigma as well as the unbreachable wall of impunity. Most participants in the study disclosed their experience of client or police violence to their peers as a way of sharing everyday troubles. Only a few disclosed violent experiences to family members or those outside their sex work environment. Disclosure of violence was linked to circumstance: some disclosed violence to those in the immediate vicinity of the violent incident to get support, or, if arrested in raids, were forced to disclose it to peers or friends for help in getting bail. Female sex workers usually called other friends who were sex workers, managers or client procurers, whereas male and trans* sex workers who had strong ties with NGO networks were able to call them for help. A 2014 study of non-disclosure of violence among female sex workers in India found that female sex workers who were not registered with an NGO or sex worker collective were 40 per cent more likely not to disclose violence (Mahapatra et al. 2014).

In case they sought medical attention for a violence-related injury, many sex workers did not disclose the cause of the injury to the health professionals attending to them, fearing they would be judged, not given treatment, discriminated against or exposed as sex workers.

There were gender- and country-specific nuances within this broader trend based on existing stigma around certain kinds of violence, and the type of relationships and community networks that existed among peers in each gender category and country.

It is also relevant to note what sex workers deliberately did not disclose. Female sex workers tended not to disclose experiences of anal rape and intimate partner violence. Trans* sex workers tended not to disclose sexual violence and intimate partner violence.

Male sex workers tended not to disclose the cause of their injury to health professionals, especially if it was self-harm.

Despite experiencing widespread violence, sex workers rarely report it to the police. Particularly where sex work and homosexuality are criminalized, reporting to the police is not the norm. In total, less than one quarter of all the sex workers interviewed had attempted to seek legal recourse by filing a report with the police. Male sex workers tended to be the least likely to report incidents of violence, including sexual violence. Sex workers in the study were more likely to report violence by thugs, strangers, clients or persons posing as clients in street settings and intimate partner violence in domestic settings than police violence. Significantly, a tiny fraction of the sex workers in the study who were supported by an NGO followed through with their complaints.

Over half of the sex workers in the study who had approached the police for help did not receive support, and were either ignored or faced extortion and harassment themselves, or were exposed as sex workers which made them vulnerable to harassment by the police in the future. The only female sex worker who approached the police to report the homicide of a co-worker was forced to reveal her identity in a statement, and was then arrested because sex work was illegal.

Most of the study participants who had not gone to the police felt that the police were not to be trusted, given that they themselves perpetrated violence against sex workers. As a result, sex workers across gender categories instinctively feared and harboured a mistrust of the police. Additionally, several sex workers feared the backlash that might ensue if they reported a client, client procurer or local thug who was likely to return to their work setting and could harm them. According to a female sex worker in Yangon: 'There was a conflict in my mind, whether I should shout out loud or report someone. But if I shouted, they'd have killed me. If I reported someone, the others would have come and given trouble. So I just kept quiet.' The few sex workers who attempted to complain to the police against police violence met with little success, their action leading in some cases to further violence against them.

The majority of sex workers across gender categories did not seek legal assistance or access any justice systems. Most of those who sought legal support did so with help from an NGO. Over half the study participants had no knowledge of the laws on sex work in their countries. Besides lack of knowledge, other barriers in seeking legal assistance included difficulties in getting a lawyer and the fear of being ill-treated for being sex workers. In a few cases, police denied sex workers access to legal representation or put pressure on them to confess to charges.

WORK AS CRIME

The study corroborates anecdotal experience that violence, especially sexual violence, is significantly exacerbated by the criminalization of sex work and law enforcement practices that increase the exposure of sex workers to police, create unsafe working conditions and reinforce impunity for men who perpetrate violence.

Laws relating to sex work and law enforcement practices, including the use of public order offences against sex workers, determine the levels and forms of police violence against sex workers. For example, ambiguities in laws around sex work and carrying condoms in Nepal and Sri Lanka enabled police to stop, search and arrest sex workers for possession of condoms. Extortion of money or sex and cases of rape and gang-rape were reported in several incidents in these countries following such searches. Ambiguities in laws regarding where sex workers could operate from allowed police to carry out raids (in several cases without warrants) and detain sex workers, which in many cases led to situations of physical and sexual violence, extortion and verbal abuse.

In Sri Lanka and Myanmar, where both sex work and homosexuality are criminalized, violence by police was acute, resulting in severe physical injuries, including several cases in which the violence resulted in a permanent disability. It is also in these countries that extreme violence in custody, in prisons and detention centres was reported by most of those who had been detained. Criminalization of sex work and homosexuality appears to exacerbate violence against sex workers by giving power to the police to pick up sex workers, detain them and incarcerate them without explanations. Even though the police perpetrated human rights violations, very rarely were they held accountable for these acts. Where sex work is illegal, the broader environment of criminalization of sex work and sex workers legitimizes these acts and creates impunity for police violence.

Different work settings influenced the type and extent of violence experienced. Certain factors across settings appeared to increase several sex workers' vulnerability to violence—such as the extent or lack of control a sex worker had over decisions related to their work. Thus, it is possible in both street settings, where a sex worker's fee is decided by a client procurer, or within an establishment, where the fee is set by the owner or manager of the establishment, that the sex worker is not in control of their labour and not allowed to refuse clients. Sex workers had less control over their conditions of work when they were homeless, excessively dependent on client procurers, in a relationship with client procurers or working in establishments with bad conditions of work. The absence of a labour framework appeared to increase the vulnerabilities of sex workers across settings. Such an absence enabled clients, client procurers and owners and managers of establishments to perpetrate violence against sex workers. Notably, however, sex workers working in establishments reported facing less client violence than those who did not work in establishments. This suggests that clients are more likely to adhere to verbal agreements or their agreement with the management in a more formal work setting.

Notably, those working in establishments with decent work conditions, responsible owners or managers, co-workers in close proximity or close-knit peer networks were more protected from violence or were able to resist or respond to client and police violence with greater efficacy. Across work settings, sex workers were more likely to face violence when they did not have autonomy over their bodies and control over their terms of work. Where collectivization or NGO interventions were weak, sex workers who were interviewed did not know about laws on sex work, perceiving their own status as being illegal or immoral, which undercut their motivation to stand up for themselves or fight for their rights.

This climate of impunity also fuelled violence against sex workers by clients and men posing as clients. In the case of client procurers and owners and managers of establishments, violence is fuelled by an unequal relationship with the sex worker where the latter is dependent on them for livelihood and can be thus controlled. Violence is also fuelled by the impunity with which they can get away with acts of violence, as sex workers have little or no recourse to justice; the assumption is that they would not be heard or believed if they reported their experiences of violence, and that no action would be taken. In the rare instances that sex workers did report instances of violence, most elicited no police action on their complaint, or further violence against them by the police.

Where sex work and homosexuality are criminalized, as in Myanmar, female sex workers can themselves be implicated as criminals if they report violence by clients or client procurers. Male sex workers or trans* sex workers can additionally be held culpable for same-sex relations. Where sex work or homosexuality per se is not criminalized, the abuse of power by the police, along with a lack of precedents involving successful complaints by sex workers, deters most sex workers from reporting client violence. Also in operation was the fear of being exposed as sex workers, which made them vulnerable to further violence by police and others. In the case of violence by owners and managers, in several instances sex workers observed that the establishment paid a commission to members of the police to prevent raids, and thus protected them from police action. In the case of violence by the police too, most sex workers did not have the confidence to report police violence to higher-level officers. Neither did they have the resources or ability to recruit lawyers, nor precedents for winning cases of redress in court.

Criminalization hampers the work and dignity of sex workers in several ways, including by fundamentally threatening their relationships with family members (who may be criminalized for living off the earnings of sex work), preventing them from accessing basic financial services such as bank accounts and insurance, and undermining their right to organize. Collectivization of sex workers and their participation in solidarity networks enable them to resist and protect themselves from violence and exploitation and ensure safe working conditions for themselves.

THE VIOLENCE OF STIGMA

While police violence appears to lie at the root of multiple vulnerabilities that sex workers face, critically undermining their access to justice and creating an environment in which violence against them is normalized and justified, it is the stigma attached to sex work that creates conditions in which others can also be violent to sex workers without being apprehended or punished.

Repeated experiences of raids and police harassment have the effect of making sex workers feel like criminals, always on the run and trying to hide from the police, including in Nepal and Sri Lanka, countries where sex work is not criminalized. Police violence has also contributed to the normalization of violence against sex workers, and has created mistrust and fear of the police among sex workers. Violence in their work settings by police, clients, client procurers or owners and managers of establishments has led to work settings which are vulnerable and unsafe, and bad working conditions, although in most cases sex workers learn through experience how to reduce their chances of facing violence. Family violence from parents and siblings results in isolation from potential support structures, and intimate partner violence leads to a cycle of violence that most find difficult to break out of.

Violence in public, in community settings and in health centres served to reduce sex workers' self-esteem and self-worth and made many sex workers across countries and gender categories feel ashamed of themselves, including before their children and loved ones, pushing them to live in isolation from family and friends. This further contributed to their fragile mental state, and resulted in almost half of all sex workers attempting suicide or having suicidal thoughts without any of them seeking mental health services.

The wider impact of large-scale violence as evidenced in this study, without recourse to justice, is that it further marginalizes a community of people and denies them their basic rights as citizens to equal protection from violence from the state. It prevents them from accessing justice and health services, and violates their human rights to live without violence, to work in decent conditions, to lead a healthy life and have equal access to redress.

The violence of stigma operates at all levels in society, built on a foundation of morality, double standards and judgemental attitudes. Historically, sex work has always been perceived negatively, as a 'sin' in religious discourse, as 'immoral' in societies or as a 'criminal' act. Sex workers experience a high degree of shame due to the stigma attached to sex work, as well as low self-esteem resulting from internalization of social prejudice, thus believing themselves to be 'dirty' and 'bad'. Sex workers spoke of high levels of depression, fear and insecurity about working, anxiety about contracting HIV, shame, helplessness, loss of confidence and self-esteem, self-harm by inflicting cuts, wounds or burns on their own bodies, suicidal thoughts and attempts to take their own lives. As sex workers who are collectivized have articulated,

> The whore stigma pushes women in prostitution outside the rights framework. It is stigmatization and discrimination that effectively de-limits their option of making money from sex, and discrimination cuts them off from the privileges and entitlements supposedly accorded to all citizens irrespective of what they do for a living. As people who experience violence as a part of our daily lives, we are being more and more penalised by increasing violence in a society that is trying to order and control our lifestyles. As women in prostitution we protest against a society that forces on us the violence of a judgemental attitude.[11]

Morality and judgementalism also seep into the legal framework, since the body of the sex worker is where lines of social codes are drawn. Transgression is met with heavy penalties, and deviance from heterosexual monogamy is penalized by the legal system. The stigma is thus borne by these 'deviants', and violence is the price paid for deviance.

Driven by social stigma and the culture of shame, emotional violence against sex workers is pervasive, taking the form of psychological and verbal abuse aimed at humiliating and intimidating. Almost 85 per cent of the sex workers interviewed had also experienced physical and sexual violence in the context of sex work from police, clients, intimate partners, owners and managers of establishments and local thugs and gangs. Widespread experience of sexual violence was reported by male and trans* research participants. The descriptions of sexual violence enacted against male and trans* participants were more graphic and detailed than those of female sex workers, even though the prevalence of sexual violence against females was higher. Violence against trans* sex workers in many instances mirrored violence against female sex workers—being stripped, left naked in a public place, insertion of objects into the anus or vagina, all reflecting misogyny or a deep hatred of women and the feminine.

The 'normalization' of sexual violence against female sex workers probably emerges from the view that 'sex workers cannot be raped since their job is to provide sex,' and also from the sheer impunity with which female sex workers are subjected to sexual violence. Male and trans* sex workers who described experiences of gang-rape most often did not use the term, perhaps due to a perception that men cannot be raped or gang-raped, or maybe due to the shame and stigma associated with rape. This selective articulation of sexual violence by male and trans* participants demands further exploration of the nuances of gender-based sexual violence.

Despite the violence and discrimination, sex workers struggle to find creative and resourceful ways to resist and cope with the violence and their marginal position in society. Female sex workers often create a tightly knit supportive community of their peers as a reaction to societal violence and societal judgementalism. Indeed, extreme performative behaviour often evolves as a shield from violence and also as resistance in and of itself; for example, 'the happy hooker', 'the flamboyant hijra', the 'uber-feminine male sex worker' are stereotypes that serve as symbols of cultural resistance.

DISMANTLING IMPUNITY

There is sufficient evidence to conclude that laws and law enforcement practices that criminalize sex work and homosexuality, and a culture of police raids under various local laws, often using possession of condoms as evidence of doing sex work, have given the police inordinate and arbitrary power. Abuse of that power takes the shape of extorting money and sex from sex workers, subjecting them to extreme, routine and brutal violence in violation of their human rights and in contradiction of the duties of the police as protectors of the civil rights of citizens. Custodial violence in country sites where sex work is criminalized is particularly severe.

How the police behave with sex workers drives the manner in which others in society behave with them. Police violence instils fear and mistrust of the police among sex workers and prevents them from reporting violence. This fuels a climate of impunity where clients, client procurers, owners and managers of establishments, local thugs, strangers, community members and health care workers are able to perpetrate violence against sex workers without being checked or apprehended.

The cumulative impact of violence has a debilitating effect on the mental health of sex workers, and the compounded violence they face greatly reduces their efficacy in responding to the violence or seeking redress. The absence of mechanisms or services for counselling or mental health support for sex workers is a critical gap. Those with strong peer networks are able to cope with violence better than those who do not have such networks. Stronger peer networks among sex workers can improve their ability to respond to violence, access information about their health, access legal services to support them in getting justice, and affirm their identity as citizens with rights.

Violence against sex workers is fundamentally driven by a climate of impunity that is built on the two pillars of: (*a*) criminalization of sex work or aspects of the sex industry that pushes them underground and exposes them to state and non-state violence; (*b*) stigma attached to sex work, homosexuality and being trans* that legitimizes violence against them and creates a protective cover for perpetrators. Sex workers face discrimination and stigma that undermine their human rights, including the right to liberty, security of person, equality and health. This results in further marginalizing sex workers to the extent that very few are able to report these violations or access rights to redress, further feeding into the climate of impunity that their perpetrators enjoy.

A crucial question that begs analysis is: why do sex workers tolerate violence? There is little data to help us understand the manner in which sex workers negotiate violence as part of their work lives, battling stigma and discrimination alongside. Indeed, a moral lens appears to be used to view their 'risk-taking' behaviour and stigmatize the choices they make to earn a living. Such stigmatization is not attached to other risk-taking action, for example, refugees, adventurers or sports persons. Likewise, there is little research, except the anecdotal reports of NGOs, about how collectivization has contributed to the reduction in violence.

It is clear that decriminalizing sex work and activities associated with it, including removing criminal laws and penalties for the purchase and sale of sex, the management of sex workers, living off the earnings of sex work and other activities related to sex work,[12] could provide an environment where violence against sex workers is not normalized or allowed to occur without any accountability. The evidence also shows that where support from NGOs is forthcoming, or where sex workers have strengthened themselves through collectivization, the solidarity generated has the potential to breach the fortress of impunity.

NOTES

1. It must be noted that no single term adequately covers the range of transactions taking place worldwide that involve sex work. The appropriate term to use for sex work is best defined relative to the local context. This definition may change over time as attitudes evolve. Priority must be given to reflecting how those involved in sex work perceive themselves in that role. Most self-identified sex workers define sex work as work.
2. For a more detailed discussion on different perspectives in the women's movement, see Seshu and Murthy (2013).
3. Trans* is an umbrella term that refers to all of the identities within the gender identity spectrum, including all transgender, non-binary and gender nonconforming identities, including (but not limited to) transgender, transsexual, transvestite, gender queer, gender fluid, non-binary, bigender, trans man and trans woman.
4. The 49th World Health Assembly passed a resolution stating that violence is a leading worldwide public health problem (Resolution WHA 49.25).
5. Although the Convention on the Elimination of all Forms of Discrimination Against Women did not explicitly mention violence against women, in 1989, the committee set up to implement the convention recommended that state parties enact legislation to protect women from the many types of violence. The Vienna Declaration and Programme of Action, adopted at the World Conference on Human Rights in 1993, affirmed that gender-based violence, including that which arises from cultural prejudice, must be eliminated since it is incompatible with human dignity and worth. But neither declaration recognizes violence against sex workers.

6. The findings of the research were published in Bhattacharjya et al. (2015).
7. The term 'non-paying clients' refers to men who approach sex workers for sexual services and refuse to pay, using their societal, caste, class or official power to get away with non-payment.
8. 'Client procurer', or a person who procures clients for a sex worker in exchange for a commission, is the less stigmatized term for a person commonly called a 'pimp'. 'Client procurers' or 'third parties'—a term used by the sex worker rights movement—are terms that recognize the diverse third-party working relationships that sex workers negotiate. In contrast, the term 'pimp' is a stigmatizing racial stereotype which posits sex workers as victims rather than as workers, denying their agency. Sex workers can be employees, employers, or participate in a range of other work-related relationships.
9. *Ponnaya* is a derogatory term in colloquial Sinhala that translates most closely as 'faggot', and has explicitly gendered connotations, referring to men who are effeminate.
10. For example, National Ugly Mugs is an initiative of the UK Network of Sex Work Projects that builds and shares a database of potentially dangerous clients and known criminals. Available from https://uknswp.org/um/ (accessed 2 August 2016).
11. Statement by the Veshya AIDS Muqabala Parishad (VAMP): VAMP, Sangli, Maharashtra, India, changed its name to Veshya Anyay Mukti Parishad in 1998 to reflect the broadening of the 'collective journey against HIV/AIDS to seek liberation from oppression and injustice'. See http://www.sangram.org/info4_1.aspx (accessed 22 June 2016).
12. As recommended in the *Consolidated Guidelines on HIV Prevention, Diagnosis, Treatment and Care for Key Populations* (WHO 2014) and the Economic and Social Commission for Asia and the Pacific Resolution 67/9 on the Asia-Pacific regional review of the progress achieved in realizing the Declaration of Commitment on HIV/AIDS and the Political Declaration on HIV/AIDS, paragraph 1(d).

REFERENCES

Baral, S., C. Beyrer, K. Muessig et al. 2012. 'Burden of HIV among Female Sex Workers in Low-Income and Middle-Income Countries: A Systematic Review and Meta-analysis', *Lancet Infectious Diseases*, 12(7): 538–49.

Barry, Kathleen. 1979. *Female Sexual Slavery*. New York: New York University Press.

Beattie, Tara S., Parinita Bhattacharjee, B.M. Ramesh et al. 2010. 'Violence against Female Sex Workers in Karnataka State, South India: Impact on Health, and Reductions in Violence Following an Intervention Program', *BioMed Central*, 10: 476.

Beyrer, Chris, A.L. Crago, L.G. Bekker et al. 2015. 'An Action Agenda for HIV and Sex Workers', *Lancet, HIV and Sex Workers Series*, 385(9964): 287–301.

Bhattacharjya, Manjima, E. Fulu and L. Murthy, with M.S. Seshu, J. Cabassi and M. Vallejo-Mestres. 2015. *The Right(s) Evidence—Sex Work, Violence and HIV in Asia: A Multi-country Qualitative Study*. Bangkok: UNFPA, UNDP, APNSW (CASAM).

Csete, J., and Meena Seshu. 2002. 'India's Voiceless Women Are Easy Prey for AIDS', *Los Angeles Times*, 1 December. https://www.hrw.org/news/2002/12/01/indias-voiceless-women-are-easy-prey-aids (accessed 22 June 2016).

Decker, Michele R., H.L. McCauley, D. Phuengsamran et al. 2010. 'Violence Victimisation, Sexual Risk and Sexually Transmitted Infection Symptoms among Female Sex Workers in Thailand', *Sexually Transmitted Infections*, 86(3): 236–40.

Decker, Michele R., Andrea L. Wirtz, Carel Pretorius et al. 2013. 'Estimating the Impact of Reducing Violence against Female Sex Workers on HIV Epidemics in Kenya and Ukraine: A Policy Modelling Exercise', *American Journal of Reproductive Immunology*, 69: 122–32.

Deering, K.N., P. Bhattacharjee, H.L. Mohan et al. 2013. 'Violence and HIV Risk among Female Sex Workers in Southern India', *Sexually Transmitted Diseases*, 40(2): 168–74.

Kerruish, Valerie. 1991. *Jurisprudence as Ideology*. Routledge. London.

Mahapatra, Bibhubhusan, Madhusudana Battala, Akash Porwal and Niranjan Saggurti. 2014. 'Non-disclosure of Violence among Female Sex Workers: Evidence from a Large Scale Cross-Sectional Survey in India', *PLOS ONE*, 9(5): 1.

Pateman, Carole. 1988. *The Sexual Contract*. Cambridge: Polity Press.

Sanghera, Jyoti. 1997. 'In the Belly of the Beast: Sex Trade, Prostitution and Globalization'. Paper presented at the Consultation on Prostitution, Asia Pacific Forum on Trafficking, Bangkok, February.

Seshu, Meena Saraswathi. 2003. 'Sex Work and HIV/AIDS: The Violence of Stigmatization'. Supporting Document, UNAIDS Global Reference Group on HIV/AIDS and Human Rights, Second Meeting, Geneva, 25–27 August.

Seshu, Meena Saraswathi, and Laxmi Murthy. 2013. 'The Feminist and the Sex Worker', in Laxmi Murthy and Meena Saraswathi Seshu (eds), *The Business of Sex*, pp. 16–24. New Delhi: Zubaan.

Sluggett, Cath. 2013. 'Sex Work and Violence: Understanding Factors for Safety & Protection: Desk Review of Literature from and about the Asia Pacific Region'. UNDP.

WHO (World Health Organization). 2012. *Prevention and Treatment of HIV and Other Sexually Transmitted Infections for Sex Workers in Low- and Middle-Income Countries: Recommendations for a Public Health Approach*. Geneva: WHO.

————. 2014. *Consolidated Guidelines on HIV Prevention, Diagnosis, Treatment and Care for Key Populations*. Geneva: WHO.

5

Visible and Invisible

Sexual Violence in Muzaffarnagar

NEHA DIXIT

In September 2013, just seven months before the Indian general elections, north India witnessed its worst communal riot of the past decade. Muzaffarnagar and Shamli, districts in the country's most populous state, Uttar Pradesh (UP), and just 100 km from the national capital of Delhi, faced sectarian violence over a week that, according to UP state government records, led to sixty deaths, seven rapes and 40,000 displaced. Unofficial figures based on a public interest litigation (PIL) filed by survivors of the violence claim 200 deaths, 120,000 people displaced and hundreds of unreported mass rapes.[1] The figures vary because many of the bodies were found months after the violence broke out.

FANNING SECTARIAN VIOLENCE

The Sugarcane Belt

Muzaffarnagar and Shamli, fall in the 'sugar belt' of Uttar Pradesh. According to the 2011 census, Muzaffarnagar, has 60 per cent Hindus, 36 per cent Muslims and a 4 per cent combined population of Sikhs, Christians and Jains. Shamli was carved out of Muzaffarnagar in September 2011. The area saw no major communal riots over the years, including the times of worst communal tensions in the 1947 Indian partition and the 1992 Babri Masjid demolition in Ayodhya. The dominant landowning Jat community that consists of both Hindus and Muslims was closely associated with the Bharat Kisaan Union (BKU) under the leadership of Mahendra Singh Tikait, who led a successful farmers' movement and agitation for over five decades in this sugarcane belt. The BKU, though, was criticized for furthering the interests of only rich farmers, while being applauded for maintaining the Hindu–Muslim unity in the belt. Tikait was sought after by major political parties, but remained largely loyal to the Rashtriya Lok Dal led by Ajit Singh, the son of farmers' leader, and former prime minister, Chowdhary Charan Singh. Tikait, in his later years, also extended support to *khap* panchayats, self-appointed caste councils within the Jat community in north India, who among other things, are opposed to self-choice marriages and regularly issue diktats against women's rights. After Tikait's demise in September, 2011, the BKU suffered a leadership crisis, which weakened the farmers' collectives, making it conducive for political parties to divide them on communal lines.

The Build-up to the Communal Violence

In March 2013, one of the first reports of communal clashes came from Gangeru village in Shamli district, where some unknown people had lit a Holika bonfire before the stipulated time. This is an annual bonfire a day before the Hindu festival of Holi. Communal motives were ascribed to this incident, leading to an atmosphere of Hindu–Muslim polarization. The real culprits were never found, neither was the case investigated by the police. In the following months, local media reported incidents where people who looked visibly Muslims—men with skullcaps and beards, and burqa-clad women—were attacked on public transport and in other places. This researcher spoke to a number of young students from Darul Uloom Deoband, an Islamic school in the neighbouring town of Deoband in Saharanpur where the Deobandi Islamic movement started, who were victims of this kind of targeted violence as well.

The next couple of months saw the rise of small groups in west UP with a clear Hindutva agenda, including viewing of women as breeders.[2] According to them, intermarriages result in the destruction of breeders. The years of this hate campaign and propaganda about Muslims overtaking Hindus in number resulted in the increasing popularity of the Muzaffarnagar-based group, Narendra Modi Sena. Set up in 2012, it had a distinct slogan: '*Hum do, humare bees*' (We two, our twenty), for Hindus to have larger families in order to outnumber the Muslim population.[3] For example, the Janeu Kranti Manch (Holy Thread Revolution Forum), also founded in 2012, was aimed at bringing several castes, including the Dalit population, into the Hindu fold by offering the *janeu*, a holy thread considered a prerogative of upper-caste Hindus, as a token of Hindu unity.

On 27 August 2013, a skirmish led to the deaths of Shahnawaz, a Muslim youth from Kawaal village and two Hindu youths from Malikpura village in Muzaffarnagar. The incident was talked about as one of 'eve-teasing', alleging that Shahnawaz harassed the sister of one of the Hindu men who confronted him. It resulted in a bloodbath, leading to the death of all three. Later, an old video from Pakistan surfaced showing the brutal killing of two men by a mob.[4] It was claimed that the two men were the same two Hindus and the killers were a Muslim mob. The Bharatiya Janata Party (BJP) Member of Legislative Assembly (MLA) from Sargana constituency in UP was said to have circulated the video on social media through WhatsApp messenger.[5]

Patriarchal Honour as a Tool

'Muslim lust for the Hindu woman' has been one of the staples of Hindu right-wing propaganda, and selective memories of rape during the partition riots are well known.[6] From Savarkar's formative writings on Muslim rule in India, the stereotype of an eternally lustful Muslim male with evil designs on Hindu women has been reiterated. While women are made to establish themselves as active political participants in the Hindutva ideology through an agenda of hatred and brutality against a besieged minority, it is the threat of 'Love Jihad' that is most invoked for their active and collective participation against the Muslim 'enemy'. (Dixit 2013a).

In Muzaffarnagar, *khap* panchayats also played a crucial role in mobilizing the Jat community. Several panchayats took place a week after the killing of the three men. They organized smaller meetings, circulating messages on WhatsApp to call the panchayat. Kadir Rana, former Member of Parliament (MP) from Muzaffarnagar, also held a public meeting where he indulged in hate speech against the Hindu community. A massive panchayat was organized on 7 September 2013 in Nangla Mandod village in Muzaffarnagar. Thousands from the neighbouring villages attended. The call was officially given by the BKU under the leadership of Naresh Tikait, Mahendra Singh Tikait's son, but it was completely taken over by the BJP, the Vishwa Hindu Parishad (VHP) and members of other Hindu organizations to the extent that none of the BKU leaders got a chance to address the audience. The panchayat was given the slogan '*Beti bachao, bahu bachao*' (Save your daughters and daughters-in-law), which was later changed to '*Beti bachao, bahu banao*' (Save your daughters, make their daughters your daughters-in-law). The meeting was attended by the BJP MP Hukum Singh, BJP MLAs Sangeet Som and Suresh Rana, and BJP leader and head of Sadhvi Shakti Parishad, Sadhvi Prachi.

The attack on women's 'honour' was not new.[7] Sadhvi Prachi's speech at the Nangla Mandod panchayat is a reminder of how women cadres of right-wing fundamentalists are trained in the same kind of sectarian, misogynist, communal politics.[8] Her speech not only incited the crowd against the Muslim community, but also encouraged them to 'protect the honour of *bahu-beti* by fighting Muslim jihadis'. The crowds armed with weapons, including spears, daggers, swords and guns, were seen in several video clips from the panchayat that day.[9]

The state government, led by the Samajwadi Party, aware of the communally volatile atmosphere, imposed Section 144 of the Criminal Procedure Code (CrPC) that prohibits assembly of more than ten people. However, it mostly remained a paper order, with the administration failing to stop the rally.

After the panchayat, on the evening of 7 September, thousands of participants returned chanting slogans like '*Musalman ke do sthan, kabristan ya* Pakistan' (Muslim belong either to the graveyard or Pakistan). As the crowds passed Jaula, a Muslim-dominated village, a fight broke out. According to media reports, ten tractors and three motorbikes were set ablaze (Bhatt 2013). Six Jats were killed and their bodies were found later. However, the rumour spread that hundreds of Jats were killed by Muslims and their bodies were dumped in the Jauli canal. Exaggerated news reached several neighbouring villages, including Lankh Bawdi, Lisad, Phugana, Kutba-Kutbi, Kirana, Budhana and Bahawdi, which were the worst affected in Shamli and Muzaffarnagar districts. That started a vicious circle of brutality and violence.

The next morning, 8 September 2013, massive violence broke out in the vicinity. Armed mobs, both from within the village and outside, attacked Muslim neighbourhoods, killing, raping Muslim women, looting an unaccounted number. The survivors were forced to leave their houses and settle in the seventeen relief camps set up initially by the community members and later supported by the state government. The hostile communal environment apart, they had to brave extreme cold weather. Living under tents led to the death of several children due to the cold.

RAPE AND THE BATTLE FOR JUSTICE

Seven Muslim women, one from Lankh Bawdi village in Shamli district and six from Fugana village in Muzaffarnagar, eventually filed cases of gang-rape with the help of activists and lawyers. The interviews that follow were conducted nine months after the incident. During this period, the women had to live in refugee camps spread across Muzaffarnagar and Shamli for months before they finally bought land with the compensation received from the government and constructed makeshift houses where these interviews took place.

S, Mid-30s, Lankh Village, Shamli District

On the morning of 8 September 2013, S's older son was down with fever. Her husband, V, had taken him to the hospital when violence broke out. 'I heard my uncle and aunt in the neighbourhood calling out to me to run. I couldn't make sense till I heard the cacophony of the mob. Before they could break down the door, I ran from the back door straight to the sugarcane fields. I stopped only an hour later to realize that I had left behind my younger son.' She hid behind Bright Zone School on the Muzaffarnagar–Shamli highway when three Jat men caught hold of her and raped her turn by turn. 'I couldn't get up till four or five in the evening till I heard a tempo, carrying several people from my village to Loni. A woman gave me a hand and I got on it.' V and her two sons found her at the Loni relief camp, three days later. 'I told him the next day about the gang-rape and he was supportive enough to say that it was not my fault. However, now, if he disagrees with me even slightly, I think it is because of the rape. In the past, when he and I fought, I used to give it back to him. Now, I keep quiet and have learnt to tame my tongue.' There were several instances of mass rapes from Lankh Bawdi, which are discussed in the later section, but S was the only one to register a case.

She says, 'I, unlike the other rape survivors from my village, decided to fight my case and I will not withdraw it because I want the other women to speak up as well.' Both, she and V, her husband, worked as tailors before everything was burnt down. 'One day, I will also open a sewing training centre,' she states. She sent her First Information Report (FIR) on 22 October 2013, five weeks after the incident, to the Fugana police station in Muzaffarnagar through registered post in which she also named the accused. However, it was neither filed nor did she get any acknowledgement from the police regarding her report. It was only during the hearing before the Supreme Court on 13 February 2014, when her lawyer handed over a copy of the complaint to the lawyer for the state of Uttar Pradesh, that an FIR was filed (dated 18 February 2014, four months after she had sent her report, and was listed for hearing on 20 February). All this while, she lived without any police protection in the refugee camps amidst threats from the dominant Jat community. Her medical test was conducted five months after her gang-rape on 22 February 2014. 'Why were we raped if a boy eve-teased a girl?" she asks.

F, Mid-20s, Fugana Village, Muzaffarnagar District

F was three months pregnant with her daughter when she was gang-raped by four men on the morning of 8 September 2013. She did not recognize the men who barged in with their faces covered, and swords and guns in their hands. 'Two held my legs and hands, while the others raped me. I remember them calling each other some names that I mentioned in my report. They said if I told anyone, they would kill me. I kept quiet because I didn't want to faint or die,' says F. Her husband, who was standing on the terrace when the men barged in, had already run away with their five-year-old son. 'Thank God, it was a Sunday or else a number of school-going children would have also lost their lives,' she says. Her son was a student of class one. She was rescued by the paramilitary forces that evening when all Muslim families were ushered to the relief camps.

F lived in the Jogia Khera relief camp for the next two and a half months. 'My lower abdomen hurt, still does, continuously. I used to bleed often and when I met the doctors at the relief camp, they said that it is because I was pregnant. I had obviously not told them about what had happened. Only my husband knew [and he] had asked me to keep quiet,' she recalls.

F had to rely on home remedies to control the pain. She underwent a Caesarean section to give birth to her baby, which was not easy since the surgery cost money and they had none to pay to the government doctors after all their assets and possessions had been destroyed during the violence. W, her husband, in his late 20s, who was a salesman with bag manufacturing companies in Rajasthan, did not return to work after the incident. He guards his wife and family all the time. F says, 'He is too scared to leave us alone. If he does not earn what will we do?' W says, 'I know that rapists have no religion, but yet I can't forget that just 20 days back when a woman was gang-raped by seven or eight Muslims in Shahpur, the police took immediate action and arrested the people involved. In our case, the same police have done nothing till date.'

F filed her report with the help of lawyer Vrinda Grover, Kamini Jaiswal and a number of activists on 29 September 2013, twenty days after the incident. Her medical examination was conducted another twenty days after the FIR, on 18 October 2013. This violates the law about an examination needing to be done within twenty-four hours of the report. The charge-sheet was filed on 24 May 2014, eight months after the FIR, instead of within three months according to law. The arrests were made only after all the seven women jointly filed a contempt petition on 15 September 2014 against the police and state administration, a year after the gang-rape.

W also faces pressure for not being 'man enough' to save his wife. He is the butt of misogynist jokes in his new neighbourhood, which is commonplace in a male-dominated society like west Uttar Pradesh. He says, 'Everyone knows that my wife was raped and I couldn't save her. My honour is lost. For now, the least I can do is fight it out in the court and show them their place. Friends and relatives of those who have been named in the FIRs keep visiting this area to get us to compromise. The other day, they said that they would burn my house. I chased them out with bricks.'

Sb, 40, Fugana Village, Muzaffarnagar District

Since news of the violence had already reached the village on 7 September 2013, Sb's mother-in-law had left with three grand-children for her relatives' place in Loni, a small town in Ghaziabad district, a day before. 'I was more scared for my teenaged granddaughter,' the mother-in-law says. 'I never thought they would do this to her mother.' Three Jat boys entered the house and put a gun to Sb's temple. 'They said if I screamed they would shoot my two-year-old son sleeping on the cot. They inserted a big stick inside my private parts and I started bleeding. They revelled in seeing that and then went on to rape me.' She fainted and only woke up to a phone call from her brother-in-law, Ashu. 'He called me when one of his hands was maimed in the violence outside, asking for help. I collected myself, grabbed my son and escaped to the common ground of the village where the PAC [Provincial Armed Constabulary] had arrived. I had worked at their [the rapists'] fields as an agricultural labourer for fifteen days last harvest season. Even after months of persuasion and pleading, I never got paid. They excused themselves by saying that because I am fat, I hardly did any work compared to the other labourers. I gave up eventually.'

Sb's FIR filed was filed on 9 October 2013 with the help of activists, but the medical examination was delayed like other cases and only took place ten days later, on 18 October 2013. The charge-sheet was filed as late as 24 May 2014, while she continued to face regular threats and intimidation from the accused.

A day before this interview, Rambeer, the father of two of the four alleged rapists and the owner of the farmland where Sb had worked, came to threaten her. He told her that she had forgotten her *aukat* (place in the social hierarchy) and it wouldn't take him a minute to make her daughter disappear. 'It is not a new thing for them,' says Sb. 'Jheemar and Chamar [Dalit] women employed at their farms are regularly raped in lieu of payment. I didn't agree to it, so they did it during the riots.' Her husband, M, who works as a salesman in Rajasthan, only came fifteen days after she was raped and escorted to the relief camps set up by the government. He left a month later, after helping her file the case. Since then, she has been by herself, taking care of four kids and an old but supportive mother-in-law.

T, Early 20s, Fugana Village, Muzaffarnagar District

At the time of this interview, in her house that was under construction in Kandhla in Shamli district, T was eight months pregnant. She had been gang-raped nine months back. This was a cruel joke that haunts her everywhere. She says, 'The investigating cop asked me, "*Kiska hai*?" [Who is the father of the child?] with a smirk. Other women also asked me, "*Itni kya jaldi padi thi*?" [What was the hurry to get pregnant?] What do I say to that?

As if the rape before or the pregnancy later were in my hands.' She is the young mother of three girls and hopes the next one is a boy.

On the morning of 8 September 2013, she was cooking when three men broke open the wood door and attacked her. 'They raped me as my little girls watched and cried. I begged them that they could do anything with me but leave me alive for my girls,' she recalls. Her husband, X, was out to meet Harpal Singh, the former *pradhan* (head of the village Panchayat) of the village, with fellow Muslims to ask for help. He says: 'While he [Harpal] was assuring us that nothing would happen, his cousins and relatives raped my wife.' Harpal has also been accused in cases of murder and rioting.

T filed her FIR along with the other four survivors on 29 September 2013 while she was living in a relief camp in Jogia Khera village. Her medical examination was done almost twenty days later and the charge-sheet was filed on 25 May 2014. Till then, the accused roamed free.

'I can only go out with the Supreme Court-provided guards now. If you step out even now, you will find some or the other Jat lurking in the vicinity to negotiate with the riot victims who have filed cases of rioting,' she claims.

Fm, 52, Fugana Village, Muzaffarnagar District

On the morning of 8 September 2013, Fm had taken her cattle out to feed when she was dragged into an empty house by five men and raped. 'Boys my son's age did not flinch for a second before pulling my salwar down. As if it was about increasing the count. They even commented on my genitals and described them to the boys in the house next door. I wondered why they didn't kill me unlike the men they murdered later. Guess it means the same for women,' she says. The five men vandalized the house after raping Fm and then left.

Her husband had passed away a couple of years back, leaving behind two sons and three daughters. Back home in Fugana, when this researcher met the accused's brothers, they said, 'We have not even seen her ever. We want a CBI investigation. These cases are politically motivated.'

Hers was the second case to be filed with the help of activists on 22 September 2013. Her medical examination was conducted a week after the report, on 29 September 2013. The charge-sheet was filed as late as 24 May 2014, like in the case of four other survivors. However, on 15 October 2014, one of the accused was granted bail by the Allahabad High Court. He was one of the first accused to be arrested in these gang-rape cases from Muzaffarnagar. Bail was granted on the grounds that there had been an inordinate delay of fourteen days in the filing of the FIR and that the survivor's testimony could not be accepted as it was not corroborated by medical evidence in the form of marks of injury on her body. The court said that while there was positive evidence against the other men accused of raping her, there was no evidence against accused, Vedpal. The state authorities chose not to appeal against this order.

Since the FIRs for all seven survivors were registered much later than the day of the incident and the medical examinations were delayed even more, this judgement of the high court did set a disappointing precedent.

Kf, 48, Fugana Village, Muzaffarnagar District

Kf was gang-raped by the local grocery shop owner, the tailor and two other men from her village. 'I fainted by the time the third one started. When the forces came to pick us up later, the *naara* [drawstring] of my salwar had broken. I held it with my hand and sat at one corner of the truck,' she says.

She was the first to file an FIR, on 15 September 2013. Her medical examination was conducted fifteen days later, on

29 September. Being the first, she suffered a lot of intimidation after filing the case. She withdrew her case in March 2014 when armed Jat men held a gun to her son's temple in the middle of the town square. 'He is my only son. I cannot even have any more children, so I got scared.'

After this incident, she submitted an application on 23 October 2013 to the state administration detailing the threats received by her and named the accused. She requested the state administration to take cognizance of the same so that she would be able to depose before the court without fear. With no action in the next five months, she wrote another application to the state authorities on 5 March 2014 stating the grave threats to the lives of her son and herself due to which she had not been able to disclose the truth about the men who had raped her before the male judicial magistrate in her statement recorded of 11 December 2013.

On that day, en route to the court of the judicial magistrate to record her statement, she had mentioned the threats and intimidation from the accused and their dominant Jat community to the investigating officer, Mala Yadav. However, Yadav gave her no assurance of any protection. Thus, fearful of the danger to the life of her only son, aged 10, Kf was constrained to not give the names of the men who had gang-raped her. In her application of 5 March, she requested to be allowed to record a fresh statement before a female judicial magistrate in order to be able to depose freely, for the men who raped her to be arrested, and for her to be provided security. Her statement was finally recorded two months later, on 1 May 2014, before a female magistrate.

On 15 September 2015, Kf, along with others, filed a contempt petition in the Supreme Court against the state administration. The state administration accused her of registering a false case for compensation. It is crucial to note that she got security only in July 2014, ten months after she was raped.

She is back to fighting the case though the charge-sheet is yet to be filed. She was given a compensation on 26 September 2014, also after a contempt of court petition in the Supreme Court. Recently, one of the Jat men came up to her husband and said, '*Ab toh apne ghar ki sarkaar aa gayi*' (Now the new government [after the general elections] is on our side). Kf says that it is nothing new. 'Sloganeering like '*Muslaman ke do sthan, kabristan ya* Pakistan' had increased a few months before the riots.' She has stopped sending her son to school. 'I feel scared.' She alleges that the current *pradhan* of the village, Thaam Singh, reached out to her on the behalf of Sanjeev Baliyan, the newly elected BJP cabinet minister, also a co-accused in the riots, to accept Rs 30 lakh (3 million) and drop the case.

K, 50, Fugana Village, Muzaffarnagar District

On the morning of 8 September 2013, K's husband, who was standing on the terrace was startled to see an armed mob metres away from their house. K was downstairs and was caught hold of by four men who raped her for half an hour. Z, her husband, is the government-appointed *pairokar* (petitioner on behalf of all seven women). Z ran a dairy in the village and had invested in small businesses of his nephews. He says, 'The *pradhan* that day confused us by telling us that we were safe and nothing would happen. We didn't even get a chance to come together to face them.'

K filed an FIR on 26 September 2013 and the medical examination took place three days later. The charge-sheet was filed on May 24, 2014. Since Z is the *pairokar*, several false cases were filed against him to build pressure and send a clear signal to all the seven survivors. In fact, during the Lok Sabha elections, the security to him and K was withdrawn, a fact which the police later accepted in court. K says, 'They laughed at me for filing a rape case. A Jat man walked up to me and said an impotent wants to feel attractive.' She says it is true that she filed the case because she does not have children. She thought it would be easier for her to fight it out compared to the other rape survivors who have the 'family's honour' to take care of before heading out for such a fight. Back home in Fugana, Mehak Singh, father of the accused, said, 'Has she seen her face? Such an old haggard. Why will my son rape her?' She says, 'Recently, Naresh Tikait, the Bharat Kisaan Union president, announced that what happened with us was a trailer and the film is still pending. What else does he want? The police are pressurizing us, the locals are threatening us, and our own people are scared to talk to us for fear of influential Jats.'

LEGAL TRAJECTORY OF THE CASES

The legal proceedings of these seven cases are crucial since Section 376(2)(g) of Indian Penal Code (IPC) was specifically introduced through the Criminal Law Amendment Act 2013, after the 16 December gang-rape protests, just six months before the communal violence in Muzaffarnagar.[10] It is also to be read in conjunction with Section 114-A of the Indian Evidence Act, whereby the burden of proof is shifted to the accused considering the coercive circumstances in which the rape is committed. Since the Muzaffarnagar sectarian violence was the first such incident after the introduction of the new law, these cases of sexual violence are precedents of sorts.

FIRs and Arrests

The First Information Reports for five out of the seven petitioners was filed within three weeks of the gang-rapes in September 2013. On 26 March 2014, the Supreme Court, in an important judgement (*Mohd Haroon and Others vs Union of India*), directed the state government to proceed swiftly with the investigations and arrest of the accused. However, the state administration brazenly flouted the directive for speedy proceedings. Only three out of the twenty-nine accused named by the seven petitioners were arrested in six months after the reports were filed. With no option, a contempt petition was collectively filed on 15 September 2014 after almost six months from the date of the Supreme Court judgement and almost a year after the first FIR was filed. It was only after this petition that the state administration got into action and arrested the other accused. This was a relief to the survivors, who were being regularly intimidated by the accused who had continued to roam free.

Medical Examination

All the seven women were gang-raped on 8 September 2013. However, there was an inordinate delay in getting them medically examined even though Section 164-A of the CrPC mandates one within twenty-four hours of filing of a report. Since their medical examinations were conducted long after the incidents, between 29 September 2013 and 22 February 2014, the reports were inconclusive in 'proving' rape, as stated in the judgement. This was also used against Fm in court. In a written submission to the Supreme court, on February 24, 2014, the lawyers of the seven women, Vrinda Grover and Kamini Jaiswal, pointed the following,

> Section 164-A CrPC, provides for the medical examination of the rape victim and casts a statutory duty upon the police, to send the woman making the complaint of rape to a registered medical practitioner within twenty-four hours from the time of receiving the information relating to the commission of such offence, as the same may provide corroborative evidence. In direct contravention of this legal provision the police knowingly delayed the medical examination of the Petitioners.

> The medical examination was thus reduced to a mere paper formality with no evidentiary value. The Petitioners are all married women having children and hence their medical examination almost 20–40 days after of the incidents of gang-rape, is unlikely to provide any corroborative evidence. The Petitioners were all gang-raped on 8th September 2013 whereas the medical examination was conducted between 29th September and 18th October 2013, exposing the farcical and mechanical nature of the investigation.[11]

There has been a longstanding debate to also pay attention to evidences other than medical reports to establish sexual violence. This includes the demand to describe the condition of the body and the genitals, as well as lacerations in a forensic report to depict the nature of violence on the victims.

Compensation

All the seven petitioners filed applications on 9 April 2014, seven months after the rapes, for compensation. They had to approach the Supreme Court since the state government had failed to compensate them despite the complaints filed by them. The Supreme Court judgement on 26 March 2014 specifically stated that the compensation was to be paid within a period of four weeks from the date of the order, that is, before 26 April. They were to be given Rs 5 lakhs (500,000) each by the state government. However, five of them received the compensation on 8 May 2014, one on 22 May and the other only on 25 October 2014, more than a year after the gang-rape.

The court had also directed the state of Uttar Pradesh to provide financial and other assistance, medical care, trauma counselling and sustained rehabilitation to the seven petitioners in addition to the compensation. Though they were provided the compensation for loss of moveable and immoveable property, which was given to all families who were targeted and displaced from their ancestral homes in the communal attacks, they did not receive any other special assistance.

It is crucial to note that all seven women are married and above the age of 30. None of the young, unmarried women had the social support to fight the stigma of rape publicly. Also, all the seven women are from working-class backgrounds—ironsmiths, agricultural labourers, carpenters and others—while the accused are from the dominant landowning Jat community who have far more money and influence over the state machinery.

THE INVISIBLE RAPES, MASS RAPES AND VIOLENCE AGAINST WOMEN

While the seven women respondents had the backing of their families, most importantly to support them along with activists and members of civil society, conversations with women across relief camps within two weeks of the sectarian violence suggested incidents of large numbers of mass rapes between the morning of 8 September and 9 September 2013.

Documenting the incidents of sexual violence was difficult initially. Most women from the eighteen relief camps, set up immediately after the riots, responded with a tutored reply when the question was brought up. 'We ran away before something happened, but we know that it happened to someone else,' they would say, and then go on to describe the scale of this sexual violence by attributing it to some other woman. The reasons for not opening up were many. Apart from social stigma, these women were facing acute crises, with dead or missing family members, loss of property and livelihood, instability, government apathy in terms of support, and pressures from the unsupportive patriarchal family setups and religious institutions. All of this was evident while investigating more such incidents.

A series of interviews conducted by this researcher corroborates one specific incident of mass rape in the compound of the house of one Sudhir Kumar, the elected head of Lankh Bawdi village, also known as Billu Pradhan. Close to thirty Muslims were given false assurances of protection from angry Jat mobs and told to gather at Billu Pradhan's house on the morning of 8 September 2013. The gates were shut and over nineteen women were raped and sodomized by twenty to twenty-five Jat men, even as they watched their children and family members being maimed in the same compound.

Shabana, 30, from the same village, who was present in Billu Pradhan's courtyard that day, recounts the horror when this author met her at the Idgah camp.[12] 'They came at eight in the morning, a group of twenty Jat men. I was cooking while my husband, a washerman, was about to leave for work. As soon as we heard the commotion, my husband, two sons and I fled. Even as we were running towards Billu Pradhan's house, we saw our house being set on fire.' It was in this mayhem that Shabana lost track of her sons. The couple reached Billu Pradhan's house and were taken inside the gated compound. 'Within half an hour, a group of men from the village entered the compound and attacked us. They hacked my husband right before me.... They stripped several of us. Took our honour.' They first beat them with batons, then stripped them and sodomized them. The men were stripped and chopped into pieces. Shabana and several others were thrown out, naked, an hour later.

Shabana's story is further corroborated by another victim, 20-year-old Rubeena from the Malakpura camp, whose cheek was bitten off. 'There were loudspeakers, Bollywood songs blaring out of them, while they were raping us. Some boys were also playing the *dhol* [a local drum], outside the gate.' That morning, her mother had asked her to leave for Billu Pradhan's house along with her younger sister. She told her she would follow with the rest of the family. 'Two men held me by my arms as they bit several parts of my body. Three men raped me then, one after the other.' Her parents and the rest of the family have been missing since then. She also informed, on grounds of anonymity, that two women from her village were made to dance naked in the mosque.

Sabra, 40, another inmate at the Idgah camp, while talking about the rape of her two daughters in Billu Pradhan's house, was concerned that no one would marry her teenaged daughter. She says, 'My husband and his first wife, who was also my elder sister, along with me and my three daughters, including Saju, were in Billu Pradhan's house that morning. My elder son had asked us to stay there while he went to arrange for a vehicle. Ajiman and Almiyat were attacked with a sickle on the neck within fifteen minutes of entering the *pradhan*'s house.' It is with difficulty that Sabra narrates what followed with her girls. 'They first pulled my elder daughter and stripped her. Two boys dragged her to the ground and took turns raping her. Then they grabbed my second daughter and hit her private parts with batons. She started bleeding and was pushed to a corner. They then proceeded to assault the other girls.'

That day, when the gates were opened after an hour, Sabra rushed out with Saju and others into the jungles close by. They had to walk a whole day and night to reach Kandhla where the volunteers of the camp there came to their aid. This is where she found Rashid, her elder son, who had gone out that day looking for help, and who was out again on the day of the interview, to the Loni camp in Ghaziabad to look for his two sisters who have been missing since that morning at the *pradhan*'s house.

It is important to note that the first response at any of these camps to questions of sexual violence is immediate denial.

In Gangeru, a small town in Muzaffarnagar district dominated by Shia Muslims, the Arabia-Islam-Hudru-Islam madrasa had provided refuge to over 400 people from the twenty-one villages nearby. The stigma associated with rape was a major impediment in accessing medical help for sexual violence survivors. Shama, in her early 20s and from that camp, says, 'It's painful to pee and defecate. I can't even tell the camp doctor. The women in the camp have given me herbal medicine.' Shama's husband, Iqbal, and his younger brother, Tahrir, were both killed in Lankh Bawdi on 8 September. Her husband ran a horse carriage for a living; it was found burnt at the house when they went there for a visit later. She says, 'I went to Billu Pradhan's house with my six children. They twisted both arms of my three-year-old daughter and threw her. They were young boys whom I had fed so many times in my house. When I ran to rescue her, they thrashed me with a baton and then used it to rape me, as they did to four or five other women.'

Similarly, Mehraz, another survivor from the Loni camp who has not filed an official complaint, says that the rioters shouted, '*Musalmanon ki laundiyaon ko rakh lo*' (Keep all the Muslim girls). 'My breasts were attacked with a sharp trowel. There were eight to ten boys who seemed to be on a mission. They'd strip a woman, attack her and rape her. Then they'd grab the next one within minutes.' Billu Pradhan, who was not named as a rapist by any of the women this researcher spoke to, had vanished after the first twenty minutes. 'When the gates of his house were unlocked, I had no clothes on me. My husband and daughter had hidden in a jute sack under a charpoy. We all ran as the Hindu boys chased us. But somehow there was news of the police reaching the village and the boys turned back.' Her 12-year-old son was left behind as Mehraz fled with her 8-year-old daughter and husband, Akbar Qureshi. The house was attacked by a group of ten to fifteen men and her son burnt alive. His charred body was found later. Mehraz, was among the few women who forthrightly talked about the sexual assault on her. However, she never registered a case because she felt too vulnerable as she was living in the relief camp at the time of this interview. While women after women in several camps talk in hushed tones about what happened on the fateful morning, the people residing in Lankh Bawdi village remain defiant.

COMPLICITY OF WOMEN FROM THE 'OTHER' COMMUNITY

Shama, one of the survivors mentioned earlier, while narrating what happened at Billu Pradhan's house, says, 'The non-Muslim men and women from the village watched us naked, bleeding, crying, but no one came forward to help. The women we had assisted during childbirth on several occasions also looked at us blankly.'

In fact, a few weeks after the riots, on 25 September, a massive public meeting was organized in the Arya Samaj temple of Lankh Bawdi village for the Hindu Jat women, which this researcher attended. The political atmosphere was tense and a resolution was taken at the meeting that no one from the ruling Samajwadi Party, which was considered close to the Muslims, would be allowed to enter the village. Since the police had started filing the FIRs and had named 114 people from Lankh Bawdi in relation to different crimes like rape and murder, it was decided that the women would be used as the first line of defence collectively to stop the police from entering the village for investigation.

Saroj Bala, whose 28-year-old son, a father of two children himself, has been accused of rape, murder and robbery during the riots, says, 'The police have arrested my son for no reason. Everybody knows him. You can ask anyone in the village if he can do something like this.' Similarly, 50-year-old Vimla claims, 'They have named my son Dharamveer in the FIR for no reason.

Why don't they arrest the Muslims who keep bombs in their mosques?' Several such statements reveal how women from families of the accused acted to shield alleged perpetrators from law and police at the time of legal proceedings and arrests.

This specific incident at Billu Pradhan's house was never taken up legally even when it was written about and widely circulated. This researcher's investigative cover story in *Outlook* 'Thread Bared' (Dixit 2013b) was rubbished by political parties and the state administration as false. The UP home secretary, Kamal Saxena, when asked if women had been raped and molested during the riots, said, 'No woman has registered a complaint with the police. The police can take action only after getting complaints.' None of the nineteen women came out openly to report the case. Billu Pradhan was absconding for several months before he reappeared during the general election campaign in April 2014. The UP State Women's Commission chairperson, Zarina Usmani, upon hearing testimonies of riot survivors, expressed the full possibility of sexual violence on women during the communal riots in Muzaffarnagar, Shamli, Baghpat, Saharanpur and Meerut districts and, in an open letter, urged women to come forward and register their complaints. She also said, 'A majority of the [victimized] women are from the weaker sections and are being threatened to stay silent.' But no action has been taken against the perpetrators and the incident is set to fade away, leaving only brutal memories—all for the lack of political will to take up the matter.

Apart from the incident at Billu Pradhan's house, there are several other undocumented episodes. Two women in Kutba-Kutbi village, Razia and Humaira, living in Gangeru camp after the riots, reported acid attacks. Their faces had been spared, but they had burnt necks and hands. Similarly, bodies of women, found in the next few months in houses, sugarcane fields and the vicinity, were mostly naked.[13] This researcher was present during the recovery of two such bodies. Some of them had also had their private organs damaged. Naked bodies of women, sometimes burnt, were recovered from trunks in Lisad village In fact, six girls from Lisad were raped in front of their parents, who told this researcher about it a few weeks after the riots. The girls are missing till date. Another such incident was reported where a woman talked about the rape of her two daughters (aged 17 and 18) on 7 September, around 7 pm. The daughters were engaged, but after the incident the fiancés broke off their engagements (Raina 2013).

ROLE OF THE STATE AND POLICE

In March 2014, the Supreme Court stated: 'We prima facie hold the State government responsible for being negligent at the initial stage in not anticipating the communal violence and for taking necessary steps for its prevention' (Angre 2014). During the riots, the police were unable to control the violence and it is only when paramilitary forces were sent by the centre that the victims could be rescued.

Abid Khan, 28, a carpenter from Lankh Bawdi village, recollects that he had called the police frantically on his mobile on the morning of 8 September 2013, but 'they arrived, but only at 12.30 pm, four hours after everything was over.' Abid's claim was further corroborated by Mehraz Bano, 27, an agricultural worker from the same village: 'The police came only two hours after we called them. When we asked them for protection, the police officer tried to arrest my husband for inciting violence. We carefully stepped back and took the way to the highway through the jungles. We later took a trolley that was carrying several other Muslims from our village.'

Saleem, 45, from Dharona village in Baghpat, recalls that when he saw a mob of 300 people, he called the police. 'The police scolded me for lying. The SHO [station house officer] later said that there are no police constables in the police station to send.' Several riot victims corroborated Saleem's claim that police accused them of lying instead of providing immediate help (Raina 2013).

Later, the state showed extreme apathy towards the riot victims. The relief material, food, milk, water and medical help all took several days to reach. The ruling Samajwadi Party head, Mulayam Singh, even made a statement that those residing in camps 'were not riot victims but paid stooges of the political parties like Congress and BJP'.[14] The Congress Party leader, Rahul Gandhi, in a public meeting in Indore on 25 October 2013, said, 'Some Muslim youths from riots-ravaged Muzaffarnagar were in touch with Pakistan`s intelligence agency, ISI.'[15] Several camps were evacuated in the coldest months of December and January, once again displacing thousands.

The investigation started a month late (Raina 2013). Kalpana Saxena, a superintendent of police in Muzaffarnagar district, said they were delayed in investigating the riot-related sexual assault cases because the initial team of officers that was formed in September did not include any female officers. Officers like Mala Yadav were brought in to deal with female victims after consideration by senior officials in the special investigation team headed by Hari Narayan Singh, the senior superintendent of police in Muzaffarnagar.

The contempt petition filed by the seven gang-rape survivors mentioned earlier states that state administration resisted the registration of the FIRs. This in itself was an attempt to shield the accused who had committed such heinous crimes. These women had also filed written complaints with the local police of the threats to their own safety and the lives of their family members by and on behalf of the accused men. They were neither provided with protection nor were any legal proceedings initiated against the accused for nine months after the first FIR was filed. This impunity enjoyed by the accused gravely jeopardized the efforts of these women to secure justice. Also, there were specific—and grave—complaints against the female investigating officer, Mala Yadav. In light of the demands of feminist activists to have more female police, this shows that in situations of communal riots, caste and religious allegiance might play more of a role than gender.

K says, 'When Mala Yadav, the investigating officer, came to record my statement, she asked people in the camp if they had seen my torn clothes on the day I reached the camp. She even told me that having a fulltime guard sent by the Supreme Court is not enough and I should compromise.' The insensitive investigation was also corroborated by Fm. She says, 'When Mala Yadav, the SIT [Special Investigation Team] inspector came to record my statement later in the relief camp, she asked the other people in the camp, "Did you see her crying? Did she tell you about the rape?"' She says that the men she had mentioned in her complaint knew each word of what she had told Yadav. 'I am a woman who is revealing that I was raped publicly, unlike so many others. Why would I lie? During the period of investigation in the camp, those who didn't know that I was raped also got to know because of police's lack of discretion.' In fact, Kf had submitted an application to the National Human Rights Commission on 29 May 2014 detailing the biased and corrupt investigation by Yadav and requesting her case be transferred to an impartial investigating officer.[16] However, action was taken only four months later when a contempt of court was finally filed. An enquiry was initiated against Yadav on 2 November 2014 and she was removed from the investigation as late as 23 November 2014.

X, T's husband, also claims that the police recorded videos of their statements and then showed them to the accused in the village: 'When the *pradhan* of Lankh Bawdi village, one of the accused, recently met me at the police station, he said, that day you were pleading in front of me. Today, you want to take me to the court." On several occasions, the police used subversive tactics to dissuade people from going ahead with their cases. In January 2014, X's cousin was booked for rioting, robbery and having links with the terror outfit Lashkar-e-Taiba (LeT). When it was reported in the media, the charges were removed overnight.

After seven months of filing the charge-sheets in five of the seven cases, no trial had commenced. The contempt petition dated 15 September 2014 says: 'The Alleged Contemnors [state administration] are deliberately and purposefully delaying the trial so that the accused persons and members of their dominant community are able to intimidate and threaten the Petitioners to coerce and compel them to withdraw their allegations.' This is despite the fact that Section 309 of the CrPC mandates that a trial in a case of rape should be completed within a period of two months from the date of filing of the charge-sheet. Also, there was no action taken against the errant officer despite the failure of the police to register an FIR despite the written complaint of S, which amounts to an offence under Section 166-A of the Indian Penal Code. Later, under pressure to arrest the accused, the police attached only articles of very little value as a token of investigation proceedings. Vrinda Grover wrote on 27 July 2014:

> As the lawyer of these seven women in Supreme Court, I must tell you that despite a judgment from the Supreme Court in March 2014, all that they have received is security guards and compensation, not justice. Here too one woman is yet to receive compensation. These 7 women are determined and want the men who committed these crimes punished. Only 3 of 26 accused have been arrested, the women and their families are being threatened and intimidated. The UP police says they are helpless and can't trace and arrest the accused. The gang-rapes took place on 8th September 2013, FIRs were filed between November–December 2013, the women have named all the accused who gang-raped them. Almost eight months have passed, no prosecution, no trial has begun. I am

> now moving a Contempt Petition in the Supreme Court. The burden to secure justice lies heavily on the women survivors and their lawyers. Ensuring justice for these women is not the responsibility of any state authority, no state functionary. On behalf of these seven women, I have filed over a dozen applications with UP Police, administration, and the Chief Minister. In the applications I have stated that the woman Investigating Officer is complicit with the accused and should be removed. Not a single application has been acknowledged by any state authority. Only the National Minorities Commission has heard them respectfully and raised their issues with the UP administration.... I am now filing a Contempt petition for non-compliance with the Supreme Court judgment. I only wish the Supreme Court knew what meagre resources I have at my disposal to keep approaching the Court for justice, while the State brazenly flouts the directive of the Court.[17]

On 18 June 2014, Deputy Superintendent of Police Shailendra Lal, one of the investigative officers, who had been praised by top politicians and the Supreme Court for 'the good work of saving property and lives' during the communal violence in September 2013, was suspended. Lal, in his writ petition filed in the Supreme Court, also mentions that in April 2014, he got distress calls from the BJP leader Sanjeev Baliyan, one of the accused in the Muzaffarnagar riots and later the minister of state for agriculture in the central cabinet after the general elections of 2014, for stopping local BJP leaders from pressurizing voters on polling day in Muzaffarnagar. Lal quotes Baliyan as saying: '*Bahot* time *se teri harkatein dekhta aa raha hun, agar hamaare khilaaf aur kaam kiya tou tujhe dekh lunga*' (We have been observing your activities for quite a while now, if your work turns out against us, we will teach you a lesson). Kf, another rape survivor also alleges that the current *pradhan* of the village, Thaam Singh, reached out to her on behalf of the Baliyan to accept Rs 30 lakh (3 million) and drop the case.

While the police failed on every possible grounds—from delay in filing FIRs to filing charge-sheets and arrests—the courts were efficient in issuing directives to help survivors each time they filed applications with the help of lawyers and activists to push for compliance. This went quite some way in helping survivors regain faith in the justice system.

INSIDE THE CAMPS

The socio-economic profile of the 120,000 people displaced is a very important element that determines the sequence of events that followed the sectarian violence. Sugarcane farming, the primary occupation in this geographical belt, is the preserve—and the privilege—of the landowning Hindu (and a handful of Muslim) Jats. Most of the people displaced were Muslims, landless agricultural labourers, carpenters, washerpeople, butchers, tailors and others in similar professions. They neither had political leadership representing them nor the means to rebuild their lives after the riots.

Initial rescue and rehabilitation efforts were proactively offered by madrasas and the Muslim community in the vicinity in the absence of state support. This has usually been the case in the aftermath of communal riots in India.[18] Rubeena, a young girl who was raped in Lankh Bawdi village, told the interviewer not to tell anyone that she was raped: 'How will I live in the camp if I complain to the police?'

'In Islam, rape is treated like adultery,' Manzar, a local lawyer from Muzaffarnagar district, says.[19] 'The women will not talk for fear of being accused of adultery.' When asked if any of the women there had reported any cases of rape, Mohammed Sanaullah, the head of the Arabia-Islam-Hudru-Islam madrassa, which had provided refuge to over 400 people, has this to say: 'Women have been raped and tortured, but it is my sincere advice to forget them. The families of these women will disown them if they come to know that they have spoken about it.' It was this fear that stopped women from openly seeking medical attention for injuries sustained because of sexual violence. Only three of the eighteen relief camps had dedicated women doctors.

CONFIDANTES: DOCTORS AND OTHER SUPPORTERS

Dr Sheba, a gynaecologist at a primary health centre in Loi village, where several displaced people took refuge, played an exceptional role in providing anonymity to rape survivors while treating them. Sheba not only nursed several such women, she went beyond the call of duty, sometimes violating government norms and at others manipulating them to help people. She says, 'Survivors of sexual violence had extremely wounded private parts, some were attacked with weapons on their chests. It took a lot of coaxing [for them to even admit] that they had injuries since there was no privacy in the camps to do a thorough physical examination.'

Several women who were pregnant had miscarriages. Some had to run with their day-old children, others gave birth on their way in sugarcane fields and jungles, and some delivered in dire situations in the relief camps that lacked medical aid. Suman Arora, the nurse stationed in the Loni relief camp in Ghaziabad, says: 'The women who ran away after delivering babies are now suffering from prolapsed uteruses because of stress. Because of lack of amenities here like drinking water, there is a risk of epidemics like typhoid. We are also ill-equipped to prevent dengue in the current situation where these refugees are living.'

In the absence of concerted state intervention, radical religious groups stepping in to provide basic amenities, find a convenient point of entry. Fm, one of the seven rape complainants, says that both her teenaged sons have become a part of the Jamaat that was managing the relief camps: 'One day, they even told me to cover my hair and I was shocked to see them become like this. But they have also heard details about their mother's rape to feel like this.' Fm hints that radicalization is the most obvious ramification of the riot. At several such camps, this researcher heard many ulemas (Islamic scholars) making daily announcements, after the evening prayers that women were raped because they did not wear the burqa. Many young girls, some who had not even hit puberty, were married off in the camps just few days after the riots. Kf says: 'I married off one of my daughters in the relief camp itself before registering the rape case. After what happened, I was not sure of being able to protect her. Also, no one would have married her thereafter. She is happy with her family now.' However, several women were sent back to their natal homes according to reports in the local media in July and August on the pretext that the grooms did not get a share in the compensation money. Many of these men remarried, while the young girls are now seen as appendages, devoid of social dignity for being rejected by their husbands.

Khurshida, a local woman from Kandhla, says, 'A lot of women didn't have clothes on them. None at all.' Locals like her collected clothes from the neighbourhood for those staying in the relief camps. Lack of tents and places to sleep out of incessant rains led many women to sleeping in the houses of locals while the men slept in the open in the madrasa compounds. Khurshida adds: 'A number of these women were preyed upon by the men from the very families who offered accommodation to these riot victims.'

Sexual abuse was also rampant within the camps on account of the extreme vulnerable situations of women who had no socio-economic agency or a place to resettle themselves. Seema, 45, a mother of three daughters, says, 'I haven't slept for days on end. I have to guard my young daughters.' In November 2013, two Jats were arrested for raping a girl who had taken refuge in a camp at Jogiya Khera village. She had stepped outside the camp to buy something from a nearby shop. While the culprits in this case were outsiders, since the displacement, women have been subjected to sexual violence from within the camp too. 'If I talk about it, we will not be allowed to live in the camp,' says another victim.

AFTERMATH

F, one of the complainants, narrates an incident that summed up the kind of polarization in the sugarcane belt, which was far less hostile before the riots: 'Recently, I had gone to the bank to withdraw money, where an old Muslim woman wearing a burqa was sitting on a chair as her son was filling a form. A Jat man walked in with another woman and said, "Jat women will sit here, you get up." No one said a word to refute him, not even me.' It is important to note that the right wing's hijacking of the BKU, which was once responsible for the unity of Hindu and Muslims in the area, was a very important reason for the subsequent polarization of the area.[20] The BJP also promised to help many accused get rid of their cases if it came to power, as Ajit Singh, the *pradhan* of worst affected village, Lisad, claimed.[21] The BJP chief, Amit Shah, famously, addressed an election campaign rally on a Jat community platform, saying, 'The coming [general] elections are of revenge and honour', inciting further communal hatred. He also stirred up an argument against the ruling Samajwadi Party, who had been extremely inefficient in stopping the riots and providing subsequent rehabilitation, saying that through police investigations, its leader was 'appeasing Muslims' and victimizing Hindus. As a result, the BJP in Uttar Pradesh, which elects the maximum number of Members of Parliament, won seventy-three out of eighty seats and went on to form a government at the centre as the single largest party with full majority. Meanwhile, it also launched on the bogey of 'love jihad' across north India. They created a myth that Muslim boys dupe Hindu women into falling in love and marry them. They then convert them and produce more children with a mission to outnumber Hindus.

Since the 2014 general elections, several Hindu religious outfits have set up 'fronts' like the Rashtriya Swayamsevak Sangh's Hindu Behen Beti Bachao Sangarsh Samiti (Hindu Society to Protect Sisters and Daughters) and the RSS' student wing, the Akhil Bharatiya Vidyarthi Parishad's Meerut Bachao Manch(Save Meerut Platform) to stop consensual interreligious marriages, which they have termed 'love jihad'. Lalit Maheshwari, the head of the VHP's Muzaffarnagar unit, told this writer before the elections, 'Once [the] BJP comes to power, they will push towards a law to stop inter-caste and inter-religious marriages.' This is in tandem with the earlier demands of *khap* panchayats in west UP and Haryana, who turned BJP supporters after the elections. *Khap* panchayats have resisted self-choice marriages and issued several death threats against violators. They also demanded a change in the Hindu Marriage Act in 2009 to prohibit same-*gotra* marriages.[22]

In fact, in September 2014, Muzaffarnagar was rocked by a case of what some Muslim religious leaders have called 'reverse love jihad' or the Hindu *dharma yuddha*, when they alleged that a Hindu man had forced a Muslim girl to convert and elope with him. This claim over women has not just affected the mobility of women and young girls across religion, but is also an attempt to control their sexuality and socio-economic empowerment in the long run.

CONCLUSION

The sectarian violence in Muzaffarnagar, like many others in India's past, is evidence of how patriarchy, communalism and political agendas connive to propagate misogyny. This essay elaborates on how the patriarchal discourse to protect women's 'honour' was used to instigate communal riots in Muzaffarnagar. As a result, women's bodies were not just used as battlegrounds to establish the superiority of one community over the other, but the survivors of this sexual violence were systematically silenced because of religious and patriarchal pressures negating the acknowledgement of violence against women in public memory.

In the cases of the seven gang-rape survivors in Muzaffarnagar, the state administration, including the police, not only failed at every possible juncture to execute legal proceedings, they deliberately delayed investigations, putting the women and their families at risk. The delay in medical tests, charge-sheets, commencement of trial, and the lack of initiative to provide security and compensation to the affected women were a reminder of the influence of the accused, who were from the dominant Jat community, and both financially and politically influential. In spite of new amendments to laws relating to crimes against women, the trajectory of the cases are evidence of how the accused continue to enjoy impunity in sexual crimes in incidents of sectarian violence. Political agendas that are fulfilled through such violence are now proving to be impediments in the fight for justice. It has helped right-wing Hindutva forces to further control women's sexuality in the name of 'honour', in resisting self-choice marriages through the myth of a 'love jihad' and reaping further benefits across the country. One and a half years late, the trials are yet to begin in the seven cases, a hint at how the Indian system treats survivors of rape. Since the crimes against these women occurred during communal violence, their cases were further isolated. The 16 December gang-rape and the Shakti Mill case did not see a similar delay because the cases were tried in a fast-track court under a lot of media attention. However, cases like those of the seven women from Muzaffarnagar did get the same amount of visibility in the public eye. With newer, stricter laws, justice within the system is possible as long as there is a political will.

NOTES

1. *Mohd Haroon and Others vs Union of India, Writ Petition (Criminal) No. 155 of 2013, Supreme Court of India.*
2. The word 'Hindutva' was coined in 1923 by Vinayak Damodar Savarkar. It is an ideology that believes in Hindu nationalism.
3. This is a spin-off from a much touted 1970s government population control slogan, '*Hum do, humare do*' (We two, our two [children]).
4. Independent investigations identified the video to be originally from Pakistan of the infamous 2010 killing of two brothers in Sialkot, Punjab province, by a lynch mob who misidentified them as dacoits.
5. As reported in the *Daily Baskar* on 21 September 2013.
6. In a press statement by Ashok Singhal, president, Vishwa Hindu Parishad, said: 'These godless Lust Jihadis donning the garb of Muslim religion as a major weapon have, for the last half a century, been targeting the Hindu girls, women, girl students (http://samvada.org/2013/news-digest/vhps-ashok-singhals-statement-on-mujaffarnagar-riots/ [accessed 4 May 2015]).
7. During the Gujarat 2002 pogrom, similar rumours were fanned when false reports circulated of Hindu women being taken off the train in Godhra and raped inside madrasas.
8. Available at https://www.youtube.com/watch?v=0EDurT3NI-w (accessed 4 May 2015).
9. Video footage available with the author.
10. The Parliament, taking note of the brutal targeting of women's bodies during communal and other sectarian violence in India, inserted Section 376(2)(g) to the list of coercive circumstances where women face aggravated rape:

> Section 376(2) Whoever,—
> (g) commits rape during communal or sectarian violence shall be punished with rigorous imprisonment for a term which shall not be less than ten years, but which may extend to imprisonment for life, which shall mean imprisonment for the remainder of that person's natural life, and shall also be liable to fine.

11. Supreme Court of India, Criminal Original Jurisdiction, Writ Petition (crl) No. 11 of 2013.
12. All names have been changed.
13. Reported by *Shah Times*, 10 October. 2013.
14. http://indiatoday.intoday.in/story/mulayam-singh-yadav-muzaffarnagar-national-commission-for-minorities-riot-remark/1/333083.html
15. http://www.ibnlive.com/news/politics/rahul-on-isi-646896.html
16. Case number 18766/24/57/2014.
17. On the public forum, Feminists India.
18. Flavia Agnes (2002) writes:

> Mosques, dargahs and madrasas are transformed into an oasis of security and solace. Women in relief camps narrated incidents of camp organisers helping out, not only with arrangements of food and first aid, but also with cleansing bleeding wounds and extracting wooden splinters buried into the deepest crevices. While women gave birth in the open in those traumatic days, the men had no choice but to help in the birthing process. Before the meagre aid declared by the government could be accessed, the hungry children were fed only through hurriedly put together community resources. Women partook in the festivity of marriage celebrations of young orphaned girls, arranged by camp leaders, which brought a semblance of normalcy to their shattered lives. They cried out, when the men were picked up in combing operations and bore the brunt of

police brutalities. The bonding between people under siege, is cemented through the adhesive of shared grief and suffering. In the struggle for day to day survival, gender concerns and patriarchal oppressions seem remote. It is here that community and patriarchal identities get forged. The secular and women's rights voices are too distant from their harrowing realities.

19. *Zinā* is an Islamic law concerning unlawful sexual relations between Muslims who are not married to one another through a *nikah*. It includes extramarital sex and premarital sex, such as adultery (consensual sexual relations outside marriage), fornication (consensual sexual intercourse between two unmarried persons) and homosexuality (consensual sexual relations between same-sex partners).
20. The pamphlet 'Radical Socialist Statement and Call for the Elections of 2014' circulated in April 2014 explains this right-wing phenomena of divide and rule:

    In 1947–8, after having stood aside from the freedom struggle, the RSS launched a bid to turn the newly independent India into a sectarian Hindu state to parallel the sectarian Islamic state of Pakistan. It was only the backlash of the murder of Gandhi that stopped them. In 1989, Advani's campaign over the Babri Masjid led to riots in 43 cities and towns. In 1992–3, the destruction of the Babri Masjid, in flagrant violation of laws saying ancient historical/archaeological monuments are to be protected, was followed by frenzied rioting in many parts of India, attacks on minorities. In 2002, there was a massive pogrom in Gujarat, which was a key to the consolidation of the BJP electorally in certain parts of Gujarat.

21. The traditional voters of the Rashtriya Lok Dal, which was seen as a farmers' party, abandoned it and a large voter base shifted to the BJP.

22. The term *gotra* refers to clan in Hinduism. It roughly means descendants from a common male ancestor, and people of the same *gotra* are regarded as kin.

REFERENCES

Agnes, Flavia. 2002. 'Transgressing Boundaries of Gender and Identity'. *Economic and Political Weekly*. EPW. Vol. 37, Issue No. 36, 7 Sep. 2002.

Angre, Ketki. 2014. 'Muzaffarnagar Riots: UP Government Failed to Protect Rights, Says Supreme Court' (edited by Deepshikha Ghosh). NDTV, 26 March. http://www.ndtv.com/india-news/muzaffarnagar-riots-up-government-failed-to-protect-rights-says-supreme-court-555147 (accessed 26 May 2015).

Daily Bhaskar. 2013. 'Muzaffarnagar Riots: BJP MLA Sangeet Som Accused of Circulating Hate Video Surrenders'. 21 September. http://daily.bhaskar.com/news/UP-muzaffarnagar-riots-bjp-mla-sangeet-som-accused-of-circulating-hate-video-arrest-4381464-NOR.html (accessed 4 May 2015).

Bhat, Virendra Nath. 2013. 'What Led to the Muzaffarnagar Communal Riots'. *Tehelka*, 8 September. http://www.tehelka.com/what-led-to-the-muzaffarnagar-communal-riots/ (accessed 25 May 2015).

Dixit, Neha. 2013. 'Holier than Cow', *Outlook*, 28 January, 2013. http://www.outlookindia.com/article/holier-than-cow/283593 (accessed 4 May 2015).

Dixit, Neha. 2013b. 'Thread Bared', *Outlook*, 30 December, 2013. http://www.outlookindia.com/article/thread-bared/288907 (accessed 26 May 2015).

Pamposh Raina, 'A Village in Muzaffarnagar Recounts Rapes and Murder', India Ink (New York Times blog), 30 September, 2013 http://india.blogs.nytimes.com/2013/09/30/a-village-in-muzaffarnagar-recounts-rapes-and-murder/?_r=0 (accessed 26 May 2015).

Shah Times. 2013. 10 October. (Hindi) http://shahtimesnews.com/epaper/

6

Developing Protocols for Medical Examinations

PADMA BHATE-DEOSTHALI, SANGEETA REGE
AND JAGADEESH NARAYAN REDDY

A 21-year-old girl who was raped and bleeding was seen by a doctor at a premier hospital after six hours. No painkiller or first aid was provided as it was a medico-legal case.

A 15-year-old girl was brought by her mother with a complaint relating to fondling of the breasts, and the doctor insisted on examining her genitals as this was part of medico-legal procedures.

A 5-year-old girl who was brutally raped and had suffered severe injuries was taken by her mother to a hospital where she was asked to first file a police complaint. So she went to the local police station, where the police refused to file an FIR [first information report] saying that it needed to be filed where the incident had taken place.

A woman who was pregnant as a result of rape came in for an abortion. She reported that a medico-legal examination had been done a month ago, but no EC [emergency contraception] was given.

> A child was brought to a hospital as she was suffering pain during micturition. The mother said the child had been raped, and that she was examined by a doctor the previous day, but no medication had been given.

These are not isolated examples but reflect the common experience of rape victims and survivors in India. They highlight how their right to treatment is systematically violated, and point also to another important aspect: the problems in forensic practice.

Since the 1980s, activists in the women's movement in India have campaigned and lobbied hard to draw attention to the question of violence against women. They have demanded the setting up of counselling centres and shelters and the provision of legal aid for survivors; they have critiqued coercive population policies, highlighted the complete lack of gender sensitivity within the system and the insensitive responses to rape, and more. Despite this, however, the role of the health sector in responding to and mitigating violence has not become a focal point. Health professionals and health systems have a critical role in providing care for survivors of sexual assault, as well as in documenting the assault and collecting relevant evidence. However, there are several gaps in the provision of care as well as in medico-legal responses that need our attention. Violence against women is not recognized as a public health issue, and it is absent in health policy and programmes. Surprisingly, medical and nursing curricula too do not include this subject. Where treatment is concerned, health providers often fail to document current and past episodes of violence and limit their role to treating its physical symptoms. Deep-rooted biases within forensic medical practice are reflected in medico-legal examinations in cases of sexual violence, as seen in the continued use of the two-finger test, the preoccupation with hymenal status and other unscientific procedures. There is a need to change such practices and to work towards creating an enabling environment, such that survivors feel they can speak out about abuse without fear of being blamed, and where they can receive empathetic support in their struggle for justice and in rebuilding their lives (Bhate-Deosthali 2013).

The health sector has certain legal obligations in responding to violence against women. The domestic violence law (Protection of Women from Domestic Violence Act, 2005) recognizes health facilities as service providers and mandates that all women reporting domestic violence must receive free treatment and information as well as appropriate referral services. The Criminal Law (Amendment) Act, 2013 (CLA 2013), now makes it mandatory for all public and private hospitals to provide free treatment to survivors of sexual violence. Dilaasa, a redesigned 'one-stop crisis centre' model in Mumbai, focuses on training hospital staff to respond to violence against women and to understand the need to deal with violence against women as part of their roles and responsibilities. The model also includes violence support services currently missing in the health sector, namely, crisis intervention and psychosocial support. Dilaasa has implemented sexual violence protocols based on World Health Organization (WHO) guidelines that include informed consent for examination, treatment, evidence collection and informing the police; use of gender-sensitive pro forma that do not record the status and type of the hymen or measure the size of the vaginal opening or make any comment on the sexual habits of the survivor; a chain of custody for management of evidence collected; and immediate first aid and follow-up care. Doctors have been equipped to provide reasoned medical opinion and explain the absence of injuries and/or absence of forensic evidence that could help survivors in courts.

HEALTH SECTOR RESPONSES TO SEXUAL VIOLENCE

Survivors of sexual violence may report directly to hospitals, or may be brought to the hospital by the police. As any incident of sexual violence is a criminal offence, doctors have an obligatory forensic role in the documentation and collection of medico-legal evidence in addition to their primary responsibility of providing treatment and care to survivors. Intervention research carried out by the Centre for Enquiry into Health and Allied Themes (CEHAT) and a situational analysis conducted by WHO in three states in India show that the current response of the health sector to these issues is fraught with problems on both fronts—therapeutic as well as forensic. Some of the problems that have been pinpointed include the following.

Mandatory Police Requisition for Examination in Cases of Sexual Violence

Despite a Supreme Court judgment (*Manjanna v. State of Karnataka*) that made it mandatory for doctors to provide treatment to rape survivors, and not wait for or demand a police requisition, hospitals across the country demand police requisitions, paralysing the entire process. Those who reach the hospital directly for treatment are not provided treatment until they get a police requisition, thus violating their right to treatment.

Inertia in Responding

Interviews with multiple stakeholders highlighted that when a case of rape is reported, there is a reluctance on the part of the providers to respond. This is in contrast to other cases that come to the emergency department, such as assault, burns, suicide, poisoning and so on, where medical treatment is initiated immediately.

This inertia in responding to survivors is reflected in long waiting periods, delays, multiple referrals and a sense of chaos. The actual examination may be completed in less than 20 minutes, but the process of delay, waiting, questioning, information gathering and so on takes a couple of hours.

A senior gynaecologist referred to this response as 'batting', where each doctor wants to avoid performing such examinations. No one wants to take responsibility for the medico-legal examination because they are reluctant to appear in court during rape trials.

No Informed Consent

Informed consent means seeking the person's consent after providing complete information about medical procedures. This has been made a legal requirement for all medical procedures, but in most places no consent is sought from the rape survivor. Providers who were interviewed said that this happens because many doctors believe that in medico-legal cases there is no need to seek consent. As a consequence, the rape survivor has no clue about what the examination entails, what its purpose is and so on.

A dominant perception among health professionals is that consent is not necessary in medico-legal cases. Providers reported that it is implicit that a survivor reaching the hospital after an assault knows why she has come there; thus, there is an assumption of consent on her part. Most activists working with survivors reported that no information was given to the survivor; a signature or thumb impression of the victim or her parent was taken in the case of children. An observational study conducted in one government hospital in Mumbai found that consent was sought by a clerk, who asked the woman whether she was 'ready for examination by a male doctor or not'. The clerk also sought the history of the sexual assault while sitting in a corridor (Contractor 2009).

No information or rationale for the examination was provided, nor were the benefits of such an examination explained. In other settings too, the consent sought was often 'blanket', and survivors were not given the option of refusing any part of the examination, nor did they have the choice of only availing treatment.

Focus on the Survivor's Past Sexual Conduct

The current procedure lays undue emphasis on the survivor's past sexual conduct as part of the medico-legal examination. There is a focus on examining and commenting on hymenal status as an assessment of virginity, and the 'two-finger test' is commonly carried out to determine the size and laxity of the vaginal opening. The forensic examination is centred around determining whether the survivor is sexually habituated or a virgin. So, irrelevant 'findings' such as old tears in the hymen, the size of the vaginal introitus and comments on 'habituation to sexual intercourse' are recorded in the medico-legal papers.

Thus, it is common to find comments such as:

> 'The finger does not go in so there is no sign of sexual abuse.'
> 'She is not a virgin.'
> 'She is habituated to sexual intercourse.'

There is no scientific basis for reaching such conclusions after an examination of the hymen or the size of the vaginal opening. Such conclusions are also inadmissible in Indian law. The Indian evidence law disallows any reference to the past sexual history of the survivor in cases of rape. An analysis of court judgments shows that such 'findings' in medico-legal papers are often used in courts to raise questions about the survivor's character or to pronounce the survivor 'promiscuous' (Human Rights Watch 2010).

The examination of the hymen is often looked upon as the most important part of medical examination in cases of rape. It is believed that the integrity of the hymen can determine whether or not sexual intercourse took place. However, research shows that an intact hymen does not rule out sexual assault, and a torn hymen does not prove previous sexual intercourse, as hymens may be torn due to other activities like cycling, horse riding, masturbation and so on. In a widely acclaimed study that attempted to diagnose, on the basis of physical examination, whether a woman had previously engaged in sexual activity, the researchers found that they had misdiagnosed 'virgins' in 50 per cent of the cases (Underhill and Dewhurst 1978). Among 20 of the 55 sexual assault cases in Mumbai who reported completed peno-vaginal penetration, 13 had no assault-related finding (such as bleeding, oedema, redness or tenderness) with respect to the hymen. Yet, the myth of the hymen continues to be relied upon by health professionals.

Build, Gait and Emotional Status

Forensic examination also includes comments on the build of the survivor—based on the idea that if a woman is well built, she can resist sexual violence. So women with above-average weight or height are considered to be stronger, and it is therefore assumed that if they are reporting rape, they are likely to be lying. This notion does not take into account the fact that there may be circumstances in which women are unable to resist, or that they may face threats or become numb when assaulted. The other common misconception is that the survivor who is raped will not be able to walk properly and will therefore be unsteady on her feet. So doctors record the gait of the victim. This is problematic, and unscientific: we know that when there is severe genital injury, survivors are likely to find it difficult to walk, but in other circumstances this is not necessarily so.

Medico-legal forms also record the emotional condition of the survivor. It is not uncommon to find phrases such as 'doesn't appear distressed', or 'is calm and composed', and so on. None of these has any scientific basis and all descriptions are subjective. The presumption is that if a woman is raped, she will be completely shattered and distraught.

Preoccupation with Injuries

Doctors look for injuries to establish the lack of consent, and if they do not find them (which is often the case—only one in three women has them, according to WHO [2003]), they opine that rape did not occur. The fact that the survivor may have been unable to resist because of threats, use of restraint or administration of intoxicants is not taken into account at all. While there is adequate evidence that most survivors of sexual violence may not report any injury on the body or genitals, this bias continues to inform medical practice.

Anti-women Attitudes among Providers

Forensic textbooks are full of biases against women reporting rape. They warn doctors that 'rape is an easy allegation to make but very difficult to prove,' then inform them that certain types of women are likely to resist rape, such as women who are well built, educated, working. Instructions on how to differentiate between women who are sexually active and those who are not are provided, which have no scientific basis. The books claim that on mere examination of the hymen, the clitoris, the labia majora and minora and the shape of the breast, doctors must first determine whether the woman is habituated to sex or not. Large sections in these books focus on false allegations, citing examples such as 'women may put frog's blood to fake injury, egg white on clothes to fake semen' (Modi 2012; Nandy 2010; Parikh 1999; Reddy and Murty 2013). There are gaps between the theory and the practice of forensic medicine, as changes in the law have not been included in the books. Further, the examinations are informed by stereotypes and misconceptions about sexual assault.

Mechanical Examination

The medico-legal examination is usually carried out irrespective of the nature of assault. Survivors are rarely asked about the nature of the sexual assault, for example, whether it was vaginal, anal or oral, whether penetration was by an object or the penis or a finger, whether it was a non-penetrative assault, and so on. Information on activities such as bathing, urinating or douching which may lead to loss of evidence is not sought from survivors. Providers reported that they just collected all swabs and whatever evidence was available as they did not want to take any risks. This practice implies that a survivor might report forced oral penetration, but the doctor often insists on the collection of vaginal swabs, as that is part of the examination. Or the doctor may not seek the history and merely collects vaginal swabs even though the victim had been assaulted with forced anal penetration. In another case, a woman who came in for an abortion, and reported that her pregnancy was due to having been raped by her cousin two months earlier, still had to undergo all the tests as the doctor said they had to be done.

Gaps in Health Care for Survivors

One of the things that emerged across the board was the pre-occupation with medico-legal procedures and a complete neglect of the therapeutic needs of survivors. Though the WHO in its *Guidelines for Medico-legal Care for Victims of Sexual Violence* (2003) states that 'the overriding priority in cases of sexual assault must always be the health and welfare of the patient,' this is far from true in the Indian context. There are no standard guidelines for treatment of sexual assault survivors, and health professionals have no training in identifying the health consequences of sexual violence. The medico-legal forms have no space for 'treatment', which often results in neglect if the survivor does not have serious physical injuries. Studies have found that in some facilities no treatment is provided at all; only the medico-legal examination is conducted (see, for example, Bhate-Deosthali 2014).

Even in tertiary care hospitals studied in two metro cities, two cities and one state capital, in spite of having state-of-the-art medical facilities, there is no standard treatment protocol for sexual assault survivors, and several patients are not provided the essential package of health services (Bhate-Deosthali 2014). In CEHAT's interventions in hospitals, we met several survivors who had reported to a public hospital where medico-legal documentation was done but no treatment was provided. As a result of this neglect, they were forced to go to another hospital, for an abortion (as no emergency contraception had been provided) or burning micturition (as this was not treated) or for infections (no treatment provided).

In hospitals in a state capital, providers were of the view that it was their job to give information about referral and follow-up services to the police, and it was up to the police's discretion what they did with this information. This included advice on treatment further tests to be conducted and follow-up services—this information was, oddly enough, provided to the police and not to the survivor herself. If the police thought it important, they would take the survivor for all the treatments and tests. But if they did not, these aspects would be neglected (Contractor et al. 2011).

Sexual assault may result in pregnancy or in sexually transmitted infections including HIV. The right to treatment must not be neglected at any cost. Often the health professional's medico-legal role is given precedence over that of care, and there have been several instances where immediate treatment was not provided for infections, pain, pregnancy prophylaxis and so on.

> When we take rape victims to the hospital, no treatment, no follow-up treatment, no advice is given. In one of our cases, the woman was brutally raped and was injured. The doctors gave an ointment and discharged her. She could not even urinate so we asked the doctor if she can be admitted till she recovers so he was angry and said 'Who is the doctor? You or me?' Her condition was bad and we had to later take her to a private hospital where she had to undergo a surgery. Can you imagine? (Social worker, Lucknow, May 2013)

> If a victim is accompanied by activists, then they may give the treatment but they still don't give medicines. We have to buy them. (Child rights activist, New Delhi, April 2013)

Given the gaps in the provision of immediate treatment, the total absence of any psychosocial support by health professionals is not surprising. Providers, lawyers, social workers and interventionists working with women and children who have accompanied survivors to hospitals reported that psychosocial services were not provided. The cities where situational analysis was carried out were large cities with well-equipped hospitals that had social workers and psychologists, but no such services were available for survivors when they reported to the facility.

Absence of 'Medical Opinion'

The biggest contradiction in the current response is the absence of any opinion provided by the doctor. Opinion refers to a doctor's conclusion or findings based on the patient's history, clinical examination and forensic evidence. A doctor cannot opine on whether sexual assault took place or not, as that is a legal term. As illustrated earlier, the medico-legal form has little scope for recording relevant details as reported by the survivor, and so it is left to the discretion of the individual doctor to record what the victim reports and what the doctor finds. As there is no training on how to do this, and the form to be filled is not comprehensive, important facts are often not noted. The examining doctor makes no correlation between the history as reported by the survivor, the clinical findings, the delay in reporting, factors such as use of threats/condom/lubricants, intoxication and so on, which impact the presence or absence of forensic evidence. All that is noted is 'awaiting FSL [forensic science laboratory] reports'.

There is often a time lapse between the examination and the court appearance. If they have to appear in court, doctors may not remember much, and they may not even have the important facts documented on paper. So they base whatever they say on an incomplete piece of paper, which does not in any case have the full information on it. Then, there is also the fact that sometimes the doctor appearing in court may not be the same doctor who treated the survivor. The incomplete report is presented in court, and specific parts or single statements in it get picked up by the defence lawyers. As a senior advocate said, 'The sad part is that there is no opinion or conclusion by the doctors in rape cases. In medico-legal reports of injuries and other complaints, there is a clear formulation of injury and clinical findings but here there is no affirmation of the opinion' (interview, New Delhi, April 2013). She gave an example of a case where a woman had a tear in the posterior fourchette, which is known to be due to sexual assault, but the doctor did not write a conclusive opinion. What then, was the use of the medical examination?

Evidence is collected and sent without any mention of whether the survivor has washed herself. In such cases when semen is not found, this piece of information is not available and the doctor does not correlate this with the FSL report. There is no one else who can put these two facts together and say that the survivor had washed herself and therefore there was no likelihood of finding semen. The medico-legal case therefore does not help the victims/survivors at all. A lawyer told us about an instance where she had seen the medico-legal case papers where medicines were prescribed which were painkillers, but the doctor had not mentioned anywhere in the report that the survivor was in pain. Thus, the whole exercise seems to be a useless one.

There are several cases where medical evidence has been interpreted by the sessions court, high court and Supreme Court very differently. For example, a hymen rupture was interpreted by the trial court as evidence of sexual assault, but was interpreted in the high court as the survivor having been habituated to sexual intercourse. Finally, the Supreme Court upheld the order of the trial court. If a doctor does not interpret and state a conclusion or medical opinion, then each fact on the medico-legal report is subject to interpretation (Modi 2012).

The preceding section has reported the most common responses to sexual violence in different health facilities in India. It is important to note that these are systemic issues and are rooted in the nature of medical education.

NO CLEAR DIRECTIVES IN HEALTH POLICY AND PROGRAMMES

Although there is a legal and ethical obligation on the part of the health system to respond to and care for survivors of violence, the absence of clear directives in policy and programmes hinders the implementation of such a directive. With regard to the forensic role of health providers, there are no uniform protocols for conducting a medico-legal examination. Indeed, every hospital and even doctors in the same hospital may follow a different practice in dealing with sexual assault survivors. The Government of Maharashtra set up a committee in response to a public interest litigation filed in 2010 for uniform protocols and guidelines for dealing with sexual violence. The CEHAT–Anusandhan Trust intervened in favour of uniform protocols that are scientific and gender-sensitive and for the right to health care. However, the Government of Maharashtra's protocols and guidelines perpetuate biases based on factors such as the height and the weight of victims/survivors, and place undue emphasis on hymenal injuries such as the type and position of tears and the elasticity of the vagina. There are no guidelines for first-line psychological support, among other problems ('Battle for Sensitive Rape Medical Test Nears End' *The Times of India* 2014).

LACK OF UNDERSTANDING ABOUT MEDICO-LEGAL EVIDENCE AND ITS LIMITATIONS

The medico-legal examination, which is often referred to as the 'medical test', is presumed to be some kind of a litmus test that will provide evidence about whether rape has occurred or not. This assumption is based on the notion that the accusation may be false and the 'medical test' will reveal the truth. The focus therefore is on so-called 'evidence' and not 'care' for a victim/survivor of rape. Having said that, the limitations of medical evidence are seldom understood or highlighted.

One of the issues related to medical evidence in rape cases is that there is rarely any medical evidence found. A systematic review of medico-legal evidence in sexual violence cases found that evidence of injuries, of semen and other material was most commonly not found in rape cases (Du Mont and White 2007). It is important to note the circumstances of the incident of sexual violence and the factors that are likely to lead to loss of evidence, such as time lapse and activities undertaken by the survivor post-assault. This approach will ensure that in most cases where medical evidence is negative, the reasons for this are explained by the doctor, so that the courts can then rely on the survivor's testimony alone and not interpret medical evidence as either supporting or contradicting her testimony.

The presence or absence of semen in the genital swabs is often considered the deciding factor in cases of sexual assault. But if one were to consider the profile of sexual violence cases reported, it is amply clear that evidence of semen is more likely to be negative than positive. This is because not all sexual assault involves peno-vaginal penetration, and not all peno-vaginal penetrative assault will result in ejaculation inside the survivor's body. Ejaculation outside the body (not on other body parts) or use of a condom would eliminate the possibility of finding spermatozoa or semen in the samples. Evidence is also lost with time: evidence of semen is likely to be found only within 72 hours of the assault. Further, evidence is lost through activities such as bathing, douching, washing private parts or urinating, that the survivor may engage in after the assault. The most basic reaction of any survivor is to wash herself, and a considerable amount of evidence is lost in this manner.

The chain of custody is a process by which collected evidence is dried, packed and sealed, and handed over to the FSL. This is an important part of the entire process of medical examination and evidence collection so as to prevent tampering or destruction or degradation of evidence. This is often not clearly spelt out in hospitals. Samples are collected and left unattended for long periods of time. As the documentation too is weak, the entire procedure is open to manipulation. The process of collection and preservation too is an issue of concern. The swabs and clothes collected need to be dried and sealed, but there is no written protocol on this, and it is possible that much of this evidence putrefies if not properly dried and preserved.

Considering the reality of how sexual assault occurs, it is, therefore, unreasonable to expect that medical evidence will be able to 'prove rape'. Yet, court trials invariably rely heavily on this evidence in order to make a judgment of rape.

A COMPREHENSIVE HEALTH CARE MODEL

Based on the understanding that health care settings offer a unique opportunity for health providers to respond to violence against women, CEHAT collaborated with three hospitals run by the Municipal Corporation of Greater Mumbai (MCGM) to demonstrate a comprehensive and gender-sensitive response to sexual violence. The MCGM had already established a hospital-based crisis centre dealing with domestic violence in 2000 (Dilaasa); therefore, initiating a response to sexual violence seemed opportune and appropriate. The sexual assault response focused on 'care' without compromising on scientificity. While upholding the principle of health care, efforts were made to steer clear of a biomedical approach. The components of the model were evolved in keeping with medical ethics, international standards for health care set by WHO, and the Indian law.[1] This model has been operational since 2008. The following table sets out the key components of the model.

Informed consent	• Enables survivors to exercise autonomy before embarking on a medico-legal examination • Gives survivors the opportunity to understand the procedures and steps pertaining to medico-legal examination • Enables them to voice apprehensions and receive complete information about the examination and evidence collection procedures

	• Age of consent for examination and treatment is specified as 12 years. This age is crucial especially in the context of incest. • A copy of the medico-legal examination report is given to the patient.
Gender-sensitive medico-legal documentation	• The documentation format ensures that no information can be sought on the past sexual life of the survivor. • The history-seeking format enables survivors to narrate forms of sexual assault such as licking, sucking, forced masturbation and so on, as against mere 'peno-vaginal assault'.
Relevant medico-legal examination and evidence collection	• Evidence collection is based on the time that has lapsed between the assault and its being reported to the hospital. Genital and physical evidence is collected only if the survivor reports to the hospital within four days of the assault. • Body examination includes looking for evidence of injuries, blunt trauma, tenderness, semen stains and so on. The genital examination notes only injuries related to assault, and not old tears to the hymen or the size of vaginal introitus.
Provision of medical opinion	• The focus of the medical opinion is on whether the assailants can be identified by any means, whether there is evidence of assault in the form of injuries, the time that has lapsed between the assault and the victim's reaching a medical facility, the actual age of the survivor in the case of minor survivors under 12 years, and reasons provided for absence of injuries and negative forensic science reports. Examining doctors are also apprised of the problems with using terms such as 'rape occurred or did not occur', as 'rape' is a legal term and outside the purview of an examining doctor.
Medical treatment and psychosocial support	• The protocol for treatment includes prophylaxis for sexually transmitted infections including HIV, pregnancy prophylaxis and management (including emergency contraception, pregnancy testing and abortion if required), surgical management, analgesics and tetanus toxoid for injuries.

	• Psychosocial support focuses on demystifying medical procedures, and addressing fears and concerns that survivors may have about their lives post the assault. It also involves carrying out a dialogue with families and friends to help them deal with the aftermath of the assault and create an enabling environment for healing from the effects of assault.
Chain of custody	• The model includes a step-by-step protocol for managing the collected evidence till the time it is dispatched to the FSL. This is done from the perspective of ensuring that evidence is dried, sealed and dispatched in a foolproof manner.

Operational Elements

The components of the model were operationalized through collaboration with municipal hospitals. This involved capacity-building workshops for examining doctors, nurses and support staff. The objective of involving all the staff was to create a positive and therapeutic approach free of biases, prejudices and loose comments across the hospital, and not just the examining room. Training content involved discussions related to the dynamics of sexual violence, its health consequences and pathways by which survivors approach the hospital. The providers were given a step-by-step manual that contained all information on aspects such as recording history, examination findings, evidence collection, age estimation, medical opinion and treatment. A system of coordination with the FSL and the police was created in order to receive feedback about the samples dispatched. A monitoring committee was set up in the hospital comprising examining doctors, nurses and administrators. External experts from the forensic science laboratory, senior forensic medicine specialists and gynaecologists with experience of working on the issue were invited periodically to conduct such training.

Learnings from the Field

- Forty five per cent of sexual violence survivors reached the hospitals voluntarily between 2008 and 2012. They reported to the hospitals to seek treatment for the health-related consequences of sexual violence.
- Detailed history seeking brought to light the fact that more than half of the survivors reported violence that involved non-penile penetration (55 per cent).
- It was seen that 38 per cent of survivors had taken a bath, which is often the immediate reaction of a survivor, 28 per cent had douched and 67 per cent had urinated before reaching the hospital and post the assault. This helped the examining doctors provide explanations for why no positive evidence was found on the survivor.
- Evidence from the examination of 94 survivors showed that only 18 of the 94 (19 per cent) survivors reported bodily/ physical injuries and only 36 of the 94 survivors (38 per cent) presented genital injuries. This finding was consistent with the WHO guidelines for medico-legal care in sexual assault, which showed that as few as 33 per cent of women report any genital/physical injuries. Hence, evidence from the model dispelled the myth that sexual violence must lead to injuries.
- Learnings from crisis intervention services showed that positive messaging, such as dealing with rape as severe physical assault, uncovering feelings of shame, helplessness, hopelessness and linking them to the social context in which rape occurs, helped in reducing self-blame. With carers of children, discussions were conducted on helping the survivor understand good and bad touch, and caregivers were encouraged to speak to children about their fears and apprehensions. The negative consequences of restricting

mobility were also discussed with caregivers. Consistent dialogue with families and follow-up for psychosocial support helped them in dealing with the rigmarole related to filing police complaints, court calls and dealing with community responses (CEHAT 2012).

Legal and Policy Changes

The definition of rape was expanded in the CLA 2013 to include all forms of sexual violence—penetrative (oral, anal, vaginal), including by objects/weapons/fingers, and non-penetrative (touching, fondling, stalking, disrobing and so on). The act recognized the right to treatment for all survivors of sexual violence by public and private health care facilities. Failure to treat is now an offence under the law. The law further disallows any reference to past sexual practices of the survivor. A strong case is made by CLA 2013 for transforming the response of the health sector to sexual violence. An evidence-based model set up by CEHAT and MCGM that had provided comprehensive care and treatment to a large number of rape survivors was discussed at various fora. A written submission was made by CEHAT along with the Lawyers Collective to the Justice Verma Committee (JVC); CEHAT also worked consistently with the media and other fora to focus on the need to upscale this model.

Taking cognizance of the lack of uniform protocols and gaps in provision of medico-legal care to survivors of sexual violence, and the recommendations of the JVC, CLA 2013 and the Protection of Children from Sexual Offences Act 2012, the Ministry of Health and Family Welfare set up a national committee of experts to formulate a uniform protocol and guidelines for health professionals to respond to sexual violence. In doing so, international standards, especially the WHO's *Guidelines for Medico-legal Care* (WHO 2003) and its *Clinical and Policy*

Guidelines for Responding to Intimate Partner Violence and Sexual Violence (WHO 2013) were referred to. The committee has drawn from the available evidence from health sector interventions, legal and other expert opinions and the voices of survivors. This is the most significant achievement, as it is the first national directive for the health sector with regard to responding to sexual violence.

However, the legal amendment brought in mandatory reporting of all cases of sexual violence by health professionals. Such mandatory reporting severely compromises the role of health professionals in instances where a survivor only wants medical treatment and care, but does not wish to register a complaint. Once the survivor is informed of the mandatory reporting requirement, she may decide not to seek health care at all, thereby jeopardizing her own health; this amounts to denying her health services. On the other hand, a health professional who does not abide by the mandatory reporting rule may invite punishment by the law enforcement machinery. This is a major challenge which has been resolved to some extent by the Ministry of Health guidelines of 2014 (MOHFW 2014) by bringing in the aspect of 'informed refusal', to be documented in cases where the survivor does not wish to inform the police.

Challenges

An appropriate response to survivors reporting sexual violence requires several agencies to work in conjunction with each other. The prosecution, police, judiciary, child welfare committees (CWCs), forensic laboratories and health system among others need to play a role in ensuring care and justice to survivors. An equally critical role is that of shelter homes, counselling centres and community-based organizations. However, the CEHAT experience shows that there are several gaps in the current response of other government agencies.

The Police

The police continue to be ill informed of the provisions under laws pertaining to dealing with sexual violence (POCSO 2012, CLA 2013). Delays in recording FIRs and refusal to record them have been discussed by survivors and their families. In case a survivor reaches a police station, police invariably delay her medical examinations, and often detain survivors and their families at the police station. Instances of women police constables being present during medico-legal examinations have been reported.

As far as their understanding of medical evidence is concerned, it is somewhat narrow, restricted to the presence or absence of injuries. A survivor is also subjected to repeated medico-legal examinations from different hospitals if the police do not find the medico-legal examination report useful. Often the police insist on getting health providers to comment on whether 'rape' occurred, whether the 'survivor [is] habituated to sexual intercourse', and the like.

The Judiciary

The judiciary too is not well versed in the aspect of medico-legal evidence and its limitations. The understanding of evidence is restricted to injuries. Health consequences such as pain during urination or defecation, tenderness or blunt trauma post-assault are not appreciated as medical evidence. There is an overemphasis on genital and physical injuries, and health providers are pressurized in the courtroom to answer unscientific questions. Several providers cited examples of such questioning, for example, 'What is the status of the hymen?,' or 'Can the injury have occurred due to a fall?' Thus, even when injuries are consistent with sexual violence, courts tend to disbelieve such evidence and claim that they could have occurred because of other reasons such as a fall.

When there are no injuries, there is a tendency to state that the act could have been consensual and as a result there were no injuries.

Efforts were made to understand the role of medical evidence in the courtrooms and whether it played a role in either acquittal or conviction. Only 14 judgments could be acquired, and these pre-dated the change in the laws pertaining to rape. There were eight acquittals out of the 14. Among the acquittals, health providers were not called as expert witnesses in court in at least two cases, neither could the public prosecutor (PP) offer a reason for the lack of medical evidence. In instances where the survivor was menstruating, the PP failed to mention this as a reason for the lack of medical evidence; the scientific fact that evidence is lost with menstrual blood was not even brought to the notice of the judges. Similarly, aspects such as delayed reporting to the hospital or the use of a condom, and therefore negative FSL results, could not be explained by the prosecutor. Neither were efforts made by the PP to bring in the examining doctor as expert witness. In instances of non-penile penetrative assault, the prosecution failed to bring to the court's notice the lack of relevance of semen or spermatozoa.

As mentioned earlier, these cases pre-dated the new law. Thus, in an offence involving finger penetration of a survivor, the police registered a case under the section on rape. However, the previous rape definition under Section 376 of the Indian Penal Code did not cover this offence. The chances of getting a conviction were thus substantially reduced because of having framed a charge under an inappropriate clause.

As far as the convictions go, examining doctors were called in to testify in 6 out of the 14 cases. Here too, most survivors did not have either genital or physical injuries, except in one case. Doctors were able to provide reasons for the lack of medical evidence, such as the use of a condom, delay in reporting to the hospital, or the nature of the assault itself, which may have involved the forced fondling of body parts, and therefore could account for the lack of collection of relevant evidence in such instances. In one instance, when asked whether the injury in itself could be from a sexually transmitted infection (STI), the doctor responded that the nature of the injury did not indicate an STI but was a genital injury. Public prosecutors were also well versed in the nature of medico-legal findings and their limitations in these cases.

Child Welfare Committees (CWCs)

The main role of CWCs in instances of child sexual abuse is to provide children and families with care and protection. But the interface of the health sector with the CWCs has brought forth the biases and victim-blaming attitudes of CWC members. They were often found to blame the parents of sexually abused children and to push for the institutionalization of these children. No efforts were made to assess and monitor the safety of the child in her place of residence, and institutionalization was suggested as the only option to keep survivors safe. For many child survivors, this aggravated their fears and those of their family members. It was also noted that the CWC did not have specific mechanisms to investigate the offence; neither did they have a set procedure for communicating with children. These concerns added to the agony of the survivors as well as their caregivers.

SEXUAL VIOLENCE IN CONFLICT

The response of the health sector to sexual violence in conflict situations is worse than in 'normal' circumstances due to the specific context of conflict, whether it is armed conflict, state repression, riots and so on. Armed conflict has a serious impact on the accessibility and availability of health care services. Migration of trained health professionals from conflict zones, breakdown in the health infrastructure, along with restricted movement of health professionals due to curfews, affect health care delivery. In all such situations, attacks on health professionals and health facilities have been reported. The political environment further acts against health professionals, as it compromises their capacity and duty to be neutral.

Abuses, murders and harassment of medical professionals drive many of them out of these regions, often resulting in the large-scale migration of trained health personnel from conflict regions. Reports point out that, like all other social services, health services too tend to collapse particularly in areas of prolonged conflict. Where infrastructure exists, personnel are often unwilling to work due to political instability and fear for their lives.

A recent fact-finding report describes the case of a government sub-district hospital in Pattan, Kashmir, which attended to several civilians who had been injured in police firing during a protest. While doctors were busy attending to the medical needs of the injured, the Central Reserve Police Force forcibly entered the hospital and threatened them with rifles (Vij 2010). They destroyed medical equipment, broke doors and windows and terrorized the hospital staff. This case illustrates how hospitals, which are meant to be safe, neutral spaces, have been turned into battlegrounds. Similar reports emerged from the communal riots in Gujarat 2002, where hospitals were attacked and victims/survivors were prevented from accessing health services. Health professionals were attacked based on their religious identity.

In Nagaland, Manipur, Assam and other states of the Northeast and in Jammu and Kashmir, the Armed Forces Special Powers Act is in force. This act gives impunity to army personnel and grants them powers to use force on the slightest doubt in the name of national security. It gives army officers legal protection for their actions. There can be no prosecution, lawsuit or any other legal proceedings against anyone acting under the law. Any complaints against army personnel for atrocities are accepted and tried only in military courts. There is a lack of transparency around such trials, which prevents civilians from filing cases. The fundamental freedoms of citizens living in areas of armed conflict are suspended as there are prohibitions on mobility, curfews, bans and search operations. Violence against women during conflict is often not recognized, or is understood as an inevitable by-product of conflict. This notion constitutes a barrier in the registering of such crimes and prevents women from reporting them. In the north-eastern states, such crimes are used as a weapon to crush struggles for autonomy and self-determination. In the states of Chhattisgarh, Odisha, Jharkhand, Andhra Pradesh and parts of West Bengal and Maharashtra, the Central Armed Police Forces are engaged in anti-Maoist operations.

The cases of Soni Sori in Chattisgarh, Neelofar and Asiya in Kashmir and Manorama Devi in Manipur highlight several lacunae in the health care system and violations of health rights, as well as lacunae in the gathering of forensic evidence. Differing or rather contradictory medical opinions and poor documentation of clinical findings of torture and violence point to the erosion of medical neutrality and lack of accountability of the medical profession.

Health professionals are often under pressure to issue reports that do not reveal human rights violations. This is particularly true in cases of rape and sexual violence. Whether perpetrated by insurgent groups or by security forces, there is always an attempt to 'hush up' rape. This is further compounded by the lack of any standard operating procedures, protocols or access to the medico-legal papers of the patient/victim.

Health professionals therefore must recognize that all victims/survivors of sexual violence in conflict areas are entitled to immediate treatment and care. Their duties must be carried out regardless of the nature of the conflict, the identity of the victim or rank and status of the perpetrator. They must ensure that the actions or instructions of police/state functionaries do not interfere with the provision of medical treatment to the survivor and the documentation of the reported incident.

In order that health professionals are able to ethically perform their duties towards survivors of violence, it is crucial that their safety be ensured and that they be allowed to function free of pressure. The 1949 Geneva Conventions clearly states:

> Medical workers shall be respected, protected, and assisted in the performance of their medical duties. The sick and wounded shall be treated regardless of their affiliations and with no distinction on any grounds other than medical ones. Medical workers shall not be punished for providing ethical medical care, regardless of the persons benefiting from it, or for refusing to perform unethical medical treatment. Medical workers shall have access to those in need of medical care, especially in areas where civilian medical services have been disrupted. Similarly, people in need of medical care shall have access to such services.

CONCLUSION

The health system has to become more sensitive to the special needs of victims/survivors of violence, and this means that the entire hierarchy needs to be motivated to have a spirit of service. Health professionals should be exposed to the concerns of victims/survivors of violence. Training has been found to lead to positive changes in provider knowledge, attitudes and beliefs about sexual assault (Donohoe 2010; Milone et al. 2010). It is also important to provide training on how to prepare medical reports so that such reports can be legally relevant.

In India, the campaign against sexual violence has demanded national protocols and guidelines that are victim-centred and that respect the right to health care for survivors of sexual violence. The amendments to the rape law (CLA 2013) where 'consent' is defined as an unequivocal agreement to engage in a particular sexual act, clarifying further that the absence of resistance does not imply consent, is most welcome, and the medical profession must accordingly make a shift in its practice. There needs to be more awareness about the amendments, and such awareness must be translated into specific directives for health professionals and the judiciary. The protocols must be made gender-sensitive on an urgent basis and the focus must shift from evidence to care in responding to sexual assault. The Ministry of Health and Family Welfare set up a national committee and issued national protocols and guidelines for responding to sexual violence in April 2014. Some states have adopted them and have issued directives for implementation. This needs to become a norm for all health professionals and facilities across the country.

NOTE

1. Section 164(A) of the Criminal Procedure Code mandates that informed consent is to be sought by a health provider for a sexual assault examination. It directs the physician to seek specific consent for each component of the examination and evidence collection, as against blanket consent. It also states that the medical examination report must state the reasons for each conclusion in the medico-legal report.

   Section 89 of the Indian Penal Code states that a person who is 12 years and above is empowered to provide consent for examination and treatment.

   Section 146 (Indian Evidence Act) states that past sexual conduct of the victim and comments about 'habituation to sexual intercourse' are irrelevant. Therefore, such history should neither be sought nor recorded for medico-legal purposes. This section made the two-finger test inadmissible in the courts.

The Indian Constitution recognizes the right to health as a fundamental right, judicially recognized as emanating from the right to life, Article 21.

REFERENCES

'Battle for Sensitive Rape Medical Test Nears End'. 2014. *Times of India*, 5 February. http://timesofindia.indiatimes.com/city/mumbai/Battle-for-sensitive-rape-medical-test-nears-end/articleshow/29875610.cms (accessed 15 June 2016).

Bhate-Deosthali, P. 2013. 'Moving from Evidence to Care: Ethical Responsibility of Health Professionals in Responding to Sexual Assault', *Indian Journal of Medical Ethics*, 10(1): 2–5.

————. 2014. 'Neither Evidence nor Care, Situational Analysis of Health Sector Response to Sexual Assault', WHO.

CEHAT (Centre for Enquiry into Health and Allied Themes). 2012. *Establishing a Comprehensive Health Sector Response to Sexual Assault*. Mumbai: CEHAT.

Contractor, Sana. 2009. An Observation Study on Response to Survivors of Sexual Assault at the Police Hospital, Mumbai, 2009. http://www.cehat.org/go/uploads/sexualviolence/policehospitalreport.pdf (accessed 28 July 2016).

Contractor, S., D. Venkatachalam, Y. Keni and R. Mukadam. 2011. *Responding to Sexual Assault: A Study of Practices of Health Professionals in a Public Hospital*. Mumbai: CEHAT and New Delhi: SAMA. http://www.cehat.org/go/uploads/Publications/R81%20SexualAssaultStudy.pdf (accessed 15 June 2016).

Donohoe, J. 2010. 'Uncovering Sexual Abuse: Evaluation of the Effectiveness of the Victims of Violence and Abuse Prevention Programme', *Journal of Psychiatric and Mental Health Nursing*, 7(1): 9–18.

Du Mont, Janice, and Deborah White. 2007. 'The Uses and Impacts of Medico-legal Evidence in Sexual Assault Cases: A Global Review'. WHO.

Human Rights Watch. 2010. *Dignity on Trial: India's Need for Sound Standards for Conducting and Interpreting Forensic Examination of Rape Survivors*. New York: Human Rights Watch.

Milone, J., M. Burg, M. Duerson, M. Hagen and R. Pauly. 2010. 'The Effect of Lecture and a Standardised Patient Encounter on Medical Student Rape Myth Acceptance and Attitudes toward Screening Patients for a History of Sexual Assault', *Teaching and Learning in Medicine*, 22(1): 37–44.

Modi, J.P. 2012. *A Textbook of Medical Jurisprudence and Toxicology*. 24th ed. Gurgaon: Lexis Nexis.

MOHFW (Ministry of Health and Family Welfare). 2014. *Guidelines and Protocols: Medico-legal Care for Survivors/Victims of Sexual Violence*. http://uphealth.up.nic.in/med-order-14-15/med2/sexual-vil.pdf (accessed 30 July 2016).

Nandy, A. 2010. *Principles of Forensic Medicine including Toxicology*. 3rd rev. enl. ed. Kolkata: New Central Book Agency.

Parikh, C.K. 1999. *Parikh's Text Book of Medical Jurisprudence and Toxicology: For Classrooms and Courtrooms*. 6th ed. New Delhi: CBS Publishers.

Reddy, K.S. Narayan, and O.P. Murty. 2013. *The Essentials of Forensic Medicine and Toxicology*. 32nd ed. Hyderabad: K. Saguna Devi.

Underhill, R.A., and J. Dewhurst. 'The Doctor Cannot Always Tell: Medical Examination of the "Intact" Hymen', *Lancet*, 1(8060): 375–76.

Vij, Shivam. 2010. 'Report #1: Attack and Killing on Pattan Hospital Premises'. Kafila, 15 November. https://kafila.org/2010/11/15/report-1-pattan-hospital-attack-kashmir/ (accessed 15 June 2016).

WHO (World Health Organization). 2003. *Guidelines for Medico-legal Care for Victims of Sexual Violence*. Geneva: WHO. http://apps.who.int/iris/bitstream/10665/42788/1/924154628X.pdf (accessed 15 June 2016).

———. 2013. *Responding to Intimate Partner Violence and Sexual Violence against Women: WHO Clinical and Policy Guidelines*. http://apps.who.int/iris/bitstream/10665/85240/1/9789241548595_eng.pdf (accessed 29 July 2016).

7

Sexual Violence and Impunity

A Psychosocial Perspective

SHOBNA SONPAR

This essay suggests the adoption of an integrated, multi-factorial framework for understanding sexual violence perpetration and the impunity that such crimes often enjoy. Eschewing single-factor explanations such as individual psychopathology or gender inequity, such an approach conceptualizes sexual violence as a complex phenomenon grounded in the interplay of individual, group and sociocultural factors. While psychological explanations help understand why individual men become rapists, they do not explain why the vast majority of perpetrators are men. At the same time, explanations based on evolutionary biology or on gender norms and power inequities fail to explain why the majority of men exposed to the same biological imperatives or sociocultural influences do not rape. As Heise (1998) points out, at a minimum, theory must be able to account for why individual men become rapists as well as why women as a class are so often their target.

In the feminist model, violence against women results from the power differentials within patriarchy that require women to be kept subdued through the use of control, including physical, sexual, economic and psychological abuse and intimidation. By focusing on the sociocultural, structural basis of this violence, feminist analysis brought the hitherto private and personal into the realm of public discourse and action. Hence, feminists have demanded public solutions to the problem of violence against women, and emphasized legislation and the involvement of the criminal justice system. Examining the discrepancy between this 'traditional' feminist perspective on domestic violence and the experience of frontline workers in agencies involved in intimate partner violence programmes, many of whom were trained in the feminist model, McPhail et al. (2007) note the need to expand feminist thinking about violence by encompassing other theories about violence while retaining the power and structural analysis which has been the core contribution of the feminist model. These additional perspectives could draw on the understandings of personal etiologies of violence and could also challenge traditional feminist theory to be more inclusive of other oppressions, including those of men.

Impunity, defined as immunity from punishment or recrimination, or exemption from unpleasant consequences, punishment, penalty or harm, commonly follows the perpetration of sexual violence. A recent large sample multi-country study on men and violence in Asia and the Pacific region (Fulu et al. 2013) found that although one in four men interviewed in the study said that they had raped a women at least once in their lifetime, between 72 and 97 per cent said that they did not face any consequences. In order to stop sexual violence, it is important to understand its causes as well as how individuals absolve themselves of moral accountability, and societies from their legal, social and moral obligations to promote social justice and ensure the well-being of all members.

Accountability and its obverse, impunity, must also be understood in a more differentiated way. The distinctions between legal, moral and causal responsibility to which Kirby (2013) in his discussion of men's responsibility for sexual violence draws attention, and the tensions between these, may be useful here. Moral responsibility concerns guilt and blame, and thus guides who should be punished and what is the ethical course of action. Legal responsibility designates the appropriate subjects of prosecution and sanction in a particular system of law and justice. Causal responsibility establishes how events come about, tracing patterns and relationships to account for a given outcome. It is causal responsibility that the paper addresses in teasing out the factors that lead to sexual violence. There are tensions between causal and moral responsibility, most evident in discussions about men's collective responsibility for violence against women and in discussions of men's agency and hence moral responsibility when structure has shaped subjectivity. A third tension is that between legal and moral accountability, and pertains to the fact that when there is broad social tolerance or condoning of ideas supportive of sexual violence, and sociocultural biases permeate civil and state institutions, there is resistance towards passing relevant legislation (for instance, against marital rape) and the implementation of anti-rape laws. Since legal accountability usually follows moral accountability, it is not surprising that the legal remedies to sexual violence are limited, notwithstanding the hard-won success of women's activism at the international level to make sexual violence a crime against humanity, a war crime or a genocidal crime. Finally, there is the question of how individuals alone and in groups disengage morally from their own conscience, compassion and empathy to inflict grievous harm.

There is, therefore, a need for a coherent framework that puts together these pieces and helps understand how so many of these crimes go unacknowledged, unlamented and unpunished. Further, the range of forms that sexual violence takes (date rape, marital rape, child sexual abuse, gang-rape, sexual torture and so on) and the variety of contexts in which it occurs (in the home, at clubs, following abduction, during war, in ethnic and caste-based violence, and so on) demands a differentiated and multi-factorial understanding.

The psychosocial lens provides such a view. A psychosocial approach to understanding perpetration of sexual violence situates any instance of such violence within the sociocultural milieu that lays the preconditions for such violent acts to be committed, in intersection with factors pertaining to group affiliation (stable or transient) and individual dynamics. The psychosocial framework views the individual, group and sociocultural domains to have a systemic relation with one another. This means that there will be complex and recursive interactions between the factors pertaining to individuals, such as individual personality and history, the factors pertaining to interpersonal and group relations, and the factors pertaining to the wider sociocultural context, such as culturally normative attitudes and practices. The framework shows how accountability can be compromised at each level. The psychosocial framework is akin to the social-ecological framework, which combines various ecologies or levels of influence to understand complex behaviour and has been fruitfully applied to the study of violence (Basile et al. 2009; Heise 1998). Such approaches are able to summarize vast bodies of research, integrate different perspectives and expose the nested relationships between the different levels of influence, and are useful to guide future research and preventive efforts (Heise 1998).

Each level of analysis suggests specific causal factors and raises different questions about accountability and impunity. None is complete in itself. The sociocultural level, consistent with the feminist model, indicates the structural and social preconditions that make sexual violence widespread and naturalizes it. These preconditions—gender-inequitable attitudes and masculinist gender norms, social acceptance of interpersonal violence, sexuality concerns, and institutional replication of the biases that contribute to sexual violence—are necessary but not sufficient in themselves to account for actual perpetration. They are predisposing or vulnerability factors.

The group level of analysis gives insight into multiple perpetrator sexual violence, the common forms this takes and the group processes involved in disengaging from individual moral radar. Masculinist gender ideology and linked practices, a theme that appears at all three levels, is starkly salient here. It also shows how sexual violence is instrumentally used in the service of identity assertion—whether of masculinity, caste, ethnicity or nation. When this happens, the justification provided by the higher system (for instance, national security, ethnic purity, caste pride, male honour) and the dehumanization of the other confounds moral accountability and enables moral disengagement.

The individual level of analysis is important in that legal and moral accountability is demanded of individuals even when their perpetration is group based or ordered from above, as may be the case in war. It is also important to consider the fact that despite predisposing sociocultural conditions and group pressures, most individuals are not perpetrators of violence. Developmental backgrounds of childhood neglect and abuse are consistently found in population-based as well as clinic studies of those who commit sexual violence. This and the finding of personality dispositions that resonate with the masculinity-related themes noted at group and sociocultural levels are significant.

Sexual violence is defined as 'any sexual act, attempt to obtain a sexual act, unwanted sexual comments or advances, or acts to traffic, or otherwise directed, against a person's sexuality using coercion, by any person regardless of their relationship to the victim, in any setting' (WHO 2002). Coercion includes physical force, psychological intimidation, blackmail or other threats, and when a person is unable to give consent as when drunk, asleep or mentally incapable of understanding the situation. The terms sexual violence, sexual aggression, sexual assault and sexual coercion are used interchangeably in the text. The term 'gang-rape' commonly used to refer to rapes perpetrated by more than one person is misleading, since in many cases perpetrators come together in a more loose and transient grouping, whereas criminal and street gangs usually have a stable membership along with shared group norms and identity. For this reason Horvath and Kelly (2009) suggest the use of 'multiple-perpetrator rape' to name sexual violence committed by two or more perpetrators with 'gang-rape' being a specific subtype. The terms multiple-perpetrator rape and group-perpetrated rape are used interchangeably in the text.

The sociocultural, group and individual levels of analysis of the psychosocial framework are applied to explore the causal factors contributing to sexual violence perpetration and the impunity such perpetration enjoys.

SOCIOCULTURAL LEVEL

The sociocultural level concerns the macrosystem that provides the 'cultural scaffolding' (Gavey 2005) that supports sexual violence. It refers to the norms, practices and discourses of sex, gender and violence prevailing in a society that set up the preconditions for sexual violence to occur. As the following section indicates, sexual violence as a phenomenon is subject to social constructions that determine whether it is construed as reprehensible and criminal, a factor intimately connected to accountability and impunity. The prominent sociocultural factors that underwrite the widespread prevalence of sexual violence include patriarchal systems, gender-inequitable attitudes, constructions of masculinity, sexuality-related concerns, and social acceptance of interpersonal violence. Also at this level of analysis are the social institutions, formal and informal (for instance, the state, legal and judicial institutions, the military and police, institutions connected to caste, tribe, religion and so on) in which are inscribed those beliefs, attitudes, practices and configurations of power that support sexual violence perpetration. These institutions, by enjoying social legitimacy, compound the problem of impunity for sexual violence.

Before proceeding to elaborate upon these, it may be useful to consider the widespread prevalence of sexual violence, a fact that indicates that the causes of sexual violence cannot be attributed to individual aberration alone but that some form of social pathology must be at work. Men's reports of perpetration of sexual violence ranged from 6 to 29 per cent in a study spanning India, Rwanda, Brazil, Chile, Croatia and Mexico (Barker et al. 2011), with 24 per cent of the men in India reporting ever using sexual violence. Meanwhile, another study in Bangladesh (Naved et al. 2011) found that 24 per cent of men reported perpetrating sexual violence. Among a sample of men frequenting alcohol shops in Chennai, India, 28.5 per cent reported forced sex with at least one partner in the preceding three months (Go et al. 2010), while in South Africa, a large community-based study found that 28 per cent of men had perpetrated rape (Jewkes et al. 2011). In the US, based on a comprehensive sample of students from thirty-four colleges across the country, it was found that 27 per cent of women reported they had suffered sexual assault that met legal definitions of rape (Koss, Gidcycz and Wisniewski 1987) and 24.5 per cent of men in a population-based study reported an act that met the legal definition of rape or attempted rape (Abbey et al. 2006). Pointing out that population-based studies of rape perpetration are few, a UN-sponsored large-sample study in six countries of the Asia-Pacific region found that 26 to 80 per cent of men disclosed perpetration of physical and sexual intimate partner violence against women, the rates varying widely between sites and countries (Fulu et al. 2013). The prevalence of non-partner rape of women ranged from

2.5 to 26.6 per cent, and the rape of men from 1.5 to 7.7 per cent (Jewkes et al. 2013).

A disturbingly large number of adolescent girls and boys are subjected to sexual coercion (Jejeebhoy and Bott 2003). In Pakistan, a pilot survey among adolescents in four cities found that 14 per cent of boys and 19 per cent of girls reported some kind of sexual abuse, figures thought to be an underestimate (Qazi 2003). In India, Patel et al. (2003) found that one-third of the students they surveyed, male and female, reported a coercive sexual experience in the past year and 6 per cent reported forced intercourse. In Sodhi and Verma's (2003) study of low-income urban youth in Delhi, nearly half reported sexual coercion, including forced sex. Both girls and boys reported coercion, including cases in which girls were raped by multiple perpetrators.

The incidence of multiple-perpetrator sexual violence is difficult to determine due to methodological issues and the figures available differ widely. Horvath and Kelly (2009) cite studies that report that one-third to half of all rapes in South Africa, 2 to 26 per cent of rapes in the US, and 11 per cent in the UK are group perpetrated. A general population study in Bangladesh found that 1 per cent of urban and 2 per cent of rural men admitted to gang-rape (Naved et al. 2011), while the rates for multiple-perpetrator rape in countries of the Asia-Pacific region ranged from 1.6 to 14.1 per cent (Jewkes et al. 2013). The incidence is probably higher in some contexts, such as that of conflict and war, and in settings such as fraternities and the military.

The Social Construction of Sexual Violence

The assumption that sexual violence is primarily a crime against women perpetrated by men has obscured the fact of sexual victimization of men by other men in the general population

(Ganju et al. 2004; Jewkes 2012; Moore, Madise and Awusabo-Asare 2012), in prisons (Gear 2005), during war and in the military (Kwon et al. 2007; Sivakumaran 2007; Turchik and Wilson 2010), sexual victimization by women, often of children (Bunting 2007; Wijkman, Bijleveld and Hendriks 2010), and women's sexual coercion of men (Ganju et al. 2004). The social construction of gender and sexuality influence the perception of harm such that coerced sex between a young boy and older woman is not viewed with as much alarm as is similar abuse of a young girl by an older man (Hayes and Carpenter 2013). Notwithstanding this, women are overwhelmingly the victims and men the perpetrators of sexual violence.

Some forms of sexual violence are simply not put on the table as crimes but are 'normalized' and come to be seen as 'natural' in everyday life. Cultures determine what kinds of coercion and violence are permissible and which are transgressive (Kalra and Bhugra 2013). To illustrate, a cross-cultural study by Rozee (1993) examined 200 ethnographic sources and identified both 'normative rape' (rape in situations condoned by that society) and non-normative rape (rape in situations not condoned). Among normative rape patterns, she found marital rape in 40 per cent, exchange rape (in which women are lent or given to guests or brothers in the course of gambling or negotiations) in 71 per cent, punitive rape (generally for transgressing gender norms) in 14 per cent, ceremonial rape (such as ritual defloration) in 49 per cent, and status rape (such as the rights of chiefs to women) in 29 per cent. In South Africa, traditional customs like *ukuthwala*, which involves the abduction and forced sexual initiation of a girl for marriage, are not considered offensive and are not called rape, and forced sex is seen as necessary to overcome obligatory feminine coyness and innate female passivity (Jewkes et al. 2011). Among South African schoolgirls, the high level of coerced sex is normalized as being inevitable in relationships, or as being a reflection of love or a natural consequence of being 'provoked'. The acceptance of widespread sexual harassment in schools by the authorities and wider community leaves girls with no clear sense that violence is intolerable and should not be a normal part of a relationship (Haffejee 2006).

'Normalized' sexual violence is most often found within marriage. The prevalence of coercive sexual intercourse within marriage is found to be 30 to 36 per cent in India (Barker et al. 2011; Koenig et al. 2006) and 17 per cent in Sri Lanka (de Mel, Peiris and Gomez 2013), along with considerable support for the view that it is husband's prerogative to physically compel his wife to engage in sex whenever he desires. The fact of early marriage is worth noting. In much of South Asia, nearly half of all women are married before the age of 18 (Chowdhury 2004; Mensch, Singh and Casterline 2005), and little heed is paid to whether she is physically and emotionally ready. An in-depth study of married adolescents in India highlights young brides' lack of preparation and ignorance about sexual intercourse until the first night. Many described their first experience as involving the use of physical force and being traumatic, distasteful and painful (George 2003). Even when the wife is a minor, marital rape is not recognized in India.

Sexual violence is also made invisible under ideological compulsions such as the suppression of cases against middle-class women by men of the subaltern class within the left movement (Roy 2010).

The 'cultural scaffolding' of rape includes the construction of rape myths that circulate in a culture. These are socially learned, stereotyped beliefs about rape, rape victims and rapists (Burt 1980) that justify sexual violence against women and advocate that women are responsible for their sexual victimization. Despite their falsehood, they are endorsed by a substantial segment of the population, permeate legal, media and religious institutors

(Edwards et al. 2011), and are also found in the texts of all major religions (Franiuk and Shain 2011). Some examples are: forced sex between intimate partners is not really rape, women secretly want to be forced and can prevent it if they really want, or women who get raped somehow deserve it (because they are promiscuous or engage in unfeminine behaviour such as being sexually assertive or going to bars alone). Beliefs about male sexuality also contribute to a distorted understanding of rape, specifically the idea that men cannot control their sexual urges. There are also myths about what constitutes 'real rape'. This prevents victims of acquaintance rape from acknowledging their rape and it may allow acquaintance rapists to engage in rape while denying it is rape (Ryan 2011). Although men are more likely than women to endorse rape myths, women also believe in them. Thus, an examination of a large number of victim narratives found that one in five women who disclosed an incident of sexual violence excused or justified it largely drawing on stereotypes that male sexual aggression is natural and normal within dating relationships, or is the victim's fault (Weiss 2009).

The social construction of sexual violence ensures that many of its forms are simply not acknowledged, thus confusing the issue of accountability and contributing to impunity.

Patriarchy, Gender-Inequitable Attitudes and Masculinity

Feminist views of rape (Brownmiller 1975) posit that the patriarchal structure of society perpetuates sexual violence against women. Various elements of patriarchal systems are implicated in this: male dominance and entitlement, rigid gender roles, gender relations that are adversarial, hostile or misogynistic, and constructions of gender, particularly of masculinity, that promote violence against women. Violence is used to maintain the hierarchy of men over women, of some men over other men, and is also self-inflicted as men struggle to mould the self into their society's version of masculinity (Kaufman 1999). This violence is perpetuated because it receives explicit or tacit permission in social customs, legal codes, law enforcement and religious teachings.

Cross-cultural studies have found reliable differences between 'rape-prone' and 'rape-free' societies. In her study of 156 tribal societies, Sanday (1981) found that 'rape-prone' societies were more gender inequitable and aggressive. The genders were more segregated, women were less powerful, ideas of male dominance prevailed, and war and interpersonal violence were common.

Gender-inequitable attitudes endorsing male domination, sexual entitlement, physical chastisement of women and rigid gender roles are found to be associated with sexual violence in a number of studies. The findings of a multi-country study on men and gender equality (Barker et al. 2011) that covered India, Mexico, Rwanda, Brazil, Chile and Croatia clearly indicate that men who hold gender-inequitable attitudes are more likely to use intimate partner violence (IPV) and sexual violence. In India, a large-sample study of domestic violence concludes that the normative pathway for domestic violence is through the fostering of norms that condone men's sense of entitlement and ownership of women, support the use of violence in conflict resolution, and condone physical punishment of women (Koenig et al. 2006). They also found that women married to more educated husbands experienced significantly higher risks of coercive sexual intercourse, and note a significant relationship between childlessness, and physical and sexual violence. It would appear that threats to conventional gender-related expectations can elicit violence and that the attenuating effects of education are limited. In Pakistan, domestic violence is normalized and justified on the grounds that men are the guardians of women, and wives deserve to be chastised if they refuse sex, are negligent in child care, or are unfaithful (Fikree, Razzak and Durocher 2005; Zakar, Zakar and Kraemer 2013). Studies in the US indicate that the strongest predictors of severe partner abuse are low sex-role egalitarianism and approval of marital violence, and that men who adhere to traditional gender roles and have adversarial attitudes towards women are consistently more sexually aggressive with women than men with more egalitarian attitudes (Heise 1998). The gender hierarchy in patriarchal systems that legitimates the use of physical violence by men to assert dominance and to discipline women also finds expression in sexual violence. Studies confirm that men who are physically violent towards a partner are also more likely to use sexual violence against partners as well as rape non-partners (Jewkes 2012).

The most common motive that men endorse for rape is sexual entitlement, as seen in settings as diverse as South Africa (Jewkes et al. 2011), Bangladesh (Naved et al. 2011), Sri Lanka (de Mel, Peiris and Gomez 2013). Female sexual rejection often leads to sexual violence since it challenges dominant male ideas about male sexual entitlement and female sexual availability, as well as contradicts what men perceive as an implicit contract between men and women, that is, resources, protection, marriage and so on in exchange for sex (Sigworth 2009).

Masculine ideals are implicated in sexual violence in different ways depending on how masculinity is defined in different settings. A study on men, masculinity and domestic violence in India found that, in Punjab, the maintenance of *mardangi* (manhood) is patterned around control over female sexuality and reproduction, and includes bodily access to women, aggressive sex and honour revenge. In Rajasthan, sex was commonly linked to violence because it is an important area where men can 'fail' at masculinity, for instance, when drunk and taunted for sexual failure (ICRW 2002). A review of sexuality research studies in India notes that frequent sexual activity, having multiple sexual partners, having many children and impregnating one's wife soon after marriage are considered significant indicators of masculinity (Chandiramani et al. 2002).

It is not that all constructions of masculinity are problematic; sexual violence is found to be linked to: (*a*) hypermasculine constructions, and (*b*) attempts to compensate for 'failed' masculinity. One of the most enduring factors promoting violence against women is a cultural definition of manhood that is linked to dominance, toughness and male honour. Mosher and Sirkin (1984) have labelled this the macho personality configuration or hypermasculinity. Hypermasculine men have calloused sexual attitudes toward women, see violence as manly and desirable, and view danger as exciting. Men high on hypermasculinity scales report a history of sexual coercion and force in dating situations (Heise 1998). Sexual aggression, because it contains attributes associated with masculinity—strength, power, forcefulness, domination, toughness—is regarded by these men as an activity that validates their masculinity. A meta-analytic study to identify which components of masculine ideology were associated with sexual aggression among men who had used sexual violence found that the strongest components were the construct of hostile masculinity and hypermasculinity, both of which involve negative, hostile beliefs about women, and acceptance of aggression against women (Murnen, Wright and Kaluzny 2002).

Another faultline for sexual violence is the disjunct between the ideal standards of masculinity and the lived reality of many men's lives (Sigworth 2009). The ideal assumes gainful employment, economic success and household headship. Failure to meet the standards set by the ideal can result in feelings of inadequacy and the need to give a 'performance' of masculinity that involves one of the hallmarks of masculinity: aggression. The taking of sex is a relatively simple but violent performance of masculinity that provides a way of feeling powerful and affirms tottering masculinity (Vogelman and Lewis 1993).

Thus, while violence against women occurs in all socioeconomic classes, it appears to be higher where men are unemployed and families have low incomes (Heise 1998). In her ethnographic exploration into group rape in an urban township in South Africa, Wood (2005) found multilayered deprivation in the lives of the young men, and a life trajectory that included childhood emotional neglect, fragmented family life, dropping out of school, leaving home or becoming street children, and a descent into petty criminality. She describes their experience of deprivation and violence transforming into an everyday violence characterized by interpersonal rage, delinquency, and a set of dehumanizing norms and relations. This provided the context for rapes of girls under 15 years of age and gang-rapes to be perpetrated 'for fun'. Another form of group-perpetrated rape called 'streamlining' is used by such men to punish women who think they are superior, who refuse sexual overtures, or who interfere with perceived masculine entitlements. Thus, the relationship of poverty to sexual violence may be mediated by ideas of masculinity and the quest for 'success' that young men from deprived backgrounds are unable to meet (Jewkes et al. 2011).

The role of the male peer group and male bonding is highly significant in sexual violence, particularly in group perpetration. This is addressed in more detail in the next section on group-level factors. Suffice it to say here that the male peer group can serve to mediate the learning and proving of masculinity through practices that may be sexually violent.

Less explored is how femininity under patriarchy mediates women's sexual victimhood. The social construction of femininity poses problems for women's sexual agency by compromising her sexual self-efficacy and objectifying her through sexualization. Conventional ideas about femininity involve relating in an inauthentic way in order to please others and avoid conflict, as well as to conform to prevailing ideas of attractiveness.

Such femininity was found to inhibit girls' sexual self-efficacy, defined as their conviction that they can act on their own sexual needs in relationships to enjoy sex, refuse unwanted sex and insist on protection (Impett, Schooler and Tolman 2006). These aspects complicate the issue of sexual consent and coercion.

The social construction of femininity also poses problems for women's sexual agency. Men's sexual script requires them to be the pursuer, their sexuality being active and urgent, while women's sexuality is supposed to be passive, awaiting activation by male desire. Where these notions prevail, forced sex is justified in the belief that women are constrained by the coyness demanded of femininity. On the other hand, women who transgress the norms of sexual modesty may be raped as a punitive measure. Perpetrators and victims of such acts of sexual aggression may not construe this as rape.

The American Psychological Association's *Report of the APA Task Force on the Sexualization of Girls* (2007) is relevant in this context. Sexualization is distinct from healthy sexuality, and occurs when a person's value is equated with sexual appeal and she is sexually objectified—that is, made into a thing for others' sexual use rather than seen as a person in her own right with capacity for independent choice and action. Societal messages that contribute to the sexualization of girls come from the media, merchandizing and girls' interpersonal relationships. Self-objectification is a key process whereby girls learn to think of and treat their bodies as objects of male desire, leading to some dissociation from their own desire and thus sexual agency. This has implications for transactional sex and its exploitation, and is relevant to instances where women have engaged in consensual sexual relations, often over a period of time, in the belief that it would secure them a marriage or a job.

Impunity for sexual violence thrives under these conditions. First, the fact that social attitudes and practices normalize, tolerate and even condone rape means that sexually violent acts can be committed without being acknowledged as a violation or as harmful. Second, gender-based structural violence melds into the direct violence of physical and sexual violence. Within patriarchy, male dominance and notions of masculinity lead to men's 'right' to use, control and discipline women. This socialized sense of entitlement along with the social devaluation of women obscures the ability to perceive sexual violence as harmful, and a violation of human rights and dignity.

A third contribution to impunity comes from the stigma and shame associated with rape, which prevents many victims from seeking justice. This is especially marked in cultures where patriarchy and the ideology of 'honour' are powerful forces, women are the repositories of honour, and female chastity is highly valued. Indeed, it is expected in some such communities that a raped woman should kill herself to avoid further dishonour to her family. The outcome is that perpetrators of sexual violence escape accountability.

Sexuality-Related Concerns

Sexuality is an area fraught with confusion, misconception and anxiety, and shrouded in secrecy and shame in the South Asian context. Analysis of data from a sexuality and reproductive health helpline in Delhi covering a period of ten years and over 40,000 calls (TARSHI 2007) reveals that people lack basic information about their bodies and sexuality, and what information they have comes from pornographic films, misinformed friends and internet sites. Common misconceptions encountered on the helpline were that nocturnal emissions and masturbation are harmful, causing weakness, infertility and pimples; women do not masturbate; sex with a virgin cures STDs and AIDS; it is a woman's duty to have sex with her husband on demand; oral sex can lead to pregnancy whereas anal sex is safe sex; and only peno-vaginal intercourse is 'real' sex. Sexual processes are defined in male terms, and arousal and orgasm are thought to occur in the same way for men and women. There is lack of information about differences in sexual responsiveness between men and women, and sexual anxieties are marked as evidenced in concerns about semen loss and sexual performance. Many men compare their performance with what they see in pornographic films or friends' accounts of sexual exploits.

From a review of Indian studies conducted in the decade 1990–2000 (Chandiramani et al. 2002), it is seen that premarital and extramarital sex are prevalent in both rural and urban areas despite being frowned upon and despite the majority of adolescents saying that sexual activity should begin after marriage. Mass media, including television, films, newspapers, billboards and hoardings, is quoted as the single most cited source of information about sexual matters. The lack of accurate information about sexuality and opposition to sex education combined with the prevalence of furtive sexual activity and double standards can make young girls especially vulnerable to sexual coercion.

Although the evidence for a causal relationship between pornography and sexual aggression in correlational, and experimental studies and in the real world violent crime data is slim (Ferguson and Hartley 2009), it is possible that exposure to sexually explicit material contributes to the construction of young people's sexual scripts, that is, their cognitive maps of what sexuality is like and, consequently, how to navigate it. Pornography can influence the scripting of sexual roles for self and expectations of partner, what constitutes sexiness and good sexual performance, and the linkage between sexuality, intimacy, emotion and power. Studies indicate that exposure to erotic films had the most effect on those males who were repressed sexually or were deprived of sexual socialization (Fisher and Byrne 1978). It is likely that where there are social restrictions on talking openly about sex, the distorted sexual world depicted in pornography becomes the source of information. Sexual aggression towards women may be derived from common pornographic portrayals of women as sexually voracious and non-discriminating, and depictions that show women enjoying forced sex.

Cultural expressions of romantic and sexual fantasy in popular Hindi films depict force and physical aggression as legitimate means of expressing romantic love. Sexual harassment involving physical force is portrayed as fun and a normal expression of romantic love, and the perpetrator is seen as a macho man (Ramasubramaniam and Oliver 2003). In a context where talk of sex is taboo and sources of information limited, films become a powerful means through which young men learn about sex and intimacy (Derne 1999). These films eroticize dominance and submission, equate love and force, portray threat and harassment as appealing to women, and teach that women exist for men's pleasure. They thus influence the sexual scripts that inform desire and influence sexual behaviour. The visual 'groping' in Bollywood 'item numbers' where the camera zooms in on a dancing woman's gyrating body parts while she exults in the male attention, fuses excitement with transgression and blurs the line between what is allowed and what is not (Geetha 2013).

Such notions are not confined to South Asia. Adolescents in Spain link attractiveness with violence so that toughness, callousness and dominance are seen as attractive in men, whereas dialogue and tenderness are boring (Valls, Puigvert and Duque 2008), and in South African youth culture, forced sex is seen as 'showing roughness in a beautiful way' (Wood, Lambert and Jewkes 2007).

Acceptance of Violence

A key risk factor for the pervasiveness of violence is the social acceptance of interpersonal violence to discipline and punish, enforce submission, express displeasure and resolve disputes. The eulogization of violence as an appropriate tool to get what one wants means that it is not socially censured, but rather provides additional social status to the perpetrator (Vogelman and Lewis 1993). This is especially so when the violence is in the service of some so-called 'noble' end such as the defence of national honour, moral order, religious sentiment and so on. Societies that have a high degree of violence in general also have greater likelihood of sexual violence. In India, a significant association between rates of violent crime and domestic violence was found with residents in areas characterized by higher murder rates having significantly higher likelihood of physical and sexual violence against wives (Koenig et al. 2006). Sanday's (1981) cross-cultural study of rape found that violence against women was more likely in cultures that condoned the use of force as a way for adults to resolve conflict. Baron, Strauss and Jaffee (1988) correlated the incidence of rape with cultural support for violence across fifty US states and found a significant association. They argue that that the endorsement of physical force 'spills over' or is generalized to spheres of life where force is not approved of, such as within the family. Acceptance of interpersonal violence, along with hostility towards women and early childhood exposure to violence, is a factor that strongly discriminates sexually aggressive from non-aggressive males (Koss and Dinero 1989).

Special mention may be made of militarized societies where the use of violent means to resolve conflict has become natural, and everyday life is saturated with violent imagery and ideas of combat, battle, fighting, martyrdom, victory, defeat, heroes and traitors. Saigol (2008) describes this in the context of Pakistan as she delineates the complex interweaving of military values, love and desire for the nation, and the gender ideology that constructs the nation-state as the mother who has to be defended and whose dishonour must be avenged. This form of nationalism frames women as symbols of the nation's culture and honour so that desecration of women through sexual violence becomes, on the one hand, a matter of national shame requiring revenge, and on the other, a triumphant violent appropriation. These dynamics have been described in the context of sexual violence during the Partition (Menon and Bhasin 1998).

State and Civil Institutions

The cultural ideology, norms and practices of gender that provide the 'cultural scaffolding' for sexual violence stretch across and into private and public spaces, and are replicated in formal and informal social institutions, including the state and its arms, such as the police, military and judiciary, quasi-formal institutions like caste and *khap* panchayats, and tribal councils, as well as the education system and the family.

The family is the primary site for socialization into society's normative gender roles and sometimes violent practices (Heise 1998), and educational institutions, instead of being sites for the questioning mind and the learning of critical thinking, replicate dominant sociocultural beliefs and attitudes. Legislation, law enforcement and the judiciary are directly involved in sexual violence prevention and prosecution. But seemingly neutral laws are deeply inscribed by the sociocultural norms of society. Thus, laws in India reflect the discourse that frames women as bearers of purity, modesty and honour (Sen 2012), and do not recognize marital rape. Law enforcement agencies like the police routinely use torture in interrogation and reports of custodial rape are plenty. The police are also known to physically chastise people who are not breaking any law but are seen as transgressing norms of 'decency', and fail to take action against civilian 'moral police' who do the same. Cases of police refusal to register complaints of rape and court proceedings that are humiliating and disparaging of victims abound.

The state is directly implicated in sexual violence when it tolerates or fails to punish its military personnel who perpetrate sexual crimes in war, allowing such violations to be immune from prosecution, for example, under laws such as the Indian Armed Forces (Special Powers) Act. The state is also complicit when sexual violence is used as a 'weapon of war' and sexual torture is part of interrogation. A state that is militarized is more likely to support the 'cultural scaffolding' of rape. Military cultures actively teach and enforce a definition of manhood that is aggressive, heterosexual and defined in terms of a negation of femininity.

Militarization involves a belief system that endorses military values in civilian life, believes in the construction of a strong masculinity and a 'muscular' state, legitimizes the use of violence to resolve conflict and dissent, and intersects with patriarchies and nationalisms in notions of national honour and national pride (Chenoy 2012). Civilian regimes can be promoters of militarization, for instance, where national chauvinistic ideology or religious fundamentalism is a dominating force in the state.

When state political power is in the hands of ethno-nationalistic groups, it is more likely that regressive actions deleterious to the position of women in society will be adopted. Ethno-nationalist movements tend to have patriarchal values, frequently demand the implementation of 'customary' laws unfavourable to women, and express their nationalism through notions of honour and shame (Srivastava 2012). Thus, for example, under the Sharia or Islamic law, victims of sexual violence are unlikely to find the required witnesses to the crime and may end up being prosecuted themselves for fornication.

The ideology of honour and shame common across South Asia also pervades local social institutions like Indian caste councils (*khap* panchayat) or tribal councils. Within this ideology, women are the repositories of honour for their families, communities and castes, while men enforce and avenge honour. Within the frame of this ideology, instead of perpetrators being punished, victims of sexual violence are blamed and shamed into silence because of the stigma of dishonour.

Caste violence frequently involves sexual violence and it is estimated that at least four Dalit women are raped every day (AIDMAM 2012). The institution of caste legitimizes the power and entitlements of higher castes, including sexual entitlement to the bodies of Dalit women (Irudayam, Mangubhai and Lee 2006), and challenges to traditional caste dominance and caste boundaries are met with punitive violence, including rape. The entrenched nature of the caste system ensures that upper-caste Hindu perpetrators will be protected at all levels of the justice system, and members of the police, judiciary and public officials often collude to keep Dalit women from filing claims and receiving justice.

Where the 'cultural scaffolding' for sexual violence extends into the state and its agencies as well as into other institutions of civil society, the task of ensuring accountability and securing justice is seriously compromised. It underlines the importance of 'untainted' or 'less tainted' spaces—human rights groups, women's activist groups, international bodies, etc.—that can be vigilant and provide critique.

The sociocultural level of analysis, dealing as it does with systemic and structural factors, raises two issues regarding accountability—that of structure and agency, and the question of collective responsibility of men for sexual violence. Men may be collectively responsible as participants in patriarchy where wrongs are linked to pervasive social norms even when they are not directly responsible for perpetration. They may be stabilizing the practice through habits of toleration and perpetuating a rape culture by speaking in certain ways or failing to speak out or intervene (Kirby 2013). But the idea of moral agency and responsibility are undermined when we think about the effects of social structure on action; moral agency and moral responsibility are possible only within social orders in which there exist milieus that sustain the relevant kind of self-understanding, critical thinking and accountability required to challenge harmful social roles (MacIntyre 1999). Paradoxically, the more rigidly patriarchal the context, the less free and conscious are participants in patriarchy in their understanding of gender and how their subjectivity has been shaped, and consequently, the less morally culpable are the actors within these roles (Kirby 2013). It has, however, been argued that since individuals must use 'compartmentalization' to create 'blamelessly compliant lives' for themselves while inhabiting harmful social roles, they are morally responsible despite the social structure in which they are embedded (MacIntyre 1999).

The sociocultural level of explanation falls short in that the damaging effects of sociocultural factors, while widespread, are not all-pervasive. In fact, the vast majority of men are not sexually violent as seen in the prevalence rates. These factors may be best understood as vulnerability or distal factors, to use public health language. Whether they will eventuate in sexually violent acts is likely mediated by other sets of factors that have to do with how groups function and with individual variation, to which we now turn.

GROUP LEVEL

Groups are powerful vehicles through which sociocultural influences work. They include primary groups, such as the family, and other ambits of involvement, such as the peer group, school, work-related groups, religious groups and so on. The group level of analysis is especially relevant to multiple-perpetrator sexual violence, which by definition involves more than one person and, therefore, must be considered a social process (Harkins and Dixon 2010).

People acting in groups are not the same as when alone. Groups exert pressure for conformity to group beliefs and norms, and members comply to belong and to reinforce their social identity. Pressures to conform to group norms and participate in group-endorsed activities become harder to resist in actual situations where emotionality is high and there is fear of mockery or rejection for refusing to participate.

Groups typically operate within certain settings and behaviour is partly determined by the 'pull' of the setting. This situationist perspective in social psychology has been usefully applied to understand how ordinary people come to act abusively, the 'Lucifer effect' (Zimbardo 2004, 2007), and demonstrates the power of situations and systems on behaviour. Early social psychological experiments showed that ordinary people regularly and reliably carry out violence when authorized to do so. In Milgram's (1974) experiments, people of varying backgrounds and educational levels were invited to participate in a 'learning experiment' that required them to administer electric shocks (faked) when a learner (who was actually a confederate) made a mistake. Under orders from the scientist looking on, they delivered shocks they believed to be high-voltage and continued to do so despite the loud distress of the learner. Zimbardo's (2007) mock prison experiment, the Stanford Prison Experiment (SPE), demonstrated ordinary people becoming abusive simply by virtue of the role assigned to them. In the study, those volunteer students who were randomly assigned the role of guards became increasingly humiliating and cruel in their treatment of prisoners so that the experiment had to be abandoned in a few days.

Extending his analysis to the highly sexualized prisoner abuse at Abu Ghraib prison in Iraq, Zimbardo (2007) also highlights the fact that abuse and violence are not just the creation of situations, but also of the system that provides the support, authority and resources that allow situations and settings to operate the way they do. Systemic power provides the 'higher authority' that allows pre-existing laws, norms and ethics to be bypassed, and explicitly or tacitly gives validation to new rules and actions. Lankford (2009) draws similar conclusions about prisoner abuse at Abu Ghraib pointing to the role of increased authorization by the US political and military leadership to use violent tactics and harsh interrogation methods to 'soften' detainees. This aspect has important implications for accountability and impunity. When the system within which the abuse takes place is a state institution like the police or the military, or an institution that enjoys social credibility, such as an educational or religious institution, a caste/*khap* panchayat or tribal council, the question of institutional responsibility arises. Institutions are morally responsible when they actively support or condone abuse, or when they fail to stop and punish it, since in the system they hold 'higher authority'. This authority is typically vested in the leaders or those in command, who then become morally accountable even if they were not directly involved in the abuse.

Group processes related to identity construction of the self and other are implicated in violence perpetration through the virtuous aggrandizement of the self (for instance, in terms of lineage, righteousness, purity, valour, honour, manliness and so on) and dehumanization of the other. These dynamics are evident in some war contexts and other inter-group conflicts associated with ethnic, caste or sectarian concerns. Sexual violence here is driven by the intersection of group identity assertion with patriarchal, masculinist dynamics. In contrast, a certain kind of hypermasculine socialization and male bonding is primary in the sexual violence typical of delinquent gangs and in contexts such as fraternity parties.

In both kinds of scenario, group processes compromise moral accountability. They reset individual moral radar through de-individuation, that is, the loss of a person's sense of individual identity and personal responsibility. De-individuation leads to diffusion of responsibility as perpetrators feel personally anonymous as identities merge with the group. Thus, much of the training of combatants involves de-individuation of both the self and the enemy. This is because it is easier for an individual to attack or kill another human being when personal responsibility is removed by his immersion in the group, and the victim is an impersonal representative of the enemy group (Castano, Leidner and Slawuta 2008).

A second process that enables moral disengagement (Bandura 1990, 1999) is by reconstructing heinous conduct as morally justified or by using euphemistic labelling that casts it in a different light. This ranges from seemingly worthy ideological objectives such as 'purifying' or 'cleansing' society albeit through rape, impregnation and murder of vilified ethnic groups, to 'streamlining' through gang-rape of women who transgress gender norms and challenge male dominance, to the national security imperatives that authorize sexual torture of detainees in interrogation.

A third process involved in moral disengagement is dehumanization and blaming of victims. Dehumanization refers to the attachment of subhuman qualities to another, thus justifying offensive behaviour towards them. It is most often mentioned in relation to ethnicity, race and related topics, such as genocidal conflicts. It is also applied to women in that women as a class are often assigned lesser humanness than men, and femaleness is associated with animality, nature, childlikeness, and lesser degrees of emotional control, reason and civility (Haslam 2006).

Dehumanization is discussed in feminist writings on the representation of women in pornography, where they are sexually objectified, by implication removing them from full moral consideration, and legitimating rape and victimization. Indeed, it has been argued that the widespread rapes in the Bosnia–Herzegovina war were preconditioned by the prior saturation of Yugoslavia with pornography, resulting in a dehumanization of women that encouraged sexualized brutality (MacKinnon 1994).

Dehumanization is also an expression of moral exclusion relevant to inter-group violence. In their theory of moral exclusion and justice, Opotow et al. (2005) suggest that our scope of justice is the psychological boundary within which concerns about fairness govern our conduct. Those who are inside this boundary for fairness are morally included and form our 'moral community'. Those outside are morally excluded and the harms that may come to them are ignored or condoned as normal, inevitable or deserved. This has significance for accountability and impunity in that by being placed outside the zone of those who belong within our moral universe, some groups are excluded from the moral considerations that would otherwise guide conduct.

Alcohol is an important situational factor in sexual violence perpetration, given its psychological effects and cultural meanings (Jewkes 2012), and is consistently reported in association with other factors in sexual violence perpetration. Abbey et al. (2004; 2006) and Abbey (2008) review relevant studies and make the important point that although half of all sexual assaults are associated with the perpetrator's alcohol consumption, the victim's alcohol consumption or both, alcohol is not a factor that causes men who would otherwise not use sexual coercion to become sexually aggressive. Research shows that it is the belief that one has consumed alcohol that provides men with justification for engaging in socially inappropriate behaviour. Indeed, many cultures or subcultures allow alcohol consumption to mitigate accountability for antisocial or aggressive behaviour.

The two dynamic strands mentioned earlier, namely, male socialization into a certain kind of masculinity, and the development of adversarial identities and inter-group conflict within patriarchal systems are described later in greater detail along with the settings associated with sexual violence.

Masculinity and Male Bonding

In her review, Heise (1998) finds that the peer group plays an important role in encouraging sexual aggression, especially among adolescent males. Having sexual access to women and being sexually active is admired in the peer group and peer pressure becomes an important factor in sexual aggression. Thus, among men who admitted to having raped a woman during a date, 41 per cent had engaged in group intercourse with a female compared to 7 per cent of men in the control group who had never raped a woman (Kanin 1985). Young men who were sexually, emotionally and physically abusive in dating relationships also had male friends who were abusive to women, had patriarchal attitudes, and exerted pressure on one another toward abuse (DeKeseredy and Kelly 1993). The male peer group is highly significant for male socialization into a masculinity that demeans the feminine, values toughness and aggression as the mark of 'real' men, encourages non-relational sexuality, constrains emotionality, and is driven by needs for dominance, power and control. This 'hypermasculinity' has been noted in the previous sociocultural-level section.

A significant aspect of this kind of male bonding is rejection and contempt of all that is feminine, including purging the self of any feminine qualities. Sexist joking is a humdrum example. Group perpetration of rape as a rite of passage into manhood is a more sinister one. Bourgois (1996) describes gang-rapes perpetrated by the immigrant Puerto Rican youth he studied as rituals through which they 'achieve their manhood' and which bond them 'homoerotically and misogynistically'. Making women drunk or drugged so as to perpetrate group rape, called 'pulling train', as documented in some fraternities (Sanday 2007), reflects extreme dehumanizing sexual objectification of women in the service of male bonding. Delinquent street gangs, college fraternities and military training institutions are settings that are commonly associated with such dynamics.

Delinquent gangs are generally contexts in which there is an exaggerated performance of heterosexuality with competition among members to demonstrate manhood. They are also contexts in which young men use substances and have weapons, all of which may situationally impact on sexual violence perpetration (Jewkes 2012). Sexually violent men are significantly more likely than others to have been members of a gang in the US (Borowsky, Hogan and Ireland 1997) and in South Africa (Jewkes et al. 2006, 2011), where they were also more likely to have been involved in other interpersonal crimes, to have raped a man and to have a weapon.

In the subculture of gangs, gang-rape cements the bonds between male members as they share the same woman as sexual object and demonstrate their virility to peers (Bourgois 1996; Harkins and Dixon 2010; Vogelman and Lewis 1993). In the US, females peripheral to a gang who want to become gang members are at risk for sexual exploitation and may be conned into participating in group sex initiations called 'being sexed in'. In some scenarios, such as that of the 'jackrollers' in South Africa, the victim is selected for degradation and humiliation because of her perceived class or status, or because she is seen as a snob who is out of reach. Such so-called 'streamlining' reflects in extreme forms of patriarchal notions that men and women are inherently in a hierarchical relation, that men can and should play a disciplining role when women are perceived to transgress—for instance, disrespecting their partner, publicly undermining their sense of masculinity, being sexually unfaithful, undermining their boyfriends' relationships with other women, refusing sex, behaving outside gender norms, being successful, or imagining she could be superior (Wood 2005).

Within some fraternity subcultures, having sex with as many women as possible becomes a critical measure of how men view themselves and each other. The use of coercion and violence to secure these conquests is normalized and becomes part of men's sexual arsenal along with the use of alcohol and drugs to weaken resistance (Lisak 2011). Highly masculinist features characterize the norms and dynamics of fraternity brotherhood (Martin and Hummer 1989). These include a narrow, stereotypical conception of masculinity and heterosexuality, a preoccupation with loyalty to the group, the use of alcohol as weapon against women's sexual reluctance, an obsession with competition, superiority and dominance, and the pervasive use of violence and physical force. The use of violent pornography may be a frequent form of entertainment, providing explicit images of rape as a sign of male virility. In some cases, a woman may consent to sex with one member but find that others have entered the room and proceed to engage in sexual activities that she may be too afraid or drunk to effectively prevent or protest (Sanday 2007).

Intergroup Conflict and Sexual Violence

Understanding sexual violence occurring in the context of intergroup aggression, such as during war and caste or ethnic conflicts, requires understanding how patriarchal and masculinist gender ideology plays into the construction—assertion and devaluation—of social identities (national, ethnic, caste, religion and so on).

The essentialist argument that holds that wartime sexual violence is an accentuation of the gender inequalities and misogyny that predates the conflict, and that all women are potential targets of a militarized masculinity (Brownmiller 1975) is not borne out by the evidence of wide variation in wartime sexual violence and the fact that men are also sexually victimized. Although militaristic norms may strengthen patriarchal social practices that support sexual violence and marital and opportunistic sexual violence may become more frequent during war, research using very large data sets indicates that wartime rape is neither ubiquitous nor inevitable, and levels of sexual violence differ significantly across countries, conflicts and particularly armed groups (Cohen, Green and Wood 2013; Cohen and Nordas 2014). Rape is widespread in some conflicts but not in others; armed groups even within the same war do not perpetrate sexual violence to the same extent or in the same forms; an armed group that refrains from sexual violence at one stage of the war may perpetrate it on a large scale at other times; and some armed groups can and do prohibit sexual violence (Wood 2006). Further, the frequency of wartime rape does not correlate with the relative strengths of pre-war patriarchy in a linear fashion and there is marked asymmetry in sexual violence patterns among armed groups that share similar patriarchal cultures (ibid.).

The patterns of perpetration also do not support the theory that sexual violence during war occurs because men get the opportunity to indulge 'uncontrollable' sexual desire. Most men, given the opportunity, do not rape; even during the chaos of war, close contact with civilians is often unaccompanied by rape (ibid.). The idea that rape of civilians is a substitute for consensual sex is not borne out by the fact that widespread rape is perpetrated by some groups in which fighters have regular access to sex workers or sex slaves, and sexual desire alone does not explain the extreme brutality of sexual violence and high frequency of gang-rape during war.

Recent research also indicates that perpetrators are not exclusively male and victims are not exclusively female. Female combatants sometimes perpetrate rape and other forms of sexual violence, as has been documented in the Democratic Republic of Congo, Haiti, Rwanda and Abu Ghraib (Cohen, Green and Wood 2013). This is attributed to the fact that female combatants face the same pressures to perpetrate sexual violence as their male peers, and the stresses on them to conform to norms of masculinity and strength is strong. Female combatant perpetration of sexual violence is also explained in terms of 'combat socialization' whereby group perpetration of sexual violence serves to strengthen cohesion among fighters who were forcibly recruited or abducted (Cohen 2013).

An alternative conceptualization of sexual violence associated with inter-group aggression is that in our heteronormative cultures, masculinity is equated with power and femininity with its lack. All victims of sexual violence, male and female, are feminized by their victimization, and by extension, their national, ethnic, religious, caste or political group is also feminized, disempowered and emasculated (Skjelsbaek 2001). Sexual violence is thus a powerful tool to humiliate and disempower the hated other. This is especially true of ethnic conflicts. Indeed, ethnic cleansing campaigns are among early warning indicators for sexual violence during conflict (Cohen, Green and Wood 2013).

Systematic mass rape has been used as an instrument of ethnically specific oppression and terror during the conflicts in Rwanda, the former Yugoslavia and during ethnic riots in South Asia. Ethnically motivated sexual violence in the former Yugoslavia (Price 2001) and during the riots in Gujarat, India, in 2002 (Nussbaum 2004) was particularly vicious, involving gang-rape, rape with objects, genital mutilation, physical and sexual torture, and humiliation. A form of sexual violence in the former Yugoslavia was the enforced pregnancy of women kept in rape camps and repeatedly raped until pregnant, the transformative 'ethnicized sperm' of the perpetrator group asserting dominance while annihilating the other (Price 2001). Similar dynamics characterized the sexual violence of the 1971 Bangladesh war for independence. Members of the Pakistani army and their supporters are reported to have raped more than 200,000 Bengali Muslims and members of the Hindu minority in erstwhile East Pakistan. The women were abducted, raped, murdered and bayoneted in their genitalia. Hundreds of women were held in 'rape camps' and forcibly impregnated (D'Costa 2013). The rapes were so systematic and widespread that it was thought to be part of a conscious policy to create a new race or dilute Bengali nationalism (Brownmiller 1975). Earlier, during India's Partition in 1947, the abduction and impregnation of women became an important weapon in the struggle of the two emerging nations to consolidate power. It also led to the killing of women by their kinsmen so that they would not be raped and impregnated by the other community, thus diluting the purity of the race (Butalia 1998).

In conflicts where sexual violence has been thoroughly investigated, as in the former Yugoslavia, the sexual victimization of men is recognized as widespread, although not at the rate of sexual violence committed against women. There is significant under-reporting as men are loath to talk about being sexually victimized, considering this incompatible with their masculinity. Sexual violence towards men in custody has been described in Sri Lanka (Human Rights Watch 2013) and in Kashmir (Sonpar 2007). Sivakumaran (2007) documents the forms of wartime sexual violence men suffer to include rape, forced sterilization, forced nudity, forced masturbation, genital violence and mutilation, and 'enforced rape' of others. He hypothesizes that power, dominance and emasculation play important roles in targeting men for such abuses. The emasculation or loss of manhood is done through 'feminization' or 'homosexualization', and damage to procreative capacity by beatings, shocks and other genital violence. Drawing on her research on war crimes in the former Yugoslavia, Zarkov (2001) suggests that the invisibility of sexual violence towards men by other men is related to the position of masculinity and the male body within nationalist discourse on ethnicity and nationhood. Sexual humiliation of a man through sexual assault and homosexualization is proof that he is a lesser man. When he is an ethnic other, his sexual humiliation is also proof that his ethnicity is of an inferior nature

Sexual violence during wartime implicating trained military forces can be traced to three factors. First, the subcultural context of militarism founded on the acceptance of interpersonal violence and the values of hypermasculinty and hypersexuality can be identified as one kind of faultline. Significantly, training and hazing often rely on abusive sexualized gender stereotypes. Several aspects of military culture are conducive to sexual violence, including sexualized and violent language, general acceptance of violence, and the learned ability to objectify other people. The removal of ordinary inhibitions against violence and killing, accomplished through training that involves endless drilling and desensitization to attacking human targets (Grossman 2009), may compromise moral judgement and behaviour. Recruits are themselves dehumanized through abuse, physical punishment and sometimes sexual violence. Turchik and Wilson (2010) report studies that show high levels of sexual violence in the US military against both women and men. While women in the military have far higher rates of sexual victimization, men who served in the military are now coming forward with long-buried stories of their rape, including gang-rape, by seniors. Once deployed, the increasing desensitization of combatants, the dehumanization of victims, the extreme dichotomies of 'us' and 'them' that make 'enemy' women fair targets, the anxiety of combat, and the threat of injury and death, pressures to acquiesce out of fear of punishment for disobedience, and conformity to the behaviour of others in the unit enhance the possibility of reprehensible conduct. The brutalizing impact of killing and witnessing death and injury contribute to a 'grotesque alienation from peacetime' (Henry, Ward and Hirshberg 2004: 548) that leads to emotional states conducive to sexual violence, while the alcohol, drugs and pornography that are reportedly widespread in war contexts act as further disinhibitors. Adding the voices of perpetrators to the analysis of why soldiers rape, Baaz and Stern (2004) show through their interviews with state army soldiers in the Democratic Republic of Congo that sexual violence may be located in the mismatch between the embodied experience of these men and their aspirations to inhabit idealized but impossible masculine positions (such as fighter and provider) within contexts of poverty, neglect, deprivation and the abnormal climate of 'warscapes'.

Second, the prevention of sexual violence under these conditions requires that strict regulatory mechanisms are in place and effective sanctions are enforced against combatants perpetrating sexual violence. Failure in this regard constitutes another faultline. If individual combatants and their units endorse norms against sexual violence and commanders prohibit violence, little sexual violence will occur. Examining the case of Sri Lanka, Wood (2009) notes the frequent instances of state-sponsored or condoned rape of Tamil girls and women at checkpoints and during military or police operations, and contrasts this with the rare allegations of sexual violence against civilians by members of the Liberation Tigers of Tamil Eelam (LTTE) despite the fact that the LTTE was known for its brutality against civilians. She holds that this is best explained by the fact that such violence was banned by the leadership and strictly enforced. This asymmetry implies that the causes of wartime rape operate at the level of the armed group, not at the level of the conflict or the country (Cohen, Green and Wood 2013), a finding with important implications for accountability. Studies also show that more sexual violence occurs within military units where the commanding officer is neutral or indifferent to abuse compared to units where there is zero tolerance for sexual violence (Turchik and Wilson 2010). Wartime rape is more frequently tolerated than ordered by commanders (Cohen, Green and Wood 2013) who do so because effective prohibition may entail disciplining otherwise capable troops or withholding what combatants perceive to be the appropriate spoils of war. In this context, accountability extends to command responsibility where military leaders are held to have certain moral and command obligations, regardless of whether they were directly involved in the perpetration of violence.

Third, sexual violence can be part of deliberate military strategy, a 'weapon of war'. Its deployment in the war for the independence of Bangladesh is thought to be the first instance of mass war rape to attract international media attention. Later, indigenous women and girls of the Chittagong Hill Tracts, the site of an insurgency in Bangladesh, were targeted for rape by the military and by Bengali settlers in a project of ethnic cleansing that has not ended (Chakma and Hill 2013). In the Bosnia–Herzegovina conflict, Bosnian Serb forces practised widespread and systematic rape of Bosnian Muslims as ordered or condoned by key military figures (Price 2001). In Guatemala, deliberate sexual violence was part of the campaign of generalized terror and repression against indigenous civilian peasantry, whereas in Peru it was selectively perpetrated on suspected opponents of the state (Leiby 2009).

A more routine use of sexual violence is in the context of custodial interrogation and torture widespread in the countries of South Asia. It was used by Sri Lankan forces against Tamil men and women in state custody (Human Rights Watch 2013) and by Indian security forces against Kashmiri detainees (De Jong et al. 2006; Public Commission on Human Rights 2006; Sonpar 2007). In Nepal, government forces raped female Maoist combatants after arrest and also targeted female relatives of Maoist suspects or supporters (Human Rights Watch 2014).

Caste conflict is another inter-group conflict associated with sexual violence, particularly in India. Sexual violence against low-caste women in India exemplifies how gender and caste intersect to doubly oppress victims. Irudayam, Mangubhai and Lee (2006), in their study of violence against Dalit women in four Indian states, found that 46.8 per cent experienced sexual harassment and assault, and 23.2 per cent were raped. The verbal abuse to which two-thirds were subjected involved caste-related epithets and sexually-explicit insults, reflecting the view of Dalit women as sexually available. Dominant-caste landlords emerged as the most prominent group among perpetrators. The majority of Dalit women were found to have faced violence in public spaces, such as streets, women's toilet area, bus stands and fields in and around their villages and towns, indicating the abusers' confidence that they need not fear social or legal sanction.

Kannabiran and Kannabiran (1991) draw attention to the many cases of sexual violence against young Dalit girls in social welfare and missionary hostels by men in powerful positions, and the failure of the government machinery in checking this abuse and bringing the aggressors to book. Sexual violence in this case arises from upper-caste sexual entitlement to the bodies of Dalit women, and also serves as punishment for transgressing caste norms, refusing sexual advances, refusing to work for the landowners, demanding higher wages, and asserting rights over resources and public spaces. Sexual assault, rape, gang-rape and naked parading are used to maintain Dalit women's subordination and to humiliate the entire Dalit community. In their analysis of power dynamics associated with caste and gender, Kannabiran and Kannabiran (ibid.) show how force is deployed by the upper castes to enforce maintenance of the traditional order and reinforce caste demarcation, even as traditionally oppressed castes are gaining power through education and mobility.

Despite the existence of constitutional safeguards and special laws, impunity for crimes against Dalits is widespread, with caste-based discrimination permeating all levels of the criminal and justice system, and convictions for caste-related crimes being less than 10 per cent. The Indian government insists that discrimination based on caste does not fall under the scope of the International Convention on Elimination of All Forms of Racial Discrimination and has yet to endorse the UN Principles and Guidelines on Discrimination Based on Work and Descent, which outlines measures to counter caste discrimination.

States are obviously complicit when government forces are involved in sexual violence perpetration. Unfortunately, in most of these cases, the excuse of national security or maintenance of troop morale enables a cover-up of gross human rights violations, including sexual violence. With regard to Kashmir, for example, Pervez (2014) delineates a giant machinery of institutional suppression of accountability for sexual crimes committed by security forces. The culture of impunity pervades all levels of the criminal and justice system—from the police stations where cases must be filed and statements recorded, to investigations that are interfered with and evidence that is tampered with, to intimidation of plaintiffs by military and other officials, to biased commissions and an inefficient judiciary, to the invocation of laws such as the Armed Forces (Special Powers) Act 1990 that shields military personnel from prosecution. Another issue regarding accountability here is that of the culpability of those who ordered or incited violence even if they were not direct perpetrators.

While the chain of command responsibility in the military is clear, civilian leaders enjoying political clout who incite mob violence may be harder to pin down and thus escape accountability.

INDIVIDUAL LEVEL

What we have seen thus far is that the preconditions—or 'predisposing' factors—for sexual violence exist in our society and culture, and that this 'cultural scaffolding' is also embedded in our civil and state institutions. Accountability is fundamentally compromised when sociocultural attitudes tolerate or condone some forms of sexual violence and, importantly, when the state, its legal and law enforcement machinery, are permeated by these same biases. The probability of these preconditions eventuating in acts of sexual violence, particularly those perpetrated by multiple perpetrators, is increased in group contexts that involve a certain kind of male socialization and identity-based inter-group conflict.

The role and extent of individual choice and responsibility remains unaddressed in the aforementioned levels of analysis. Also unaddressed is the fact that the vast majority of men within the same sociocultural milieu do not perpetrate sexually violent acts. In spite of systemic, structural and group-situational contexts that are highly conducive to committing sexual violence, some individuals refrain despite considerable pressure and even threat of harm (Henry, Ward and Hirshbert 2004; Price 2001). Disputing the idea that contexts and situations invariably cause ordinary people to enter an agentic state in which judgement and moral restraint are suspended, Haslam and Reicher (2007) re-examine the evidence from the Stanford Prison Experiment (Zimbardo 2004, 2007)and the description of the 'ordinary' men of the Reserve Police Battalion 101, a mobile killing unit that roamed German-occupied Poland and murdered at least 38,000 Jews in 1942–43 (Browning 1992), and note considerable individual difference. In the Stanford Prison Experiment, some role playing prison guards sided with the prisoners, some were strict but fair, and some actively humiliated and abused prisoners. Similarly, a closer look at the men of the RPB 101 showed that some were 'enthusiastic killers', others confined action to the jobs assigned to them, and yet others refused or avoided killing. They conclude that while groups may push some individuals to act in consonance with group norms, many individuals are drawn to certain settings in the first place because of their personality dispositions.

The study of sexual violence had been biased towards individual pathology until feminist research revealed that sexual violence was not separate from the gendered continuum of violence that women suffer, and that structural, sociocultural conditions played a significant role. However, critics of the feminist and cultural theory of sexual violence decry an overemphasis on the concept of a 'rape culture', asserting that rapes are not caused by cultural factors but by the conscious choice of a small percentage of men. The focus on cultural factors removes the focus from the individual at fault and seemingly mitigates personal responsibility. Some support for this argument comes from studies of US college men who admit to rape. Like the majority of incarcerated sexual offenders, these 'undetected' college rapists tend to be serial rapists who commit multiple sexual assaults (Lisak 2011; Lisak and Miller 2002) so that the vast number of campus rapes is committed by a small number of men. Similarly, a general population study in Bangladesh found that 2 to 3 per cent of men said that they had sexually abused more than ten women (Naved et al. 2011). What is important to note is, first, that these men fall within the 'normal' range on the normality–abnormality spectrum unlike clinic or incarcerated populations of sex offenders who usually manifest dysfunction at many levels. Second, they display personality dispositions that echo themes that emerged earlier regarding gender inequitable attitudes and masculinist gender norms. Third, an adverse developmental history of childhood abuse and neglect characterizes their history. It seems that although not all perpetrators of sexual violence have a background of developmental adversity and not all those who suffer such adversity end up as sexual predators, there is considerable overlap in the terrains of gendered violence perpetration and developmental adversity. With respect to the latter, it is to be noted that the widespread extent to which children are subjected to harshness, abuse and neglect, and the consequences thereof have only begun to be gauged in the recent past.

What are these personality dispositions? Largely based on research with American college men, two types of personalities were found to result in sexual aggression when they converge: hostile masculinity, and impersonal sex reflecting sexual callousness and the willingness to engage in sex without closeness or commitment. Based on this confluence model of sexual aggression, researchers were able to correctly predict ten years later which of the men would be in distressed relationships, commit sexual aggression and engage in impersonal sexual encounters (Malamuth et al. 1995). In another set of studies on the same population, college men who admitted to date and acquaintance rape were found to be serial 'predators' who were measurably more angry at women, more driven by the need to control and dominate women, more antisocial and disinhibited in their behaviour, and more hypermasculine in beliefs and attitudes (Lisak 2011). They were also more sexually active than other men, and engaged in consensual and coercive sex far more than typical of men in their age group. Sexual activity was an important component of their masculine identity and sexually aggressive behaviour reflected their view of women as sexual objects to be conquered, coerced and used for self-gratification. This combination of misogyny and impersonal sexuality are repeatedly encountered in the research. This echoes the findings from a large sample population study of men in the Asia-Pacific region (Fulu et al. 2013) that men who perpetrate sexual violence but not physical violence are strongly associated with having multiple sexual partners and engaging in transactional sex, suggesting a preoccupation with demonstrating heterosexual performance and sexual dominance over women. It is likely that such individuals will seek out others holding similar dispositions and be drawn to groups, settings and institutions that place a premium on similar values.

These personality dispositions are linked developmentally to family violence and childhood experience of abuse by both Malamuth et al. (1995) and Lisak (2011). This association is also found in studies of known sex offenders. In a meta-analysis, a history of child sexual abuse (CSA) was five times more common among adolescent sexual offenders than among other adolescent offenders (Seto and Lalumiere 2010), and it is estimated that approximately one of ten victims of CSA are at risk of being convicted of a sexual offence in adulthood (Craissati, McClurg and Browne 2002). In a national survey of youth in South Africa, it was found that 66 per cent of males and 71 per cent of females who had abused someone sexually had themselves been forced to have sex (CIETafrica 2004).

The evidence for exposure to physical abuse, emotional abuse and neglect as risk factors for sexual violence perpetration is inconsistent (Jewkes 2012), but witnessing parental domestic violence in childhood is positively associated with adult violence against intimate partners (Heise 1998) and also with later sexual aggression (Malamuth et al. 1995, 1996). Adverse childhood experiences associated with trauma and domestic violence are common in general population studies of men who admit to sexual violence perpetration in South Africa (Jewkes et al. 2006; 2011), in the US (Borowsky et al. 1997; Lisak 2011; Malamuth, Heavey and Linz 1996; Malamuth et al. 1995) and in India (Barker et al. 2011; Koenig et al. 2006). The findings underscore the importance of inter-generational transmission of domestic violence. Husbands in India who had witnessed their fathers beating their mothers as children were nearly five times as likely to beat their wives and three times more likely to sexually coerce their wives (Koenig et al. 2006).

The exact mechanisms involved in translating the experience of family violence and personal abuse into sexual violence perpetration in adulthood are unclear but probably lie in the emotional scars that damage the developing self, and in learning to use violence as an instrument to secure personal or group goals and desire. Ward and Beech (2006) point to four areas of psychological vulnerability arising from developmental adversity: (*a*) interpersonal relationship difficulties that make it hard to have an intimate relationship; (*b*) cognitive distortions about people and relationships formed through their own adverse experiences and which support sexual offending; (*c*) deviant sexual interests, for example, in children or in sadism; (*d*) problems with emotional regulation and behavioural control.

The willingness of individuals to inflict harm may also be the result of developmental deficits. The capacity to be pro-social, that is, to feel emotions such as compassion, caring, empathy and sympathy, to want to help, to refrain from inflicting hurt, to have a moral sense and to inhibit aggression when angry or frustrated, is a normative developmental achievement. It is perhaps the development of these pro-social faculties that explains why most men do not engage in sexually coercive behaviour despite being exposed to the sociocultural and group influences described earlier. However, this achievement is mediated by 'good enough' attachment and learning experiences when growing up and may be severely compromised when developmental histories are marked by lack of secure and loving relationships, violence, abuse and neglect. Thus, Malamuth (1996: 281) argues that abusive home environments 'interfere with the mastery of critical developmental skills, such as managing frustration, delaying gratification, negotiating disagreements, and forming a pro-social identity'. It also compromises the capacity to be empathic when angry, stressed or sexually aroused (Varker et al. 2008). Not only can self-regulatory mechanisms and pro-social orientation be relatively weak, exposure to abusive experiences during critical periods of development lead to the learning of aggressive patterns of behaviour and adversarial attitudes that reinforce the willingness to inflict harm.

People in everyday life use certain psychological mechanisms to switch off their moral radar. As described in the section on group-level factors, regulatory self-sanctions can be selectively disengaged for inhumane conduct by converting harmful acts to moral ones through linkage to worthy purpose, obscuring personal causal agency by diffusion and displacement of responsibility, misrepresenting or disregarding the injurious effects on victims, and vilifying the recipients of abuse by blaming and dehumanizing them (Bandura 1999). Based on his work with a large number of Catholic priests who were sexual abusers, Lothstein (2004) concludes that the defensive use of cognitive distortions such as denial, minimization and rationalization by these priests allowed them to sexually abuse despite their idealized self-image. Many who identified themselves as heterosexual had sex with teenage boys (the population most at risk from clergy) and rationalized that since they were not having sex with a woman, they were not violating their celibacy or priesthood. Thus, they continued to act perversely while rationalizing that their errant behaviour was actually protective of celibacy and priesthood. The Church, by its failure to punish errant priests and its efforts to cover-up these sexual crimes, failed as an institutional authority to uphold its own stated ideals, thus allowing, instead of interrupting, the offenders' rationalizations.

CONCLUSION

Causal responsibility for sexual violence is multi-factorial and calls for an expansion of the feminist model of violence against women to integrate other perspectives while retaining its feminist core of structural power and gender analysis. This essay uses a psychosocial framework to present an integrated perspective that examines sexual violence perpetration at the sociocultural level, the group level and the individual level of analysis. These levels influence each other recursively and understanding any particular case of sexual violence will mean examining it simultaneously at all levels.

The sociocultural factors encompassing gender-inequitable attitudes and masculinist gender ideology, along with the acceptance of violence in social life, and confusions about sexuality and the expression of desire set the ground for acts of sexual violence to occur. Since these sociocultural conditions apply widely, yet the vast majority of men are not sexually violent, other factors must come into play for sexual violence to occur. These factors may lie in group processes and/or in individual personality dispositions. Group processes are especially important in multiple-perpetrator sexual violence. Group processes are involved in short-circuiting individual moral radar and in promoting violent social identity assertion in inter-group conflict. The combination of social identity assertion and patriarchal, masculinist gender ideology underlies sexual violence associated with inter-group conflict, particularly those that have an ethnic dimension. Importantly, the compulsions of masculinity appear as a thread through all three levels, suggesting that interventions that specifically target boys and men in a bid to modify harmful notions of masculinity to versions that are equitable and non-violent will be particularly useful.

Impunity for sexual violence can also be understood to operate at all three levels of analysis. State and civil institutions are riddled with the same gender biases that characterize sociocultural life, so that the law and the criminal justice system fail to hold perpetrators accountable. At a more fundamental level, the social construction of sexual violence ensures that certain forms are not seen as violations or as harmful. Also, when constructed in terms of honour and shame, victims of sexual violence avoid seeking justice because of the stigma. At the level of the group, processes that facilitate de-individuation, diffusion of responsibility and dehumanization of victims enable groups and individuals to avoid taking moral responsibility for their crimes. Similarly, individuals use psychological defence mechanisms to evade conscience.

REFERENCES

Abbey, A. 2008. *Alcohol and Sexual Violence Perpetration*. Harrisburg, PA: VaWnet, a project of the National Resource Center on Domestic Violence/ Pennsylvanian Coalition Against Domestic Violence. Retrieved on 29 August 2013, from http://www.vawnet.org.

Abbey, A., M.R. Parkhill, R.BeShears, A.M. Clinton-Sherrod and T. Zawacki. 2006. 'Cross-Sectional Predictors of Sexual Assault Perpetration in a Community Sample of Single African American and Caucasian Men', *Aggressive Behaviour*, 32(1):54–67.

Abbey, A., T. Zawacki, P. Buck, M. Clinton and P. McAuslan. 2004. 'Sexual Assault and Alcohol Consumption: What Do We Know about Their Relationship and What Types of Research Are Still Needed?' *Aggression and Violent Behavior*, 9(3): 271–303.

All India Dalit Mahila Adhikar Manch (AIDMAM). 2012. *Violence against Dalit Women*. New Delhi: AIDMAM.

American Psychological Association. 2007. *Report of the APA Task Force on the Sexualization of Girls*. Washington, DC: American Psychological Association.

Baaz, M.E. & Stern, M. 2009. 'Why do soldiers rape? Masculinity, violence and sexuality in the armed forces in the Congo (DRC)', *International Studies Quarterly*, 53: 495-518.

Bandura, A. 1990. 'Selective Activation and Disengagement of Moral Control', *Journal of Social Issues*, 46(1): 27–46.

————. 1999. 'Moral Disengagement in the Perpetration of Inhumanities', *Personality and Social Psychology Review*, 3(3): 193–209.

Barker, G., J.M. Contreras, B. Heilman, A.K. Singh, R.K. Verma and M. Nasciemento. 2011. *Evolving Men: Initial Results from the International Men and Gender Equality Survey (IMAGES)*. Washington, DC, and Rio de Janeiro: ICRW and Instituto Promundo.

Baron, L., M. Strauss and D. Jaffee. 1988. Legitimate Violence, Violent Attitudes and Rape: A Test of Cultural Spillover Theory', *Annals of the New York Academy of Science*, August, Vol. 528: 79–110.

Basile, K.C., D. Espelage, I. Rivers, P. McMahon and T.R. Simon. 2009. 'The Theoretical and Empirical Links between Bullying Behaviour and Male Sexual Violence Perpetration', *Aggression and Violent Behavior*, 14(5): 336–47.

Borowsky, I.W., M. Hogan and M. Ireland. 1997. 'Adolescent Sexual Aggression: Risk and Protective Factors', *Pediatrics*; 100;e7. Retrieved on 10 September 2013 from http://www.pediatrics.org/cgi/content/full/100/6/e7

Bourgois, P. 1996. 'In Search of Masculinity: Violence, Respect and Sexuality among Puerto Rican Crack Dealers in East Harlem', *British Journal of Criminology*, 36(3):4312–4427.

Browning, C.R. 1992. *Ordinary Men: Reserve Police Battalion 101 and the Final Solution in Poland*. London: Penguin.

Brownmiller, S. 1975. *Against Our Will: Men, Women and Rape*. London: Penguin.

Butalia, Urvashi. 1998. *The Other Side of Silence: Voices from the Partition of India*. New Delhi: Penguin.

Bunting, L. 2007. 'Dealing with a Problem That Doesn't Exist? Professional Responses to Female Perpetrators of Child Sexual Abuse', *Child Abuse Research*, 16(4): 252–67.

Burt, M. 1980. 'Cultural Myths and Supports for Rape',*Journal of Personality and Social Psychology*, 38(2): 217–30.

Castano, E., B. Leidner and P. Slawuta, P. 2008. 'Social Identification Processes, Group Dynamics and the Behavior of Combatants', *International Review of the Red Cross*, 90(870): 418–28.

Chakma, K. and G. Hill. 2013. 'Indigenous Women and Culture in the Colonized Chittagong Hill Tracts of Bangladesh', in K. Visweswaran (ed.), *Everyday Occupations: Experiencing Militarism in South Asia and the Middle East*, pp. 132–57. Philadelphia: University of Pennsylvania Press.

Chandiramani, R., S. Kapadia, R. Khanna and G. Misra. 2002. *Sexuality and Sexual Behaviour: A Critical Review of Selected Studies (1990–2000)*. New Delhi: CREA.

Chenoy, A.M. 2012. *Militarization in India*. Chennai: Prajnya Trust.

Chowdhury, F.D. 2004. 'The Sociocultural Context of Child Marriage in a Bangladeshi Village', *International Journal for Social Welfare*, 13(3): 244–53.

CIETafrica.2004. *Sexual Violence and HIV/AIDS: Executive Report on the 2002 National Survey*. http://www.ciet.org/_documents/2006316174822.pdf (accessed 2 September 2013)

Cohen, D.K. 2013. 'Female Combatants and the Perpetration of Violence: Wartime Rape in the Sierra Leone Civil War', *World Politics*, 65(3): 383–415.

Cohen, D.K., A.H. Green and E. Wood. 2013. *Wartime Sexual Violence: Misconceptions, Implications and Ways Forward*. Washington, DC: United States Institute of Peace.

Cohen, D.K. and R.Nordas. 2014. 'Sexual Violence in Armed Conflict: Introducing the SVAC Dataset, 1989–2009', *Journal of Peace Research*, 51(3): 418–28.

Craissati, J., M. McClurg and K Browne. 2002. 'Characteristics of Perpetrators of Child Sexual Abuse Who Have Been Sexually Victimized as Children', *Sexual Abuse: A Journal of Research & Treatment*, 14(3): 225–39.

D'Costa, B. 2013. Victory's silence, *Forum*, 7(1). http://archive.thedailystar.net/forum/2013/January/victory.htm (accessed 10 November 2013).

De Jong, K., S. Kam, S. Fromm, R.Galen, T. Kemmere, H. Weerd, N. Ford and L. Hayes. 2006. *Kashmir: Violence and Health.* Amsterdam: Medecins Sans Frontieres.

DeKeseredy, W. and K. Kelly. 1993. 'Woman Abuse in University and College Dating Relationships: The Contribution of the Ideology of Familial Patriarchy', *Journal of Human Justice*, 4(2): 25–52.

De Mel, N., P. Peiris and S. Gomez. 2013. *Why Masculinities Matter: Attitudes, Practices and Gender-Based Violence in Four Districts in Sri Lanka.* Colombo: CARE International Sri Lanka.

Derne, S. 1999. 'Making Sex Violent: Love as Force in Recent Hindi Films', *Violence Against Women*, 5(5):548–75.

Edwards, K.M., J. Turchik, C. Dardis, N. Reynolds and C. Gidycz. 2011. 'Rape Myths: History, Individual and Institutional-Level Presence, and Implications for Change', *Sex Roles*, 65(11–12): 761–73.

Ferguson, C.J. and R.D. Hartley. 2009. 'The Pleasure Is Momentary… the Expense Damnable? The Influence of Pornography on Rape and Sexual Assault', *Aggression and Violent Behavior*, 14(5): 323–29.

Fikree, F.F., J.A. Razzak and J. Durocher. 2005. 'Attitudes of Pakistani Men to Domestic Violence: A Study from Karachi, Pakistan', *Journal of Men's Health and Gender*, 2(1): 49–58.

Fisher, W. and D. Byrne. 1978. 'Individual Differences in Affective, Evaluative and Behavioural Responses to an Erotic Film', *Journal of Applied Psychology*, 8(4): 355–65.

Franiuk, R. and E.A. Shain. 2011. 'Beyond Christianity: The Status of Women and Rape Myths'. *Sex Roles*, 65(11–12): 783–91.

Fulu, E., X. Warner, S.Miedema, R. Jewkes, T. Roselli and J. Lang. 2013. *Why Do Some Men Use Violence against Women and How Can We Prevent It?* Bangkok: UNDP, UNFPA, UNWomen and UNV.

Ganju, D., W. Singer, S. Jejeebhoy, V. Nidadavolu, K.G. Santhya, I. Shah, S. Thapa and I. Warriner. 2004. *Sexual Coercion: Young Men's Experiences as Victims and Perpetrators.* New Delhi: Population Council.

Gavey, N. 2005. *Just Sex? The Cultural Scaffolding of Rape.* London and New York: Routledge.

Gear, S. 2005. 'Rules of Engagement: Structuring Sex and Damage in Men's Prisons and Beyond', *Culture, Health & Sexuality*, 7(3):195–208.

Geetha, V. 2013. 'On Impunity', *Economic & Political Weekly*, 48(2): 15–17.

George, A. 2003. 'Newly Married Adolescent Women: Experiences from Case Studies in Urban India', in S. Bott, S. Jejeebhoy, I. Shah and C. Puri (eds), *Towards Adulthood: Exploring the Sexual and Reproductive Health of Adolescents in South Asia*, pp. 67–70. Geneva: WHO.

Go, V.F., A. Srikrishnan, M. Salter, S. Mehta, S. Johnson, S. Sivaram, W. Davis, S. Solomon and D.D. Celentano. 2010. 'Factors Associated with the Perpetration of Sexual Violence among Wine-Shop Patrons in Chennai, India', *Social Science & Medicine*, 71(7): 1277–84.

Grossman, D. 2009. *On Killing: The Psychological Costs of Learning to Kill in War and Society*. New York: Back bay Books.

Haffejee, S. 2006. *Waiting Opportunities: Adolescent Girls' Experiences of Gender-Based Violence at Schools*. Braamfontein: Centre for the Study of Violence and Reconciliation.

Harkins, L. and L. Dixon. 2010. 'Sexual Offending in Groups: An Evaluation', *Aggression and Violent Behavior*, 15(2): 87–99.

Haslam, N. 2006. 'Dehumanisation: An Integrative Review', *Personality & Social Psychology* Review, 10(3): 252–64.

Haslam, A.S. and S.Reicher. 2007. 'Beyond the Banality of Evil: Three Dynamics of an Interactionist Social Psychology of Tyranny', *Personality & Social Psychology Bulletin*, 35(5):615–22.

Hayes, S. and B. Carpenter. 2013. 'Social Moralities and Discursive Construction of Female Sex Offenders', *Sexualities*, 16(1–2): 159–79.

Heise, L. 1998. Violence against Women: An Integrated Ecological Framework. *Violence Against Women*, 4(3): 262–90.

Henry, N., T. Ward and M. Hirshberg. 2004. 'A Multifactorial Model of Wartime Rape', *Aggression and Violent Behavior*, 9(5): 535–62.

Horvath, M.A.H. and L. Kelly. 2009. 'Multi-Perpetrator Rape: Naming an Offence and Initial Research Findings', *Journal of Sexual Aggression*, 15(1):83–96.

Human Rights Watch. 2013. *'We will teach you a lesson': Sexual Violence against Tamils by Sri Lankan Security Forces.* New York: Human Rights Watch.

————. 2014. *Silenced and Forgotten: Survivors of Nepal's Conflict-Era Sexual Violence.* New York: Human Rights Watch.

International Centre for Research on Women (ICRW). 2002. *Men, masculinity and domestic violence in India: Summary report of four studies.* http://www.icrw.org/files/publications/Domestic-Violence-in-India-4-Men-Masculinity-and-Domestic-Violence-in-India.pdf (accessed 15 November 2013)

Impett, E.A., D. Schooler and D.L. Tolman. 2006. 'To Be Seen and Not Heard: Femininity Ideology and Adolescent Girls' Sexual Health', *Archives of Sexual Behavior*, 35(2):131–44.

Irudayam, A., J. Mangubhai and J. Lee. 2006. *Dalit Women Speak Out: Violence against Dalit Women in India.* New Delhi: National Campaign on Dalit Human Rights.

Jejeebhoy, S. and S. Bott. 2003. *Non-consensual sexual experiences of young people: A review of the evidence from developing countries.* New Delhi: Population Council.

Jewkes, R. 2012. *Rape Perpetration: A Review.* Pretoria: Sexual Violence Research Initiative.

Jewkes, R., E. Fulu, T. Roselli and C. Garcia-Moreno. 2013. 'Prevalence of and Factors Associated with Non-Partner Rape Perpetration: Findings from the UN Multi-Country Cross-Sectional Study on Men and Violence in Asia and the Pacific', *Lancet Global Health*, 1(4):e208–18.

Jewkes, R., K. Dunkle, M.P. Koss, J.B. Levin, M. Nduma, N. Jama and Y. Sikweyiya. 2006. 'Rape Perpetration by Young, Rural South African Men: Prevalence, Patterns and Risk Factors', *Social Science & Medicine*, 63(11):1277–84.

Jewkes, R., Y. Sikweyiya, R. Morrell and K. Dunkle. 2011. 'Gender Inequitable Masculinity and Sexual Entitlement in Rape

Perpetration in South Africa: Findings of a Cross-Sectional Study', *PLoS ONE*, 6(12): e29590.doi:10.1371/journal.pone.0029590

Kalra, G. and D. Bhugra. 2013. 'Sexual Violence against Women: Understanding Cross-Cultural Intersections', *Indian Journal of Psychiatry*, 55(3):244–49.

Kanin, E.J. 1985. 'Date Rapists: Differential Sexual Socialization and Relative Deprivation', *Archives of Sexual Behavior*, 14(3): 219–231.

Kannabiran, K. and V. Kannabiran. 1991. 'Caste and Gender: Understanding the Dynamics of Power and Violence', *Economic & Political Weekly*, 26(37): 2130–33.

Kaufman, M. 1999. *The 7 Ps of Men's Violence.* http://www.michaelkaufman.com/1999/the-7-ps-of-mens-violence/ (accessed 13 November 2013)

Kaufman, M. 2003. *The AIM framework: Addressing and involving men and boys to promote gender equality and end gender discrimination and violence.* New York: UNICEF.

Kirby, P. 2013. 'Refusing to Be a Man? Men's Responsibility for War Rape and the Problem of Social Structures in Feminist and Gender Theory', *Men and Masculinities*, 16(1): 93–114.

Koenig, M.A., R. Stephenson, S. Ahmed, S. Jejeebhoy and J. Campbell. 2006. 'Individual and Contextual Determinants of Domestic Violence in North India', *American Journal of Public Health*, 96(1): 132–38.

Koss, M.P. and T.E. Dinero. 1989. 'Discriminant Analysis of Risk Factors for Sexual Victimization among a National Sample of College Women', *Journal of Consulting and Clinical Psychology*, 57(2): 242-250.

Koss, M.P., C.J. Gidcycz and N.Wisniewski. 1987. 'The scope of Rape: Sexual Aggression and Victimization in a National Sample of Students in Higher Education', *Journal of Consulting and Clinical Psychology*, 55(2): 162–70.

Kwon, I., D. Lee, E. Kim and H. Kim. 2007. 'Sexual Violence among Men in the Military in South Korea', *Journal of Interpersonal Violence*, 22(8): 1024–42.

Lankford, A. 2009. 'Promoting Aggression and Violence at Abu Ghraib: The US Military's Transformation of Ordinary People into Torturers', *Aggression and Violent Behavior*, 14(5): 388–95.

Leiby, M.L. 2009. 'Wartime Sexual Violence in Guatemala and Peru', *International Studies Quarterly*, 53(2): 445-468.

Lisak, D. 2011. 'Understanding the Predatory Nature of Sexual Violence', *Sexual Assault Report*, 14(4): 49–50 and 55–57.

Lisak, D. and P.M.Miller. 2002. 'Repeat Rape and Multiple Offending among Undetected Rapists', *Violence and Victims*, 17(1):73–84.

Lothstein, L. M. 2004. 'Men of the Flesh: Evaluation and Treatment of Sexually Abusing Priests', *Gender and Sexuality*, 5(2): 167–95.

MacIntyre, A. 1999. 'Social Structure and Their Threats to Moral Agency', *Philosophy*, 74(3): 311–29.

MacKinnon, C. 1994. 'Turning Rape into Pornography: Post-Modern Genocide', in A. Stiglmayer (ed.), *Mass Rape: The War against Women in Bosnia-Herzegovina*, pp.73–81. Lincoln: University of Nebraska Press.

Malamuth, N.M. 1996. 'The Confluence Model of Sexual Aggression: Feminist and Evolutionary Perspectives', in D.M. Buss and N.M. Malamuth (eds), *Sex, Power, Conflict: Evolutionary and Feminist Perspectives*, pp.269–95. New York: Oxford University Press.

Malamuth, N.M., C. Heavey and D. Linz. 1996. 'The Confluence Model of Sexual Aggression: Combining Hostile Masculinity and Impersonal Sex', in E.J. Coleman, M. Dwyer and N.J. Pallone(eds), *Sex Offender Treatment: Biological Dysfunction, Intra-Psychic Conflict, Interpersonal Violence*, pp.13–37. New York: The Haworth Press.

Malamuth, N.M., D. Linz, C. Heavey, G. Barnes and M. Acker. 1995. 'Using the Confluence Model of Sexual Aggression to Predict Men's Conflict with Women: A 10-Year Follow-up Study', *Journal of Personality and Social Psychology*, 69(2): 353–69.

Martin, Y. and R. Hummer. 1989. 'Fraternities and Rape on Campus', *Gender & Society*, 3(4): 457–73.

McPhail, B., B. Bush, S. Kulkarni G. Rice. 2007. 'An Integrative Feminist Model: The Evolving Feminist Perspective in Intimate Partner Violence', *Violence against Women*, 13(8):817–41.

Menon, R. and K.Bhasin. 1998. *Borders and Boundaries: Women in India's Partition*. New Delhi: Kali for Women.

Mensch, B., S. Singh and J. Casterline. 2005. *Trends in the Timing of Marriage among Men and Women in the Developing World.* New York: Population Council.

Milgram, S. 1974. *Obedience to Authority: An Experimental View*. New York: HarperCollins.

Moore, A.M., N. Madise and K. Awusabo-Asare. (2012). 'Unwanted Sexual Experiences among Young Men in Four Sub-Saharan African Countries: Prevalence and Context', *Culture, Health & Sexuality*, 14(9): 1021–35.

Mosher, D.L. and M. Sirkin. 1984. 'Measuring a Macho Personality Constellation', *Journal of Research in Personality*, 18(2): 150–63.

Murnen, S.K., C. Wright and G. Kaluzny. 2002. 'If "Boys Will Be Boys," Then Girls Will Be Victims? A Meta-Analytic Review of the Research That Relates Masculine Ideology to Sexual Aggression', *Sex Roles*, 46(11–12): 359–75.

Naved, R.T., H. Huque, S. Farah and M.M. Shuvra. 2011. *Men's Attitudes and Practices Regarding Gender and Violence against Women in Bangladesh: Preliminary Findings*. Dhaka: ICDDR,B.

Nussbaum, M.C. 2004. 'Body of the Nation: Why Women Were Mutilated in Gujarat', *Boston Review*, 1 June. http://www.bostonreview.net/martha-nussbaum-women-mutilated-gujarat (accessed 3 May 2014).

Opotow, S., Gerson J. & Woodside, S. 2005. 'From moral exclusion to moral inclusion: theory for teaching peace', *Theory Into Practice*, 44(4): 303-318.

Patel, V., G. Andrews, T. Pierre and N. Kamat. 2003. 'Gender, Sexual Abuse and Risk Behaviours in Adolescents: A Cross-Sectional Survey in Schools in Goa, India', in S. Bott, S. Jejeebhoy, I. Shah and C. Puri (eds), *Towards Adulthood: Exploring the Sexual and*

Reproductive Health of Adolescents in South Asia, pp. 99–102. Geneva: WHO.

Pervez, A. 2014. 'Sexual Violence and the Culture of Impunity in Kashmir: Need for a Paradigm Shift?', *Economic & Political Weekly,* 49(10):10–13.

Price, L.S. 2001. 'Finding the Man in the Soldier-Rapist: Some Reflections in Comprehension and Accountability', *Women's Studies International Forum,* 24(2): 211–27.

Public Commission on Human Rights. 2006. *State of Human Rights in Jammu and Kashmir.* Srinagar: Coalition of Civil Society.

Qazi, Y.S. 2003. 'Adolescent Reproductive Health in Pakistan', in S. Bott, S. Jejeebhoy, I. Shah and C. Puri (eds), *Towards Adulthood: Exploring the Sexual and Reproductive Health of Adolescents in South Asia,* pp. 77–80. Geneva: WHO.

Ramasubramaniam, S. and M.B. Oliver. 2003. 'Portrayals of Sexual Violence in Popular Hindi Films, 1997–1999', *Sex Roles,* 48(7–8): 327–36.

Roy, S. 2010. 'The Grey Zone: The "Ordinary" Violence of Extraordinary Times', *Journal of the Royal Anthropological Institute,* 14(2): 316–33.

Rozee, P.D. 1993. 'Forbidden or Forgiven? Rape in Cross-Cultural Perspective', *Psychology of Women Quarterly,* 17(4): 499–514.

Ryan, K.M. 2011. 'The Relationship between Rape Myths and Sexual Scripts: The Social Construction of Rape', *Sex Roles,* 65: 774–82.

Saigol, R. 2008. 'Militarization, Nation and Gender: Women's Bodies as Arenas of Violent Conflict', in P. Ilkkaracan (ed.), *Deconstrucing Sexuality in the Middle East: Challenges and Discourses,* pp. 165–76. Aldershot: Ashgate.

Sanday, P.R. 1981. 'The Socio-Cultural Context of Rape: A Cross-Cultural Study', *Journal of Social Issues,* 37(4): 5-27.

————. 2007. *Fraternity Gang-rape: Sex, Brotherhood and Privilege on Campus.* New York: New York University Press.

Sen, R. 2012. '"Neutral" Laws or "Moral" Codes: Controlling and Recreating Sexualities/Intimacies', in S. Pilot and L. Prabhu (eds),

The Fear That Stalks: Gender-Based Violence in Public Spaces, pp.143–72. New Delhi: Zubaan.

Seto, M.C. and M.L. Lalumiere. 2010. 'What Is So Special about Male Adolescent Sexual Offending? A Review and Rest of Explanations through Meta-Analysis', *Psychological Bulletin*, 136(4): 526–75.

Sigworth, R. 2009. *'Anyone Can Be a Rapist...': An Overview of Sexual Violence in South Africa*. Braamfontein: Centre for the Study of Violence and Reconciliation.

Sivakumaran, S. 2007. 'Sexual Violence against Men in Armed Conflict', *European Journal of International Law*, 18(2): 253–76.

Skjelsbaek, I. 2001. 'Sexual Violence and War: Mapping out a Complex Relationship', *European Journal of International Relations*, 7(2): 211–37.

Sodhi, G. and M.Verma. 2003. 'Sexual Coercion among Unmarried Adolescents of an Urban Slum in India', in S. Bott, S. Jejeebhoy, I. Shah and C. Puri (eds), *Towards Adulthood: Exploring the Sexual and Reproductive Health of Adolescents in South Asia*, pp. 91–94. Geneva: WHO.

Sonpar, S. 2007. *Violent Activism: A Psychosocial Study of Ex-Militants in Jammu Kashmir*. New Delhi: Aman Public Charitable Trust.

Srivastava, S. 2012. 'Masculinity and Its Role in Gender-Based Violence in Public Spaces', in S. Pilot and L. Prabhu (eds), *The Fear That Stalks: Gender-Based Violence in Public Spaces*, pp.13–50. New Delhi: Zubaan.

TARSHI. 2007. *Talking about Sexuality: A Report of Preliminary Findings from the TARSHI Helpline*.http://www.tarshi.net/downloads/tarshi_helpline_report.pdf (accessed 15 December 2013).

Turchik, J. and S.M.Wilson. (2010). 'Sexual Assault in the US Military: A Review of the Literature and Recommendations for the Future', *Aggression and Violent Behavior*, 15(4): 267–77.

Valls, R., L. Puigvert and E. Duque. 2008. 'Gender Violence among Teenagers: Socialization and Prevention', *Violence Against Women*, 14(7): 759–85.

Varker, T., G. Devilly, Y. Ward and A. Beech. 2008. 'Empathy and Adolescent Sexual Offenders: A Review of the Literature', *Aggression and Violent Behavior*, 13(4): 251–60.

Vogelman,L. and S. Lewis. 1993. *Gang-rape and the Culture of Violence in South Africa.* Braamfontein: Centre of the Study of Violence and Reconciliation.

Ward, T. and A.Beech. 2006. 'An Integrated Theory of Sexual Offending', *Aggression andViolent Behavior*, 11(1): 44–63.

Weiss, K.G. 2009. '"Boys Will Be Boys" and Other Gendered Accounts: An Exploration of Victims' Excuses and Justifications for Unwanted Sexual Contact and Coercion', *Violence Against Women*, 15(7): 810–34.

Wijkman, M., C. Bijleveld and J. Hendriks. (2010) '"Women Don't Do Such Things! Characteristics of Female Sex Offenders and Offender Types', *Sex Abuse: A Journal of Research & Treatment*, 22(2): 135–56.

World Health Organization (WHO). 2002. *World Report on Violence and Health.* Geneva: WHO.

Wood, E.J. 2006. 'Variation in Sexual Violence during War', *Politics and Society*, 34(3): 307–41.

Wood, E.J. 2009. 'Armed Groups and Sexual Violence: When Is Wartime Rape Rare?' *Politics and Society*, 37(1): 131–62.

Wood, K. 2005. 'Contextualising Group Rape in Post-Apartheid South Africa', *Culture, Health & Sexuality*, 7(4): 303–7.

Wood, K., H. Lambert and R. Jewkes. 2007. '"Showing Roughness in a Beautiful Way": Talk about Love, Coercion and Rape in South African Youth Culture', *Medical Anthropology*, 21(3): 277–300.

Zakar, R., M.Z. Zakar and A. Kraemer. 2013.' Men's Beliefs and Attitudes toward Intimate Partner Violence against Women in Pakistan', *Violence Against Women*, 19(2): 246–68.

Zarkov, D. 2001. 'The Body of the Other Man: Sexual Violence and the Construction of Masculinity, Sexuality and Ethnicity in Croatian Media', in C. Moser and F. Clark (eds), *Victims, Perpetrators or Actors? Gender, Armed Conflict and Political Violence*, pp. 69–82. Delhi: Kali for Women.

Zimbardo, P. 2004. 'A Situationist Perspective on the Psychology of Evil: Understanding How Good People Are Transformed into Perpetrators', in A. Miller (ed.), *The Social Psychology of Good and Evil*, pp. 21–50. New York: Guilford.

———. 2007. *The Lucifer Effect: Understanding How Good People Turn Evil*. New York: Random House.

8

Headlining Sexual Violence

Media Reporting After the Delhi Gang-rape

DIVYA ARYA

The Indian media, on most days, feels somewhat like a large hot-air balloon high up in the sky, with thousands of small balloons inside, jostling for space in a cluttered, busy, almost saturated space. The market is huge and so is the rapidly increasing number of players inside, the pressure forever mounting as the race to attract the limited reader/listener/viewer attention heats up. Evidently, it wasn't always this packed. In the 1970s, there were 876 newspapers and the sole national television broadcaster was Doordarshan. This has grown to 13,761 newspapers and 400 privately owned television news and current affairs channels in India. Add to that 85,899 magazines, the national radio broadcaster All India Radio, its 413 radio stations, 243 private infotainment FM radio stations, and the innumerable news portals, blogs, social media and news aggregating websites, and it should start feeling fairly stuffy inside that hot-air balloon (Ministry of Information and Broadcasting 2014; RNI 2014; TRAI 2014b).[1]

The past decade has seen significant trends in the news media that help in understanding news consumption patterns. The census of 2011 reveals that less than 20 per cent of Indian households own a radio. Radio listenership of the traditional shortwave bands that broadcast news through the national radio network, All India Radio, has steadily declined, and though private FM radio stations have grown, the government does not allow them to broadcast news yet. The global print industry is suffering from lower circulation as the internet has changed reading habits. The 2013 Indian Readership Survey (sample based analysis of all media consumption) says that 20 per cent of the Indian population read a newspaper. But Indian publications are still registering growth at a moderately average rate of approximately 6 per cent.

In the recent past, access to TV and the internet has seen rapid growth, bringing into its fold smaller towns and villages as well.[2] Half the country's 1.2 billion-plus population has a TV set, and the potential power and influence of the media is attracting companies and advertisers to invest in this busy, competitive market. It is noteworthy that within the TV universe, news channels have an unusually large share (400) in the total number of channels (813) in India. But the television audience measurement agency, TAM Media Research, points out that news only gets 7 per cent of the average viewer's time, while 53 per cent gets taken up by general entertainment and 14 per cent by movies ('Indian Media Scenario' 2011: 37).

The internet's share in the media pie seems small as only 10 per cent of Indians have access to a computing device and internet reach is 2 per cent. But it is growing, as the global digital measurement and analytics firm, comScore, in its report, *India Digital Future in Focus* (2013: 10, 53), points out: 'India has bypassed Japan to become the world's third largest Internet user after China and the United States, and its users are significantly younger than those of other emerging economies.'

It is important to note that each medium (TV, radio, print, web) in the Indian media universe operates in multiple languages spread over different regions of the country. For example, in the print media, publications are registered in 172 languages. Hindi leads the list (40,159), followed at a long distance by English (13,138), Marathi (7,155), Urdu (4,500) and Gujarati (4,401). Many media companies have publications in multiple languages, some with national and/or regional circulation. Then there are big networks that not only work in different languages but also across multiple mediums.

SO, FINALLY, THIS IS WHAT OUR WORLD LOOKS LIKE! WELCOME!

Media is a business deeply guided by technology and invention, constantly changing and adapting to find newer ways to stay relevant, stand out and get noticed. It is in this environment, the complexities of which shall be explored further in the sections that follow, that we need to situate the 'editorial' or indeed the 'news' aspect of things.

'News', for the purposes of this research, is sexual violence, which, arguably, has been the subject of intense media attention since the brutal gang-rape of a young woman in Delhi in December 2012. The media named her Nirbhaya, a Hindi word meaning 'fearless'. She was a college student who was raped on a moving bus by a group of six men and later died as a result of the injuries inflicted on her. The case provoked large-scale protests and was extensively covered by the media (locally and internationally). It became the catalyst for government action on the women's movement's longstanding demands for legal reform. The government set up a committee to review the existing laws pertaining to sexual violence against women. Its recommendations, though, were only accepted in part by the government and it introduced the death penalty as a punishment in rare cases of rape. During the trial, one accused committed suicide in jail and all others were found guilty of rape and murder by a fast-track court in 2013. Four were sentenced to death by hanging and the fifth, being a minor, was given three years imprisonment in a reform facility.

The coverage of that case brought a renewed focus on sexual violence on the part of the media. It is significant that an analysis of the representation of gender in media by the Global Media Monitoring Project (GMMP) in 2010 found that, '73% of the news stories on crime and violence analysed from India, reinforced gender stereotypes'.[3] So, could December 2012 turn the tide and become what the media loves to call a 'game-changer' in relation to all the cases of sexual violence that were reported or not thereafter? The answer lies in understanding how the media functions. What governs its response to stimuli? How does it set agendas? What are its motivations or, indeed, what keeps a watch over it?

THE MEDIA MACHINE

Broadly, the news media functions in a three-step process of selection, newsgathering and presentation. According to the National Crime Records Bureau (NCRB 2012), the government agency tasked with collecting crime data nationwide, on an average sixty-eight rapes were committed every day in India that year. The report also says that 98 per cent of rapes were committed by friends, family or acquaintances, and only 2 per cent by strangers. With 24,923 cases reported to the police in a year, rape is indeed a crime far too common and numerous to hit countrywide headlines. But the same could be said for other violent crimes like kidnapping (47,592), murder (34,434) or robbery (27,343) registered with the police that year. Suffice it to say then, that media reportage of crime is in essence and practice 'selective', as it possibly cannot be exhaustive. But the coverage could at least strive to be representative especially in a country that is in many ways an amalgamation of many countries, many realities and many differences in one.

Selection

The first stage in the life of a news story, when it is selected from a crime statistic to be explored, understood and eventually reported on, is critical for many reasons. First, for deciding the birth and consequent life of the news report of that crime; second, for the added attention and impact that may potentially draw to that incident consequent to the media exposure; and finally, and critically, in a wider pool of news coverage, this selection goes a long way in building, reinforcing or challenging perceptions and facts about the crime and its incidence. This, of course, is not a simple choice and is governed by many factors, some intrinsic to the workings of the industry, some to the individuals involved, and some to existing perceptions.

Despite the earlier comparison of rape with other violent crimes as an argument and basis for selective coverage, rape is indeed different from other violent crimes. The sexual component inherent in rape puts it in an altogether separate category for the news media. For the news audience too, sex crimes have the unique ability to touch upon their deep-seated beliefs about gender roles. In her book *Virgin or Vamp: How the Press Covers Sex Crimes*, journalist and novelist Helen Benedict argues that 'sex crimes have the ability to evoke such beliefs because they involve aggressive sexual interaction between men and women, and call into play age-old assumptions about rape and sex' (Benedict 1992: 3). For decades, feminists across the world have argued that rape is not just an act of sexual desire but a tool of exerting power and subjugation. Media reportage of sexual violence though, often fails to follow that argument, falling short of making those connections, especially in cases where economic, social, cultural, national and other contexts play a decisive role in the crime.

Newsgathering

The second stage in the news story's life cycle depends heavily on the newsgatherers, their sources of information, and also the resource persons they tap into for context and perspective. By virtue of being a crime, rape is most likely to be written about by correspondents specializing in crime reportage. The police would be their main source of information with eyewitness accounts sometimes being used to supplement or question this. It is hard to ascertain whether the audience can be won over by presenting new leads in a crime story first or by in-depth or contextual analysis of the crime. What does emerge, though, from patterns of broadcast in the mainstream media is that the general consensus is to pay more attention to the former.

Thus, merit is placed on speedy, accurate and minute details of the crime. As news is available 24/7 these days, whether via television or web portals of newspapers, the challenge is not only quick initial reporting but also continued fresh and distinctive takes to sustain interest. However, a sharp rise in the total number of journalists looking for scoops has made it harder to be the first in getting exclusive reports or breaking leads in a developing story. This is not to imply that path-breaking or niche reporting has become extinct; just that it is a rarer feat to achieve now. One route to distinctive reporting is the telling of the story. To an extent, this explains the sensational revelatory tone in crime reports, sometimes bordering on overstepping into the realm of speculation about character, motivation and even the guilt of the people involved. The use of re-enactments or reconstructions of events through video or graphics add drama and detail to the coverage.

Presentation

The final stage, when crime statistics are ready to be presented as a story of real characters, motivations and context, is a continuing test to win the reader/listener/viewer's attention. Another tool employed for this is taking ownership of the coverage. What is now being increasingly understood as campaign journalism implies the process by which a news outlet will claim credit for successfully owning or leading the coverage, and 'achieving impact'. By continuous follow-up coverage and by calling government, police and other power-wielding bodies to account, news outlets collectively play an important and potent role in the arrest of an accused, reopening of an investigation, speedy trial or pursuing legal reform. And they have done so, both before and since the gang-rape in December 2012.

But in a rush to take credit, individual news organizations may often up the tempo of their coverage, trying to outdo the competition. And the good practice of sustained reporting sometimes runs the risk of building panic, crossing the line into opinionated media campaigns that may lose all sense of balance and proportion. Reasoned debate could risk being drowned in a cacophony that pushes for quick solutions to fix individual cases being highlighted by the media at that moment.[4] This is especially true when the media's self-regulatory bodies, such as the Press Council of India, Editor's Guild and News Broadcasting Standard's Authority, have not been seen actively intervening or calling for order until recently.

* * *

To build on this broad understanding of the media machine and find specific trends or themes that form the general consensus on the coverage of rape cases, I spoke to some journalists.

The interviews probed the unwritten rules on rape reporting that the individuals or their organizations abided by, and the specific experience around the coverage of sexual assault in a two-year period after the gang-rape in December 2012. The purpose was also to find common threads in their responses to spot distinct patterns that may be unique to the medium or language.

The news media is an extremely diverse universe, with multiple platforms and languages, each with their different audiences and reach. For the purposes of this research, this universe was narrowed down to a broadly representative sample of what is understood to be 'mainstream traditional news media'.[5] A cross-section of correspondents and editors from newspapers and television news channels, published and broadcast in English and Hindi on a national level, were interviewed.

The conversations were insightful and not just for information on the working of the news producing machinery. I found some profound and telling beliefs, notions and expressions on my table. These will be peppered over the following pages, and here is the first one to start with:

> Rape is a fashion statement in terms of media coverage. Rape comes and goes out of fashion. It became fashionable when Nirbhaya happened. Right now it's out of fashion again.

This statement by a senior editor accurately outlined that media coverage of violence against women has seen a cyclical pattern of lull periods interspersed with interludes of intense attention. There is a sort of bonhomie, an understanding almost, among the mainstream media when it comes to following this pattern. This is reminiscent of the 1980s, when the media made 'rape' the subject of their collective attention.

HISTORY: THE FIRST TIME...

Rape became a major public issue in 1980 after the Supreme Court judgement acquitting two policemen accused of raping a minor tribal girl, Mathura, in the premises of a police station came to light.[6] Outraged at the judgement, four university law professors wrote an open letter to the Supreme Court in 1979 raising the issue of absence of consent in cases of custodial rape (Baxi et al. 1979). This is considered by many to be a landmark in the consolidation of the women's movement in India in its focus on the issue of sexual violence.

After the letter became public, women's groups highlighted the definition, causes and impact of rape on victims, held demonstrations across the country, and campaigned for legal reform. The media took note of this reverberation and many articles and op-ed pieces found their way into national newspapers. In their book, *Whose News? The Media and Women's Issues*, journalists Ammu Joseph and Kalpana Sharma (2006), compiled the coverage during this period. They observed that the anti-rape campaign's media coverage was 'explained partly by the involvement of journalists in the campaign, as activists or sympathizers, and partly by the fact that some women activists and commentators contributed timely articles that were promptly used'. They concluded that, 'This kind of serious media attention cannot but have had some impact on the government of the day' (ibid.: 115).

The Supreme Court judgement in Mathura's case was preceded by another custodial rape that was again highlighted by progressive voices in the region. In 1978, an 18-year-old Muslim woman, Rameeza Bee, was raped by four policemen, who also beat her husband to death.[7] The feminist legal researcher and sociologist Kalpana Kannabiran noted that the agencies of the state had communalized an issue that had nothing to do with religion and that 'during the entire proceeding, the police never denied that the rape took place. Their defence was based on questions about the legitimacy of Rameeza Bee's marriage and on allegations that she was a prostitute' (Kannabiran 1996).

In another case of police brutality, in 1980, a pregnant woman, Maya Tyagi, was brutally assaulted, stripped and paraded naked by policemen. Her husband and two others were shot dead by the police. A commission set up to probe the incident asserted that it was incorrect to say that the police had raped Maya Tyagi.[8] A report in the People's Union for Civil Liberties' *Bulletin* noted that the media failed to see the problem with the commission's findings:

> To touch a lone women sitting in a vehicle and pass vulgar remarks, to drag the woman out, bare her breasts and touch them and shove a stick into her body, are not rape? Then what is rape?... That only if there is a forced physical intercourse it will be considered rape is the male chauvinistic notion on which the commission has based its judgement. ('Baghpat Report Supports Oppression' 1981)[9]

Following these cases and women's groups' relentless pursuit, the government amended laws around rape and added many clauses including one on consent in 1983. According to it, in cases of custodial rape, gang-rape and the rape of a pregnant woman, if the victim states in court that she did not consent, then the court shall presume that she did not and the burden of proving consent shall shift to the accused.[10] Pointing to media's sporadic attention to the issue, Joseph and Sharma said: 'Notwithstanding the extensive coverage provided to the issue at the height of the campaign, little notice was taken of the new rape law when it was finally passed nearly four years later—only one paper commented on it in an edit' (Joseph and Sharma 2006: 116).

It was only in 1988 that six men of the Uttar Pradesh Police were found guilty and sentenced to death and four to life imprisonment on charges of murdering Maya Tyagi's husband and two others. The weekly news magazine *India Today*'s report on the verdict had no reference to the 1981 commission's observations on rape (Pachauri 1988).

All of this, of course, was before the times of TV news, and one should not compare the widespread protests after the December 2012 gang-rape, the role of women's rights activists at the time, the consequent changes in law and the media's role in any of this with the events and context of the Mathura rape case. It is also important to note that in the thirty-five years since the Mathura case, many others have periodically caught the media's eye and received extensive coverage.

Which brings us back to the underlying question: why does the media give attention to particular rape cases and not to others, and what was the media's trajectory after the coverage of the gang-rape in December 2012? In my attempt to look for answers, I found that two forces work simultaneously in the selection–newsgathering–presentation process of the media. On the one hand are certain assumptions built in partly by personal perceptions and common social stereotypes, and on the other are factors like the concept of news and journalism per se. In the following sections, I outline both aspects, trying to point out at the same time the few exceptions when media breaks this mould in its coverage of sexual violence.

'REAL' RAPE

It is at this point that one could stop imagining the media as the big hot-air balloon and move to thinking of it as a machine of real people and motivations. The first information of any crime reaches crime reporters through the police and/or what are called 'sources'.

These might be local leaders, activists, low-rung police constables, reporters of smaller media start-ups, freelancers or the common public. The initial information is scrutinized, facts cross-checked and then reported back to the media organization to gauge interest for coverage. If the news organization is found to be interested, then the reporter will delve deeper to write about the crime. All of this happens in a few hours, depending on how the information originated and how clear/complete it is.

Tanima Biswas, associate editor at the English news channel, NDTV 24/7, specializes in investigative journalism. She told me that as crime reporters, they have to have, 'a very hawkish eye to sift through the rape cases, because when one is reporting them, there cannot be a question mark on the woman involved. Media reporting, though unbiased, is victim-sympathetic, and so they wouldn't want to get it wrong.' In all my interviews, this concern and emphasis on 'real rape' and 'true victim' was clear. I was told that the category of rape by a stranger, gang-rape and rape of minors, therefore, were more likely cases to be picked up by the media, as in those, it seems improbable that the victim could have had a role in bringing the assault upon herself. Journalist Helen Benedict analyses this social stereotype in her book *Virgin or Vamp*:

> As a result of rape myths, a sex crime victim tends to be squeezed into one of two images—she is either pure and innocent, a true victim attacked by a monster—the 'virgin' of my title—or she is a wanton female who provoked the assailant with her sexuality—the 'vamp'. (1992: 18)

So, when is the victim perceived to have had a role in inviting her assault? Rajeev Ranjan has been covering crime for the past fourteen years, initially with one of the most read and circulated Hindi newspaper, *Dainik Jagran*, and now leads a team of five crime reporters at another Hindi daily, *Rashtriya Sahara*, as chief correspondent. He explained,

> Law and order is the responsibility of the police, whereas if something happens in the house, the girl is responsible to some extent. If you invite a boyfriend over and something happens, then if not 100 per cent, you are involved at least 50 per cent in that situation. You had an idea of what could happen.[11]

There are two points to be noted here. First, that media has always had a preference to report on rape cases where the perpetrator is a stranger; and second, that after the December 2012 coverage, this preference has increased. The reason for this, as most reporters explained, is the new Criminal Law (Amendment) Act 2013. The Act passed in the aftermath of the December 2012 gang-rape case, has made it mandatory for the police to register an FIR in all rape cases at the first instance of getting a complaint, that is without any preliminary investigation. This had been done to prevent the police from turning away rape victims and led to a rise in the number of cases being reported in the following months.

But as Ananya Bhardwaj, crime correspondent with the English news daily, the *Indian Express*, explained,[12] 'The new rape law started getting misused and most of the cases would be a result of fall-out with a live-in partner or boyfriend, and refusal to fulfil [a] promise of marriage.' This was a perception that was shared by all the crime correspondents I interviewed, and how pervasive this has become even amongst editors (who have an important say in the selection of news stories) was highlighted when Bharadwaj elaborated, 'They are considered to be personal matters that a woman may have decided to bring to the police station. The editors feel that by giving more space to this, it would encourage the filing of more "false cases".'

Rajshekhar, senior correspondent at the English daily, the *Times of India*, the largest circulated multi-edition daily in India, also told me that there is a mutual understanding within the media that these were 'false cases' of rape and they would not report on them. He said, the police sources also would not tip reporters about these 'as they felt that such cases would not stand trial and mostly a compromise would be reached'.

This understanding that a high proportion of rape complaints are in cases where sex was consensual was furthered by a recent analysis by Rukmini S., national data editor with the English daily, the *Hindu*. She analysed the 600 rape cases reported to Delhi police for a particular period of six months and found that:

> Of the cases fully tried, over 40% dealt with consensual sex, usually involving the elopement of a young couple and the girl's parents subsequently charging the boy with rape. Another 25% dealt with 'breach of promise to marry'. Of the 162 remaining cases, men preying on young children in slums was the most common type of offence. (Rukmini 2014a).[13]

This data was then decoded and understood through interviews with the police, judiciary, complainants and activists. It brought out the complexities of inter-caste and inter-religious relationships, parents' disapproval and the police's role in filing 'scripted' FIRs that would often lead to arrest of young men in consensual relationships. This was a Delhi-based study and the countrywide picture, especially in smaller towns and villages, is likely to be even more complex. But such in-depth investigation is hard to find and the mainstream media mostly highlights rape cases in urban areas, against foreigners, brutal in nature and generally where the victim was an educated, working professional, attacked either by a stranger or by an influential person.

NDTV's Tanima Biswas gave another reason for the media's preference to cover rape by strangers. She said that the media could ask tough questions of the police and government, around law and order, street lighting, etc., in such cases and hold someone to account. 'But if rape happened inside the house, who could be questioned? It would just be an "unfortunate crime".'

Marital rape was not part of the broad understanding of 'rape inside the house', and none of the correspondents had ever come across any such complaint. Some in the Hindi media were not sure of what encapsulated marital rape and also referred to the fact that it was excluded from the Criminal Law (Amendment) Act 2013. Another assumption was that the audience is not interested in cases of sexual abuse that either happened within a family or in consenting relationships.

Under the Indian Penal Code, sexual intercourse or sexual acts by a man with his own wife, the wife not being under 15 years of age, is not rape. As the additional solicitor general, Dr Kamini Lau, explained in a recent judgement:

> In India, marital rape is not covered by the ordinary rape laws and is a form of non-criminal domestic violence.... Some cases, however, are in fact covered by the ordinary laws relating to assault and unnatural sex/sodomy as in the present case, for use of violence to claim sex is clearly not acceptable. (Jain 2014)

The *Rashtriya Sahara*'s Rajeev Ranjan said that rapes that happen within the boundaries of the house are not as important as those on the street, and that 'most perpetrators known to the victim felt remorse after the crime', the guilt and assumed self-reform, probably becoming another reason to invisibilize these rapes.

It appears that both in cases of consensual relationships (rape by boyfriend/live-in partner, breach of promise to marry) and when rape takes place inside the four walls of a house or family (in cases of marital rape, incest, rape by a relative), most of the media's interest in the crime's coverage goes down. More often than not this is guided by the notion that by virtue of the perpetrator being known to the woman, she is partly to blame for the assault. In her study of the British and American media's reporting of three rape cases, researcher Shannon O'Hara (2012: 256) notes that, 'If the perpetrator is a devious monster, rape becomes a random act of violence rather than a societal problem.' She then quotes E.K. Carll from his 2003 work, 'News Portrayals of Violence and Women: Implications for Public Policy':

> By presenting stories of violence against women as separate isolated events, the news media reinforces the idea that the violence was an isolated pathology or deviance. Maintaining this mirage of individual pathology, the news media denies the social roots of violence against women and absolves the larger society of any obligation to end it.

At the outset, the December 2012 gang-rape ticked all the right boxes. As one reporter put it: 'She was a classic victim. She wasn't being judged, she wasn't alone, she wasn't wearing provocative clothes, and you just couldn't point fingers at her. The media focus in fact shifted to the perpetrators and the brutality they inflicted.'[14] This case was one of the 2 per cent rapes committed by strangers that year (2012) in India. But media's deliberate attention on such cases and not the other 98 per cent reinforces a particular notion about the prevalence of rape as a crime committed by a deviant few and does not push the larger public to ask uncomfortable questions of themselves and society.

REPORTER PRESENCE

Arguably, the public outpouring on Delhi's streets also drove the media's coverage of the gang-rape in December 2012, and it in turn propelled them further. Historian Uma Chakravarti makes a very telling observation about these protests and the attention media gave to them in the 6th Anuradha Ghandy Memorial Lecture that she gave on 'Nirbhaya, Muzaffarnagar, Badaun and Beyond: Sexual Violence in Contemporary India' (2014):[15]

> Activists in Delhi have only been allowed to hold protests at New Delhi's Jantar Mantar area for many years now. For us this is the only 30 square feet of democracy left. A place that is invisible, tucked in a corner and does not give an opportunity of any engagement with the public. Now, in December 2012, the protesting students did not confine themselves to Jantar Mantar and spilled on to Vijay Path, the seat of power, the Government's Secretariat.

I would add that Vijay Path also happens to be an area where most TV news channels have their outdoor broadcasting vans parked, enabling quicker and easier coverage. So would the media have given similar attention to a rape case that sparked public outrage in a small city? To answer that, it is useful to first outline how media organizations are structured and how they make their resource deployment decisions, which in turn impacts how much coverage a case would be given.

The bulk of the reporting staff in most news organizations is based in their headquarters in metropolises like Delhi, Mumbai, Kolkata and Chennai. The second tier of reporters are stationed at news bureaus set up mostly in state capitals. The third tier, that is, for coverage of news in small towns and villages, is managed through a network of stringers/freelancers. And when particular news gains prominence or momentum in that area, the reporters based either in the nearest bureau or from the headquarters are rushed for coverage.

Jyotikamal, senior editor at the twenty-four-hour English news channel CNN-IBN, based at the Chandigarh bureau, had this to say:

> [The] media did a great job in sustained coverage of Nirbhaya, but it happened in Delhi and snowballed in terms of media coverage as each news channel tried to outdo the other, when brutal rapes happen in faraway places, no channel can afford long term continuous coverage.[16]

Jyotikamal is in charge of coverage from the north-Indian states of Punjab, Haryana, Himachal Pradesh and the Jammu region. He pointed out that massive coverage is given to rape incidents that happen where channel bureaus are based. The moment the location shifts to small towns, the level of media interest goes down.

> Leave alone sustained campaign-like coverage, even for initial detailed coverage of the crime, for TV channels there is an economic equation to it. If the money is flowing and payments are being made to freelancers that give information from smaller cities, coverage will happen. On its own, it won't happen.

He went on to explain that once the initial information is shared with the channel, they have to decide if the incident merits the movement of the bureau-based staff reporter, which is an extra cost of Rs 20,000 to 30,000 (US$ 330 to 500 approx.). So the decision is whether to incur that cost, get the incident covered by a freelancer and pay only Rs 2,000 (about US$ 33), run it as an update with news agency-provided information and footage, or not run it at all.

Raju Raj has been covering crime for ten years now and is principal correspondent with the 24-hour Hindi news channel

Zee News. He too believes that the perception of Delhi being the 'rape capital' is not true, and more cases are being reported from the city because there are so many reporters stationed here. The presence of larger reporting teams means that they have the time and ability to check information coming in through the police, to know whether cases should be reported upon or not. 'The channel would also then be more confident in coverage, knowing that these were "true" rape cases,' he told me.

> Last year, the NCRB said most rapes were reported to the police from Madhya Pradesh, but we don't see many media reports from there. And what about places like Orissa? I don't remember even one case of rape being reported from there. It's more about where the correspondents are stationed.

But this by no means is the general understanding or perception of reporters. Rakesh Kumar Singh has been working with the Hindi news daily *Dainik Jagran* for 14 years. He is now the metro crime head, leading a team of seven reporters. He firmly believes that the maximum rapes in the country happen in Delhi. One reason could be the floating population or because millionaires live next door to poor people, he reasoned.

> In cities, there are fifteen, twenty rape cases every day, but in other districts or villages there would hardly be any. Maybe one or two cases, those too would either not be reported to the police because of shame or probably be dealt with at the level of the panchayat only.

Examining this perception against crime data throws up a different picture. For the purposes of its tabulation, the NCRB counts crime in eighty-eight big cities in India as a separate category. For the year 2012, only 3,025 cases of rape were reported to the police from these eighty-eight cities out of the total

24,923 cases reported from all twenty-eight states and seven union territories (NCRB 2012).

It is noteworthy that newspapers do not have as huge a cost differential as TV news channels in moving reporters from big cities to smaller areas as there are no camera crew and broadcast costs. Despite that, much like TV, there is a preference to report on crime that happens where the reporter is stationed. Despite that, even rape cases in Delhi may not get the media's undivided attention.

NEWS CONTEXT

About sixteen months after the gang-rape in December 2012 brought the media's spotlight back on the issue of sexual violence, in March 2014, when the country was getting ready to vote for its next government, survivors of another rape tried to get their voices heard. Four minor girls were allegedly raped by men belonging to the upper caste in a village in the north Indian state of Haryana. The village, Bhagana, had been witness to a two-year caste conflict, which had led to a boycott of lower-caste families, having their access to water, work and education cut off, and finally culminated in the attack on the girls.

The girls' families fled the village along with scores of other families of their caste, initially demanding justice from the Haryana chief minister and finally camping at Jantar Mantar in Delhi. Jantar Mantar, which the historian Uma Chakravarti somewhat sadly called 'the 30 square feet of democracy', according to Hindi newspaper *Rashtriya Sahara*'s Rajeev Ranjan: 'is a picnic spot in Delhi [where] all kinds of fraudulent people also come here to protest, have tea and snacks and leave at the end of the day. It is unfortunate, but the protestors are not taken seriously by the media now.'[17] The protesting families stayed at Jantar Mantar for over two months. Apart from coverage by the English daily *Indian Express* in April (Bhardwaj 2014), an article in the Hindi news magazine *India Today* ('Yahan Dar ke Saaye mein Rehte Hain Dalit' 2014), and a long article by the investigative English news magazine *Tehelka* in May (Sonar 2014), there were only short reports filed in a few Hindi dailies.

Some of the reporters I spoke to mentioned missing links in the versions of the families and legal complexities of the case, while some said the case was very strong but the police had weakened it by not taking prompt action. Yet others felt it was not highlighted by the local media because of political pressure. Everyone agreed on one point, though: that when the case came to Delhi, other news simply overshadowed it.

It was only after elections were over, the new government put in place and the prime minister sworn in that the media focus shifted. Not to the Bhagana case, but to Badaun, a village in the north Indian state of Uttar Pradesh where two girls were found hanging from a tree. Shocking pictures of the hanging drew the media's attention to the case. After initial investigations and post-mortems of their bodies, the police filed a case of rape and murder. And here too, the suspected perpetrators were higher up in the social hierarchy to the victims.[18] It was then that most national media took note of the Bhagana protestors. However, there was no media-led campaign or call for justice, and the sporadic reports generated no substantial impact for the victims.

It was noteworthy, though, that most of the coverage of the Bhagana and Badaun cases, in both the English and Hindi media, interpreted sexual violence as being a tool to oppress lower castes. Some of the headlines were: 'Rape is being used as a weapon to humiliate Dalits' in a report in the Hindi daily *Dainik Bhaskar* (Thakur 2014), or the link between Dalits protesting their social boycott, in a report in the Hindi daily, *Navbharat Times* ('Bhagana

Gang-rape: Ab Tak Nahi Jaagi Sarkar' 2014), and a discussion marking the links between the Badaun and Bhagana cases on the English news channel NDTV ('Bhagana to Badaun: Caste Conspiracy' 2014).

Chandigarh-based senior editor Jyotikamal explained that

> Reporting one rape with a caste context after another made sense. Rape coverage is not consistent. It depends on news flow, news vacuum, news context or latching up to another rape incident. Like Nirbhaya or Badaun. Because these cases gain prominence, for a while lots of rape cases will start being reported upon.

This phenomenon of news fighting other news for space and prominence was explained by Bhavatosh Singh, deputy news editor at the twenty-four-hour English news channel Times Now. He recalled a case as brutal as the gang-rape in December 2012 that took place in February 2012, when a girl was abducted, gang-raped, tortured and murdered on the outskirts of Delhi, in the neighbouring state of Haryana. 'However it wasn't reported widely because it coincided with the attack on an Israeli diplomat in the city. It only gained prominence two years later in February 2014, when the court sentenced the accused to death' ('Haryana Gangrape Murder' 2014). Singh further explained that resources becomes a big factor in such a situation:

> When the chief crime reporter is already deployed on one crime story and he gets information about a second one, then someone else will be sent there by the news organization. That other person may not cover [the] crime beat. He may treat this incident as just another story and may not cover it with as much involvement or tenacity.

NEWS IS NEW

Zee News' principal correspondent Raju Raj felt that by the time the Delhi-based national media reported on the Bhagana case, it was too late

> The case was old, there was no new news angle and it could not be made into a campaign. It was only covered as one story. Sometimes, old cases do get picked up because of a new development, like the Ruchika Girhotra case, and then media makes it into a campaign for justice.[19]

The media picked up Ruchika Girhotra's case when the court handed a six-month sentence to a former senior police officer convicted of molesting her when she was 14 years old.[20]

Raju Raj went on to mention the Soni Sori sexual assault case, pointing out that TV news again lagged behind local and national newspapers on reporting this and hence struggled to find a news development or hook. Soni Sori, a tribal school teacher, arrested in October 2011 on charges of helping an insurgent group in the east Indian state of Chhattisgarh, had alleged sexual torture by a senior police officer at the police station she was kept in soon after her arrest. The reporting on her cases was championed by the investigative news weekly *Tehelka* (Chaudhury 2011). In fact, she had sought refuge at *Tehelka*'s Delhi office before her arrest, alleging that she was being falsely accused.

The arrest itself was covered extensively by the media. But Soni Sori's allegations of sexual torture, which surfaced soon after, were not. A Hindi article in *India Today* even declared them 'misleading' apart from calling her a Naxal supporter, though nothing had been proven yet. The article titled, 'Gumrah Kar Rahi Hai Giraftar Naxali Samarthak' (Arrested Naxal supporter is trying to mislead) (Mishra, V. 2011) went on to say that Soni Sori was becoming a 'headache' for the police and the hospital where she is admitted for 'minor injuries'.

Tehelka and the *Hindu*, continued to report on the progress in all her cases—the charges of helping an insurgent group levelled on her and her allegations of sexual torture at the hands of Superintendent of Police Ankit Garg. Another English news magazine, *Outlook* (Mishra, N. 2011) and the English news channel NDTV reported on the case. According to Raju Raj:

> By the time the national TV news channels [Hindi] woke up to this story, there was nothing new to say. Also, this happened in Chhattisgarh. Had this been Bihar or someplace which is a TRP area for Hindi channels and where there is a reporter present, probably the case would have got attention.[21]

Contrary to Raju Raj's claim, there were regular developments in Soni Sori's case, including when SP Ankit Garg was given a police gallantry award on the country's Republic Day in January 2012 for leading an ambush against insurgents in 2010. NDTV carried a report at that time, which concluded:

> While the jury is still out on Mr Garg's complicity, the case itself highlights one of the biggest dilemmas of a security force faced with a hostile rival, where the rules of war are blurred, where any tactic becomes fair game so much so that one person's villain becomes another man's hero and justice ends up having more than one meaning. (Mehrotra 2012)

A few months later, an investigative report in the English newspaper the *Indian Express* caused much outrage (Bhardwaj 2012). The detailed report set out to explain the context of tribals stuck between Naxals and the security forces in Chattisgarh, and went on to cast doubts over Soni Sori's links with Naxals, downplaying her sexual torture and suggesting that she had been lying. Women and human rights activists, who had spearheaded the legal fight in her case and tried to bring it into Delhi media's radar, wrote an article critiquing the newspaper report ('Anything but the Truth' 2012). The article highlighted factual inaccuracies in the report, questionable ethics of 'journalism of courage', and said that it was distressing that it wasn't found worthwhile to investigate 'why a whole generation of adivasis [tribals] is being put behind bars on the basis of such false cases, why it is taking years and their entire family's savings to get them out'.

Despite medical examinations confirming sexual torture, Soni Sori's allegations of custodial abuse did not outrage people anywhere in the country and the national media too did not choose to 'campaign for justice' for her. However, after the sexual abuse was confirmed in a medical check-up in Delhi directed by the Supreme Court, the tone of the media softened. Some Hindi TV news channels and newspapers finally gave space, albeit insignificant, to the later stages of trial in the case ('Soni Sori Jagdalpur Jail Mein Shift Hogi' 2013; 'Soni Sori ke Jail Sthanantaran ko Supreme Court ki Hari Jhandi' 2013).

Now, the basic ethics of reporting were followed. Since nothing had been proven yet, Soni Sori was not labelled a Naxal supporter, nor were the allegations of sexual torture dismissed as frivolous. Also note that by now it was January 2013, the media was in the midst of the continuing coverage of the gang-rape in December 2012, and the news context, as some would say, was 'right'. The English news channel CNN-IBN did a report in January 2013, titled 'Rape Cases We Forgot: Soni Sori, Chhattisgarh's Prisoner of Conscience'.

Soni Sori was exonerated in seven out of eight cases filed by the state. In November 2013, she was finally given bail by the Supreme Court in the one remaining case on allegedly helping insurgents. She then stood in the general elections in April 2014 on the ticket of the year-old Aam Aadmi Party and lost. Her case pertaining to allegations of sexual torture is still in court. Despite her coming into prominence as a tribal leader in the elections and the medical report that confirmed torture, there has been no reporting on her case since.

Of all my interviewees, only one admitted, on the condition of anonymity, the hidden reason behind some media's discomfort on reporting about Soni Sori's sexual torture: 'Most of the times, in Naxal issues, there are channels which have an anti-Naxal line. It's like you have killed hundreds of paramilitary forces, if something happens to you, then you pay the price. Much like, say, what happens in Kashmir." It is important to note in this comment that Soni Sori's guilt was already assumed at the stage of arrest. Second, sexual torture is deemed to be a minor cost/repercussion of the Indian state's larger struggle against the Naxal-led armed rebellion in Chhattisgarh or the Indian army's actions against militants in Kashmir. In the context of national security, this attitude is pervasive in both English and Hindi media. Custodial rape in conflict areas in India (Kashmir, the North-East and Chhattisgarh–Jharkhand) is often ignored, considered less credible, too complex and a small price in the pursuit of a larger goal (of the state) to report on. It is in many of these areas that the Armed Forces Special Powers Act (AFSPA), which gives protection to security forces, is in force.[22] The misuse of this impunity in cases of sexual assault has not been highlighted much by the Indian media.

CARPET BOMBING

While discussing their coverage of the Soni Sori case, Kirandeep, senior editor at the Hindi news channel IBN7, told me that since Chhattisgarh was far, and there was no reporter stationed there, they could only cover this as a single story. There was no 'carpet bombing'. 'Carpet-bombing coverage depends on how soon and what elements you can get in a story, what resources and reporters can be deployed. Some of it also depends on how the story came to you, how the reporter pitches it, and some on how the other media and newspapers play it up.'[23]

In a saturated news universe, mere coverage of a crime does not garner much impact any more. What Kirandeep calls 'carpet bombing', that I referred to as 'campaign journalism' earlier, that is, sustained coverage over a period of time, which tends to stand out and builds pressure on the government, police, judiciary and general public. Hence, it becomes even more important to mark why some cases get undivided media attention and others do not. She explained that some cases fall through the cracks because the reporter does not pitch them with a distinctive hook and some because the distance would make them difficult to get lots of elements around the story in a short period of time for sustained coverage. Though in the same breath, she added that with technological advancement, it is now cheaper than earlier to send reporters with equipment that enables them to send visuals and data or give live updates from locations away from Bureaus. For Hindi news channels, Kirandeep told me, 'Smaller towns and villages are the new market, the new TRP areas, so there is an eagerness to cover incidents happening there. Also discussion shows organized there often throw up interesting views as news points, as villagers are getting more and more vocal.' Of course, this trend is limited to the Hindi-speaking belt and hence north and north-west India (Chhattisgarh is a state in eastern India and Hindi is not the local language spoken there).

The other enabling feature for extensive coverage is the increasing role of news agencies, for example, the Press Trust of India, United News of India and Asian News International. News agencies have extensive reporter and stringer networks that aim to provide information and updates quickly to all news channels and/or newspapers that subscribe to them. News agencies have been providing this service in India and across the world for decades. But in the past few years, as media houses have pruned their reporter strength, the dependence on agencies has increased. According to Kirandeep, reporters are now deployed to cover these crime stories in depth and give live coverage from their locations, while the additional developing elements like political reactions, police press conferences, protest, etc., are covered through agency inputs. With fewer resources, the coverage is kept fast-paced and alive, giving it the feel of a 'campaign'.

While talking of 'media campaigns', it is worth pointing to the Badaun case, where two girls were found hanging from a tree in the north Indian state of Uttar Pradesh (identified as a TRP area by both Hindi and English language media). In this case, once initial investigations confirmed rape and, more importantly, the shocking photos and video of the hanging became available, the media decided to go there and 'carpet-bomb' with its coverage. This, despite Badaun being a remote village, a torturous nine-hour bumpy road journey from Delhi.

Crimes like rapes, in most cases, are not supported with any visual material. Hence, photos or videos in any rape case generally increases the media interest in it manifold. Raju Raj pointed out that especially in cases taking place in villages or towns where no staff reporter is stationed, photos or videos become a strong way to tell the story 'remotely' or till someone is deployed there. This was seen in the case of molestation of a girl outside a club in Guwahati, the capital of Assam. The video of the act became available on YouTube and started being shared widely. The case was then picked up by the national media three days after it took place and led to eventual arrests.

In the case of Badaun too, the intense media coverage led to the quick arrests of the accused, suspension of police officers on allegations of helping the accused, and the investigation was handed over from the state police to the Central Bureau of Investigation (CBI). The media highlighted the role that the girls' lower caste may have played in the rape, as also the issue of lack of toilets in villages that exposed women to violence when they used open fields for defecation. The 'story', though, changed over a period of time and the CBI, after its own investigation, ruled out rape and murder[24].

Times Now's chief crime correspondent Bhavatosh Singh travelled to Badaun too and told me that due to the immense pressure in such a situation, it was tough to scout for correct leads from the police investigation: 'When there so many channels, there is a certain amount of competition, and you tend to get sucked into doing live updates and running around. You don't spend as much time on the story as you should.' Kirandeep also explained that with the exponential rise in the number of news channels, speed has become more important than exclusivity: 'It is hard to get exclusivity between twenty channels. It is more important as to who gets it first.'

The pressure to get accurate information first has become very high for newspapers too. Most newspapers have web portals now, but only the big few can afford a separate team that can file original content for the website. It is then up to newspaper reporters, who earlier filed only for the print edition, to at least provide information updates for the website, which may then be supplemented from news agency reports. *Indian Express* reporter Ananya Bhardwaj said that according to each newspaper's general focus on crime news, crime reporters may be expected to file stories from at least two to even five angles on the day of a big crime incident. Bhavatosh pointed out that in the Badaun case, there was a general mistrust of the police as they was alleged to have helped the accused (who belonged to the same caste) and hence an over-reliance on the victim's family's version of events. However, the same media that unquestionably believed the victim family's version of events was quick to believe the CBI later when it gave a different theory on the crime.

It is important to remember though that unlike the local police, it is very hard for reporters to get information from the CBI and special investigative agencies. Crime reporters divulge that more often than not they end up publishing and reporting whatever is handed out to them by these agencies as there is very little scope of corroborating or verifying these 'leaks', which they then present in their reports as information attributed to 'sources'. Because of the secrecy surrounding these investigations, most of the media will indeed race to be first in reporting the leaks as that is the only forthcoming information. Some media organizations have reporters dedicated to covering the 'CBI beat' and they arguably have better access to information.

None of this is to suggest that the CBI-led investigations are faulty or work to present a pre-decided theory instead of the actual truth. It is to point out that media's role as an independent verifier of facts in such cases can be highly compromised. Especially when, as in the Badaun case, the victims' family vehemently denied the CBI's claims. The *Indian Express* though did carry a report questioning the CBI theory, which quoted, among others, one police officer accused in the case ironically saying that none of the evidence they had collected 'could remotely link to a possible suicide' (Chatterjee 2014).

OPENING SPACES

Even earlier, the Indian media had picked up certain crime incidents and highlighted them enough to cause a stir, raise questions and result in action. But things are different now. After the gang-rape in December 2012, sexual violence started getting discussed widely in TV debates ('Rape and Punishment: Time for Tougher Laws?' 2012). Women's rights activists got invited to these panels and many of these were new voices in the mainstream, providing an informed opinion on an issue they had spent years understanding. NDTV's Tanima Biswas pointed out, 'We had to be circumspect about the new voices because all kinds of people were speaking at that time. We had to be careful to choose the sane voices.' She added that the new trend of extensive coverage meant that media was getting into the 'activist role' very openly. She said, 'There is huge response from audience in the interactive shows that the channel organizes around such cases. It is also a way of getting the mood of the country and telling your viewer that the channel is very interested and engaged with the issue.'

I would argue that a small but new space has been created, not just among audiences, but even between the media community, which now does look towards the new voices for opinion and context much more than earlier. The information circulated through activists and organizations is taken more seriously and responded to. And this change has not only been seen in the English news media, but across Hindi newspapers and news channels too.

An editorial that appeared in the Hindi daily *Dainik Jagran* after the December 2012 gang-rape judgment came in highlighted many broader issues around justice for victims of sexual violence including that of selective outrage and application of laws when it asked, 'Why don't we see the speed with which courts delivered justice in the Nirbhaya case, in other rape cases too?' ('Rahat Bhara Faisla' 2013). It further goes on to mention cases such as the gang-rape of a woman (Manorama) by security forces in Manipur in 2004.

This important media attention and public outrage led to the setting up of a commission to look into changes in the Criminal Law dealing with sexual violence against women. Women's groups from across the country, including those from the North-East and

Kashmir (the two regions where army has special powers) and representatives of LGBT groups laid their suggestions in front of the commission headed by a former chief justice of India, J.S. Verma. In record time, the commission came with what many hailed as progressive recommendations (Justice Verma Committee Report Summary 2013). The amendments that the government finally passed did bring about some very positive and affirmative changes, but ignored the commission's key recommendations on criminalizing marital rape and reviewing controversial sections of the AFSPA. It also overlooked the commission's opposition to capital punishment and introduced the death penalty in rare cases of rape ('Rape Law Ordinance' 2013).

It is noteworthy that the issue of death penalty made its way into TV news debates and newspapers within two days of the Delhi gang-rape being reported in media. For example, on 18 December 2012, the Hindi news channel ABP News organized a discussion around the question 'Will capital punishment stop rape?' ('Phansi se Rukega Balaatkar?' 2012). It is undeniable that some of these discussions were shrill and often ended up drowning the new feminist voices as was evident in a debate on the death penalty on the English news channel Times Now ('Newshour Debate: Justice through Death Penalty?' 2014).

Sangeeta Tiwari, executive editor with the Hindi news channel ABP News felt that in the coverage after the gang-rape in December 2012, the media represented both sides of the capital punishment debate fairly. She felt that women's rights activists opposing the death penalty were accorded a special space in these debates.

> The media was never in support of death penalty, it was only reflecting the debate within society. It might be that the demand for death penalty was very impassioned at that moment and so it seemed that media was also supporting that, but this was absolutely not the case.

The interactive element of 'campaign journalism' was being employed as a tool by newspapers too, and they organized audience polls to reflect public opinion. The *Times of India* issued a quarter-page ad asking people to cast their votes in response to the question: 'What's the punishment for a man who takes away a woman's life while she's still alive?' And the options were: (*a*) life imprisonment; (*b*) death sentence; (*c*) bobbitization; or (*d*) chemical castration ('Crime and Punishment in TOI' 2012). I would argue that the headlines of debates, or indeed the questions and options for opinion polls, made certain assumptions (like rape takes away a woman's life while she is still alive!), giving a particular direction to the discussion on the death penalty.

This clamour for stricter punishment for rapists was so fierce that a press conference was organized by women's groups and human rights activists to unequivocally condemn capital punishment and bring forth the reasons why it would not be an effective deterrent to reduce the crime rate, as was being espoused everywhere (Arora 2012). Even though the death penalty is handed out for many serious offences in India, the execution and actual hangings are rare as the convicts have the option of making a mercy plea to the president to commute their punishment to a life sentence.

The last four death penalties carried out in India have been of Yakub Memon (30 July, 2015) convicted of conspiring in the 1993 Mumbai serial bomb blasts; Afzal Guru (9 February, 2013) convicted of conspiring in the 2001 attack on the Indian parliament;[25] Ajmal Amir Kasab (21 November, 2012) the lone surviving gunman of the 2008 Mumbai terror attacks;[26] and Dhananjoy Chatterjee (14 August 2004) convicted for the rape and murder of a teenage girl.[27]

The media has generally been very laudatory in such cases. Zee News used the term 'Aatank ko Phansi' (Terrorism hanged) in the case of the hanging of Afzal Guru, while only a few editorials critiqued the execution that had been given, by the Supreme Court's own admission, 'to satisfy the collective conscience of the country' (Roy 2013). One may note that the call for capital punishment and executions becomes loudest when violations of the nation's integrity or of the woman's body are in question. Debates are impassioned, and politicians and the general public too whip up this call for immediate resolution or setting an example through strict punishment.

In 1998, in the aftermath of the gang-rape of four nuns in Madhya Pradesh, when Home Minister L.K. Advani called for the death penalty as a punishment for rape, he was supported by opposition leaders as well. In 2013, during discussion around amendments in the rape laws, parliament witnessed passionate appeals for the death penalty from various members, including the popular film actor Jaya Bachchan. She broke down while speaking, saying that the 'act of sexual assault should be treated on par with attempt to murder' and demanded that 'Section 307 of the Indian Penal Code [which has a provision to award death penalty] should be amended to include rape under its purview' ('Delhi Gangrape Shakes Parliament' 2012).

In September 2014, after a considerable time had lapsed from the aforementioned sequence of events, the Law Commission of India decided to take another look at capital punishment in India, issuing a consultation paper open to the public to send in their views on the issue ('Death Penalty: Law Panel Seeks Reviews' 2014).

MORAL CRUSADES

The toughest test perhaps for media reporting on rape since December 2012 came in the form of the alleged sexual assault of a woman journalist by Tarun Tejpal, the editor of the investigative weekly news magazine *Tehelka*, where she was employed. Tejpal, a journalist of considerable repute, is well known for the hidden-camera technique in exposing crime. He is the founder of the newspaper *Tehelka*, which was later re-launched in a magazine format. An influential person, he had friendly relations with many senior editors in the media. No doubt, intense discussions followed across Indian newsrooms when the first newspaper reports of his decision to step down after having been accused of sexual assault came out.

Kirandeep of IBN7 told me that some media houses were reluctant to pick up the issue initially, but then Tarun Tejpal's case became a moment when the media was faced with the issue of moral responsibility. And without any official FIR or complaint, leaked emails between the woman, Tejpal and the managing editor of *Tehelka*, Shoma Chaudhary, became the basis for immediate media coverage in the case ('Accused of Sexual Assault by Staffer, Tehelka Founder Steps down for 6 Months' 2013).'Even though, an FIR was not registered, we had to cover it; else it would look like we don't want to speak about one of our kind. Also, it is rare that someone would speak up against a powerful and influential person like him.'

An FIR did get lodged eventually and Tejpal was arrested. There were two distinctive features of the coverage that followed. First was the intense scrutiny of Tejpal. Instead of questioning the victim, this time media focused on the accused, at least initially. Detailed profiles of Tejpal, tracing his journey as a journalist ('Tejpal ka Tehelka Kaand' 2013) were titled as sensationally as rape victim profiles are. Some went to the extent of digging out information about his finances ('Tarun Tejpal ne Khoob Kamaai Daulat aur Shauhrat, Scandal ne Kar Diya Barbaad' 2013). The second aspect was media's absolute disregard of the right to privacy in divulging the intimate details of the assault. Within the first few days, full transcripts of emails that were part of internal official communication in *Tehelka* and contained full description of the assault were leaked and published by the media. This unethical and sensational treatment of the case has made sure that these details are still easily accessible on the internet ('The Complete Email Trace of the Tarun Tejpal Sexual Assault Case' 2013).

The conflict within the media on reporting this case did simmer at the surface, and assertions of Tejpal being targeted politically because of his journalistic crusades would find mention in various reports. His accuser eventually came out with a detailed statement ('Tejpal ne Jo Kiya Woh "Dushkarm"' 2013), rubbishing these allegations and also making it clear that what happened with her was indeed 'rape' as per the expanded definition in the Criminal Amendment Law of 2013.[28] But the unease with Tejpal's arrest and denial of bail for months did spark off articles and counter opinions questioning the 'severity' of his offence and even the woman's allegation, specifically in the English news magazine *Outlook* (Grover 2014; Joseph 2014).

It is worth mentioning that Tarun Tejpal's case was followed by two separate complaints of sexual harassment by law interns against two former Supreme Court judges within two months. Contrary to the general hesitation around airing any allegations against judges for fear of contempt of court, these too were widely reported by the media and the intense questioning around policies to check sexual harassment at the workplace continued. The media was encouraged in part by the effort of the activist-lawyer and additional solicitor general of India, Indira Jaising, in making the details of harassment faced by one intern public (with her consent). This was carried as a front-page banner headline by the *Indian Express*, with what many termed a sensational headline, 'When I Tried to Move Away, He Kissed My Arm, Repeated He Loved Me: Law Intern's Charge against Ganguly' (Jaising 2014).

Within the media, these cases led to an internal tidying up. Kirandeep agreed that these cases served as a reality check and many media houses subsequently set up the legally mandated sexual harassment committees in their organizations to deal with complaints of sexual harassment.

RAPE IN COMMUNAL VIOLENCE

In sharp contrast to the news space given to the Tejpal case or the sexual harassment cases referred to earlier (where media coverage preceded the filing of formal police complaints), the rape horrors faced by women in riots in the north Indian state of Uttar Pradesh got belated and scattered attention only after police FIRs 'legalized' the rape complaints by women.[29] As has been characteristic of communal riots, in this one too sexual violence against women was used as a tool to 'shame' the community. And women were scared to report rape to the police in the vitiated atmosphere that prevailed after the rioting. They did have faith and were willing to speak to the media and human rights activists, though. Tanima Biswas of NDTV, who travelled to Muzaffarnagar, told me that the national media literally camped there for two weeks:

> There were some people who would come up to the media and bring women with them, and they'd give us accounts of molestation and assault, but they were not filing complaints with the police. Now, we cannot report on rape cases, till they are registered with the police.

Biswas also explained that they did not know the scale of sexual violence since they were only meeting a few of the thousands of people affected and displaced. Except for one report in the English newspaper, the *Hindustan Times* (Singh 2013) that suggested that large-scale sexual violence took place during the riots, the national media did not report on this issue for one month. This report quoted unnamed police officials, doctors at the relief camps and a human rights activist.

It was only with the help of women's rights activists that the first rape complaints were made to the police on 25 September 2013. By that time, the national media had gone back to Delhi and the news was carried as an update in some news channels and newspapers. There was no reporting from the ground, which would have versions of the victims or any other context (Ghosh 2013). Information provided by activists and lawyers working with victims in the camps continued to be the basis of a few reports like one in the Hindi daily, *Amar Ujala* ('Dangon mein Hua Tha Mahilayon ke Saath Durachaar' 2013) that came thereafter, suggesting that rape was more widespread than the few official police complaints.

Journalists Ammu Joseph and Kalpana Sharma point to a similar role played by women's rights activists after the communal riots in Gujarat in 2002:

> It is an established fact that the mainstream, nationwide media, which covered the horrific, intense and prolonged communal conflagration in Gujarat in 2002 quite boldly and critically, were surprisingly slow to report the rapes and other forms of sexual violence that characterised the carnage. In fact the first to report these gendered crimes were two reports, one by an independent fact-finding team of women (and one man) from different parts of the country and the other by a team from the All India Democratic Women's Association (AIDWA).... Media coverage of the communal crimes against women in Gujarat appears, by and large, to have been catalysed by these reports emerging from the women's movement. (Joseph and Sharma 2006: 52)

There were at least twenty independent fact-finding reports on the Gujarat riots by women's groups and other rights organizations from inside and outside the state. 'The Surviviors Speak' report by a six member team focused specifically on sexual violence against

Muslim women (Hameed et al. 2002). Amongst the details of the horrifying experiences of women, the report also highlighted the problems faced by women in filing official police complaints in a post-riot situation.

Little seems to have changed during the Muzaffarnagar riots. It was *Tehelka* that did the first detailed article in October that explained how a rape victim had to hide even after filing a complaint with the police, as the five accused continued to roam freely in the village (Anand 2013). There was a long lull after this. Newspapers and news channels only carried small updates sourced from news agencies. The investigation into the riots was handed over to the Special Investigative Team (SIT), and medical tests followed the registering of FIRs of rape. Finally, in November–December, the national media revisited Muzaffarnagar and sporadic reports highlighting the plight of rape victims and the lack of police action in making arrests started appearing in the media ('Rape Peediton ko Insaaf Kab?' 2013; Bhonsle 2014; Siddiqui 2013; Vohra 2013). This generated no furore. Unlike the en masse reporting on a rape case that puts a spotlight on the issue and generates a wave of questioning of police, judiciary and government, these reports did not make any impact. This second round of reporting from Muzaffarnagar was otherwise focused on poor conditions in relief camps, which were leading to disease and the deaths of children. The most notable report on sexual violence during this period appeared in *Outlook*, in December 2013, detailing an incident where nineteen women were allegedly raped in one village (Dixit 2013). None of them had filed any complaints with the police.

Hindi newspapers, noticeably, did not report even on the officially registered rape cases in any detail, and restricted themselves to only printing updates supplied by news agencies. Tribhuvun, resident editor of the Udaipur edition of the Hindi newspaper *Dainik Bhaskar* (the second largest circulated multi-edition daily in India), believes that there is a difference between the English and Hindi or vernacular media's coverage of all minorities in general. Making a broader observation, he shared the insights he derived from working in Hindi newspapers for almost three decades now:

> The English media is more sensitive to crimes against religious minorities, Dalits, tribals and women. [The insensitivity of the vernacular media] is due to the biases of some reporters working in the vernacular news industry. There is a lacuna in their education and media training where there isn't enough sensitization to these issues. Their own social influences are more powerful and they lack progressive thinking.

This analysis is a common understanding within the media. Local reporters are often considered too close to the story and themselves part of the social hierarchy in the area to effectively contextualize and balance their reporting. Even though it is a general trend for channels and newspapers to send correspondents from the nearest bureau or head office for in-depth reporting once a news incident gains more attention, in cases where minorities are involved, the preference for such in-depth coverage is even more so.

Tribhuvun also felt that there was an increasing tendency by reporters in smaller cities and villages to get information from the police on the phone rather than make visits to locations to meet victims and assess the situation on their own. This, he felt, could work in incidents of small crimes, but not in a communal violence context or in crimes where women or Dalits or tribals, or Dalit women or tribal women, were involved. These cases, according to him, needed more nuanced understanding, and whenever editors in the bureau could persuade a reporter to visit the location, new and different information emerged.

Perhaps this explains the lack of any remarkable local coverage on such incidents. Instead, more often than not, reporting would only be championed by reporters sent from Delhi, and once they left, it would fade. The same factor may explain the lack of interest in the Hindi language media in the coverage of allegations of sexual assault by the tribal teacher Soni Sori.

In August 2014, the English news magazine *Caravan* did a long article with testimonies by all the seven women who had filed police complaints of rape during rioting in Muzaffarnagar (Dixit 2014). Until then, not a single arrest had been made in these cases. Only by the end of October 2014, a full year after the first complaints were registered, did the SIT make the first arrest ('Muzaffarnagar Riots: Four Gangrape Accused Arrested' 2014). There was no shock or outrage at how long this had taken, and these media reports again became updates supplied by news agencies.

CLOSING THOUGHTS

In navigating the journey of a rape crime statistic to its news report from the perspective of the media that has chosen or ignored it, I have tried to give an insight into the working of our industry. While the nature and structure of the industry in many ways limits and directs how and how much it covers sexual violence, I want to state categorically that I believe the media can do so, and has shown agency and broken boundaries when it deems fit and compelling. And that's why I want to conclude by discussing this quote from one of my interviews: 'News finds its own space.'

The interviewee further explained that they believed the media is not prejudiced in any manner, and a relevant and powerful news item is always able to carve space and prominence for itself in the wider news agenda, forcing news organizations to give it its due coverage. I disagree. Through the various themes that I chart out in this research, it is clear that the media makes active choices about what is given how much prominence and for how long.

In the specific context of sexual violence coverage, it emerges that correspondents and editors allow themselves to be susceptible and pliant to the widespread stereotypes of 'real rape' and 'true victim', and ignore 'marital rape', rape by family members, etc. Consequently, certain perpetrators who already enjoy social impunity to their acts of sexual violence continue to do so as the media almost consciously does not expose them. Instead, it focuses on reporting on particular kinds of rape, perpetuating incorrect notions on its prevalence, incidence, reasons and society's collective responsibility.

Like any service industry, the media too has a market whose needs it has to service. It is inevitable that it would focus on audience interest as determined by language and region. Media companies are run on money. Decisions on deployment of reporters and resources will always have to be a cost-benefit analysis. Hopefully, newer markets will lead to more representative journalism.

But it is worth remembering that the news media is the fourth estate and its responsibility cannot be explained away by practices. As senior journalist Sevanti Ninan and media critic Subarno Chatterji noted, 'Media is ubiquitous, taken for granted, and influences ideas, prejudices, notions of "normal", or "Indian", or "Muslim", or "merit", or "terrorism", or "development". Media bias, ethics and practices are not merely professional matters for journalists' (2013: xvi). Since rape in the custody of the police is a horrific crime that violates dignity and trust, it should be reported on without being clouded by the context of region, reporter presence or context of national security. Rape of women as a tool to shame a community during communal violence is double victimization and needs strong coverage, which should actively seek to verify accounts and expose the lack of faith in governance at such tense times. There could not be a more 'real rape' or 'true victim' than in these cases.

From 1980 to 2012 and beyond, the media has changed. Reportage on sexual violence is not being spearheaded only by feminist journalists, more incidents are getting covered and they are being given increased news space. Journalists are engaging more with feminists and progressive voices, which has brought forth fresher perspectives and newer sources of information into their radar. There are efforts to tell the complex story of rape being used to perpetuate caste-based inequalities. Sexual harassment at the workplace has been acknowledged as an important issue, with even judges being questioned. The media has not hesitated to speak against its own and not shied away from raising uncomfortable questions.

Despite a cut-down on the number of reporters, media houses are making an effort to judiciously use resources such as news agencies to ensure continued in-depth investigative reporter-led journalism. The media market continues to get more competitive with multiple organizations and newer platforms, a trend that has led to the 'campaign-style' coverage. This effort at looking 'distinctive' has had its pitfalls, but, it can be argued, has also been impactful.

On balance, the mainstream English media appears to be more sensitive in the treatment of rape stories, but does seem to be afflicted with a focus on its urban incidence. The mainstream Hindi language media, on the other hand, caters to a different and more mixed urban, semi-urban and increasingly rural audience base. Their coverage of rape comes across as more sensational and afflicted by stereotypes. Some assumptions around coverage of sexual violence, though, are similar across languages (English and Hindi) and platforms (TV and newspaper).

Clearly, this journey has had stops and starts, and may well continue to do so, but there is hope. In a medium where the only thing constant is change, changing audience, changing technology and changing ideas may force it to change its understanding and priorities even more in the coming years.

NOTES

1. Also see the All India Radio website, http://allindiaradio.gov.in (accessed 18 November 2015).
2. The Indian television industry grew by 16 per cent in 2011 and internet subscribers saw an increase of 14 per cent (TRAI 2014a).
3. Every five years since 1995, the GMMP's research has taken the pulse of selected indicators of gender in the news media, studying women's presence in relation to men, gender bias and stereotyping in news media content. The fourth research in the series was conducted in 2009–10 by hundreds of volunteers in 108 countries around the world (GMMP 2010).
4. This issue is explored in detail in the section on the debate on the death penalty.
5. These interviews were conducted in November 2014. The interviewees spoke for themselves and not as representatives of their news organizations. However, their experiences reflected the general beliefs and codes of the workplaces they had been with. The news organizations that the interviewees in this research were working with are: *Dainik Jagran*, *Dainik Bhaskar*, *Rashtriya Sahara*, *Times of India* and *Indian Express* (newspapers); and ABP News, Zee News, IBN7, Times Now, NDTV 24/7 and CNN-IBN (TV news channels). Journalists working in English were interviewed in English and those working in Hindi were interviewed in Hindi. The quotes from the Hindi interviews have been translated.
6. Mathura was raped in a small town in the western Indian state of Maharashtra in 1972. Over the course of the next eight years, the lower court acquitted the policemen of rape, the high court held them guilty, and the Supreme Court again acquitted them. The Supreme Court based its judgement in part on the assumption that

Mathura had been habituated to sex and consented to intercourse with the policemen.

7. The incident took place in a police station in Hyderabad, the capital city of the southern Indian state of Andhra Pradesh (now in Telangana). It sparked protests by women's groups, human rights organizations and the youth, and led to the formation of a one-man commission of enquiry that found the policemen guilty. But the case was transferred to a district judge who acquitted the men and an appeal filed against that acquittal by a women's group was dismissed.
8. Maya Tyagi and her husband were attacked in the small town of Baghpat in the north Indian state of Uttar Pradesh. The outrage that followed forced the home minister to take note and order a judicial enquiry. But according to the commission's recommendations, the policemen were only charged with Section 354 of IPC—assault or criminal force on woman with intent to outrage her modesty.
9. http://www.pucl.org/from-archives/may81/baghpat.htm
10. For the amendment regarding consent in 1983, see http://www.lawyerscollective.org/wp-content/uploads/2008/08/Annexure_3_CONSOLIDATED_TIMELINE.pdf (accessed 19 November 2015).
11. Interview with author November 2014
12. Interview with author November 2014
13. See Rukmini S.'s three-part series published in the *Hindu* (2014a, 2014b, 2014c).
14. Interview with author November, 2014.
15. A video recording of Uma Chakravarti's lecture is available at http://hillele.org/2014/07/20/sexual-violence-in-indian-society-uma-chakravarti-6th-anuradha-ghandy-memorial-lecture/ (accessed 18 December 2015).
16. Interview with author November 2014
17. Interview with author November, 2014
18. The investigation in the case was later handed over to the Central Bureau of Investigation (CBI) from the local police on the demand of the girls' families. The CBI has now said that there is no evidence

of rape or murder; rather, it is a case of suicide. The accused are out on bail and the CBI is in the process of filing a closure report.

19. Interview with author November 2014
20. Ruchika complained of her molestation in 1990, but the harassment that followed drove her to committing suicide three years later. In 2009, the 'light' sentence after a nineteen-year-long trial caused outrage and extensive media coverage. Following this, the sentence of the accused, S.P.S. Rathore, a former police officer, was increased to eighteen months and CBI, the investigative agency in the case, filed fresh FIRs, adding 'abetment to suicide' as a charge against him. That case is still being heard. For more details, see 'Ruchika Molestation Case: Chronology of Events' 2010.
21. TRP or television rating points is a measure of viewership and is used by media outlets, advertisers and sponsors for better targeting of their content and products. In recent years, the method of estimating TRP has been contested and an alternative TV ratings management system is being evolved under the Broadcasting Audience Research Council (BARC). See http://www.barcindia.co.in (accessed 21 December 2015).
22. The AFSPA was introduced in 1958 in Nagaland to fight the Naga secessionist movement and was later applied in Manipur, Jammu and Kashmir, and some other parts of the North-East. It was drawn from the colonial Armed Forces Special Provisions Ordinance, 1942, which had been used to quell the Quit India Movement during India's freedom struggle. The AFSPA's special provisions give the security forces unbridled powers to raid without evidence or warrant, and use force, even fatally. Prosecution can be initiated only if the Government of India sanctions it. Activists have raised the issue of human rights violations in the guise of this impunity. The Justice J.S. Verma Committee set up to look into legal reforms related to violence against women (in the aftermath of the December 2012 gang-rape) called for a review of the AFSPA, noting that 'impunity for systematic or isolated sexual violence in the process of internal security duties is being legitimised by the AFSPA' and 'women in conflict areas are entitled to all the security

and dignity that is afforded to citizens in any other part of our country'. This recommendation was not accepted by the Indian government.

23. Interview with author November 2014
24. *Indian Express* August 19 2014. 'Rape of Badaun victims doubtful: CBI'. – http://indianexpress.com/article/india/india-others/rape-of-badaun-victims-doubtful-cbi/
25. Zee News (9/02/13) – आतंक को फांसी (Terrorism hanged) http://zeenews.india.com/videos/afzal-guru-hanged_19762.html
26. The Wall Street Journal (22/11/12) – Kasab Hanging Sparks Debate on Death Penalty – http://blogs.wsj.com/indiarealtime/2012/11/22/kasab-hanging-sparks-debate-on-death-penalty/
27. The Hindu (15/08/04) – Dhananjoy hanged – http://www.thehindu.com/2004/08/15/stories/2004081509770100.htm
28. The amended law has expanded the definition of rape from 'an act of penile intervention' to now include 'insertion of any object or body part into a woman'.
29. At least 60 people were killed and more than 50,000 were displaced in communal riots in Muzaffarnagar in August–September 2013. Most of them were Muslims, a religious minority community in India.

REFERENCES

Articles

'Accused of Sexual Assault by Staffer, Tehelka Founder Steps down for 6 Months'. 2013. *Indian Express*, 21 November. http://indianexpress.com/article/news-archive/regional/accused-of-sexual-assault-by-staffer-tehelka-founder-steps-down-for-6-months/99/ (accessed 22 December 2015).

'Afzal Guru Hanged'. 2013. Zee News, 9 February. http://zeenews.india.com/videos/afzal-guru-hanged_19762.html (accessed 21 December 2015).

'Anything but the Truth'. 2012. Sanhati, 18 August. http://sanhati.com/articles/5417/ (accessed 21 December 2015).

'Baghpat Report Supports Oppression'. 1981. *PUCL Bulletin*, May 1981. http://www.pucl.org/from-archives/may81/baghpat.htm (accessed 19 November 2015).

'Bhagana Gang-rape: Ab Tak Nahi Jaagi Sarkar' (The government has still not woken up). 2014. *Navbharat Times*, 28 April. http://navbharattimes.indiatimes.com/metro/delhi/crime/bhagana-gang-rape/articleshow/34340080.cms (accessed 21 December 2015).

'Bhagana to Badaun: Caste Conspiracy'. 2014. NDTV, 4 June. https://www.youtube.com/watch?v=H2c9d7d8Wpo (accessed 21 December 2015).

'Crime and Punishment in TOI'. 2012. The Hoot, 21 December. http://blog.thehoot.org/crime-and-punishment-in-the-toi/ (accessed 24 August 2015)

'Dangon mein Hua Tha Mahilayon se Durachaar' (Women were assaulted during riots). 2013. *Amar Ujala*, 9 October. http://www.lucknow.amarujala.com/news/city-news-lkw/rape-in-muzaffarnagar-riots/ (accessed 25 December 2015).

'Death Penalty: Law Panel Seeks Reviews'. 2014. *Times of India*, 24 May. http://timesofindia.indiatimes.com/india/Death-penalty-Law-panel-seeks-views/articleshow/35531638.cms (accessed 21 December 2015).

'Delhi Gang-rape Shakes Parliament; Jaya Bachchan Breaks down, Sushma Swaraj, Others Seek Death Penalty'. 2012. *Indian Express*, 24 December. http://archive.indianexpress.com/news/delhi-gangrape-shakes-parliament – jaya-bachchan-breaks-down-sushma-swaraj-others-seek-death-penalty/1047359/ (22 December 2015).

'Haryana Gang-rape-Murder: Court Gives Death Sentence to Convicts'. 2014. CNN-IBN, 19 February. http://ibnlive.in.com/news/haryana-gangrapemurder-court-gives-death-sentence-to-convicts/452985-3-244.html (accessed 21 December 2015).

'Indian Media Scenario'. 2011. March. http://www.aidem.in/downloads/Indian%20Media%20Scenario.pdf (accessed 18 November 2015).

'The Newshour Debate: Justice through Death Penalty?'. 2014. Times Now, 18 December. http://www.youtube.com/watch?v=Vh2WHdRnAtk and http://www.youtube.com/watch?v=nm1ampGOqqk (accessed 21 December 2015).

'Muzaffarnagar Riots: Four Gangrape Accused Arrested'. 2014. *Indian Express*, 21 October. http://indianexpress.com/article/india/india-others/muzaffarnagar-riots-four-gangrape-accused-arrested/ (accessed 21 December 2015).

'Phansi se Rukega Balaatkaar?' Will capital punishment stop rape?). 2012. ABP News, http://www.youtube.com/watch?v=wwoI1BrR4y0 (accessed 21 December 2015).

'Raahat Bhara Faisla' (Judgement brings relief). 2013. *Dainik Jagran*, 14 September. http://www.jagran.com/editorial/apnibaat-full-relief-decision-10723812.html (accessed 21 December 2015).

'Rape and Punishment: Time for Tougher Laws?'. 2012. NDTV, 22 December. http://www.youtube.com/watch?v=yE2xU5lroGY (accessed 22 December 2015).

'Rape Cases We Forgot: Soni Sori, Chhattisgarh's Prisoner of Conscience'. IBNlive, 4 January. http://ibnlive.in.com/news/rape-cases-we-forgot-soni-sori-chhattisgarhs-prisoner-of-conscience/313817-3-235.html (accessed 21 December 2015).

'Rape Law Ordinance: Govt Rejects J.S. Verma Panel's Recommendations on Marital Rape, Review of AFSPA'. 2013. NDTV, 2 February. http://www.ndtv.com/article/india/rape-law-ordinance-govt-rejects-js-verma-panel-s-recommendations-on-marital-rape-review-of-afspa-325492 (accessed 21 December 2015).

'Rape Peediton ko Insaaf Kab?' (When will rape victims get justice?). 2013. IBN7, 13 November. http://khabar.ibnlive.in.com/news/111796/1/ (accessed 21 December 2015).

'Ruchika Molestation Case: Chronology of Events'. 2010. *Indian Express*, 25 May. http://archive.indianexpress.com/news/ruchika-molestation-case-chronology-of-events/623455/0 (accessed 21 December 2015).

'Soni Sori Jagdalpur Jail Mein Shift Hogi' (Soni Sori will be transferred to Jagdalpur jail). 2013. *Dainik Bhaskar*, 9 January. http://www.

bhaskar.com/news-srh/CHH-RAI-sony-sodhi-will-shift-in-jagdalpur-jail-4142821-NOR.html (accessed 21 December 2015).

'Soni Sori ke Jail Sthanantaran ko Supreme Court ki Hari Jhandi' (Supreme Court agrees to Soni Sori's jail transfer request). 2013. *Dainik Jagran*, 8 January. http://www.jagran.com/news/national-supreme-court-accepted-soni-soris-jail-transfer-appeal-10019233.html (accessed 21 December 2015).

'Tarun Tejpal ne Khub Kamaai Daulat aur Shauhrat, Scandal ne Kar Diya Barbaad' (Tejpal earned a lot of money and fame, but a scandal made him lose it all). 2013. ABP News, 28 November. http://aajtak.intoday.in/story/tarun-tejpal-earned-a-lot-of-money-and-fame-but-lost-all-1-748059.html (accessed 25 December 2015).

'Tejpal ka Tehelka Kaand' (Tejpal's Tehelka saga). 2013. India TV. 29 November. http://www.youtube.com/watch?v=3xmwePIczgY (accessed 25 December 2015).

'Tejpal ne Jo Kiya Woh "Dushkarm"' (What Tejpal did is 'rape'). 2013. *Dainik Jagran*, 29 November. http://www.jagran.com/news/national-tehelka-sexual-assault-case-it-was-a-rape-not-a-sexual-harrassment-10897825.html (accessed 25 December 2015).

'The Complete Email Trail of the Tarun Tejpal Sexual Assault Case'. 2013. CNN-IBN, 28 November. http://ibnlive.in.com/news/the-complete-email-trail-of-the-tarun-tejpal-sexual-assault-case/436601-3.html (accessed 25 December 2015).

'Yahan Dar ke Saaye mein Rehte Hain Dalit' (Here, Dalits live in the shadow of fear). 2014. *India Today*, 5 May. http://m.aajtak.in/story.jsp?sid=763561&secid=66 (accessed 21 December 2015).

Books

Anand, Deevakar. 2013. 'Muzaffarnagar Riots: Rape Accused Roam Freely as Victim Hides in Refugee Camp', *Tehelka*, 6 October. http://www.tehelka.com/rape-accused-named-in-fir-roam-freely-as-victim-hides-in-refugee-camp/ (accessed 21 December 2015).

Arora, Kim. 2012. 'Women's Collectives and human Rights Groups Oppose Death Penalty for Rape', *Times of India*, 25 December.

http://timesofindia.indiatimes.com/india/Womens-collective-and-human-rights-groups-oppose-death-penalty-for-rape/articleshow/17748493.cms (accessed 21 December 2015).

Baxi, Upendra, Vasudha Dhagamwar, Raghunath Kelkar and Lotika Sarkar. 1979. 'An Open Letter to the Chief Justice of India', 16 September. http://pldindia.org/wp-content/uploads/2013/03/Open-Letter-to-CJI-in-the-Mathura-Rape-Case.pdf (accessed 18 November 2015).

Benedict, H. 1992. *Virgin or Vamp: How the Press Covers Sex Crimes.* New York: Oxford University Press

Bhardwaj, Ananya. 2014. 'Dalits Flee Haryana Village after Four Women Raped, Seek Justice in Delhi', *Indian Express*, 20 April. http://indianexpress.com/article/india/india-others/dalits-flee-haryana-village-after-four-women-raped-seek-justice-in-delhi/ (accessed 21 December 2015).

Bhardwaj, Ashutosh. 2012. 'Soni's Story', *Indian Express*, 5 August. http://archive.indianexpress.com/news/soni-s-story/983928/ (accessed 21 December 2015).

Bhattacharya Malabika. 2004. 'Dhananjoy Hanged', *Hindu*, 15 August. http://www.thehindu.com/2004/08/15/stories/2004081509770100.htm (accessed 21 December 2015).

Bhonsle, Anubha. 'Muzaffarnagar Riots: Four Months on, No Rape Accused Arrested', CNN-IBN, 15 January. http://ibnlive.in.com/news/muzaffarnagar-riots-four-months-on-no-rape-accused-arrested/445432-3-242.html (accessed 25 December 2015).

Chakravarti, Uma. 2014. 'Nirbhaya, Muzaffarnagar, Badaun and Beyond: Sexual Violence in Indian Society', 6th Anuradha Ghandy Memorial Lecture. http://hillele.org/2014/07/20/sexual-violence-in-indian-society-uma-chakravarti-6th-anuradha-ghandy-memorial-lecture/ (accessed 18 December 2015).

Chatterjee, Pritha. 2014. 'Badaun Case: Why Few Are Buying CBI's Suicide Theory', *Indian Express*, 1 December. http://indianexpress.com/article/india/india-others/in-badaun-why-few-are-buying-the-cbis-suicide-story/ (accessed 21 December 2015).

Chaudhury, Shoma. 2011. 'The Inconvenient Truth of Soni Sori', *Tehelka*, 15 October. http://archive.tehelka.com/story_main50.asp?filename=Ne151011coverstory.asp (accessed 22 December 2015).

Carli. E.K. 2003. 'News Portrayals of Violence and Women: Implications for Public Policy', American Behavioral Scientist. 2003;46(12):1601–1610.

comScore. 2013. *India Digital Future in Focus*. https://www.comscore.com/Insights/Presentations-and-Whitepapers/2013/2013-India-Digital-Future-in-Focus (accessed 18 November 2015).

Dixit, Neha. 2013. 'Thread Bared', *Outlook*, 30 December. http://www.outlookindia.com/article/Thread-Bared/288907 (accessed 25 December 2015).

————. 2014. 'Has Anyone Here Been Raped and Speaks English? Chilling Accounts of Muzaffarnagar Rapes', *Caravan*, 11 August. http://caravandaily.com/portal/has-anyone-here-been-raped-and-speaks-english-chilling-accounts-of-muzaffarnagar-rapes/ (accessed 25 December 2015).

Ghosh, Deepshikha. 2013. 'Muzaffarnagar's New Horror: Five Women Allegedly Raped by Rioters', NDTV, 1 October. http://www.ndtv.com/article/india/muzaffarnagar-s-new-horror-five-women-allegedly-raped-by-rioters-426080 (accessed 25 December 2015).

Global Media Monitoring Project (GMMP). 2010. *Who Makes the News? GMMP Report*. http://whomakesthenews.org/gmmp/gmmp-reports/gmmp-2010-reports (accessed 18 November 2015).

Grover, Vrinda. 2014. 'Look before You Creep', *Outlook*, 3 March. http://www.outlookindia.com/article/Look-Before-You-Creep-/289599 (accessed 25 December 2015).

Hameed, Syeda S., Ruth Manorama, Malini Ghose, Sheba George, Mari Marcel Thekaekara and Farah Naqvi. 2002. 'The Survivors Speak: How has the Gujarat Massacre affected minority women—Fact-Finding by a Women's Panel', *Outlook*, 2 May. http://www.outlookindia.com/article/The-Survivors-Speak/215433 (accessed 25 December 2015).

Jain, Akanksha. 2014. 'Non-Recognition of Marital Rape Is Hypocrisy: Court', *Hindu*, 5 October. http://www.thehindu.com/news/cities/Delhi/nonrecognition-of-marital-rape-is-hypocrisy-court/article6473013.ece (accessed 18 December 2015).

Jaising, Indira. 2014. 'When I Tried to Move away, he Kissed My Arm, Repeated He Loved Me: Law Intern's Charge against Ganguly', *Indian Express*, 16 December. http://archive.indianexpress.com/news/when-i-tried-to-move-away-he-kissed-my-arm-repeated-he-loved-me-law-interns-charge-against-ganguly/1208135/ (accessed 25 December 2015).

Joseph, A. and K. Sharma. 2006. *Whose News? The Media and Women's Issues*. New Delhi: Sage Publications.

Joseph, Manu. 'What the Elevator Saw', *Outlook*, 7 April. http://www.outlookindia.com/article/What-The-Elevator-Saw/289993 (accessed 21 December 2015).

Justice Verma Committee Report Summary. 2013. http://www.prsindia.org/parliamenttrack/report-summaries/justice-verma-committee-report-summary-2628/ (accessed 22 December 2015).

Kannabiran, K. 1996. 'Rape and the Construction of Communal Identity', in K. Jayawardena and M. Alwis, *Embodied Violence: Communalising Women's Sexuality in South Asia*. London: Zed Books

Mehrotra, Sonal. 2012. 'Outrage over Gallantry Award for Chhattisgarh Police Officer', NDTV, 30 January. http://www.ndtv.com/article/india/outrage-over-gallantry-award-for-chhattisgarh-police-officer-171391 (accessed 21 December 2015).

Ministry of Information and Broadcasting. 2014. 'Status of Permitted Satellite TV Channels in India (as on 15-09-2014)'. http://www.mib.nic.in/writereaddata/documents/Status_at_glance_of_Private_Permitted_Satellite_TV_Channels_as_on_30-04-2014.pdf (accessed 18 November 2015).

Mishra, Neelabh. 2011. 'Oh, It Happens', *Outlook*, 31 October. http://www.outlookindia.com/article/oh-it-happens/278713 (accessed 21 December 2015).

Mishra, Virendra. 2011. 'Gumrah Kar Rahi Hai Giraftar Naxali Samarthak' (Arrested Naxal supporter is trying to mislead), *India Today*, 15 October. http://aajtak.intoday.in/story/Chhattisgarh-Maoist-soni-sodhi-accuses-police-of-harassment-1-66079.html (accessed 21 December 2015).

National Crime Records Bureau (NCRB). 2012. *Crime in India 2012: Statistics.* http://ncrb.nic.in/CD-CII2012/Statistics2012.pdf (accessed 18 November 2015).

Ninan, S. and S. Chatterji. 2013. *The Hoot Reader: Media Practices in Twenty-first Century India.* New Delhi: Oxford University Press

O'Hara, S. 2012. 'Monsters, Playboys, Virgins and Whores: Rape Myths in the News Media's Coverage of Sexual Violence', *Language and Literature*, 21(3): 247–259. http://lal.sagepub.com/content/21/3/247 (accessed 25 December 2015).

Pachauri, Pankaj. 1988. 'Death Penalty: Court Indicts Policemen in Ishwar Singh Tyagi Case', *India Today*, 15 February. http://indiatoday.intoday.in/story/ishwar-singh-tyagi-case-six-uttar-pradesh-policemen-sentenced-to-death/1/328903.html (accessed 18 December 2015).

Roy, Arundhati. 2013. 'A Perfect Day for Democracy', *Hindu*, 11 February. http://www.thehindu.com/opinion/lead/a-perfect-day-for-The democracy/article4397705.ece (accessed 21 December 2015).

Rukmini S. 2014a. 'The Many Shades of Rape Cases in Delhi', *Hindu*, 30 July. http://www.thehindu.com/data/the-many-shades-of-rape-cases-in-delhi/article6261042.ece (accessed 18 December 2015).

————. 2014b. 'Young Love Often Reported as Rape in Our "Cruel Society"', 31 July. http://www.thehindu.com/news/national/stories-behind-sexual-assault-rulings-shine-light-on-reality-of-rape/article6265285.ece (accessed 18 December 2015).

———— 2014c. 'Rape Cases: Scripted FIRs Fail Court Test' 1 August. http://www.thehindu.com/news/cities/Delhi/rape-cases-scripted-firs-fail-court-test/article6268958.ece (accessed 18 December 2015).

Siddiqui, Furquan Ameen. 2013. 'Muzaffarnagar's Gang-rape Victims Sentenced to Silence', *Hindustan Times*, 4 December. http://www.hindustantimes.com/india-news/muzaffarnagaraftermath/muzaffarnagar-s-gang-rape-victims-sentenced-to-silence/article1-1159173.aspx (accessed 25 December 2015).

Singh, Rajesh Kumar. 2013. 'Women Raped by Rioters in Muzaffarnagar', *Hindustan Times*, 13 September. http://www.hindustantimes.com/lucknow/women-raped-by-rioters-in-muzaffarnagar/story-kdHQyryCultrG54GWircxL.html (accessed 22 December 2015).

Sonar, Nupur. 2014. 'I Didn't Know What They Do to Women. But Now I Do', *Tehelka*, 24 May. http://www.tehelka.com/i-didnt-know-what-they-do-to-women-but-now-i-do/ (accessed 22 December 2015).

Stancati, Margherita. 2012. 'Kasab Hanging Sparks Debate on Death Penalty', *Wall Street Journal*, 22 November. http://blogs.wsj.com/indiarealtime/2012/11/22/kasab-hanging-sparks-debate-on-death-penalty/ (accessed 22 December 2015).

Telecom Regulatory Authority of India (TRAI). 2014a. 'Consultation Paper on Issues Relating to Media Ownership', 15 February. http://www.trai.gov.in/WriteReadData/ConsultationPaper/Document/CP_on_Cross_media_%2015-02-2013.pdf (accessed 18 November 2015).

Telecom Regulatory Authority of India (TRAI). 2014b. 'Indian Telecom Services Performance Indicator Report for the Quarter Ending March, 2014', press release. http://www.trai.gov.in/WriteReadData/WhatsNew/Documents/quarterly%20press%20release%20-final.pdf (accessed 18 November 2015).

Thakur, Manoj. 2014. 'Ladkiyon se Gang-rape ke Mamle mein Do Guton mein Bata Hissar ka Gaon Bhagana' (Hisar's village Bhagana divided into two groups on the issue of girls' gang-rape), *Dainik Bhaskar*, 9 May. http://www.bhaskar.com/news/c-3-969611-NOR.html (accessed 25 December 2015).

The Registrar of Newspapers for India (RNI). 2014. *Press in India Report 2013–14.* http://rni.nic.in/pin1314.pdf (accessed 18 November 2015).

Vohra, Aanchal. 2013. 'Knife to Son's Throat, She Was Allegedly Raped during Muzaffarnagar Riots,' NDTV, 30 December. http://www.ndtv.com/article/india/knife-to-son-s-throat-she-was-allegedly-raped-during-muzaffarnagar-riots-464883 (accessed 25 December 2015).

9

Reflections on Sexual Violence in Gujarat

Feminist Friends in Conversation

UMA CHAKRAVARTI AND FARAH NAQVI

Farah Naqvi is a feminist writer and activist who works on gender and minority rights. In this three-part interview with Uma Chakravarti, she reflects on the nature of mass sexual violence in the context of the 2002 Gujarat riots, with a focus on the Bilkis Bano case. In the first part of the interview, she offers an analysis of the identity politics that defined her experiences as a 'Muslim' feminist activist working in post-2002 Gujarat. This shared experience of the varying degrees of injustices faced by her, as an activist; and by Bilkis Bano, as a survivor of violence, is reflected in her able 'companionship' of Bilkis through her legal and ethical struggle for justice, which she discusses at length in the second part. She speaks of the need to create a space for reparation that allows the survivor to define her path to justice. The third and final part of the interview is an exercise in feminist sense-making of an overwhelming and unprecedented situation. She discusses several issues, such as the collective nature of trauma, by focusing on the 'metanarrative' of mass sexual violence during communal unrest; and the need to broaden definitions of sexual violence, to remove it from the limiting context of peno-vaginal penetration.

I
THE SURVIVORS SPEAK[1]

Let's begin with something basic; how did you get involved with the Gujarat situation in 2002?

When the violence happened in 2002, Ahmedabad groups put together a citizen's initiative fact finding team, to focus on what had happened to women during this massacre. I joined the team from Delhi. After that report – 'The Survivors Speak' – came out, the continued involvement was a given. We went to Gujarat at the end of March, and the report came out in April 2002, a quick turnaround. It felt urgent. I suppose most fact-findings are.

Actually, we will get to this point about how the team was assembled, but what is striking is that even before your report came out a couple of other reports had come out – for instance, the AIDWA (All India Democratic Women's Association) did a report on Gujarat 2002 that was out very soon. So tell us something about how the team was assembled and what did you feel?

I was a member of the team. But it was assembled by the Gujarat group, Gagan [Sethi], Martin [Macwan] and others, so I can't say much about why and how that was done. I was approached by Malini Ghose, a friend and colleague from Delhi, to join the team. Basically the team split up, and went to different areas; I went to both Panchmahal and Ahmedabad – which is why my involvement with both Panchmahal and Ahmedabad. What did the fact-finding feel like? Well, to be honest, I haven't thought about it for so many years, Uma. Nobody's asked me actually, what that *felt* like. People ask about facts, not feelings, generally. I think one was so, um...(pauses).

You know, I suspect I will still get emotional when I talk about it, it was...it was a completely life changing fact-finding.

I've never seen or heard or experienced anything quite like it... it was – it was everywhere, you couldn't escape it. In most other fact-findings, it's contained, and you have pockets of normalcy, and then you have an aberration. Here, it was *all* an aberration – you couldn't breathe normal air in Gujarat anywhere at that time. It was overwhelming. Just the inhumanity was overwhelming, the violence was overwhelming, the women, the children, the starvation. It's interesting, the things that the human mind zones in on, when it finds itself incapable of absorbing the magnitude of the horror it must confront. I will never forget the multitudes lying around, broken, bandaged, displaced, in the relief camps, but what struck me immediately was the hunger. That while these people had been denied basic rights of citizenship, they were also hungry, and they needed food and water. It was a combination of denials – from basic human needs [all the way] to rights violations. It was just a denial of everything that we thought was normal, and the idea that this was happening in a so called democratic nation, within the framework of a Constitution, under the rule of law...it violated every fundamental principle that had made me feel secure in this country. And – and the fact that you needed to run away from Gujarat to breathe. At that point, certainly wherever you turned it was there; so much violation, so much human debris, strewn around.

Politically, Gujarat did a thousand things and more. But it also changed some things for my own identity. Before this, I had constructed my identity primarily as a feminist activist. That's who I was. All of a sudden over there, while meeting certain people for the fact finding – and this is a story I have told friends subsequently – I had to keep taking my *bindi* off and on depending on where I was going, because markers of identity were so important when, in a short period of time, you were asking deeply, brutally violated people to trust you. They were looking for identity markers, constantly. Are you Hindu? Are you Muslim? Can we trust you? So, entering the Shah-e-Alam relief camp, I had to take off my bindi. Meeting Maya Kodnani I could put on my bindi.

Also, meeting Maya Kodnani was the first time in my life that I was meeting someone whom I considered to be a murderer, and she was a woman to boot. And some strange behavior around purity and pollution played itself out when we went to her house – because most of us couldn't drink water in her house. She sat there brazenly, justified the murders, rapes, denied all involvement. We were sitting across her like I am sitting across you. And it was an out of body experience because I felt like I was watching ourselves talking to this murderer with – with – reasonable politeness, with a semblance of normalcy. There was something really eerie about that conversation. And I remember none of us drinking water, and not drinking chai, and it often made me wonder. Did we feel we would become morally polluted if we took water from the hands of a murderer?

It's actually more like – 'How can I be beholden for paani (water), which is such a sustaining thing, from someone who is a killer, and my gut is totally against her!' But, yes, it's interesting this bindi business – even I do that. Sometimes I wear it, if I'm going to a place where it will immediately mark me as a woman of the 'other' community, then I don't wear it, you know?

But you know Uma, *humne toh zindagi bhar bindiyaan pehni thi. Meri amma toh ab tak bindi pehenti hain. Humaare yahan kabhi bindi se parhez ya rok nahin thi.* (Uma, all my life I wore bindis. My mother still wears them all the time. There was never any restriction on it.) It was an aesthetic habit. I couldn't see my face without a bindi. It felt naked without one. After Gujarat I never wore a bindi again. It was a small personal thing that changed in my gut. This one marker became so fraught and tainted with memory of those days, and so burdened with 'meaning' that it lost all joy for me as an aesthetic or pleasurable thing. It was a personally troubling journey that started with Gujarat. I felt vulnerable in ways I hadn't ever before.

I remember vividly one experience of personal fear. This was during the election in December 2002. I was in Godhra with fellow activists from Anandi (a Gujarat-based women's NGO) when the results came out. A BJP victory rally was announced in Godhra. And there were these Babu Bajrangi types with gigantic *tilaks* on their foreheads. They were all drunk I think, crowded atop various trucks and jeeps, shouting victory slogans. Crowds lined the jam-packed tiny streets of Godhra. So here they were, fresh on the heels of a carnage, murderers on trucks – yet I wanted to be there rather than hide; to confront and absorb this painful moment. I was quite traumatized that they had won the election on the heels of this carnage. And I remember making eye contact with one man on his truck. And I felt a deep, personal, pulverizing fear. I can't remember if it was Neeta, Sejal or Jhanvi (from Anandi) with me, but I remembering saying, '*Niklo yahaan se boss.*' (Let's get the hell out of here) And they said, *kya hua* (what happened)? And I said, look I haven't got the passport you have. If they find out I have a Muslim name, they might kill me. That momentary alienation from my fellow activists – we may be feminists in this together but I am more vulnerable than you. That fear I felt for the first time in my life.

Jab humne kaha ki hum Panchmahal mein kaam karenge – un dino, one's *aukaat* was only to take the train. *Main train se aaya jaaya karti thi.* Often alone. *Panchmahal Express jaati thi, Dilli se Godhra.* (When I told my family that I was going to work in Panchmahal for a while, and in those days I would come and go by train. Often alone. It was the Panchmahal Express I remember from Delhi to Godhra). For the first time my parents said – book the train under another name. Why? They said the reservation chart stuck on the bogey has names and you will be recognized! For the first time, I was being told in my country, by my own liberal parents, to travel under a false name. It was awful – change your name, be careful, don't travel by train. I said – I can't go by flight, I'm going there every ten days! And I won't change my name.

So these small moments – the bindi business, being asked to change my name, feeling fear – apart from being a journey of justice, it was also personally difficult. And it was a double whammy because I was a woman and our focus was on violence and the sexualized torture of women.

I approached Gujarat very much as a women's rights activist. My antennae were ten times more tuned to a woman's pain than to a man's pain. And I honestly admit that I was biased in my assessment of pain because I was so focused on women's pain. That sense of identification with them and the fear they were feeling – I acutely empathized. I was in complete sync. An aside to this is that though in my politics I dislike clubbing women and children together (I can't stand the construction of 'motherhood as an essential determinant of being a woman' in our culture), physically on the ground, in the relief camps, I had to admit they were a club. Large numbers of survivors in the camps were women with children, who had to be looked after as a unit.

This is coming to me right now – why was it an all-woman team that [went to Gujarat]? Gendered violence has been happening, but around that time there was a lot of information about sexual violence that had happened, and therefore, you needed an all-woman team? An all-woman team will capture something more than the "usual" team that goes – dange samajhne ke liye (to understand a riot.) That might be the reason why you people were assembled as an all-woman team?

I think at that stage there was a sense that there had been a great deal of violence targeted specifically at women. But I don't think there was any knowledge of the extent, of the depth, of the numbers. There were certainly indications, so I think the purpose of this team was not 'sexual violence has happened, go and investigate.' It was more, '*auraton ke saath bahut kuch hua hai*' (a lot of awful things have happened to women) – in a general sense, so an all-woman team needed to be sent. I don't think we were prepared at all for the extent of the violence we encountered. Not at all. It wasn't like going into Bastar or Dantewada today. One has a sense of what horrors are going on there, and they have been going on for a long time. And despite the state's attempts at clampdowns, information has been coming out from Chattisgarh. But in Gujarat I don't think we were prepared for what we saw. I think the entire team was shell-shocked.

It was very, very overwhelming – it was the kind of overwhelming experience that I don't think any human being ever recovers from, Muslim or non-Muslim. It was tough for anybody who engaged with it. I don't think anybody who was on that fact-finding has emerged untouched or completely whole, in how they understand the nature of this beast called communal or targeted violence. I think they've seen the most barbarous face of it and I think anyone who's understood Gujarat, some part of their insides will always be aware of the tenuousness of the nature of democracy and the rule of law. You will never take it for granted. You will never assume that things will ultimately be fine because you've seen it when they went so wrong. The fragility of what we have to fight for every day – you do not take your state structures for granted, you do not take the Constitution for granted, ever.

Having been an activist for as long as I was before Gujarat, I was amazed at my own naivety for having taken a lot of these basic structures for granted – taking their health for granted, assuming that they will work somehow at some basic level when the chips are down. But this was a complete Banana Republic. So, that fundamentally changed for me. A lack of trust for the security of the state as a frame that guarantees us any dignity and security and safety and rights and all of that. I mean, we've always fought against the state to enhance those rights, to improve them, but that the very structure itself is so tenuous. It can go [snaps fingers]. So that changed for me as an activist, in terms of my own politics. To be always aware of that danger.

So now let's get to the report itself. The fact-finding was done in March. How many days were you in the field – about seven or eight?

Less. Five days

And then the report itself came out roughly within a month.

No, we released it in about fifteen days on April 16, 2002

Wow! So the report writing must have been frenetic and I want to address that – because I think what marks that report out was the manner in which you rethought the question of sexual violence [outside of earlier frameworks] in those fifteen days, not only did you have to process all of the material that you got and all the notes that you would have taken, but you actually had to think about sexual violence in some fundamentally changed ways. And I think that's what you should tell us about, because that's really quite important.

It was a process of 'sense-making' – to make meaning of what had happened. Not just call it communal violence. Me and Malini [Ghosh] anchored and wrote the bulk of 'The Survivors Speak' report. I remember days and nights in my tiny flat in Press Enclave, when the two of us sat with our closest friends and partners (men, women, all feminists!) who had been called in to help. It was an 'all-hands-on-deck' kind of urgent moment in all our lives. Kilos of paper were generated in a 10-day frenzy. Notes were typed all day and night. Edited. Corrected. Organized. It was to try and be as honest about what we had actually experienced, as far as humanly possible from the perspective of the survivors. And it was also to do exactly what many fact-findings do, which is to be as accurate as possible, recognizing that this was going to be an endless litany of legal cases that was going to happen, so we could not afford to get our facts wrong about numbers, dates, witnesses, who saw what – all of that.

You have to remember we were feminist activists going in there, and sexual violence was already a part of our understanding and our consciousness. What we had never seen was *mass* sexual violence. And we had no framework to begin an engagement with that as a concept – and that too, embedded in a community context. We were only used to dealing with that as a women's rights issue, in the context of patriarchy – a woman violated by a man, end of story. And I think those were the shifts one begins to make and while we were aware of Dalit activism, and violence against Dalit women, yet the nature of identity in sexual violence was not something that really informed large sections of the so-called 'mainstream' women's movement; in fact there was actually little engagement, or articulation about the nature of identity in sexual crimes, whether Mathura or Rameeza Bee. That understanding is something we now take for granted, many, many, many years later. Fifteen years ago that was not our prime understanding of sexual violence, and our task was to put those two together, and engage with mass sexual violence in the context of identity-based targeting. Because sexual violence had not happened in this manner, on this scale in a communal violence situation post-independence. You see, even the facts we now know about the anti-Sikh pogrom in 1984, emerged later – the five '84 affidavits that spoke of sexual violence, the facts about them emerged in our consciousness much after

'The Survivors Speak.' Because after Gujarat one began intellectually reconstructing a history of sexual violence in communal episodes in India, and in hindsight, our narrative now says we know it happened in '84 as well, it just never got any attention.

We had some gut understanding of communal violence certainly, but not like this. This was not communal violence. To some extent, we had to open our frame. We couldn't just keep calling this a communal riot because it was clearly not. While many of us had done fact-finding on cases of violence against women, very few of us had recorded communal riots before this, which was a good thing. Because we were not restricted by a familiar framework of communal violence, which looks at it generally as an episode to seek legal accountability – documenting what happened, how the police behaved or what the trigger for the attack was, who pelted the first stone etcetera. Our instincts were different – to zero in on notions of – "targeting", "identity", "subjective experience of women" and "make meaning". This was a targeted attack. We were a) freer to work with that, and b) identity issues were increasingly part of our consciousness as well. (Curiously enough, Malini Ghose was constantly being called a Muslim, because despite being a good Bengali (Hindu), she never wears *bindis*, so various people would say – "*lekin aap toh bilkul Muslim lagti hain*" [but you look just like a Muslim!], whatever that means.) We were all made acutely aware of each of our personal identities being so fraught during this fact-finding. And gradually we arrived at a gut understanding of sexual violence in the context of targeted crimes – there was a performative aspect to these crimes, women were specifically targeted, they were not attacked just by chance because they happened to be there, or just as part of the larger attack. There were 'signs' and there were 'signifiers' and there was a message being sent to Muslims. Because this we knew quickly – Gujarat was something new, a new phenomenology of violence against women that we had to describe in frameworks and phrases that we did not then have. I think those were the pushes we had to make.

I think one of the shifts we also made – not a legalistic but a conceptual shift in understanding mass violence – is the idea of the metanarrative that emerges in communal violence. You sit with a group of survivors and hear their stories and you wonder, as you look at each face in turn: is this your story? Is it her story? Or, is it their story? Because they all seem to speak for each other, and overlap, and congeal in the telling. And we said, it really doesn't matter, because this is the 'truth' of it: when you're suffering so much trauma, there is really no notion of reality or falsity. It's all one big traumatic cloud that this group of people is suffering, and that does not make their case any less legally tenable. There were many moments when we felt there was an entire crowd speaking in a single voice of things that actually may not have happened to any of them – and maybe it happened to [one woman] and didn't happen to [another woman] – this merging of pain is both frightening and beautiful, at a human level. It is rare that a human being can experience their own pain in complete sync, in complete empathy with another human being's pain. It's frightening that this happened to a group of people, but it was human beauty – being able to experience another human's pain on par. People were not being able to distinguish 'my pain' from 'your pain', because they had all suffered such gruesome pain. There was something incredible – it sounds odd to put it in a positive light – but there's something amazing about that sharing of human horror, and to lose yourself within that, because otherwise I only feel my cut – I can never feel your cut in quite the same way. But here I saw people experiencing your cut. Looking at mine but describing yours! The idea of the collective is also very important – I'm trying to remember moments and triggers – the idea of the collective pain, the idea of the collective community, and the idea that this level of violence can never be dealt with as an individual crime, it is a crime against a collective. Now, these notions have been there in international law certainly, but in India, at the level of a fact-finding, and our own experiential intellectualizing, these are the trigger points that made those things happen – there is a metanarrative, and that doesn't make it any less solid. It's real, it's true. It is collective pain, and we have to acknowledge that. This is how ideas of targeted violence against a community, and targeted sexual violence come – from those moments of actually seeing and hearing stories in the camps, you know? In hindsight, I think it fundamentally shifted my own understanding and approach to sexual violence itself. To learn to look at the context and not just the act. To discern what that act of violence is 'saying' in a larger sense.

The meta-narrative point you are making is actually crucial from the perspective of the congealed narrative. Do you think that the sexual violence also became that kind of a collectively experienced thing?

Sexual violence was less a part of what you are calling 'the congealed narrative' – less so than the other forms of brutality we heard about – the maiming and torturing and burning and murdering in cruel painful ways. You see tragically, far too many of the women who were raped were burnt. They were simply not there to bear witness to what had happened. Just a few survived to tell that story. So, what you did have was people describing it – at that level there was congealing happening. The victims themselves – a bulk of them were killed. And so, when you actually got someone to say, did it happen to you, it took a long time to figure out that this didn't happen to them. They are describing in first person what happened to somebody else.

So in that sense it did become a congealed narrative. But also in a gendered way. That would not be the story of every man?

Yes…in that sense it did. Sexual violence against men, pulling down their pants, hitting them in the groin, crushing penises to a pulp – these acts were not even recorded, let alone entered into any narrative. But the other new thing about sexual violence against women – that now has become a common enough part of the Gujarat narrative – but at the time it was a new shift we noted in 'The Survivors Speak' report – how open it was. I'd never heard sexual violence being talked about so openly anywhere, the way it was in those camps, the relief camps. There was no hiding it! I feel sad that we had a window, although a very brief window, and we as feminist activists did not push it wide open. We had a window during which much more litigation on women's violations could and should have happened, and we didn't act then. A window, when it was just out there and nobody could possibly deny it! Because it happened to so many women and there were so many witnesses and they were all there in those camps. The denial that always happens in sexual violence, couldn't happen in the immediate aftermath of such violence, but it did happen soon after, which we discovered to our great sadness. After 'The Survivors Speak', Malini and I went back to do a follow up – 'The Survivors Speak Part 2' – which we did not circulate very widely at that point. We discovered even more and more and more cases of sexual violence in the hinterland, but which had now been subjected to all the denials that generally accompany sexual violence – parents were in denial, no one wanted to pursue cases. Shutters were now downed. In that first flush after the violence – that was when people wanted to pursue cases because it had happened so publicly that there was no denying it and we could and should have acted then on a far greater number of cases.

But I remember when we did the International Initiative for Justice for Gujarat (IIJG) report, I think there was a very important way in which the thinking around 'The Survivors Speak' fed very dramatically into the IIJG formulations.[2] *At that stage, the argument of, why was it not public? Why were there not that many more cases? Because the public-ness of the public violations was very clear. Why was it that it did not actually lead to much more litigation? The thing that we all denied but that came out of 'The Survivors Speak' is that it is because they didn't think they were going to get justice. The public-ness was not denied, there was nothing to hide, because everyone knew it had happened. That it did not lead to litigation is another question around the way that justice is delivered, and the faith that you have in the justice system. And I think that was part of the reason we didn't have enough cases.*

Yes. Perhaps. Also, in Gujarat, the legal desire was to go for the low hanging fruit, which was the mass murders. To prove rape, beyond a reasonable doubt, with no body, and certainly no forensics, was difficult. This is what was being said – if you lose the rape, you are going to weaken your murder rap as well, please don't burden this case with too much, whether they get punished for murder or theft, how does it matter to you? If the same guys have killed also, let's get them on the murder, because we have a body. To prove the killing all we need is the body, to prove rape, we have to prove that they first raped that body, which is now half charred and has no evidence. So, these conversations were happening often when we were sitting with a group of lawyers – by the way all male lawyers, for the most part. Many of them Muslim male lawyers and perhaps for them there was discomfort with taking on sexual violence. There was no collective of women lawyers. And certainly at the trial court level where we were hanging around in Panchmahal, it was all a bunch of men, expressing a desire to keep rape off the radar. "*Aap kyun kar rahe ho yeh? Yeh sab cases aap chhod dijiye, is mein se yeh charge hata dijiye, nahi toh aapka yeh bhi charge jaayega aur murder bhi jaayega. If they disprove it, aap kaise prove karoge?*" (Why are you doing this? Leave all these rape cases, drop the rape charge, otherwise the charge will not stick and they will get off on murder also. How will you prove the rape?) Legally, it seems like rubbish. Why would it weaken the case? But, on this issue of supression of rape cases, I feel there were probably two things going on – one just a simple and male-centric lack of interest in focussing on specific violations experienced by women qua women. But also, in hindsight, I think *baad mein samajh mein aaya also, ki yeh sexual violence humaare liye bahut important tha, but un logon ke liye bahut sari aur cheezein bahut zyada critical thi. Bilkis ke liye bhi.* (I think I understood it later, that while sexual violence as an issue was important for us as feminists, for the survivors a whole lot of other violations were perhaps more important, even probably for Bilkis) She was brutally raped, but that was not the most egregious hurt she suffered.

In those months, you were actually trying, you were trying to bring more visibility to the rape cases and you were trying to pursue them. In some report there was a case of forty rapes happening in a certain area, but when you went back, not even three would come forward. So actually there was that difference, that was the level of suppression.

Women stripped, women being made to walk naked, women not talking about it… moments of sitting at night in a room in a village in Dahod district, a closed room, lit by a *laalten* (lantern), packed with women, and initially nobody would talk, and when they started talking, I felt I was drowning.

A dam burst!

I felt I was drowning. I couldn't take notes, I could barely hear. It was just being surrounded by an ocean of pain and violation. You're just another activist. You have nothing to offer immediately. And that moment of helplessness that you experience – all I've got is my pen, I can do nothing immediately for these women, so all you can promise is, 'I will make sure this story never dies.' But in the middle of this tragedy there are also so many moments that restore your faith in humanity – a moment when a completely ravaged fellow human being looks you in the eye and trusts you enough to tell you their story, that's a completely human moment. They have no reason to trust anybody in the world. Who do we trust anymore when human beings can do this to each other? And they trust you, and that is affirming of the power of humanity. Those moments of human connect are so deep that you don't emerge from them completely dead. Otherwise you can't emerge from this a whole human being, but I did, and so did everyone else who went. Because you also have these incredible powerful moments of human connection, which feel like, my god! At a completely gut level. *Itna sab hone ke baad koi aapko trust karta hai, bahut badi baat hai, bahut badi baat hai.* (After all that has happened someone is willing to trust you, it is a very big thing, a very big thing)

II
THE SIGNIFICANCE OF BILKIS [3]

Why is the Bilkis case so significant according to you? There were other cases also of women...?

Many. Medina and Sultana also. Medina [from Eral Village] won her case – this was her daughter and her niece, both of whom were raped and killed, and she and others were the witnesses to that. You see, this was actually a very important case which didn't get the space it deserved – neither girl was alive to tell her story and the rape charge stayed on the evidence of eye-witnesses. And that was a very important breakthrough in sexual crimes in a targeted, mass violence context. So the Eral case was won in the trial court. I'm not quite sure what happened to Sultana's case – she was under enormous pressure, she was alone, her husband was killed. Local activists in Kalol were already working with her, so we did not.

So how come the special significance of the Bilkis case?

She represents and represented something powerful in the context of impunity for Gujarat. She represented a living witness, a living survivor who was talking about mass murder and gang-rape; she wasn't hiding anything, and she was saying she wanted justice. This was a powerful combination of factors. Bilkis at one level was simply a woman in distress who needed help to get justice, but she also symbolized something so vital. She was many things – a woman, a survivor, a symbol and a strong human being through a difficult six year journey – from the Supreme Court to an entirely new CBI investigation, and transfer of the trial to a Mumbai Sessions Court and the trial itself for three years from 2005 to 2008, and then the appeal process in the High Court, over nine years later. As feminist activists, it was incumbent on us to not allow it to be erased from history that women were brutally sexually tortured in Gujarat; to create that historical record, to legally prove it; to collectively support her struggle.

Let us talk about the group dynamics of a bunch of you feminists. On the one hand there was this terrible territoriality regarding the cases in Gujarat. But in complete contrast to this proprietary air, there is this other collective and low profile process that you were involved in. Something of that is also critical as we record the history of feminist struggle, that sexual violence happened in Gujarat and there was a living witness to testify to it, that's one of the things that we put down and leave for history. But another thing we need to leave for history is how should we ensure that a case is actually fought on the principle that you are not interested in the personal victory of A lawyer or B lawyer, or A activist or B activist. For me when I hear the Bilkis story – although I did meet her in August and December – I think this process is very important for us to document.

You know, this process has no conscious intellectualizing around it. It just emerged because of our shared politics and activism – me, Huma [Khan], Malini, Madhavi [Kukreja], and Gagan, and the many, many others who were involved and cared about the outcome of this struggle. We knew no other way to do it.

And this was friendship based?

This was commitment based! Above all else. Yes, we all knew each other, we had worked with each other before. And each of us subscribed to an unspoken work-ethic that says these struggles are about the survivors, not about activists. We were ambitious, very ambitious – and we fought hard for that ambition. But there was no 'my case or your case'. Visibility never occurred to us, except maybe to instinctively stay away from it. I don't know. We were and are a team, and it was just an intuitive, determined, collective push to a goal – bring out the truth of what happened to women in Gujarat – the truth, the undeniable truth, in a court of law. It was a limited goal, but a clear goal.

We kept focus on sexual violence, because this was an issue on which we felt we had a far better handle, deeper commitment, and experience than most other groups that were taking up legal cases. And in this respect, we felt we could and we should make this contribution to the larger struggle against impunity for Gujarat. We saw ourselves very much as partners in a larger struggle, for that is how it should be when something like Gujarat happens. That, at least is how we approached and discussed it among ourselves. We said – this is what we are good at. Our job was to use our expertise – which was not just as feminists in a theoretical sense, but as feminist activists, with a strong political impulse to defeat communalism, and years of experience of working with survivors of sexual violence. How do you get a sexual violence survivor to express herself? What is the kind of consistent support they need over an extended period of time? It's not easy to get them to live and relive and have that comfort with you and to understand what lies ahead of them.

To my mind the single biggest lacunae in getting legal justice for women is the absence of support before, during, and after. In a mass violence situation, in communal and targeted violence even more so, because the survivor's traditional, familial sources of support have literally been decimated, killed. Then there is physical displacement – you're uprooted from your home. And the survivor really is alone. A framework that embraces rehabilitation of an entire community is absolutely critical for legal justice.

The feminist lawyering-activism that is needed in a communal violence situation for a sexual violence survivor has to include all of this – daily sustenance and long term trust. You are helping people reconstruct their entire life, and the legal battle is part of that reconstruction, but it's just a part. I find our conception of what a legal battle requires is so narrow. Relief, rehabilitation, witness protection, hand holding, supporting, reassuring again and again, restoring confidence not just in the survivor but in her entire community that you will be there for the long haul, helping them resist pressures, standing solidly with them – all of that is key. You need to be there on the ground physically, visibly with them. The community needs to see your presence as a tangible tactile thing. This can include making sure that when family members are sick we are there for them as well. It's not just about filing legal papers or arguments in courts. You may need to be there on call when there is the inevitable friction in the home, to get involved in domestic disputes. In a post-trauma situation, for a sexual violence survivor there is generally a lot of tension between husbands and wives, on so many things – about kids, about jobs, the daily struggle of living again. Men, in these situations have lost everything, their work, ability to protect their wives and children. As patriarchs in a traditional framework, they see themselves as having failed, so tensions have to be released somewhere, somehow. Displaced children need to be helped to get admission into schools – all these are aspects of real life – there is no demarcation of just the legal battle. You work with the understanding that a victim-survivor is more than a 'case'. She is a real live human being with flaws and strengths, and a wounded heart and a tortured mind, and moments of weakness and anger and irrationality, even with you. And you embrace all of it, take her community along, so witnesses don't falter, and only then can you work towards legal justice with her. The legwork that builds a relationship with her entire community is really critical in order to get legal justice for a sexual violence survivor in these mass violence circumstances. At the end of the day, activists and survivors are companions in a journey, and we all win, legally and ethically, when these journeys are open, honest, communicative and collective.

Do you feel Bilkis sees her own struggle for legal justice in the same way others saw her struggle for justice, or was there some difference in the way she thought about it?

You'd have to ask her. I think there was some difference. Perhaps for Bilkis, the sexual violence that she experienced was not the prime violation. For her there were far greater violations that happened. You can see it all in her press statements.

They killed her daughter and child.

They killed her entire family, 14 members, barring a father and one brother, women were raped before being killed, she herself was gang-raped and her daughter was killed by having her head smashed on a rock. So what was the space occupied by sexual violence in the series of violations this woman experienced – losing her home, losing her entire family, mothers, aunts, *chachis*, uncles, *bhais*, and losing – watching her child be killed in front of her? I think for Bilkis that was the big thing – losing Saleha in this way was singularly the most traumatic. Yet Bilkis will probably be recorded in history primarily as the gang-rape victim. That is her dominant identity and image. But the truth of her own subjective experience is perhaps different. There were other many powerful moments of her tragedy. And, I do not believe, she related to this only as woman qua woman. It was not – *main aurat hoon, aur mere shareer ko violate kiya gaya hai* (It was not – I am a woman and my body was violated). This was not the language in which she framed her own tragedy or constructed that entire episode in her head. Again, read her statements, and in this context the first statement she made in Delhi, after the Trial Court verdict in 2008, is clear. For her, it was much more of a community issue. She articulated it largely as a Muslim woman, that she was brutalized because she and her family and her daughter were all Muslim, and that was the hatred which destroyed her life.

And she lost her child because that little child was Muslim.

Yes. As activists we need to see – *hamaari approach kya hai aur uski approach kya hai.* (We need to see what is our approach to the tragedy and what is the survivor's approach?) But we need to have the honesty to recognize these differences through the battle and allow every survivor the space to approach it the way she wants to approach it… And I think that gives us cause to pause and reflect on our own – on the primacy that we give sexual violence and our own understanding as feminists on the nature of violation itself. Why do we give it the primacy that we give it? I think we need to theorize it better and in more accessible ways to younger activists, otherwise it simply becomes sexual violence for the sake of sexual violence, and it stands the danger of becoming just a women's issue, which it is not. I think we need to nuance our own position, when we talk about marital rape for instance, let us think about the numerous violations within marriage, and articulate better why we focus on marital rape, for our focus appears to pedestalize it as a more privileged violation than a host of others?

But as long as our goals were not dissonant, as long as they did not cause us – as feminist activists and as Bilkis, or any other survivor – to push and pull in different directions, and as long as there was space for all articulations to be made, and for them to become part of a larger legal goal, I think that's all right. But to also have enough of an open mind to be able to reflect on what that meant, for us as feminists as well, to engage with a case that we thought was defined as a feminist or women's rights issue, but it may not be for the survivor.

In a sense I think fundamentally you're interrogating the hierarchization of the violence that the survivor experiences – that is, the rape over the loss of the – watching the child die. Certainly the abiding memory is going to be the child that she lost, the innocent child that is killed before her eyes, and she cannot save it. There is nothing that she can do to save her child. To that extent there's something wrong with our feminist formulations if we think that this is worse than that. For her it would have to be that, this is the brutality, in which the child is killed in front of its mother, what can be more brutal? Do you think that is one reason why, when the first judgment came, the Trial Court judgment – and I remember talking to you about this, that how important was it, how validated did she feel? I remember, one of the things that all of us, including you, were concerned about was that the state had not been indicted, despite police complicity in placing salt on the bodies, and burying evidence – only one of them got punished by the Trial Court – from our point of view it was a major disappointment. And then comes the High Court judgment nearly nine or ten years later, which finally convicts the state officials. Historic. I think the first Gujarat case where they are indicted in such strong words. So tell us something about your reaction to both judgments. Did her response change?

Again, I do not speak for her, but I believe she was extremely happy with the core of the Trial Court judgment in 2008 – the conviction of the prime accused. Out of twenty accused, the eleven main accused who had murdered and raped got life sentences, (there were twelve, but one of them passed away during the trial) and one policeman who had directly threatened her with a lethal injection when she tried to lodge her complaint got three years. But seven accused – five policemen and the two doctors – were acquitted.

You have to remember that Bilkis may not necessarily be articulating this to herself *primarily* in terms of a violation by the state, above and beyond the physicality of the actual perpetrators. Yes, she knew how much the state/government was complicit in what she suffered, and yes, she has spoken with pain about betrayal by the '*sarkar*' (government), but the perpetrators that she knew from her village, that was something very deep and personal. She needed to see them punished. Because they had looked her in the eye and killed her child; they had looked her in the eye and raped her; they had looked her in the eye and killed her mother and her aunt and her brother. And these were people she grew up with in her village. I think there is a very strong aspect of seeking justice for that personal betrayal from a survivor's perspective. For us as activists, for you, for me, for all of us who have cared about the outcome of her journey, it was equally framed in terms of state accountability. And so yes, that the police officers and medical doctors who presided over a massive cover-up didn't get jail-time, that senior policemen accused of criminal conspiracy were not convicted by the Trial Court, was disappointing. But, like I said I think for Bilkis, the fact that the main perpetrators were convicted, the killers were convicted, was deeply satisfying, and like she said herself publicly – a vindication of her truth. That is what she wanted. Her truth upheld.

Now with the High Court judgment of 2017, she has achieved a more complete and greater moral victory, and she has done it with such grace and resilience. Both she and Yakub have. They have held themselves together for fifteen years. 'Holding the state accountable', these are not the phrases in which she speaks, but the fact that she had to leave the land of her birth, her very own Gujarat, to seek justice elsewhere (in Mumbai) has always hurt both her and Yakub very deeply. He broke down when he said this at the Press Conference in Ahmedabad after the High Court verdict in May 2017. And the fact that that 'her' sarkar was complicit in her torture, and even afterwards it did not seek to correct, help, did not inquire about her, offered her nothing, not even a sorry, has angered and hurt her. To see officers of that same 'sarkar' convicted has meant a lot to both of them. To find the courts on her side has affirmed her faith in some small way in the system. Her own articulation on the '*phaasi*' (capital punishment by hanging) issue, on death penalty, has been nuanced. She has said that she wanted the maximum the law could give them. But as she said most recently, she also did not want any blood on her hands, or more killing in the name of Saleha, the daughter she lost in the carnage. When she said at the Delhi Press Conference just after the High Court verdict, that she wanted 'justice not revenge', she meant it, from somewhere deep down, emotionally. And she and Yakub want a safe future for their children, their daughters especially.

Particularly now… when so much time has passed…. Did you know she had a third daughter? She had another Saleha.

Oh, she had another Saleha?

She named her first child Hajra (the child she was pregnant with when she was attacked), but it was her third daughter who she named Saleha. And I think that was a moment of some closure for Bilkis. Maybe she was finally ready to seek closure.

She's making her own statement then. "I got my child back".

She needed some closure to heal the wound of Saleha's loss, and perhaps naming another one of her children Saleha was the way she did it.

How did you react to the High Court verdict, amid the great public mood that has been howling for the death penalty for sexual violence?

Our politics, as activists, was always categorically against the death penalty. It was never the quantum of punishment, but the accountability of the accused and of the state that mattered. But, yes, it once again stuns you, this bizarre legal standard of "rarest of the rare". I mean, how much rarer do you need a crime to get? You've got a combination of mass murder, gang-rape, murder of a child and complete political cover up and conspiracy, and yet it's not the rarest of rare and the worst of the worst? So that is a curious moment, of realizing that while you so much want legal acknowledgement of the egregiousness of what a human being has suffered, the 'rarest of rare' is ultimately a subjective standard. It is a moment of emotionally accepting what one intellectually knows – that this is precisely why we need to do away with death penalty, the completely capricious and arbitrary and yes, prejudiced history of awarding death penalty in India.

We've all had many discussions about it, about the High Court judgment, how Bilkis and Yakub feel, how all of us felt, and I think that her public stand – 'I want justice, not revenge' – is ultimately what makes the women's movement and feminist politics proud. Because what she has achieved is not just a legal, but a moral victory.

III
REFLECTIONS ON MASS SEXUAL VIOLENCE

I remember in more reflective mode, you have spoken on various occasions – the difficulty of actually keeping Bilkis at the centre of one's thinking. And when the community decides to appropriate her as a symbol. She becomes the ideal witness. And yet actually in the rhetoric, it is a celebration of the husband – the greatness of the husband in taking her back. And I remember you being very critical – tell us something about that, because I remember you speaking about this at one of our meetings also. You remember Mr. Bandukwala? He was so appreciative of the husband's role in all of this...

I've carried a report with me so let me read it to you – this report of a 'memorializing' event in Ahmedabad, in 2012 where Professor J.S. Bandukwala said, "All praise according to me goes to Bilkis' husband Yakub Rasool who has not only stood by his wife despite [the fact that] she was raped several times during the riots in 2002, but, he also protects her and takes full care of her. He earns petty money by selling milk pouches but has been looking after his wife. I feel such MEN should be awarded and rewarded with 'Bharat Ratna' awards for their real bravery. Yakub is indeed a living example of resilience and commitment."

This completely normal act of a normal human being was pedestalized because our standards of expectations from Indian men are so lousy. This reasonably normal behaviour, that you simply don't abandon a wife who's been gang-raped and who's lost her child...and you don't need to garland the man for doing that! The response of secular male activists to the 'greatness' of Yakub was very problematic, and it came from a very patriarchal place. In other words, the abandonment of a woman who has been violated is to be expected; it is the 'normal', and anybody who doesn't do that therefore deserves the Bharat Ratna. It's problematic for Yakub, because it exceptionalizes him, and he should not be exceptionalized. Our attitude to him should not be – '*Aap bahut mahaan ho, aap aisi luti-piti biwi ko waapas le rahe ho!*' (You are so great for taking back this beaten, raped wife!)...But I think we also need to make it possible for men in these situations to remain normal. Often people (especially male lawyers) tend to address themselves to the accompanying male (husband), even if the woman is the victim. Or, at the other extreme, the female-victim is put on a pedestal, and treated like an isolated atom. But if you're working with a survivor not extracted as 'the victim', or treated like an isolated atom, but within the context of her entire family and community, the husband is naturally an important part of her story and her tragedy, and we engage with them as a composite context for the harm she has suffered. With this approach, he feels secure, not threatened about being displaced in the narrative that he is after all a key part of also, and so he does not act out or compensate in strange patriarchal ways, or feel the need to behave exceptionally macho, or feel he deserves a Bharat Ratna!

And I also think, gratefully, that in some cases in India, we have begun to dent the hypocrisy of purity and pollution around sexual violence. The fact is it was always a hypocritical position. No one is so *doodh mein dhula* (No one is pure as driven snow). To use this as an excuse to leave a woman, is now more and more being seen exactly for what it is. It's merely an excuse. And the notions of *izzat* (honour) are less and less salient. And I think that these are all positive shifts that are happening in general around rape.

It is one form of harm, and not more than that.

Yes and no. It is a specific form of crime and torture. That it is about power and not sex is our staple feminist mantra. But we need to unpackage it and articulate it better – what sexual violence does to subjective sexuality? How the messaging around it in a mass violence context constructs itself through both notions of violent sex with the 'female of the other community' and the power in that act? How it feeds a public discourse? And we need to put centre stage that there is a titillating, performative aspect to all descriptions of sexual violence in the public domain. It works in the mind's eye; it is an over-visualized crime. A gang-rape victim gets stared at like an object of lascivious curiosity. It gets greater eyeballs. A murder as an issue will not get as many television eyeballs as gang-rape. And how do we deal with this reality in our feminist-activism? Even post-Gujarat, even while doing 'The Survivors Speak', one was constantly aware of this. That we are constantly talking about rape and rape and rape, and for the audience, or the reader, there is the titillating nature of this. Why do rape stories sell more than murder stories? As feminists we should put that centre stage, and ask what are we doing with it? Are we feeding this? And I think that post-Gujarat, and everything after, has given me a lot of reason to introspect on my own approach to it. Which is why maybe when we discuss the marital rape issue, I find myself getting equally exercised by domestic violence and other forms of violence against women including psychological harm. I think that having travelled these conceptual journeys, we need to stop and pause on how we engage, and project, and hierarchize issues of rape, sexual violence, and violence against women in general. We need to engage with it without taking positions, without judging each other's feminisms or mistrusting each other's politics.

I think the "obsession" with marital rape actually is coming from a reverse logic. It is because the non-acknowledgement of it is coming from the notion of this sacred contract between men and women, within which women don't have agency, and that's where the discomfort comes in. And I remember it was a shock for me was to find the Army General arguing the case on television after the Verma committee's [position on] marital rape and the AFSPA [Armed Forces (Special Powers) Act], or rape by the soldiers – in a sense, the two things that we never got after Verma. And the argument that was being put forward by the Army General was that AFSPA is a sacred document. And how can you talk about marital rape, am I going around policing every single one of my jawans on whether he is committing marital rape or not? I mean, it was quite extraordinary, you know! So, my understanding – my irritation with the whole thing, my annoyance, is coming not from the feeling that it's the worst thing, or priority number one, but it's the boundaries that you're putting – there are definitions within which you are working, and it's not to do with us. If we are hyper about it, it's in response to the refusal of everyone around you to acknowledge that such a thing happens. If a rape is a rape is a rape, and it's not consensual, then it has to be that in every single location. And if we haven't got it now, we have to look at the politics of why we haven't got it until now, rather than saying it is the number one issue for us to be pursuing.

The politics of why we haven't got marital rape on our statute books yet is very simple, it's not rocket science...it's patriarchy, institution of marriage and the conception of the domestic space and home. Marriage is the real problem – the institution of heterosexual marriage. At its core it is about the man's promise to protect and provide financial upkeep, in exchange for access to a woman's body and womb. As long as we accept the fundamentals of the institution of heterosexual marriage itself, we will face resistance to criminalization of marital rape, because acts that you and I consider marital rape are so much part of the essential definition of the marriage contract, not in a legal sense but a societal sense. So, the feminist project of questioning institutionalized heterosexual matrimony is deeply relevant.

[Laughing] Guys saying, "I'm very happy, I can have sex whenever I want because my wife lets me." It's like as simple as that. It's like – "Theek hai, she's my property, mai uske saath jo bhi kar sakta hoon." (Okay, she is my property, so I can do what I want with her.)

It's true that – I think it's the refusal – first, I think the delicacy with which you have to step around that – that is irritating. Not that it's the greatest violation, but certainly on this question of the rape and surviving rape as some kind of extraordinary trauma. And on this note, I had completely forgotten this, but when we did the fact-finding in Bhagalpur, Urvashi – we were all on that fact-finding together, we were trying to figure out kya hua (what happened), we never got actual cases of sexual violence. Because all there was, was verbal sexual violence, and breasts that had been cut off and so on – that was a thing. But nobody mentioned a case of rape. Urvashi says that she remembers asking, and they said, "Woh kya hai, woh to hota hi rehta hai", big deal. Woh to gharon mein bhi hota hai. (What about rape? It keeps happening. What's the big deal? It even happens within homes.) So they weren't privileging that as a wrong. Instead, there is this extraordinary account where a young Hindu woman watches a crowd go after an old Muslim man, and says, "Uske peechhe kyon ja rahe ho, woh to bachcha paida nahi kar sakta hai, iske peechhe jao." (Why are you getting behind him [the old man]? He can't even reproduce. Try to get to someone like him instead.) – a young man who can still reproduce. And that was much more shocking in terms of women's complicity in the fact of violence.

Yes. How do we deal with that? Women's complicity and sexual violence against men? All vital questions. I think we did deal quite directly with the issue of women's complicity in violence, even in sexual violence, post-Gujarat. And there was insightful theorizing around the role of women in right-wing mobilization, but on sexual violence against men, there is a lot to be said and done.

But I hear you, Uma, on marital rape. If they would just put it in the damn law and get it over with, we can move on. But it is the most egregious of all violations in the domestic sphere? Burning her, beating her, torturing her psychologically – among the many violations in marriages. Martial rape is also not the same as the rape that socially shames (and shame is an internalized thing for many women, no matter how hard we rail against it in our discourse), because it is a socially legitimized rape. So we need to engage in more nuanced ways. Yes, the blanket denial around marital rape, the normalizing of it, is unacceptable. So I hear you. And that impulse – to rail against 'normalization' of violation – that's what prompted support for Bilkis as well…that you're not even admitting that sexual violence happened in Gujarat. Why should women tolerate even a slap as normal?

And what is your intent in doing it? It's the hatred that drives sexual violence targeted at a certain community that is the problem. Not the surviving of sexual violence itself.

Yes that is what is important – the hatred that drove it. But this articulation of sexual violence as the worst of the worst, and a rape victim as being a '*zinda laash*' (living dead), and all of this, we need to change this….

Haan, zinda laash, uff!!

No, no, but Uma you know, the 'zinda laash' mentality may be articulated by Sushma Swaraj, but even in feminist or liberal understanding, that sense vaguely hovers, that you treat a rape-survivor with an 'exceptional victim-hood'. Like I said, I do believe sexual crimes are a specific and horrific set of crimes, a specific form of torture, dissimilar to others. We can neither normalize it nor minimize it. And no one should have to suffer anything, but I think we all agree that it is not the worst thing that could happen to a woman. I think what happens in making sure that it's not invisibilized, we willy-nilly come across as appearing to pedestalize it and we need to be watchful of that line constantly.

But equally, I think there have been huge gains from placing a feminist lens on mass sexual violence. We are subject experts. There is no denying that. One of the big things of Gujarat for me was to expand and stretch the notions of what is sexual violence, sexual torture. And that has fed directly into the Verma committee report, new definitions in the rape laws, and those changes have very much come about because we all collectively placed a feminist eye on the phenomenon of sexual violence in Gujarat.

Stripping and parading and all of that?

Yes.

That's actually the learning we got, watching Gujarat. That and the tragedy of a society, which says we can't get justice, therefore we don't proceed with the law. For me, that's a greater tragedy – the idea that justice will not be delivered, for me that's the worst tragedy because it means that the same Constitution is a dead letter and the Right to Life and the Right to Bodily Autonomy is a dead letter, and the law will not protect me on that. It's that impunity that I am concerned with rather than the sexual violence. You don't speak about it, you sweep it under the carpet. If you treat it like everything else, mera naak kata, mera hath kata, (my nose has been cut or; my hand has been severed)- I was raped, and there was also this thing. It's a series in a continuum of targeted violence. And there is a politics to that targeting. That's the bottom line as far as thinking about sexual violence in this context.

Yes. I agree. The struggle against impunity is the core battle. For that, to dent impunity – definitions expand *karna bahut zaroori tha.* (There was an urgent need to expand the definitions of impunity.) There need to be expansive definitions that describe the nature of sexualized torture on women's bodies.

That – that I think is a great expansion.

Cutting, stripping, parading, burning – all of this is within the rubric of sexual violence that also feels good as a feminist because it gets you away from the peno-vaginal penetration.

And the reproductive logic, and the purity of the sexual property, can be [done away with]. Fantastic!

The expanding of these definitions gets us away from the notions of *izzat* (honour), because it takes us away from the peno-vaginal focus. And I think that was another gain.

Big move. I think those were big moves. And I think my irritation with Partition studies has been that the – I was so fed up of the formulation that said the nation's honour is built on the bodies of women. I just hate that, that line was just the most offensive line to me because it just hides so much.

Much more than it reveals.

The bodies of women? What do we say about male sexual violence? Why don't they speak about it? It's not the shame – in fact, there is greater shame on the part of men. But then it's not being built on the bodies of men. So you have to think in a way that captures all the complexities -

And the burden on those women on whom – *Pehle to family honour. Phir community honour. Ab nation ka honour! Humaari body par aa gaya!* (First family honour, then community honour, now national honour. All laden on our bodies!)

Exactly!! [laughs] Even the idea is frightening! And the feminists are doing it – the nation's honour is being built on the bodies of women. It's like too much. To say the least.

It's one of those catch-phrases that one heard used and that one may have unwillingly or unwittingly used!

And we feminists have put it into place! So it's like – it was useful at one point, but now it's not. And I think that's the big shift in Gujarat. The public-ness – everybody knew that the person had been raped. And I have never gotten over that description that one of the men who hid in Gulbarg Society described – of men standing around on the low walls and the women being raped. So it's actually a spectacle – a performative thing. It's so public, and yet – it's so complex that you can't just write it off as a simplistic thing, that yeh hua (this happened) and the aurat's (woman's) a 'zinda laash' or whatever. I think the burden that is being put on that act is congealing around the range of ways in which people have been trained to think and feel that they are victorious in some way, they have made some sort of statement on it, and that's the bestiality of it, which is offensive. Otherwise the idea that I won't go to court and I won't seek justice, because I will bring it to light, it doesn't fit that reality, which is that it was known that all of this had happened. So Gujarat was frightening for so many reasons.

Gujarat was actually uniquely frightening. Yes. And I'm not entirely sure that some of the theoretical or feminist learning from Gujarat that all of us articulated in the IIJG report can apply in a general way to other situations of targeted violence, even if there is sexual violence during the attack. Gujarat was extraordinary. I think we learned and evolved a theoretical understanding of the way many things need to come together to create a Gujarat situation – a community is targeted, state presides over it, an ideology is invoked and implicated, there are many messages about masculine construction of community that are implicit in the act, the messages of (Hindu) power you're giving the victims and society at large, the public 'spectacle' of the attacks on women, the visible triumph of the attacker, the emasculation of the Muslim male, and so on. I'm not sure all of that necessarily occurs every time. I think in terms of sexual violence there was a particular signature moment in Gujarat, and little elements of it may surface in subsequent episodes of communal violence in other parts of India. But in the centrality of sexual violence to the 'meaning' of the carnage, I think Gujarat remains qualitatively different.

Absolutely true. And the nature of the complicity between civil society – "the great civil society" – and state power in the way that signature is established, and the fact that is so impossible to disentangle it – when you think of it, the horror of it was that the State was so much implicated in all that had happened – the Advocate General, the prosecutors, the VHP. The nature of penetration by the Hindutva [ideology] into all of State structures was the frightening thing.

Unprecedented. And I don't think it's been repeated since, in other places.

And I think all that we did derive from there – from the understanding from Gujarat, which will stay and be applicable elsewhere – is the idea of targeted violence. And as you rightly pointed out, it also comes from the experience of caste. So in a sense caste and community, and the targeted nature, is the central idea – or, even in the Northeast, it's targeted. You're targeting a bunch of people who live in that area. That, I think, has been the way in which one could make the move from the particularities of each of these cases, to something larger that is also happening.

I don't think we used that word [targeting] in previous instances of so-called communal violence. I think first of all we must rethink this phrase 'communal violence'. Also the word 'riot' is a complete misnomer, and ninety per cent of the time, the word 'communal' is a misnomer. Before Gujarat, to my mind, the most hideous fresh memory would be '84 in Delhi, and even that is called communal violence, but it is not. It is something else. The idea, the horror of what the nature of targeting means – I don't think we ever articulated it in those words in 1984. It's a very visceral animal-like act, this targeting of another human being for who he or she is, because they smell different. And it zeroes in on what this country has been escaping, and blinkering around – the reason for the targeting, is the concept of identities and how they are constructed and experienced. We've been blinkering around it in all our public policies, even the women's movement has been like this about it. But in the past 20 years, it's like the dams have burst. We need to re-engage with the idea of identity, and targeting on the basis of identity. Those notions were not really explored in the past. For one the phrase 'communal violence' in the historical context of India has come to signify only Hindu-Muslim. And that too in a – 'they are equal opponents in the battlefield' kind of way. The reality is that in most episodes there is no equal attack, and these attacks are not restricted to Hindu-Muslim alone. The violence against Sikhs in 1984 does not theoretically fit into the traditional, historical, ideological framework of 'communalism' in India. It will always be seen as an aberration. 'Targeting' as a concept works for 1984, it's broader.

That's true. So now winding down this conversation. Let's look back and look forward, do you think after all this time we have some handle on the tools that are needed to address or give justice for sexual violence in a mass violence communal situation?

We need to first ask ourselves what were the potential routes to justice for sexual violence survivors in a communal mass conflict situation like Gujarat. I mean 'justice' defined broadly, beyond its narrowest definition of criminal prosecution. If we look globally, many tools present themselves – recognition; criminal prosecutions; truth and reconciliation type of mechanisms; public apology; lustration (public naming and shaming), banning perpetrators from public office; memorializing; reparations programmes that repair the material and moral damage of violation; material and symbolic benefits, including financial compensation; literary and historical writings; narrativizing and 'making meaning'. Clearly in a situation like Gujarat there was a need to use several tools. No single mechanism could fully repair such enormous damage. But there was a difference here, because globally we've seen these tools deployed in 'transitional justice' types of situations - accompanying societies in transition from a violent past to a more democratic future. Like say, South Africa, which is the most obvious example. In Gujarat, on the other hand we faced communal mass crime in a society and polity that did *not* appear to want to transform itself in any way. Where there was purportedly no over-all break down of the structure of society; it was not a system in transition. The challenge was to create justice mechanisms in a communalized system that pretends to be stable; create justice without state support, with no guarantees of non-repetition (because state was complicit); address impunity that has widespread social and political sanction; where the crime itself has widespread social sanction (through adherence to a communal Hindutva ideology). So the challenges in India, in Gujarat were enormous.

Okay. So, from the menu of potential justice mechanisms, what do you feel were our dominant responses to sexual violence in Gujarat 2002?

Recognition of sexual violence - making it visible was perhaps the dominant and most successful response. And let us underscore that it was a struggle to visibilize sexual violence - even among our larger *biradari* (community) of secular activists; for whom this violation was not a priority. There was also writing and narrativization - making meaning. Then criminal prosecutions, though far, far, fewer than needed, did take place. And finally, there was some amount of memorializing - for example, some memorializing events marked the 10th anniversary of the Gujarat Pogrom.

When you speak of writing and narrativization which we've all been part of, do you see these exercises in 'making meaning of it all' as really meaningful in the search for justice?

Yes, I believe so. I believe they were actually critical. As you said Uma, you and I have both been part of these 'sense making' initiatives including as partners in the International Initiative for Justice in Gujarat (IIJG) report. So you will recognize how important these were, for us to evolve a coherent feminist frame for what happened. And well beyond 'The Survivors Speak' or IIJG, sexual violence in Gujarat did generate a lot of welcome writing by both academics and activists. Writing about how acts of violence against the Muslim community, and women in particular, were a product of the communal political and discursive practices of the Hindu Right. And in many of these writings, certainly by activists, sexual violence against Muslim women was located centrally (not peripherally) in the discourse of the Gujarat carnage.

And yes, it is true that after a point it began to seem futile and frustrating because it did not dent structures of impunity (state failure to pin responsibility, provide justice, reparations and guarantees of non-repetition). But we must understand that these crimes were not crimes in the understood sense of an aberration from a socially accepted moral norm or universe. These crimes were a normal and normalized part of the Hindutva project. Without these attempts at understanding, the full truth of the Hindutva project (as it revealed itself in 2002) could not be told. Without it, we could not arm ourselves to attack the discourse that enabled and justified sexual violence. This 'sense making' was a component of the overall scheme of justice. It was critical. But obviously it could not be the only or dominant component/element

So, then lets talk about the other response – criminal prosecution for sexual violence. How do you reflect on what you achieved in the Bilkis case? I know that there are issues that trouble you? Insights that make you feel it was significant or not? What did this process of justice for a 'Communal and Targeted Crime of Sexual Violence' mean? Lets talk about the troubling aspects.

The joy of legal justice from the successful prosecution of Bilkis's case was immense, and I've already shared with you why that felt so important for her and us to create an indelible historical record of violation of women's rights, with state complicity, in the face of staggering denial. But the dilemmas continue. And they are many. Ironically, some of them are to do with precisely the nature of 'legal justice'. Bilkis's case was *one* successful prosecution for sexual violence in Gujarat 2002. There were scores of women violated. Many killed. Some survive. First, that is a huge symbolic burden for one woman to bear. But more importantly, in mass violence, how does one celebrate legal justice in one or a few cases without privileging legal justice as the dominant mechanism for all victims? What of the many victims who never enter the criminal justice system? How much do symbolic cases make a dent in the overall structures of impunity? What do we do when the state appropriates this symbol? For example, in so many forums I have stood up, angrily, when one speaker after the other, used the Bilkis case as evidence of the ultimate health and resilience of India's criminal justice system, including senior judges. They've all said – '*Dekhiye* ultimately the system works and it is fair, look at Bilkis, justice *mil to gaya*'. (Look ultimately the system is fair. Look at Bilkis, she did get justice after all!) And I've had to stand up and ask them if this is symbolic of success or of failure of the criminal justice system? Is this the level of extraordinary human struggle and support needed for the average survivor to get justice in this system? No. Bilkis was the exception. Not the norm. That is something often hard to communicate, because it seems counter intuitive.

So she was merely a symbolic success?

Yes, but not symbolic of the success of criminal justice. She was symbolic of the *truth* of what happened, in the absence of being able to establish the truth for all the other women who were similarly and brutally violated. And that brings me to the other dilemma – the feminist dilemma of 'symbolic' appropriation.

Where actually, in a discursive sense, the individual (woman) is less important than the principle they serve. There is fungibility of the individual (a woman) with subjective experience. It could be any woman, right? So, taking this further, and going back to what I said were the differences in the response of many activists to the verdict and Bilkis' response. Did conviction of the 12 accused who actually raped and murdered, serve any symbolic purpose? Put differently, were these convictions less useful than the conviction of the accused state officials, the policemen? Probably, yes. Because conviction of the police, even symbolically, addresses impunity of the communalized state machinery.

But you also mentioned earlier issues arising from the legal procedures, the depositions, the entire criminal justice machinery itself? What were those? As feminists, how do we enter this system? Do we do it on our terms?

Is the successful conclusion of a criminal trial, and a successful prosecution of a sexual violence case in a *mass violence* context, 'the truth' from a feminist perspective? It is a question in my mind. In this case is it truth telling, in a larger sense, if it could only speak to the immediate and limited question of the culpability of the twenty defendants? In a criminal trial of this nature what you have is human suffering rendered appropriate, in a language deemed appropriate, for a judicial proceeding; the human suffering we speak of was inflicted because of communal targeted violence, but the law has no space for recognizing the 'targeted' nature of the attack. That, when you reflect on it, is surely a strange and terrible way of claiming 'truth' for what happened in Gujarat. The 'stickiness' of that shame was never actually transferred to the accused; because there was no acknowledgment of the hate-based nature of their crime. There could not be, because the Indian Penal Code does not recognize either the identity-based, communal or targeted nature of these crimes. And lastly, in a case like this, the 'victim', no matter how much one rails against it, is inevitably 'constructed' in the mind of the court, as a sexually vulnerable woman (victim, not survivor), deserving of protection by a paternal state (read: court). Does any of this, as a process, result in a 'healed self'? These are the dilemmas that haunt my feminism.

Add this dilemma to the other issue of 'hierarchies of violence' that we've already spoken about!

Yes. Those are ongoing. Is death more important than rape? Which do we prioritize? Does the feminist focus on sexual violence, privilege it over other brutal forms of violence in which sexual violence may be embedded? Do we inadvertently perpetuate a patriarchal discourse that constructs sexual violence (particularly in community-based communal conflict) as a crime worse than all others? You will remember during the International Initiative for Justice for Gujarat (IIJG), many conversations all of us in the team had about international law with Rhonda [Copelon]. And she came with a strong feminist position on sexual violence in mass conflict which was that – in mass conflict, rape of women be treated under international law "with the same fervor as war crimes which happen routinely to men." I agreed. You did too. Unfortunately, the graver we make it, the deeper it seems to get embedded in the Indian narrative of honour. In the Indian context, we saw in 2004 Dhananjoy Chatterjee hanged to death for rape and murder of Hetal Parekh. In the same year, in fact the same month, Akku Yadav was lynched to death, and it was seen as morally justified because he was a serial sexual assaulter. We've also seen demands for the death penalty surface with alarming regularity in India. And in 2002 in Gujarat, make no mistake, Muslim community honour was certainly seen to have been violated, because Muslim women were raped.

So, the honour narrative surrounding sexual violence is even more resilient in the context of targeted violence?

Yes. How do we get away from that? In [terms of] how the act is seen by perpetrators and victim both. I think also there is a need to really understand the idea of mass rape or mass sexual violence. Does it have the same 'meaning' as a single act of sexual violence, only multiplied many times i.e. is it the same act only the scale is larger? Or, is the targeted, communal and mass nature of the crime itself distinct in what it signifies to the participants? Particularly when state actors are involved. Is it – for lack of a better word, and back to the hierarchies of violence – a greater evil? It is a hate crime. But both a gendered and communal hate crime. And because it is on a mass scale, what does it say for political and social complicity and political and social participation in the meanings that are generated?

I think if we look at the site of law, present law simply does not account for the targeted and identity based nature of sexual assault in a Gujarat-like situation. What we have achieved subsequently is that we have categorized 'rape in communal and sectarian violence' as an aggravated crime in both POCSO (Protection of Children from Sexual Offences Act 2012) and in the Criminal Law Amendment Act, 2013 (the new 'rape' laws), which means a higher mandatory sentence. Is that what we were after? More jail-time? But we have still not made it a distinct substantive hate crime or a specific form of sexual torture. And we still have no changes in CrPC or the Evidence Act that respond to the specific situation of mass violence, with breakdown of normalcy, with women on the run.

So many questions, then, and few answers...And the Communal Violence Bill, in which all of us so painfully defined and crafted sexual assault provisions, not just in terms of the many forms of sexual torture, but in how to make legal justice achievable through women-sensitive legal procedures, taking into account the ground situations of targeted violence to really dent structures of impunity. Has it all fallen by the wayside?

Yes. Tragic, really. That loss of a moment to collectively push that Bill through as political activists. And we're left with, as you say, many questions, few answers… And of course, the core of the problem, no law can address that. Of crimes that enjoy widespread social and political sanction. Crimes that inhabit a self-contained moral universe (of the Hindu Right). Denting that communal moral universe remains a much larger political project for secular justice. And denting the dominant meanings of sexual violence in identity based communal mass crimes remains a larger project for feminist justice and feminist memorializing. For my part, along with dealing with these conceptual and political dilemmas, my desire after Gujarat was to focus on larger ideas of justice, which must include rebuilding lives after violence; and all that it entails to a restore sense of self at a human level, and restore citizenship rights at a political level. This may include legal battles but is not restricted or defined by that framework alone. This, the concrete stuff of rebuilding lives – this is the stuff that actually makes survivors trust again, and as we learnt, it also wins the legal cases. Justice for women means more than punishment of the guilty, it also means the wherewithal to rebuild lives.

Interviewed by Uma Chakravarti
in Delhi

NOTES

1. 'The Survivors Speak' was the first detailed report on the violence against Muslim women during the Gujarat massacre of 2002. A

national level all-women's fact-finding team, put together by the Citizen's Initiative (Ahmedabad), released the report on April 16, 2002. It immediately caused a national stir, and remained a key document about the events of Gujarat.

2. The International Initiative for Justice in Gujarat brought together a panel of feminist jurists, activists, lawyers, writers and academics from all over the world and was initiated by Citizen's Initiative (Ahmedabad), People's Union for Civil Liberties (PUCL), Shanti Abhiyan (Vadodara), Communalism Combat, Awaaz-E-Niswaan, Forum Against Oppression of Women (FAOW), Stree Sangam (Mumbai), Saheli, Jagori, Sama, Nirantar (Delhi), Organised Lesbian Alliance for Visibility and Action (OLAVA, Pune), and other women's organizations in India. Its report – *Threatened Existence: A Feminist Analysis of the Genocide in Gujarat* was published in December, 2003. [Forum against Oppression of Women, December 2003.]

3. On March 3, 2002, during the Gujarat massacre, Bilkis Rasool was gang-raped and fourteen members of her family, including her three and half year old daughter, were murdered. Bilkis was the only adult survivor and eyewitness to the massacre. Her case was closed by the local police and magistrate. In a journey to justice that lasted six years, Bilkis, with the help of feminist activists, moved the Supreme Court, got her case reopened, re-investigated by the CBI, got the trial transferred outside Gujarat to a Mumbai Sessions Court. After a trial lasting three years, the verdict on January 18, 2008 convicted the twelve main accused, as well as one police officer. Seven accused were acquitted including two doctors and five police officers. The Mumbai High Court verdict on appeals in the case on May 4, 2017, for the first time categorically upheld state complicity in these crimes, by setting aside the Trial Court acquittals and convicting seven officers of the state, policemen and doctors, of falsifying and tampering with evidence with intent to shield the accused and save them from punishment.

   The case was landmark because it was the only case of sexual violence in Gujarat that progressed this far; the only case of sexual violence in which the victim was alive to testify and sought redress from the Supreme Court; the only Gujarat carnage related case to be handed over to the CBI, and the only case that proceeded to trial on the basis of fresh investigation (by CBI) instead of on the basis of biased investigations by local police in Gujarat. It became a case that had the power to silence those who claimed with impunity that no sexual violence took place in Gujarat, and then tried to stop legal battles from even beginning. Justice for Bilkis, exposed this lie, and prevented the reality of sexual violence in 2002, and the reality of state complicity in these crimes, from being erased from the history of Gujarat and of India.

10

The Limits of Law

Interview with Vrinda Grover

URVASHI BUTALIA AND UMA CHAKRAVARTI

Vrinda Grover, a Delhi-based human rights lawyer who has had a long involvement with the women's movement describes the beginnings of her engagement with law as an instrument in the search for justice. She goes on to reflect on the major issues she has been involved in, from working with survivors of the violence of the 1984 anti-Sikh pogrom to many other instances of injustice, discrimination and violence where she has provided legal counsel to survivors. This interview, though touching upon only some parts of her wide-ranging work, provides insights into both the possibilities and the limitations of law.

I

Can we begin by talking about what led you to take up law?

I was involved with issues of women's rights while studying in college. And I had got an important exposure to them through the feminist street theatre group that I was part of; [we worked] on issues of dowry deaths, domestic violence etc. It seemed to me that law was a very good field if you wanted to canvass for rights, whether it was of workers or women. These were the two areas I was interested in. I also had some familiarity with the field of law because my father, Mr. P.P.Grover, was a renowned criminal lawyer. My father was actually not very enthusiastic about my joining the legal profession, because in the late eighties there were few women in it, and hardly any in the Trial Court.

[But] I was determined that that was what I must study. And I actually thought that it was the best way advance any cause or issue. While I was studying at the Law Faculty, I went regularly to [the resettlement colony] Jahangirpuri, which is not far from Delhi University and where [the NGO] Action India had set up a group called Sabla Sangh. I would try and go [there] at least once a week. It wasn't that I was working with them. I became friends with many of them, Gyanvati, Sudha, Virmati, Reshma. I was trying to understand their lives, because they came from a different class. What were the issues they were negotiating? Just being in the slum for a stretch of three or four hours is an experience which is necessary if you want to understand lives that are different from our middle-class privileged existence. How do other people live in this city? So, I would [regularly] go there. For me it was a very important learning process.

Criminal law…was actually something [I found] important and interesting. I did initially think of working in labour law but perhaps the opportunity did not come my way. I was also familiar with the work of [Advocate] K.G. Kannabiran, and his engagement with human rights through criminal and constitutional law. And of course I could join my father's law chamber to learn, much against my father's wishes – he said that criminal law was definitely not something that women should practise. So I told him not only will I practise criminal law, but I will work with you because you are good at your work and I need to learn from you. Well, since he was undeniably a trial lawyer par excellence, learning from him was a phenomenal experience. Quite soon, he grudgingly, admitted that

I was good at my work. Eventually, I know he was happy, almost proud, that I had followed his lead.

And this takes us in the direction of what happened in Delhi in 1984, the anti-Sikh pogrom following the assassination of Indira Gandhi.

Yes, 1984 happened while I was studying at St. Stephen's College. My parents' home is in West Patel Nagar, where I used to live. So we actually saw the violence unfold before us. It was a very early lesson in state complicity; learnt not through abstract theory but actual real-life experience. I remember we saw a crockery shop – because the market can be seen from our house – we saw the Sardar Crockery Shop (a large corner shop) being set on fire and burning. We saw the mobs wreaking havoc. I actually saw a man break bricks and hand out stones to the mob. There was a family living two lanes away which was a Sikh house which was targeted. And when all this was happening, as per instinct, I picked up the phone and I repeatedly dialled number 100 and repeatedly dialled the Patel Nagar police station. Of course, no phones were answered whatsoever. Two Sikh families took refuge in our house, because my father being a big-shot lawyer, people knew that no mob would dare enter our house.

It was an interesting phenomenon, what was happening inside our house. My extended family, including my maternal grandmother and my mother's brother lived in Amritsar; and my father's brother and sister lived in Chandigarh. Being in Punjab, they had witnessed the years of militancy. In Punjab, Hindus were targeted during the years of militancy, and this created social tensions between Hindu and Sikh families. That fear and tension spilled into our home in Delhi also. I remember this completely schizoid behaviour that I witnessed in my own family in Delhi, in 1984, where two of my father's Sikh colleagues with their entire families were given shelter and my father had assured them that over his dead body would anybody dare to enter his house, and that they could stay safely with us for as long as they wanted. At the same time, my grandmother, my *Dadi*, standing at the gate, was saying: 'Good, the Sikhs deserve what is happening to them because this is what they did to people in Punjab.' It was very odd to understand where our family stood in all this. A friend of mine, Jyotsna, she comes from a Sikh family. Her father – they also used to live close by – was in touch with my father just in case they were under any threat. I also saw how rumours were fuelled and the complete polarization [that happened] between the Hindu and Sikh communities. There was absolutely no help whatsoever provided to the Sikhs by the state till the army came in. And I actually saw that only when the army trucks started patrolling, that was the first time that rioters were picked up. And then I went with my friend Jyotsna to Farash Bazaar where a refugee camp [for those affected by the violence] had been set up. It was actually quite far – we would take a bus and go there and talk to Sikh families who had lost family and homes and everything.

And I learnt about Nagarik Ekta Manch, [Citizens Forum for Unity, an initiative for communal harmony that emerged post-1984] met a whole new set of people, actually both through Farash Bazar and Nagarik Ekta Manch. It's just that each thing led me to meet new people, who were engaged with this kind of socio-political work, and of course my own understanding, thoughts and insights developed. It was a very natural way of learning and growing.

Is 1984 marked in your mind because you did a very important piece of research work that never got published, which was a study of the state of the cases? If you could speak about that as well as address the cases of sexual violence.

For me, looking at the targeted violence against the Sikh community in 1984, I saw the burning, the looting – I did not see any killings fortunately in my neighbourhood. There were people who were killed in Patel Nagar, but not in my immediate vicinity. I saw what happened. I know it was allowed to happen. And I also knew that I was not attacked because I was a Hindu. For me, doing this research [as part of Oxfam (India's) Violence Mitigation and Amelioration Programme] was important. It was my way of, in a way, seeking forgiveness for what had happened. I had to do this research because I knew what had been done to the Sikh community was wrong. As a citizen, as an individual, what do you do? And what is the way in which you can contribute to moving away from the injustice? So, for me actually this has remained with me for years – this happened in 1984, I finished my law in 1988; I did this research much, much later – but it was something that I wanted to do for a very long time, because it was the only way I could come to terms with the targeted violence and the brazen impunity I had witnessed at that time. Also, it was an area of study where I found complete silence. Nobody was looking at it, not as lawyers, not as activists. At the same time, the victims had turned to the legal system in a very big way for redress. More than redress, I think, it is acknowledgement that a very, very grave crime had been perpetrated and the legal forum becomes an important site for this acknowledgement, this record of the truth, of injustice.

So, in a sense concepts of impunity were central to the way in which '84 happened and was sort of allowed to die, without any redressal?

Absolutely. I think impunity was staring at me in the face. When I did the legal research, I found evidence to substantiate the claims of impunity even in the court records. When the Nanavati Commission was set up, during the NDA (National Democratic Alliance) rule – the first NDA rule – I submitted my affidavit to the Nanavati Commission, based on my research and analysis of the role of the police during the 1984 pogrom, and I went and deposed before the Commission. Interestingly, it was at the Nanavati Commission that I was cross-examined for the first time in my life. I felt that if my research and analysis could feed into the understanding of what is the origin of communal violence; what is the nature of communal conflict; and how it has a very, very direct bearing on politics, particularly electoral politics [then it would have been worth it]. The report that the People's Union for Democratic Rights, or the book that you Uma [Chakravarti], and Nandita [Haksar][1] wrote, were obviously part of my learning in trying to grapple with the role of the state in the targeting of the Sikh community.

When you went to the Nanavati Commission, did you actually in any way flag the sexual violence, because in your reports you do talk about cases of sexual violence?

No. There was no FIR [First Information Report] lodged about sexual violence during the 1984 attacks, prior to the Nanavati Commission Report. My affidavit to the Nanavati Commission only examines the role of the police as it emerged starkly from court records and where the link with state complicity and impunity was writ large. So, I had culled out from various judgements what the courts said about the actions and inactions of the police.

And at what stage did you get involved in the actual cases?

Much, much later because I had to actually first finish my law and then get into practice, so that comes much, much later.... Many years later, I was asked to represent the widow of a man who had been killed by a mob when a Gurudwara had been burned and where Jagdish Tytler is alleged to have instigated the mob.

I remember very well an occasion where the personal and the political got entangled. So, (Congress leader) H.K.L. Bhagat was someone my father knew through his professional work. When my sister was getting married, Bhagat's name was on the guest list. I told my parents that if H.K.L. Bhagat was invited to this wedding, then I would not be attending it because he has been named as an accused who instigated the attack on the Sikhs. Many years later I interviewed Darshan Kaur at her house and I had a conversation with her, a conversation that remains vividly with me even today.

And Darshan Kaur is central to H.K.L. Bhagat?

Darshan Kaur is the main complainant and witness. She saw H.K.L. Bhagat's white ambassador car come to her locality. She deposed in court, saying H.K.L. Bhagat came, incited the crowd, instigated them, told them go ahead and kill the Sikhs. And her husband, a young autorickshaw driver, was brutally killed. So fortunately, H.K.L. Bhagat's name was struck off the guest list. And I attended my sister's wedding.

How did you come to do this interview with Darshan Kaur at all?

During my '84 research, I looked at what the legal aftermath of the complaints was, the FIRs, the cases that were filed by the Sikh victims. For the legal research I examined primary data in the form of 100 odd judgments of the Trial Court, which is an arduous story by itself. I also analysed cases relating to prominent Congress leaders like Tytler, Sajjan Kumar and H.K.L. Bhagat. And I tracked those cases very carefully, because while there will be accused whose hands will be stained with blood due to the actual killings, burning, looting but the charge of conspiracy, the people who mastermind, incite, abet, plan, sponsor, orchestrate the attack, those who stand to gain from it – we know how the Congress reaped an electoral windfall in the elections thereafter – invariably are let off the hook, if they are booked at all in the first place. So I specifically tracked the cases against these three Congress leaders. And in H.K.L. Bhagat's case, Darshan Kaur was the star witness. And what she has done… I mean, it's nothing short of heroism, to testify against H.K.L. Bhagat. And she paid a very heavy price, including being thrashed on the way to court with sticks – this lead to her being hospitalized. It was absolutely ghastly, she was accorded no protection whatsoever. So I interviewed her as part of my analysis and research on '84.

When I was reading the Trial Court judgments, I found references, stray fragments of references, to sexual violence. And I had, of course, at the time, read *Manushi*, the volume that documented the sexual violence that was perpetrated on Sikh women during the attacks. And then I never heard about the sexual assaults against Sikh women again. There were no cases, no complaints, no FIRs. I have been to Tilak Vihar [resettlement colony for survivors of the ani-Sikh carnage] a few times but I never heard about it ever again....So the issue of sexual violence was never mentioned even in whispers. And it was not until I went back to studying the judgments for my research, that I started finding these stray references. I remember reading one woman's evidence where she is deposing about a mob attacking her brother, who was eventually killed. In her testimony she describes how her brother was lynched and killed by the mob that chased him. In her statement she states how some men in the mob opened her *nara* (drawstring of her salwar). Then, as suddenly as she says this, she stops and you lose the thread. Nobody asks her a further question, because it was seen as not relevant to the crime that the Court is prosecuting. The judge doesn't ask what happened with her, the Public Prosecutor does not ask her to complete her narrative. It just tapers off and there is total silence.

That is an important issue because I [Uma Chakravarti] also, despite doing that fat book [Three Days in the Life of a Nation] in one of the cases there was a suggestion of sexual violence because there is the account of the doctor, and she says that many women came to her and asked her what would be the consequences. Then they would drop it and not pursue it. But then I found that there were four references even in our collection, that actually did refer to [it]. And we didn't make an issue of it; we didn't even mention it in the introduction. There was a way in which we were not foregrounding the sexual violence issue over there because it seemed to be overwhelmed by-

The killings and the brutality of killings.

There was a conspiracy, I think, to some extent that the men don't want to talk about it. And also because this was put out in the public domain, it was an attack on the masculinity of Sikh men.

Because the Sikhs are supposed to be militaristic…

And they were also seen as the prehistory of the militancy or whatever. It was a man to man thing and important social scientists actually put that gloss on it. They treated it as if women and children were safe from the violence.

Justice Nanavati made precisely this comment in a Supreme Court judgment in which he commuted the death sentence of Kishori, who was a butcher in Trilokpuri and who was convicted for many of the killings in Trilokpuri. While commuting the death sentence, one of the mitigating circumstances Justice Nanavati cites is that the mob did not kill women. Therefore the death sentence can be commuted. The death sentence, as we all believe, should be commuted. But the reasoning that he gives is very, very alarming.

In a sense, the men, the Sikh men, even while they were pursuing the law, didn't want to push that question. The women themselves were not able to push it. And even those of us who are, say, on the citizens' response side, even we let it drop. I think that [journalist] Manoj Mitta's point, somewhere he writes, he says that you couldn't acknowledge the sexual violence because then what would you do with the story this was a –what's it called– sorrowing mob, grieving for their mother being killed. So, how can they be raping? You know in a sense you put a gloss on it which makes it men versus men. And then you can't acknowledge this in one way or the other.

II

Let us now turn a bit to your current work. I know you have been thinking a lot on the issue of consent and the ways in which it is now understood in law. Can you tell us a bit about that?

I was recently reading that in the U.S, apparently, except for California and maybe a couple of other states, the law is, that you can withdraw your consent even during the sexual act. In fact, in California, they say the law is regressive because it does not permit women to do so. And the reason why this is being raised is because there have been acquittals in certain rape cases. If one looks at the facts of those cases, one understands why consent is important, not only for the act at that time, but also the reason why continuing consent becomes important. So, if the woman said that, 'Yes I gave my consent in the beginning to have sex with him. But later, when we started, the sex became violent. The manner in which the sex was performed was violent. I did not agree to violent sex with him and therefore, I should have a right to now withdraw my consent.' Because consent is given on a certain set of factual terms or assumptions. But if in the process of the sexual interaction, the man indulges in violence, then the woman should have the right to withdraw her consent, as the terms have clearly been altered.

Now, in India, it would be considered provocative to say that the sexual interaction may begin with consent and the woman can withdraw her consent even during the sexual act. But if you look at the facts that so many women are putting out, then surely, as with any other issue, consent is given on a certain set of assumptions, and if the terms change then so may consent. Consent has been specifically and clearly defined by the 2013 Criminal Law Amendment Act – it is detailed in the explanation to Sec.375 IPC., as otherwise it was left to the courts to infer from a set of circumstances whether consent had been given or not by the woman; and invariably that inference would draw upon inherent prejudices and biases which would deny women any sexual agency or autonomy. Now, the law clearly says that there should be an unequivocal voluntary agreement to that specific sexual act. Consent for the sexual act cannot be construed because she agreed two days ago, or that they are hanging out together at a party etc. Let me just clarify why the elucidation of consent is important. This has two significant implications. Firstly, in law, there is now a very clear and explicit statement of what should be understood as consent. It is important for all concerned, particularly men, to understand that this is what consent means, so it's not just to set a normative standard. It is a public declaration so that men no longer say, 'I didn't understand that this was not consent.' So, if the man is confused, then the law requires that he should make sure that he is not misreading the signs or the situation. Of course consent can be given through a gesture, non-verbal conduct or by words, but it has to be an unequivocal and voluntary agreement. It is good that the law is now stating this boldly and explicitly, because in our societal culture, male privilege and entitlement over women's bodies is embedded and women's self-determination of their sexuality an alien concept. Secondly, what this elucidation of consent does, is that it provides guidance to the court to glean consent while appreciating evidence, because of course, in many cases, the defence of the accused is going to be that it was consensual. So, the woman's clothes, the hour of the night, her demeanour, even her work, her background; all those are not issues that should influence the decision of the court whether the case is within the category of consensual or non-consensual sexual activity. This clarity in law, I would have imagined, should have been welcomed by one and all, not just by women. What we do see however, is that very soon – even before the law was used effectively by women to counter the pervasive crime of sexual assault – a PIL [Public Interest Litigation] has been filed by Madhu Kishwar before the Delhi High Court challenging many provisions of the new law – including the expanded definition of rape and the definition of consent – where she argues that this definition should be deleted and the court should be allowed to infer consent from the circumstances. That was exactly what went against women [earlier] in the criminal trials, where evidence was dislodged by social prejudices and embedded biases, and the woman victim's conduct, her life choices, her character, acquired centrality in the court. Therefore by defining consent, the law has taken a progressive step in this manner. The crux of the legal challenge filed by Madhu Kishwar is against the expanded definition of rape, beyond forced peno-vaginal to forced oral sex; forced anal sex; sex by [using] an object etc., because it will in most situations be incapable of medical corroboration. So, actually, what the petition asks for, is to go back to pre-Mathura time, where once again, the medical evidence will determine whether the woman has been raped or not. [Interestingly] studies both globally and in India show that injuries are not the norm in sexual assault incidents. In a majority of cases, you will not have injuries and you will not have bruises, so there will be no medical evidence. There are circumstances in which many women are raped, in the home, by men known to them or part of the extended family, in situations of fear and helplessness, where there may not be physical resistance which will produce physical injuries on her body. However, physical resistance and the absence of consent are two very different things. It's after a lot of hard work by the feminist movement that the distinction between submission and consent is grudgingly finding its way into jurisprudence. So, it's very unfortunate that a legal challenge of such a regressive nature is pending. There are many other stereotypes and biases that afflict rape jurisprudence, for instance, if the woman complainant belongs to the lower strata of society, or is an *adivasi* women, or belongs to a particular caste, there is a lurking notion even in the court room, that they are promiscuous women, and this interferes with their right to justice. To that extent, the 2013 Amendment could actually filter a lot of these biases. I don't think you can ever totally exclude prejudice and bias, but the law can, even in its articulation and vocabulary, filter a lot of it and the rest of it really has to be done through public discourse and discussions. And I, for one, believe that we are living through a very significant phase for the women of this country. I think post 2012, despite the very high rate of violence against women, including sexual violence against women, and the low rate of conviction, I feel that we are at a very exciting moment of change. There is today, an assertion and it is coming from the younger women and it is an unstoppable assertion from across classes. But of course, the media only foregrounds the articulations of young middle class women, so we hear more of and about them. But those of us who work and engage with women from all classes, witness them asserting themselves. And what they are laying claim to, is not only equality but also their sexual autonomy. They have infused life breath to the phrase 'bodily integrity', and 'dignity'. The assertion of equality, to my mind, is actually an assertion of equal citizenship. What I hear them saying is not just that I have to be equal, but that I am an independent citizen of this country and therefore, all these rights must accrue to me, I must be free to enjoy them and I will not accept anything short of this. Which actually, in another sense, (since I have worked not only on women's rights but on a host of civil and human rights issues) is a very interesting moment, when you see that citizenship is being eroded in all other forms, and here there is a very powerful assertion, a claim by women. The other day I was watching on television, two young women who were groped and sexually harassed, [and were subjected to] lewd calls at a Gurgaon liquor store. When asked [about this harassment they faced], the women said that they feel it's their social responsibility to be in such public places. And yes, they know that there is a risk if you're going to be out late at night at a liquor store buying wine or beer or whatever, there is a likelihood that this is 'an unsafe place' to which their response is, 'We know it, but we are going to do it and we are going to do it again and again, because only then will this become acceptable...In order to make it acceptable we are going to have to take this risk.' In fact, at a town hall meeting in Bangalore which was telecast, the Police Commissioner was talking about some safety app [mobile application] which, except for one woman, nobody else had downloaded. I think that itself was a very telling comment. All advice given to them by the politician and by the Police Commissioner, to not go to certain areas was loudly booed by the women [who] said , 'We will take the risks that it asks for because we don't want to tell our daughters to not go here and there.'

So you're saying this is a very strong assertion of citizenship on the part of women, mostly young women?

Yes, the private and the public congeal here; it's about citizenship and it's about self-determination over your body, your sexuality and laying claim to public space, public facilities and freedoms. It's an assertion which has the potential, at certain moments, to cross class, caste, and religious barriers. Not always, but at certain moments those alliances may be forged, which is necessary for the challenges to be transformative. So to my mind, a lot of the change that you see today – since I engage mainly with the legal system whether it's at the police station or in the court room – is being shaped by this bold articulation from outside [the criminal-legal system]. It is compelling the legal system to grapple with what these women are saying. Very often the legal system doesn't quite understand it, and when you read judgements you can sense that confusion.

Yes, that's so true, reading court judgments today is quite an experience.

Because courts now know that the times and the law have changed, they are grappling with this change. They also know that if a judgement is particularly atrocious, there will be a debate and comment. Perhaps at times the legal system is uneasy with the pace of the change,...that the young women are asking for too much, too soon. And it's not even that they are just asking, they are taking, demanding, snatching their rights through street-based activism, fierce activism....

They really think this is asking for too much too soon?

Yes, perhaps. I think there is a very interesting push that is coming from the outside and that is really where a lot of the hope rests [even without the support of the media]. I think this is one of the worst phases for the media in India. You don't even need the state to clamp down on them anymore, they themselves have [taken those steps] ...you know? They exude arrogance as they serve the agenda of the government and the state. Interestingly, on the issue of the rights of middle-class women, the media has been taking consistently progressive stances; which is not because the media is necessarily progressive but because there are just many more women today in the print and electronic media holding positions where they can determine the content of the programme. The showcasing and foregrounding of those voices is pushing for developing a better understanding of what sexual violence is; why it is wrong; why women are not to be blamed; and why victim blaming is wrong.

But will this affect the course of justice for the women?

Well, it'll depend very much on who the woman is and where she is located and it's... so let me complete the middle-class women context and then I'll move into the other sectors because there, gender will intersect with so many other axes that they cannot be understood only through that one lens. In so far as justice is concerned, women are actually making very interesting choices. A lot of women who come to consult me, talk about the actual incidents of sexual violence – harassment, stalking, molestation, rape – and are calling out the offender, publicly or within a circle of friends, or are informing their family, definitely telling the person [the perpetrator] that he is the one who is in the wrong, and then they make a choice whether to seek redress through the formal legal system or not.

There are two things here which took me a long time to grapple with, for myself, to comprehend why women are raising the issue in other fora and not approaching the police and the court. The way I understand it, presently, is that if we say that a woman should have agency – agency to walk out of an abusive violent relationship of any kind – then she will continue to exercise that agency to identify and choose where, when and how she will seek redress for the violence and abuse. There is no 'higher/superior/politically or morally correct route' here...not in my mind at all. I do not categorize the hierarchies of these routes and choices [of dealing with violence]. When the feminist movement has over the years repeatedly held that rape is not a 'fate worse than death', then if a woman walks away from the sexual assault without going to the court at all, actually, she has dealt with it precisely on those terms. She is saying, 'Yes I've been raped, yes I've been wronged, yes he has committed a crime. I am moving away from this completely. I am severing all my association with this man. But at this moment, I don't want to invest my life, my time, my energy in prosecuting this man, by filing a police complaint, by giving evidence, by going to court. I am moving away from this and focusing my energy on recovering myself.'

I personally find this very important for us to understand, because a lot of people around us, including the media, are with righteous indignation telling the woman, 'go and file a complaint with the police.' As though that is a superior thing to do. Of course, no will bother to see that we have yet to make either the police station, or the court room, accessible, sensitive, less harsh, less difficult or less time consuming for the woman survivor. And therefore, I believe that till the legal system is gender sensitive you cannot tell the woman that she must go to the police station.

This demand was raised very significantly when the young [law] intern made a complaint against Justice A.K. Ganguly, a former judge of the Supreme Court of India. [In November 2013] she very importantly wrote [about being sexually harassed/molested by a judge] on her blog, disclosing her own name, but did not reveal the name of the judge. I think that was a very important moment for us to mark, where she revealed her own identity and the incident of sexual harassment that had occurred a while back.[2] She felt that she had to share her experience and how she coped with it. She decided to write about it and not keep the sexual crime committed by such a reputed and high profile man a secret. The Supreme Court set up a fact-finding Committee of three Supreme Court judges to enquire into the matter. This Committee examined the law intern, and affidavits filed by three witnesses on behalf of the law intern. And Justice Ganguly submitted a written statement. Importantly, it was the Supreme Court Judges Committee that made the name of Justice Ganguly public, as till then there was much speculation over the identity of the retired judge. The Committee believed her truth and held that it was its considered view that prima facie her statement discloses sexual harassment by A.K. Ganguly in a hotel room. Many people, including BJP leader Subramaniam Swamy, maligned the intern, saying that she was part of a conspiracy, she was linked to Mohan Bagan football team to the 2G scam. Swamy and others remarked that if there is any truth in the law intern's complaint, she should lodge a complaint with the police and take her case to the criminal court.[3]

I spoke about this with the law intern. I tried to understand why she first made that public disclosure, and why did she then not complain to the police? She, actually, was very clear about her choices. She felt uneasy about remaining silent about her sexual harassment at this juncture in 2012-2013 when society was publicly grappling with issues of sexual violence. She felt that she needed to say it, but she needed to say it on her terms, in her voice, and not necessarily with anger and rage. And I respect her for the tone, tenor and the manner in which she disclosed. Quite thoughtfully, she said, 'If I file a FIR now against someone who has recently retired as a judge of the Supreme Court of India and is highly reputed and quite powerful by virtue of his position,... I've just passed my law. I want to work in a certain area of law. If I start this litigation, quite clearly, I will have to invest a lot of time, a lot of energy in just pursuing this case for many years to come. It will shape everything that I will do for the next ten years. And that's not how I see my future, that's not what I want to do.' I think this is a choice that she or any other woman must make for herself. It does not mean her complaint is false. It does not mean that she has chosen a weaker or an inferior route. I completely respect a young woman who decides otherwise. And she moves on. Everybody, including the Chief Justice of India, has said on innumerable occasions that the criminal-legal system is a broken system. Why do you want to push women into a broken system without any assurance that there will be any healing for them in this process? So, women must have the freedom, the autonomy to choose, given their specific set of circumstances. Some will choose to go to court, some will choose not to go to court. And we, in the feminist movement, should not be pushing women into the criminal-legal system without necessarily assuring them of all manner of support, till the end of that journey – whether it is legal, or social, or rehabilitative support. I think there is a perverse reason why women are being compelled to seek recourse only through the criminal-legal system. In my view, men know that the criminal-legal system can be controlled, can be manoeuvred, can be manipulated, and they know that the chances of women getting a conviction, the chances of them getting justice are actually very bleak.

Before I speak about the criminal-legal system, I just want to add another dimension. To go back to the sexual harassment issue, I think it's very important that the public sphere has been impacted and reshaped by the feminist movement, by young people, by social media, and [this has] reshaped the discourse around the articulation sexual violence. We are also seeing a growing trend of the courts issuing gag orders against the media for speaking on these issues. In the Justice Swatantra Kumar case, where the media has been gagged from discussing the complaint except to report about the case. The Delhi High Court judgment, while injuncting the media, says that the integrity of the judicial institution is involved, which in my view, is a totally wrong understanding. A man who held the office of a Supreme Court judge, at the time of the incident, and then held another very important judicial position, as Chair of the National Green Tribunal, had a complaint of sexual harassment made against him by a law intern. It wasn't a complaint against the Supreme Court of India. The High Court order should have drawn a distinction between the individual and the institution. If you examine the Court Orders, they record that appearing on behalf of the judge are at least seventeen to eighteen senior lawyers of the Delhi High Court; and standing up for the woman are barely three or four of us. So, that in a nutshell tells the story of where power lies and how it plays out within the court room.

To go back to the silencing [shrinking] of the social space. This injunction order was passed in the Swatantra Kumar case. Thereafter, Pachauri [R.K Pachauri, former chairman of the Intergovernmental Panel on Climate Change, who had to resign in 2015 following allegations of serial sexual harassment] filed a suit in which he has sought a gag order against the media, monetary damages against the second woman who has complained against him, and against me. The issue has reached a new low, where the lawyer who is speaking in the public space is now being targeted. So if, as a lawyer, or as an activist, or as a feminist you speak out about the cases of sexual harassment against high profile men, there is a high risk of being sued for monetary damages. This to my mind is an extremely dangerous direction in which things have been moved because the one area where we have been able to create support is the social space. And that social space is extremely important to access not only because, as I said, it impinges on what's happening inside the courtroom, [but also] because prejudices and biases don't disappear with the passing of a new law. It is the social sphere that is critical to the process of change, where a different narrative develops, one that pays keen attention to women's articulation of what is wrong with a lewd comment and why it's not a minor 'eve-teasing' issue. That social space is important because it will shape our understanding of the issues, both inside and outside the court room. If, *that* social space is gagged, if it is closed – and it is shrinking very rapidly – for me, that is one of the most serious challenges to our work in the near future.

Even otherwise, we do know that rape trials can be extremely harrowing for women. Many changes have been made through the law. Are those changes being implemented in court rooms? My experience is mixed. It depends on the accused; it depends on the counsel; it depends on the court; it depends on the location of the court – metropolitan city, mofussil town, rural; and it depends very much on the power inequivalence between the victim/survivor and the accused. If the in-camera trial is actually going to be perversely interpreted to close that space completely from scrutiny, I think it would become a dangerous space for women. So, this is an area where I think we need to challenge the court. Very interestingly, on the one hand you have a growing jurisprudence on freedom of speech and expression, and on the other hand, when it comes to high profile and powerful men, principles of freedom of speech and expression get trumped by concerns of reputation. I think this is not just an issue of freedom of speech and expression, it is an issue of women's right to dignity, and that is really what is at stake. It is unfortunate that most media houses accept the gag orders after a murmur, and are not seriously committed to fighting these gag orders. The challenge against the gag orders is being mounted by women, with no resources to fight these long drawn legal battles. I have been told by lawyers representing major media houses that, 'We've been told it's all right, we can live with this gag order.' My response is, 'Yes, you can live with a gag order, but women will not be able to live with the gag order, because this will signal impunity for further sexual violence'.

Can you also briefly address the issue of investigations? How good or bad are they? How much are police trained to conduct investigations?

In almost ninety per cent of cases in this country, regardless of what the crime is, we have very poor, shoddy, unprofessional perfunctory investigation. It does not matter if you've been cheated of your life savings, or you've been murdered, or there has been a theft in your house, or you've been raped. The general standard of criminal investigation by the police is abysmally low. I've always said this to my friends in the feminist movement that if you don't engage with the larger issues of police accountability and professional investigation, change will not miraculously come in the investigation of the new sexual offences defined under the new law. The same police man or woman will not perform competent forensic investigation in a woman's case, simply because that cop has never investigated an offence professionally. Let me give you a very small innocuous example – a friend has filed a case of sexual harassment. She says the man sexually harassed her over the telephone. He would repeatedly call, be sexually abusive over the phone. So it's a case of stalking and sexual harassment on the phone. Not a hard case to investigate. She is an upper-class woman, the guy was from a lower class. One would imagine things would fall into place quite easily. The police investigates the case and the investigating officer [IO] is a woman which is a demand that was made [by the complainant.] I personally think that we need to move away from this [idea of the] woman investigator and woman judge. I don't think it's helping us at all. We need people who are professional and have an understanding of the issues. The CDR (Call Data Records) that have been filed with the charge-sheet are of a month, other than the month on which she had been abused on her mobile phone. So, the most crucial piece of evidence is missing. By the time the case came to me, it was already quite late, I moved an application in court, saying that if you read her FIR, the dates on which he sexually harassed her are clear, and the relevant CDR must be summoned from the mobile service provider.. By the time the application was heard, which took another six months [or so] in the mahila [women's] court, the service provider informed the Court that the CDRs have been destroyed. Thus the most important and readily available piece of direct evidence in this case is missing. It's missing because the IO did not read the complainant's statement carefully, where she says, 'I arrived on this date and then on Sunday he called me.' Is this corruption? Is this inadvertence? What is this? Will this missing CDR cause an acquittal? It is the simplest case to investigate. I don't think the IO was in cahoots with the accused. This ordinary example reflects the dismal state of police investigations in this country. So my point is that basic competent criminal investigation is lacking in this country, and we are not paying any attention or investing to improve this.

III

So it's interesting to see that impunity builds up at different levels. One wouldn't have thought something as simple as CDR records could be an instrument of impunity. Could you talk of some of the other ways in which impunity for perpetrators is strengthened?

Gender intersects with other forms of deeply entrenched inequalities, discrimination and prejudice to produce a heightened vulnerability and an extraordinary impunity. This could be the intersect of gender with religion or caste or ethnicity, or in conflict areas, and here there is no semblance of justice for the survivor of sexual violence. This is a scenario where law enforcement, or maintenance of law and order intersects with the perpetration of violence against women. For instance, quite a few women in Chhattisgarh, have complained of gang-rape by security forces and the patrol team, which comprises of the CRPF [Central Reserve Police Force], the local police and the District Reserved Guards, the Special Police Officers (who are often local surrenderees) working as police informers. To register an FIR, to file a complaint with the police, the women have to walk for miles on end, because the nearest police station is many many kilometres away from their village. So, when questions are raised about the delay in lodging the FIR – why is she telling us today, why didn't she tell us earlier? – we also need to see what is the accessibility that women have to the legal system. In these cases, because there is an inbuilt delay, there is no prospect of any medical evidence, being available. Our conceptualization of the crime, its investigation and evidence, cannot be only through the lens of where we are located, in urban metropolitan cities. Let us not forget that these adivasi women are stepping forward to complain against men in uniform, men whose force dominates and controls the area. Even the complaints documented with the NHRC of sexual violence would disclose that the adivasi women step forward to make a complaint only when they get some support, whether of adivasi leaders, adivasi organizations or feminist activists. I think it's important for the law to recognize – that due to their extreme marginality, some communities of women will not be able to simply walk into the police station to lodge their complaints. The power inequivalence will have to be mediated though adivasi leadership and feminist activism. The reason why I am underlining this is because the legal system tends to look at an adivasi leader like Soni Sori[4], or the feminist activists with suspicion and accuse them of misleading the 'innocent adivasi woman' and charge them with maligning the security forces in conspiracy with the Maoists. Just as the law has learnt that sexual harassment is a crime, a misconduct, a violation of the right to equality and dignity and not a trivial issue; the law must grasp the different marginalizations of diverse constituencies of women and how it impedes their access of the legal system. Let me give you a different example, the NALSA (National Legal Services Authority), as part of delivery of legal aid in India has made provision for para-legals to help the poor access their legal rights. Then why do courts view adivasi organizations or feminist activists who help these women reach the police station to record a complaint of rape, with such marked suspicion? How are these women going to identify these men? The men will be in uniform. The women will in all probability not recognize their faces; not know their names. In such coercive circumstances, steeped in fear, individual recognition and identification of the accused is usually impossible. Both in the Northeast and in Kashmir, not just in rape cases but even in cases of enforced disappearances and extrajudicial execution, the particular unit that is accused of human rights violations, is quickly moved out of that area and a new unit is brought in, making any identification of the accused men impossible. So, how will the legal machinery respond in such egregious circumstances? Will such rapes and sexual abuse be treated as collateral damage? Place the burden on the women victims to identify, name and locate the accused? Let me point out two aspects, one the law has recognized and the other the law is reluctant to incorporate. In the 2013 Criminal Law Amendment, a very important amendment was that to the list of coercive circumstances under Sec. 376 (2) of the Indian Penal Code, more circumstances of aggravated rape were added. This legal provision with respect to power or custodial rape was introduced in the post-Mathura phase, to recognize that position, authority, and state power, contributed to a woman's vulnerability. Police custody was recognized as an aggravated circumstance in law, post Mathura, as a category of aggravated rape. In 2013, the IPC expanded the scope of this section to bring within the ambit of coercive circumstances, rape by a member of the armed forces and other security forces, in an area where they are deployed. The first FIR against the security forces (the CRPF and the others), under the new provision of the 2013 amended law was lodged by adivasi women of Chhattisgarh against CRPF [personnel] and others who were a part of the patrolling group[5]. Of course, there is no progress in the investigation of this complaint but the law recognized it as an instance of aggravated rape. Yet the absolute impregnable impunity that existed is being slowly disturbed, by at least recognizing it as a distinct crime that takes place in a set of coercive circumstances. But there is still a very big chasm between women seeking and securing justice. Gaps remain in the law itself. These aggravated rapes cannot be examined only as individual criminal acts. The law must ask who is at the helm of affairs. And that is where the criminal law doctrine of command or superior responsibility steps in. It's an internationally recognized criminal law doctrine, not only by the Rome statute governing the International Criminal Court, but in many other jurisdictions. In the absence of this legal doctrine in our legal lexicon, accountability will not be secured. These men in uniform work through a chain of command, in a formal hierarchy, they work through orders. The superior or commander exercises authority over them, and therefore, if some security personnel or unit has transgressed official duty and the same is within the knowledge of the commander, there is a legal obligation on him to take action; failing which the commander will be individually criminally liable. Not only is the doctrine of command responsibility missing in our law, it is aggravated by laws like AFSPA (Armed Forces Special Powers Act) which through the clause of prior sanction for criminal prosecution, effectively obstruct any prospect of a punishment. Thus a culture of impunity has spawned, whether in the case of Manorama in Manipur[6], or the adivasi women in Bastar, or the women of Kunan and Poshpora in Kashmir.[7] So, to my mind, in the absence of the international criminal law doctrine [of Superior/Command Responsibility], impunity will remain firmly entrenched. To go back to the complaint of the Bastar women, those complaints were investigated by the NHRC [National Human Rights Commission]. NHRC's investigation has confirmed the veracity of these complaints; and found more complaints of rapes, in the course of its investigation. The NHRC has asked for compensation to be paid to the women. The Chhattisgarh state is taking time even in replying to that. What the compensation would do – whether the women accept it or not is for them to say, I don't know, but what the compensation would do, is to acknowledge that yes, these women were sexually assaulted by the security forces. Now my question to the CRPF and the Chhattisgarh police is that, if there are verified complaints of rape by men in your force and service, what have you done about it? The state cannot seek refuge behind the fact that the women are unable to name or identify the men in uniform. I think the feminist movement needs to change this discourse, because quite conveniently and callously the burden has been placed entirely on the woman victim. Because what I hear and see in all this, is actually both a backlash and a push back taking place.

Can we talk a bit about the Soni Sori case? I know from bits and pieces, mostly anecdotal evidence, that Soni Sori called you when she surfaced in Delhi. How did she actually pick on you? What were the dynamics? And tell us about how you got involved with the Soni Sori case because that, from the point of view of the sexual violence question, becomes quite interesting, no?

When Soni Sori was arrested in Delhi, I was asked by some friends to intervene because she needed a lawyer. I had learnt then that she was going to be produced in Saket court for transit remand, to take her to Chhattisgarh, and that is when I met Soni for the first time – I don't think I had met her before that. So I went to Saket court and I informed Uma Chakravarti and Vani [Subramanian] from Saheli. When Soni was produced by the Delhi police she very clearly told me that she didn't want to go to Chhattisgarh, as she knew the police would torture her and coerce her to make statements implicating activists, based in Delhi and Chhattisgarh, who were exposing human rights violations taking place in Chhattisgarh. Soni said to me, 'Look they will misbehave with me, they will abuse their power, they will torture me. So you have to do whatever you can to stop this remand being given to the Chhattisgarh police.' Unfortunately, while torture is an open secret, and the NHRC each year documents innumerable cases of custodial violence, the police overwhelms the court with references to national security or Naxal links, and courts presume good faith on the part of the state functionaries.

I knew that our chances of halting the transit remand were quite bleak and that is why I told Soni that while I would strongly argue for her, I wanted her to also address the court and express her fears directly to the judge. Otherwise it appears that lawyers routinely say these things to obstruct a transit remand. But if Soni speaks it may have a different impact and also because I wanted the Magistrate to quote Soni's apprehension in the judicial order. In fact, I recall Soni telling the judge in Hindi that the Chhattisgarh police will not spare her and will torture her, and the judge noted it in her Order. However the court granted transit remand to Chhattisgarh police and Soni was taken back to Chhattisgarh, where she was sexually tortured at the police station.

Are you saying that you actually succeeded in the judge recording that she had apprehensions?

Yes, I recall that it was noted in the written record. So there is a paper trail recording her grave fears, and this is very important in law. And that is why I asked Soni to speak in court. But even that did not deter the police from sexually torturing Soni in police custody. Which tells us how entrenched the impunity is.

A petition was filed against the sexual torture of Soni before the Supreme Court. An independent medical examination in Kolkata confirmed that small stones had been inserted into Soni's private parts. Soni has named the senior police officer on whose instructions she was sexually tortured. However no one has ever been held accountable for this. In a country where everyone expresses such concern about sexual violence, what Soni's case tells us is that in certain circumstances, sexual violence and sexual torture does not attract state disapprobation.

And is practised by it, also?

In certain political exigencies, sexual violence is sanctioned by the state through multiple acts of omission and commission, and the institutions that can hold them accountable, just look the other way. Particularly when women human defenders challenge injustices, or discrimination or deprivations, which the state views as a challenge to its power, sexual violence is deployed, sexual torture is the weapon that is used against women activists and women leaders will be used against them. If the judiciary shies away from strongly and promptly bringing and holding such perpetrators accountable, then the impunity for sexual torture is confirmed and as a natural corollary the vulnerability of the activist women, engaged in political life, is severely aggravated.

Soni Sori and her journalist nephew Linga Ram Kodopi were both implicated in a case, alleging that they were a conduit for channelling funds from the Essar company to Maoists. The case was fixed for arguments on charge before the Trial Court, and I was requested to argue for their discharge. This took me to Jagdalpur, where Soni and Linga were held in prison; and then to Dantewada, where the court is located. At that time, Soni and Linga were both imprisoned in Jagdalpur Central Jail. I sought permission and met them. Soni was lodged in the women's barracks and Linga was in the male section of the jail. Quite a few years had passed since my first meeting with her in Saket Court in Delhi. She had since been in jail, and had not been given bail despite the sexual torture inflicted on her. When Soni first saw me in the jail, she looked at me very tentatively because she wasn't sure if I was the same person, her lawyer. However, she quickly recognized me and her first words to me were, '*Maine aap ko kaha tha, mujhe yahan mat bhejo.*' (I had asked you not to send me here.) That is the thing with Soni Sori – she is unrelenting, both to herself and others. So, I said, '*Haan, par maine tumhe kaha tha main aaungi*, and I have come.' (Yes, but I had told you I would come, and I have now.) She said, '*Aapne bahut der kari*'. (But you came too late.) And I said, 'Yes, I accept.' But now I am here to represent you in court.

Did she say 'aap ne bahut der kari' (you came too late) ya 'bahut der ho gayi' (it is too late now).

Perhaps she said '*bahut der ho gayi*'. I don't remember her precise words, but what she communicated to me would translate as 'a lot has happened and it is very late now'. And I said that yes, I am aware of what has happened and I had told you I would come. And I am here and will do what needs to be done. I told her that I will be appearing on her and Linga's behalf before the Dantewada court. I said I will see you in Dantewada court tomorrow. When I went to Dantewada court, the next day, they had not brought Soni and Linga from judicial custody, which is also one of the reasons why these cases get dragged endlessly, because the accused are not produced before the court on the dates of hearing. When they did finally arrive in Dantewada court, it was quite late. I went to meet them in the lockup in the court. And Soni informed me that she had a huge argument with the Jail Superintendent, to make arrangements for them to be taken to Dantewada Court. She told them 'my lawyer has come from Delhi and you cannot today tell me that due to lack of facilities you cannot make arrangements for our court appearance; my lawyer has come all the way from Delhi and I cannot afford to miss the date of this hearing'. As both Soni and Linga were tagged as "high risk Naxal undertrials", certain security arrangements are required to be made by the state for their travel from Jagdalpur to Dantewada.

It is a basic rule of criminal law that the trial must be held in the presence of the accused persons, so after they were produced in the court I argued the case on charge. At the Dantewada court, there was a woman judge, a woman Public Prosecutor, a woman defence counsel (me) and a woman accused (Soni Sori). The Public Prosecutor first sent word that she was very busy and sought an adjournment. I strongly opposed this adjournment and informed the court that I was willing to wait there the whole day if required but that I had come from Delhi and today was the date fixed by the court for arguments on Charge, and my clients were suffering incarceration. So, then the case was heard. The Public Prosecutor, I recall, came and made a rather short three-point submission, to the effect that this is a Naxalite affected area; these people are associated with Naxals; and such dangerous persons should not be discharged. None of the PP's arguments spoke to the facts of the case, or the charge sheet which had no evidence at all to make out any offence against either Linga or Soni. The PP made this brief submission and in fact left the courtroom. Soni and Linga were brought to the court and made to stand at some distance near the back of the court room. The arguments took place in Hindi and English. I don't know how much they could hear or understand. Often the person whose life and liberty is at stake has very little clue about what's transpiring in court. Soni's father's leg was in plaster and he was walking with the aid of crutches, had travelled a very, very long way to meet with Soni. He didn't get to meet her or Linga in the court lockup because family members are not allowed to meet high-risk undertrials. He momentarily saw his daughter, Soni, when she walked past him in the corridor outside the courtroom, and when she exited the courtroom, escorted by armed police. They barely exchanged a word or two and a smile, more than that, he had no opportunity. He had travelled a very long way with an old friend because he could not travel alone in his present condition, just to have one fleeting glance of his daughter. Linga later told me that every time his sister came to meet him either at the court or at the jail, she didn't travel alone, and on her return her escort was harassed by the police, saying that 'you too must be linked to Naxalites'. Later both Soni and Linga were released on bail.

So, let's continue along the sexual torture part of it...

In fact, if you remember, an NCW [National Commission for Women] team went to examine the complaints of continuing sexual torture that Soni had made, after women's groups repeatedly petitioned them. The NCW team, in which Annie Raja of the NFIW was the external member, went and met with the women inmates in prison. It's actually the statutory mandate of the NCW to study and review the condition of women in jail. So, that mission was of course sent only afterwards.

And finally gheraod [protested against] them-

That was done later asking them to release the report. This was...

No, no, no. It was before they went.

Oh, I see. Yes, this was when letters were coming from Soni saying that in addition to the incident of sexual torture at the police station at the time of the investigation, she was suffering repeated sexual torture and humiliation as she was strip searched at the jail. Most aggressively and very obtrusively she was frisked and strip searched by the prison staff, all this amounts to varying forms of sexual torture. She was able to somehow communicate this to her lawyers through letters. The letters were placed before the Supreme Court. Despite all this women's groups had to move heaven and earth to get the NCW to undertake a prison visit to Chhattisgarh, which is anyways their statutory mandate.

Soni has named and identified the police officer under whose charge she alleges that she was sexually tortured in police custody. She has named him. She has identified him. She has made a detailed accusation. The system has remained unresponsive. No enquiry, no investigation, no probe, nothing into such serious allegations. Would it be wrong then to infer that the state is complicit, and the state through its inaction, through its omissions, through its silences, provides protection and the patronage to sexualized torture and rape of women activists, here a woman adivasi leader. This is a form of state domination of the adivasi community.

I think, therefore, it is very important to note that the feminist movement no longer restricts itself to highlighting certain kinds of sexual violence cases. It's actually raising its voice and speaking out against this kind of institutionalized impunity in which the state is complicit.

Now, looking at the way in which systematic torture is being used against the adivasi population...

I recall, when I got a call late at night that there were women, who wanted to file a FIR for rape by security forces in Bijapur district of Chhattisgarh. They wanted to know about the new section introduced in the Indian Penal Code, in 2013. Criminal law as you know was amended post the gang rape of December 2012. One significant amendment to my mind was that of, "rape by armed forces or other security forces' being recognized as a specific form of aggravated rape in the Indian Penal Code. The phone call from Bijapur was from women activists asking for the relevant legal section under the IPC, as neither the District Magistrate nor the S.P were aware of the amended legal provision and what the section was. This complaint referred to the rape and molestation of adivasi women by security forces who while on patrol went to the village for a search and cordon operation.

In Bijapur perhaps the first FIR under this new provision Sec. 376 (2)(c) IPC of rape by armed forces was lodged by adivasi women against security forces.

In January, there were a whole slew of complaints. Five women I think went up and down trying to make a complaint, that included the peculiar thing they were doing of pinching the women's breasts and nobody could make any sense of it also.

For lactation[8].

Yes.

So really it's all forms of sexual torture and sexualized humiliation. But what must be underscored is that these adivasi women are coming forward and making these complaints against sexual violence before multiple fora. However, these cases are not necessarily in any way progressing. So whether it is the assault in a communal violence situation on a targeted minority community, or the assault on the adivasi community, the perpetrators may be state actors or non-state actors – but sexual violence and torture and sexualized humiliation seem to be a component of the manner in which a community is attacked, and women's bodies are targeted.

So, I think the natural progression in this would be to discuss your work on Muzaffarnagar. That I think is very important because it brings up critical issues around how the targeted community can stand in actually pursuing cases. So, from the point of impunity, how can we challenge impunity unless we have some structures of support that make it possible for people to continue the legal struggle?

Just before I speak of Muzaffarnagar, even in Chhattisgarh we have seen that women who are living deep in the interior, their community does not necessarily engage with the formal state or the formal legal system at all, are stepping out and filing complaints. In fact, one of the earlier cases of rape was during Salwa Judum.[9] Five of those women had come forward. Private criminal complaints were filed in court, and Sudha Bharadwaj, a human rights lawyer, had represented these women.

Was this rape by the Salwa Judum cadre?

Yes, by the Salwa Judum cadre. Five women rape survivors had filed cases in court. Their evidence was recorded. They had named the accused men and the court issued warrants for their arrest. However the police said that they can't locate the accused men. One of them was a SPO [Special Police Officer] of the Salwa Judum, who was on the payroll of the state. While the police claimed helplessness to locate the accused and ignorance about their whereabouts, the photograph of one of the accused appeared in the local newspaper as part of a group of SPOs. In fact, these women, faced severe threats and intimidation, leaving them with absolutely no choice but to retract their statements. They were threatened by the Salwa Judum cadre with the elimination of their children and family. So, adivasi women of Chhattisgarh, whether it is Soni or other adivasi women, have at different points of time knocked the proverbial door of the court, given cogent evidence, named the accused men, but on each occasion, the legal system has failed them.

Let me now talk about the cases of gang rape of women during the communal attack on the Muslim community in September 2013, in Western Uttar Pradesh. I think we need to think: what is it that we mean when we say that women targeted during sectarian violence, whether caste or communal, should ask for justice for sexual assault? And what is it that women must sacrifice to pursue this justice? Should they, in order to fight for dignity, stake their life? That seems to be what the legal system today is asking of them. If the rape survivor is to secure a conviction – forget a conviction – if she wants to take forward her case of rape, her life and the lives of her family members could be in danger…which is an unacceptable risk to ask any woman to take. Why should she risk her life? The legal system offers her no protection, no time frame, no assurance, no solace, no support.

In Muzaffarnagar in 2013, once again, as we have seen in almost every episode of communal violence, the attack was state engineered and state orchestrated. Once again rape was an element of the targeted violent attack on the minority community. Adult married women, with children, roughly in the age group of 30 to 50, were gang raped by men known to them, with whom they had social and commercial interactions, belonging to the same village, but from a different religious community. The women were Muslim and the men Hindus. As the women knew the men, there was no confusion and they were able to name and identify the rapists in the FIR.

The Muzaffarnagar communal violence was part of the politics of polarization on the eve of elections in Uttar Pradesh in 2013. One of the most serious consequences was the massive rural displacement and permanent ghettoization, which will obviously have repercussions in the years to come. The Hindu Jat community, which was the aggressor here, didn't want anyone to raise the issue of the rape cases. They said, '*Humare ladke murder kar sakte hai but rape nahi karte.*' (Our boys may murder but they don't rape.) I've never completely understood this, because it seems that killing Muslims is an act of valour, but not raping Muslim women. If one looks at Western U.P., it has such a dreadful history of killings of women, even within the Jat community – any woman who dares to transgress caste, sub-caste boundaries, is routinely killed in cold blood. But clearly this is something of which there is no public acknowledgement. Silence shrouds the killing of women. And there was a huge effort to actually suppress the rape cases. [They said] that murder cases, '*...toh hum lad lenge, ki humne unko mara toh accha kiya. Magar rape humare ladke nahi karte hai.*' (We can fight [murder cases] easily. It was a good thing that we killed them or beat them. But our boys would never rape.) While working in these cases I gained a few interesting insights. One, I think that the discourse that emerged, post the 2012 gang-rape of Nirbhaya in Delhi is actually reaching quite distant and different spaces. The women rape survivors came forward with their families only because there was a social activist who assisted them and supported them in lodging FIRs. These women came to my office accompanied by their husbands. When they narrated the sexual assault to me, their husbands were sitting by their side. This is very, very different from what happened in 1984, where the Sikh community also hushed up the incidents of rape, advised the women to remain silent and only stray comments were heard. In 2002, [in Gujarat] it was mainly due to the intervention of feminist activists who visited the relief camps, that the narratives of sexual violence were known. It was again due to the support and commitment of these activists that Bilkis Bano fought her legal battle and won. In 2013 post the Muzaffarnagar riots, it was the women survivors, accompanied by their husbands, who came forward and told me about the incidents. What was striking was that the women and their spouses spoke about the gang rape incident without attaching any shame or stigma or victim blaming. In fact, interestingly one woman told me that she was apprehensive of telling her husband as it is her second marriage, her husband is younger than her, and she was fearful that due to the gang-rape he may leave her. This thought had crossed her mind and so she didn't tell him immediately. But she did tell him later and he didn't think that she had done anything wrong and he stood by her. So, I think there is a shift, in the understanding and response to rape. Of course, it was just seven women who stepped forward and [formally] complained. We do know that many more Muslim women were sexually assaulted during the communal attack. It's also true that soon after the riots some religious organizations arranged mass community weddings so that young women were not at risk of sexual violence. So, it's not as though there has been a complete shift but one can see the glimmers of change, both among the women and their families.

However, tragically, it is the legal system that completely and totally let them down, and it wasn't an accidental or an incidental omission. I strongly believe that the Muzaffarnagar rape cases tell the story of institutional apathy. These are instances of institutional complicity. Let me underscore that it was in the Muzaffarnagar rape cases that for the first time the new penal provision that was introduced in the IPC through the Criminal Law Amendment

Act 2013, which recognized rape during communal or sectarian violence as an aggravated form of rape, was invoked. The first FIRs under this new offence i.e. under Section 376(2) (g) IPC, were registered in Muzaffarnagar. Why is this new criminal provision very critical in these cases? As I said earlier, in these seven cases the women knew the men who had gang raped them, as they belonged to the same village and they had accordingly named these men in the FIR. Significantly, the police, in the beginning. did not mention this specific section of aggravated rape committed during communal violence in the FIR. On behalf of these seven women, I filed a Writ Petition in the Supreme Court, where rebutting my argument that these cases squarely fall within the purview of adding Section 376(2) (g) IPC, the counsel for the state of U.P. said, 'Oh, but we have lodged the FIR as a case of gang-rape, and Section 376D of the IPC, attracts a higher sentence", implying therefore that no malafide can be attributed to the state of UP. Now this is a very misleading statement, because to get to the issue of sentence we first need a conviction. I think it's also about erasure of the official record. If you don't put the cases under gang-rape during communal violence, you are actually erasing, sanitising the official record. After all *gang-rape toh kabhi bhi ho jata hai. Gang-rape toh bohot saare hote hai.* (Gang-rapes are very common, a lot of them happen all the time.) These gang rapes are part of that specific history of targeted attacks on the Muslim community, which is sought to be erased and supressed.

Right, and you are raising that issue.

Yes, despite the issue being raised in my petition, the U.P. police still did not add the offence. There was a woman Investigating Officer in charge of the investigation of all these seven cases, who was totally in cahoots with the accused. She tried her level best to dissuade the women from taking their complaints forward. Eventually, I filed a Contempt of Court application in the Supreme

Court and only then did the state of U.P. include this particular IPC provision, that recognizes rape as a weapon for targeted attack on a religious community during communal riots. Now, how does this impact the case, the trial? This new offence, of rape during communal violence, is linked to a provision of the Indian Evidence Act, where a rebuttable legal presumption is raised against the accused. If the women testify before the Trial Court that the sexual act was without their consent, then it will be presumed to be a non-consensual sexual act, because in the middle of a riot, when your house is being burnt, and your family is fleeing, you're not about to start having sex with six men from your village and from the aggressor community. A rebuttable presumption in law is raised against the accused and the accused has to counter it. That is why, whether it is in the case of the Chhattisgarh adivasi women raped by security forces or it is the case of Muslim women raped in Muzaffarnagar, the amended law puts the rape survivor on a stronger footing. If she steps into the witness box and she testifies before the court, the likelihood of conviction is quite high. It's important to note that in the Muzaffarnagar cases, there is no possibility of medical evidence as the women were taken to the hospital two months later only after their case was heard by the Supreme Court. The Supreme Court asked why their medical examination was not conducted after they lodged FIRs. What purpose can a medical examination of married women serve after two months?

The local BJP political leaders were prominently reported by the media to have said that they will support the rape accused. These media reports were presented to the court, stating that if the sitting MLAs and the sitting state party leader are going to be actively supporting the accused, these women are not going to be able to come forward and testify in the court. We don't have a witness-victim protection programme. We asked for robust protection, which was answered in the form of two constables assigned to each of the women. I am not very sure what kind of security this provides. What I did discover, however, was that when these two constables come and stay in the house of the women, their food, boarding, lodging becomes the responsibility of that family. And suddenly, all the families who have just been displaced from their ancestral home, they have no work, they are living in camps, these families now also have to feed the constables. Of course, the threats are so insidious and covert that two constables stationed at their homes, obviously can't counter them. I also sought reparations for the rape survivors from the Supreme Court. And I think for the first time, in one case, even before a FIR was lodged, Rs 500,000 were awarded as compensation by the Supreme Court, recognizing rape as a harm, an injury to her person. I recall the court said to the state of U.P., 'You're compensating for death, you're compensating for injury, you're compensating for loss of property, why are you not compensating for this?' However, what I had asked for was not compensation, but rather reparative justice. In my petition I cited international law on the victim's right to reparative justice. Unfortunately, in India, reparation and compensation are used as interchangeable terms. Although the two are distinct, both conceptually in law, and the consequences and the obligations that they impose on the state. Compensation is only one element in the larger conceptual category of reparative justice. The Supreme Court unfortunately did not recognize the right to reparations. However, the judgment of the Supreme Court recognized that in situations of communal violence rape is a specific form of gender-based crime and there is an obligation on the state to compensate for the failure to protect and the harm caused.

There is this mirage that is blindly chased by many, including women's groups. There's a constant clamour for this entity called 'fast-track courts'. The state knows that if you perform certain gimmicks, it serves the purpose of satisfying society. So, the fast-track courts were set up, predictably in Muzaffarnagar also. It is a minor detail that for eight months there was no judge appointed to the fast-track court. The Bar in Muzaffarnagar was very hostile. There was a Special Public Prosecutor appointed and at the time it was a Samajwadi Party government so at least some superficial sympathies were expressed. I myself went to Muzaffarnagar district court, which is a three and half hour run by car from Delhi. It's one thing to say – and this I feel is something the women's rights movement, the human rights movement is very quick to ask and very slow to stand by – we want justice, the guilty must be punished. So, what is the process of securing that justice? What is the process of punishing the guilty? It's very slow, very arduous, very difficult and all forms of resources are required – social, physical, monetary, emotional, legal, to go through the legal process. Let me give you a glimpse of the Muzaffarnagar legal process. So, Muzaffarnagar court was a fairly chilling and intimidating experience. It is the first time that I asked for security for myself, police security at the Muzaffarnagar court. Because at Muzaffarnagar court, it is possible that somebody will pull out a gun and shoot the witness, or the lawyer, or both. The lawyer's Bar is very male, very hostile and sharply polarized on religious lines. In the court I was tagged as a specimen and attracted unsolicited attention for being 'an English-speaking Supreme Court woman lawyer.' At that time, the National Commission for Minorities [NCM] was very supportive and on my request ensured that the local police provided some formal police protection. I received a lot of support from ANHAD [Act Now for Harmony and Democracy, New Delhi]. Shabnam Hashmi, an indefatigable activist, would ensure that some ANHAD activists would accompany us as it was not safe for me and my junior, two women lawyers, to be alone at Muzaffarnagar court. We would also invariably inform some journalist. These are ways in which I made a circle of...some kind of security. Whether it works or not, I don't know. I feel that people need to understand that this is what pursuing justice entails...that when you say that the guilty must be punished, then you have to stay with these cases for a very long time. And I feel groups and movements don't have stamina, they don't have tenacity. They flit from incident to incident. The one [thing] that I have learnt is – and I say this for all my cases…and I have particularly learnt his from my experience in representing the victims of the 1987 Hashimpura massacre, is that the legal system's silent but lethal weapon against us is delay.[10] This year marks 30 years since the Hashimpura killings. The Ishrat Jahan trial has barely begun, 14 years later.[11] The Muzaffarnagar cases are dragging. So, it's important for groups and movements to know that the state will try to exhaust us, wear us down and frustrate us. Delay is a weapon in the state's armoury. I feel initially everyone is charged up, enraged, everybody visits the women but later, finally it is just the women survivors and their lawyers, who are left fighting a very lonely and protracted battle for that elusive justice. A lot of the women drop out of the legal system, exhausted, helpless and hopeless, because there is nobody around to hold their hand, give them hope, express solidarity. As a lawyer I cannot provide all forms of psycho-social support. It's not my role to play.

Let me narrate an interesting case proceeding in Muzaffarnagar court. Out of the seven rape cases, in one case the police had filed a closure report, saying that it was a false case. I moved an application challenging the closure report and seeking further investigation. I told the court that to present my arguments, I have to read out the rape woman survivor's statement about the rape incident and so it should be heard in-camera. The judge looked very puzzled, because in Muzaffarnagar, which is only three and a half hours away from Delhi, the judge had not heard of the concept of 'in-camera' trial. He asked the Public Prosecutor to check the veracity of my application on this point. I sat with the Prosecutor and I showed him the relevant provisions of law in the statute book, under the Indian Evidence Act. The PP went back to the Judge and said, '*Yeh thik bol rahi hai, aisa law mei likha hai*' (She is right. This is written in the law.) I was both amused and surprised. We think, that with the momentum created by the women, courts are changing, legal systems are changing. However, what this brought home starkly was that we are living in a little bubble of our own in Delhi. Not much is changing even a few hundred kilometres away. I don't know if there are any judicial trainings ongoing in districts like Muzaffarnagar, where there is a very high rate of sexual violence and rape, even in ordinary times. So, after the endorsement by the PP that my application was legally valid, the judge said, 'Okay...you wait then, I will hear your case last.' The CJM's court had a rather long daily cause list so I said, 'If I am asking for an in-camera hearing, it doesn't mean that I will be heard last in line. Please take up my case in the sequence it is listed.' There were a large number of lawyers and others present in the court room, so the judge asked how could he hold an in-camera hearing? I said, 'You ask them to leave and close the court doors and the Prosecutor and myself will be present and we will argue.' The judge looked quite puzzled and said, 'Oh, I can do that?' I said, 'Yes, that's what is done for in-camera hearings in courts in Delhi.' So, all the lawyers were sent out. And they looked rather annoyed that why is this woman lawyer getting preferential treatment! Now, there was an infrastructural problem, in even executing an in-camera trial in that court. The district court in Muzaffarnagar is housed in an old building of colonial vintage; and in the large court room, which is a massive hall, at the rear end there is an iron cage where the accused of all cases who are in custody are brought from jail and kept through the day, while the cases are being heard. How can it be an in-camera trial when the audience comprises of many accused persons, unrelated to the rape case? Thus, even the spatial architecture of the court was not aligned to the law.

In the case of another rape survivor of Muzaffarnagar, her case was fixed for recording her evidence. She appeared with me before the trial judge, to give evidence that day. As soon as the accused saw that rape survivor had come to testify, (there were four accused) three of the accused raised an objection against her being examined saying, 'We have no lawyer!' And the judge said, 'Oh! If they don't have a lawyer, I can't record her evidence.' I argued that the defence counsel was present in court and the judicial record showed that the same lawyer has been representing all the accused men, at the stage of Charge etc. Almost on cue the defence counsel said, 'No, no, no! I am only representing one of the accused.' I persisted and informed the court that, 'Today, the rape survivor has come to give evidence and that is why the accused are orchestrating this false plea. They are buying time hoping to pressurise her and silence her.' Regrettably, the judge accepted the argument of the accused and in spite of my protests, the hearing was adjourned. On that very day I filed an application and placed on record the rape survivor's affidavit stating unequivocally that, 'I am being threatened and intimidated. Please record my statement at the earliest. I will not be able to withstand this pressure from the accused.' The Sessions Court adjourned the case for a fortnight. After a fortnight I again travelled to Muzaffarnagar and appeared with the rape survivor before the court for her evidence to be recorded. Once again, the accused men loudly informed the court that her evidence could not be recorded as they were not represented by a lawyer and that the defence lawyer of their choice was asking for a high fees. I suggested that the court should in such circumstances appoint legal aid lawyers for them as it was evident that they were using this as a ruse to delay the recording of the rape survivor's testimony, which would nail the case. and moving forward, that's what you do for most people. The court heard the accused men and adjourned the case on their request for another fortnight. On the next date of hearing, my client the rape survivor did not contact me. She went to court, deposed and in her testimony stated that she was gang-raped but could not identify any of the rapists. Let me remind you that in this case the woman had named the rapists in her FIR itself. Is this not a case of a hostile witness foretold? Who is responsible for this? The answer is available in the judicial record, in the adjournment orders, the rape survivor's affidavit pleading for her evidence to be recorded. Significantly neither the Sessions Judge nor the Public Prosecutor, paused the trial when the rape survivor turned hostile.

In the case of another rape survivor, where the woman remains undeterred and is determined to give evidence, the case is dragging endlessly. I argued against the application filed by the accused seeking discharge in October of 2015. The Sessions Court reserved the order. Till June 2016 the Sessions Court had not passed an order although arguments by both parties concluded eight months ago. Then the judge was transferred. So now the application has to be argued all over again before the new judge. Unless this application is disposed off and the charges are framed against the accused men, we cannot reach the stage of evidence. And only then will the rape survivor's testimony will be recorded.

Of the seven Muslim women who filed FIRs of gang-rape during the communal attack in 2013, one woman died during childbirth; five have turned hostile in court; and one is patiently but determinedly waiting to give evidence against her rapists in court. With good reason the seventh rape survivor has no confidence in the Muzaffarnagar court, so I filed a petition before the Allahabad High Court seeking transfer of her case out of Muzaffarnagar district. From 2016 to 2018 the case was not decided by the High Court and the accused kept seeking adjournments. In the interim, media reports mentioned that the Yogi government is seeking to withdraw the cases pending against the riot accused. In such circumstances, I am once again moving the Supreme Court seeking a transfer of her trial outside the state of U.P. From 2013 to 2018, she is still waiting for a court that will hear her, record her evidence and then maybe hold the accused men who gang raped her accountable. It is a deeply unequal fight for justice. However as long as these women wish to pursue justice, we have no choice but to be very determined and tenacious.

Interviewed by Uma Chakravarti and Urvashi Butalia in Delhi

NOTES

1. Chakravarti, Uma and Nandita Haksar. 1985. *Three Days in the Life of a Nation*. New Delhi. Lancer.
2. James, Stella. *Through my Looking Glass*. November 6, 2013. https://jilsblognujs.wordpress.com/2013/11/06/through-my-looking-glass/
3. https://www.indiatoday.in/india/north/story/law-intern-harassment-case-subramanian-swamy-lends-support-to-justice-a-k-ganguly-221582-2013-12-21
4. Soni Sori 43, is an adivasi school teacher and warden of a government-run school for adivasi children in Dantewada district of Chhattisgarh. She was implicated in several cases by the Chhattisgarh police, arrested, tortured and sexually assaulted in police custody in 2011. She is now a fierce human rights advocate and campaigns relentlessly against state excesses.
5. The security forces allegedly went on a rampage between October 19 and 24 in 2015, in the villages of Chinnagelur, Peddagelur, Gundam, Burgicheru and Pegdapalli, about 70 km from Bijapur district headquarters. The incidents of rape, gang-rape, stripping and other forms of sexual violence in these remote villages were brought to light and documented by activists of the Women Against Sexual Violence and State Repression (WSS). In January 2017, the National Human Rights Commission found 16 women prima facie victims of rape and assault by police personnel and was waiting for recorded statements of 20 others. https://www.hindustantimes.com/india-news/nhrc-notice-to-chhattisgarh-on-bijapur-rapes-few-dare-to-tread-ground-zero/story-aN41KlPSrxAb9SkSWMplQI.html

6. Thangjam Manorama Devi, 34, was picked up from her home in Imphal by personnel of the paramilitary Assam Rifles on the night of July 11, 2004. The next day, her mutilated, bullet-ridden body was found, with signs of gang-rape. None of the perpetrators has been brought to book for this crime.
7. On the night of February 23, 1991, Indian army personnel carried out a search operation and also allegedly raped over 30 women in the twin villages of Kunan and Poshpora, Kupwara district of Kashmir. The survivors have been fighting for justice ever since, and in 2013, in response to a petition on behalf of the survivors, the Jammu and Kashmir High Court ordered reopening of the case.
8. This was a crude method employed by security forces to surmise whether or not an adivasi woman was a Maoist cadre, since it was assumed that female cadre would not be married, bear children or breast feed them.
9. Salwa Judum (which in Gondi translates as 'Peace Hunt') was an armed vigilante movement sponsored by the State, financed by private capital, and used by the police and security forces to wipe out the Maoist movement in Chhattisgarh. Under the reign of the Salwa Judum, thousands of villagers were evicted and confined in camps, their homes razed to the ground and livelihoods destroyed. Mass evictions were accompanied by extreme violence and also sexual violence. The Salwa Judum was active from 2005 until 2011 when the Supreme Court declared the group illegal and unconstitutional.
10. On May 22, 1987, during communal riots in Uttar Pradesh, 19 personnel of the Provincial Armed Constabulary allegedly rounded up 42 youth from the Muslim community and shot them in cold blood on the outskirts of Meerut city and dumped their bodies in an irrigation canal. In March 2015, a trial court acquitted all 16 accused citing "insufficient evidence". It was only in May 2015, 28 years after the massacre, that the UP government announced a compensation of Rs 5 lakh to the families of the victims. The case is pending appeal in the High Court, Vrinda Grover is counsel for the National Human Rights Commission on behalf of the victims' families.

11. The "Ishrat Jahan encounter case' refers to the alleged encounter on June 15, 2004 by officers of the Ahmedabad Police and Subsidiary Intelligence Bureau who shot dead four persons on the outskirts of Ahmedabad on suspicion of being members of the banned militant group Lashkar-e-Taiba. Vrinda Grover is representing Shamima Kauser, mother of 19-year-old Ishrat Jahan in her writ petition alleging that her daughter was killed in a 'fake encounter'.

11

A Fighter's Story

Interview with Suzette Jordan

RAJASHRI DASGUPTA

Suzette Jordan, a single mother of two children was gang-raped on February 5, 2012 in Kolkata. In the process of her fight for justice, she transformed herself into a women's rights activist. In this journey, a year later, she waived her right to anonymity as a rape survivor to further her work as an anti-rape activist. Her fierce will to not just survive but to celebrate life, challenged the dominant cultural discourse of the 'pure' victim whose life has been destroyed by 'a fate worse than death.' In this interview, she narrates her harrowing experience of sexual violence and her subsequent fight for justice. She highlights the problematic nature of the institutional and social response to sexual violence and impunity and narrates the many ways in which the state government, the police, the courts, the medical community and her own community failed in their duty to protect her fundamental rights as a survivor. She concludes with the kind of institutional and cultural change she would like to see for women who seek help, and the ways in which that help can be offered to them.

On March 13, 2015, a few months after this interview, Suzette Jordan passed away in Kolkata. She was only forty years old when she succumbed to encephalitis. The repetition of parts of her story throughout the interview is a part of her narrative of trauma and consequent recovery and healing. As we did not wish to change it without her consent, the transcript has been retained with minimal edits.

I

Suzette, I have been wanting to interview you for a very long time. I knew you were going through a traumatic time.

First, I want to let you know from me and all our friends that we are extremely pained by what happened to you, it should not have happened at all, it should not happen to anybody. We are very ashamed of how the administration dealt with the incident. By speaking up, you have provided us with a lot of courage and strength

Thank you.

Let me explain the purpose of this interview. Some of us are doing research on sexual violence and on the role of the state: how it handles it [sexual violence], counselling, treatment for the woman [and so on]. We are trying to understand what can be done, it's an ongoing battle and struggle. Any time you are uncomfortable with my questions, stop me. Any question you don't want to answer, don't answer. I completely understand. Any time you realize you have said something, you don't want to be said, alert me.

Sure.

I'm trying to understand what happened that night. The objectives of the questions are not so much about the brutality of the violence you faced; but that such a thing could have happened at all in the first place in Park Street in the heart of the city, at that time of the night.

I trust people very easily. I have always trusted people very easily from a very young age. I have never looked at any person thinking, you know, that person is bad. I look at everybody thinking that everyone is good. Throughout my life I have been let down all the time, by my closest friends, because I think that they love me and…I have always [been there] for everybody, they tell me their problems. When it comes to *trust*, the optimist person that I am, I have trusted, [and sometimes this] is bad, then I have to deal with it. I think that every person is good. I can't judge anybody just by talking or anything like that, it's not in me to judge anybody.

That evening I had gone to our family club. The problem was I had lost, actually, I was cheated of my business, which my sister and I had started, in the month of September 2011. It was a small call centre that we had started. Later, we hired a couple of boys and girls to work with us and some chap cheated us out of the whole business and we had to shut down. So that was a very big setback for me. I wasn't working for anybody, and for so many years had something of my own. So when you lose that, it hurts a lot.

I have never really had a business of my own [but] have had experience of a call centre since 2005 when I began working in one. [T]he experience of having my own was a completely different story. Seeing two women, you know, we got cheated and me being the quiet one, and stupid (laughs) and trusting you know…when I and my sister weren't around, that was the time when cheating went on and I didn't even know it. I started my business in 2011 on the 14th of September, and in January of 2012 I lost it.

So then the blame game started, with my sister saying, 'It's your fault, it's your fault', you know what it is like, and my sister and I who have never before fought because we always stuck together since boarding school. And I was always her protector, I am five years older than her. So I was always being, you know, her protector and guide and her bodyguard kind of a thing. So we never fought; we have fought over stupid things like t-shirts or deodorants but this was serious.

It put me into, not only me, but my mom also into depression and I started to feel that my mom was picking more for my sister and I got more depressed and then I went through a bad phase.

[That day] I was extremely depressed. So in the evening I called one of my friends, an old friend of mine and I asked him, 'What are you doing? Let's meet in our family club.' He said he was free so I said we will meet up at my family club in Park Street. I need to get out of the house, I need to be with friends. You know I just needed to unwind, really I was in a very bad mental frame.

He said, okay, fine. So I was there by 9:15 [pm] as usual. Then we went to the club, he came up later. We were all sitting and drinking and talking. There were other older members there who joined our table, so we were all sitting and talking and laughing, you know… for that moment you are not in the world. You are out of the world and you are in a different world, you are in a world of friends and it took my mind completely off [my worries] and I was actually having a lot of fun. In that time I saw another group of friends come in and I joined them and then we all decided to go to a pub, which is again in Park Hotel, which is like three or four minutes' walk from there. So we went there, it was pretty empty, being a Sunday night, so we were having fun and…[The club we went to closes at 10:30]. And because I have been going there since I was so small and my father, my grandmother and everybody, uncle are all members, they allowed me to sit there and finish our drinks … till about 11: 15 or so.

You are comfortable with your friends? You knew them?

Yes…of course…In fact, one girl was my childhood friend. And my friend who was waiting for me, he has been a friend of mine for the past fifteen years. So it's not like, you know…of course there were two more friends there, my friend's friend who he had introduced me to on one occasion before and that was the second time I met them. They were also fun to be with because I wouldn't have been in this company if they weren't fun, you know...we were really enjoying [ourselves], they left around 11:20 or so ...I didn't want them to go. I wanted them to stay. I didn't want my happiness to stop, I wanted to carry on.

So we went to Someplace Else [bar on Park Street, Kolkata]. It was my treat because they were all low on cash. So I promised that I would treat them...we were all having fun there, being a Sunday, next day was a work day, it [the bar] closes early. Around 12: 30 [am] the pub shuts down. And I was still not ready to end the night. I talked to them and I dragged them all to Tantra, [bar on Park Street, Kolkata] which is just a walk away.

We entered Park Hotel and the disco, sorry, Tantra, was empty again being a Sunday and when we entered we saw on the right-hand side there was a group of ten to twelve guys, and in front there were two three couples, and the four of us.

I went straight to the bar and ordered another drink and all of us were having fun and one guy from that group constantly smiled at me. There is no harm in smiling, you are at a social place, it's a club, you know, and I am not a person who won't smile, I am a person who *will* smile so I smiled back and he waved back to me couple of hand gestures now and again, and then I didn't bother. When my friends and I decided to go to the dance floor, we went to the dance floor usually like everybody else at the nightclub. We were dancing and it's around about 1:10 or 1:15 [am], then my friend said, 'Sue come on, come on let's go, let's go.' I was still not ready to go. So I told them like you know...in any case we all live in different directions. One friend lives in Lake Gardens, one in Rajabazar side and one lives on Park Street, and I live in Behala. So either way we are all going home separately, the only thing was we will walk out together but when we go to the main road, we would all go our separate ways.

It's a fact that for eleven years Rajashri, I have been a single mom, I have been alone everywhere and I have mastered the art of being alone, kind of, you know, and nobody can mess with me and I want to be the tough person. Besides that, I've not only been alone, travelling, but I have brought up two kids by myself, and also taken care of my mother. My sister who lives with me, we both work together, sort of share everything…I've always been confident, [right] from school I have been a rebel. From my school days, I fought. I have always been a strong person. If you ever chance to meet my friends you know, they will all tell you that from school I have been a terror, bold, very bold, a fighter, always getting suspended for fighting for a cause for some other girl. In fact, I was suspended because of my sister, because the matron shouted at her for bed-wetting and said she would have to carry the mattress with her around the whole school. I knew this would affect my sister very much so I got mad and I jumped up and I gave her a rap. Of course, the school suspended me for one month for that…but the thing that I am telling you that is if I thought that it was for a good cause, I fought. I always have been a strong person.

So my friends and I often go to the disco, [maybe] once in a month, we go twice, thrice and we all leave when we have to go home, we all leave when go to our respective homes by taxi…if somebody has the car then if he is good enough he will drop us. Otherwise we take a taxi and go back. You know, it's no big deal.

So that night was not different from any other night. In fact, I was actually at peace with myself. I had completely forgotten about what I am going to do with my business over, now I have to look for a job… so many thoughts I didn't want to think of it at all. That place really was a change because of my friends, laughing, fun, dancing…then they decided they wanted to go home. Of course I wanted them to stay longer, but two friends had work the next day so they left. When they left… my drink was still there because we were dancing and drinking, so my drink was there so I finished… I told them I will finish my drink and then I will leave, they could carry on, not a problem. They left me.

I was standing there having my drink and this guy comes up to me and…the guy that smiled and waved at me a couple of times… he comes up to me and he introduces himself. First he says to me, 'My name is Ruman Khan.' And then he smiles, smirks rather. Then, you know, in a split second, he said, 'Nae, it's…Kadir Khan' – he changes his name.

I didn't think that…guys [are] stupid you know, they do stupid things. Since I was alone, he came up and I have to finish my drink and so I thought, 'Why not? Somebody standing will chat.' So I chatted, that's like, no big deal, you know.

We were chatting and there was no sexual gesture from him, there was no sexual talk from him, there was no indecency, it was a casual conversation…he was asking where I work, and I said I was in the call centre line and then he offered me a job…He said, 'I have a call centre, we are looking for a manager, would you [be interested]…?' And at that point talking about a call centre, something I was running away from, and then the job, it was not going [anywhere]…so I pulled myself like, you know… and I gave him my number instantly…I didn't judge him, I didn't think he was a bad guy or he might be a bad guy or he might be a murderer…no…I had nothing to hide myself, I just gave him my number and said, call me when [you are] awake in the morning.

I gave him the number. I don't wear a watch, so I checked my mobile and it was about 1:30 [am]. Not far from the time my friends had left, so my beer was coming to an end, the bartender had my card so I asked him to charge me and then I left my beer there and then went to the toilet. I had to travel a long way back. Behala is a long way back, so I went to the loo. When I came back the bartender handed me my card and I stood there for a while to finish the rest of my beer and he was still talking to me.

So by the time I finished my beer it was about 2 [am], around 2 or little bit after 2, I am not sure. I didn't check again. Then I said, 'I am leaving, it's pretty late, nice meeting you', and I walked out. Just before walking out, I don't know what made me turn back, I turn back and he had joined his friends where they were all looking at me. He had a finger pointed at me, I didn't say anything and I didn't wait, again I carried on walking. If you have been to Tantra...have you been to Tantra? You know at the reception where you sign to get in just there he comes running up and when I see him running up to me, his four other friends slowly walk behind him; the two friends, he has introduced to me, two more friends while he was talking to me, they kept coming to him and whispering to him while he was talking to me on two three occasions and he introduced me to them but besides saying hello there was no other interactions with them. And they went back to their group. So he came running up to me and he said, 'Please Suzette let me drop you home.' 'No, no,' I said, 'It's okay, cool, I will take a taxi, you don't have to worry.' 'Don't be mad *yaar*...I will drop you. Look my car is already parked in the parking edge.' He showed me a Honda City parked...then he said, '*Achha achha thik hai*...[Okay, okay, that's fine] let me drop you to a taxi, I promise I will drop you to a taxi, *thik hai?*' So I said okay. I saw the guy was decent enough to offer me [a ride] and I saw no problem. He was so persistent, I said okay.

So he walked and his friends were also walking behind. Then I think it's not unusual, probably they are also going home. So I got into the car at the back and he didn't get in as I got in and I was wondering why he didn't get in with me, you know. I said, *thik hai*, and we left. I thought he would drive. So he went around and he came to the right hand side, I got in from the left and he went to the right hand side. Then I saw another friend of his...in the front, the driver's seat.

He was also inside, I had seen him inside but I was not introduced to him. He was there in the group, the fair guy was there...so he gets into the driver's seat and I am still waiting for this guy to get in because you know we were getting late and I had to get home. And I saw two of the guys, who he had introduced to me as his friends, they haven't got in, they were standing there and talking to the bartender. I was waiting for him to come because I was getting late and I had to get home. And then I saw the bartender hand them a packet and the bartender leaves. Then the guy that befriended me ... soon as the bartender leaves, he gets in from the right side. He gets in and he sits down.

As soon as he gets in, they get in. So when they get in I sit forward. Because it was like four of us. So obviously we were stuck. So I sit forward, and it bothered me. Like, you know, I mean it was not quite ... then I thought I am going to get off at the nearest taxi stand. They are probably taking a ride back too, you know. And then I felt a little bit ... but I didn't want to get into that thought you know...young man.

If you don't feel like talking, don't. We can stop.

No, no...it's okay, it's okay.

You don't have to.

No, it's okay...no, it's okay...it's okay. I like to talk because I don't want another girl to get into a similar situation. This is again under the pretext of being friends but everything was actually planned, at that point I didn't think...it is, ah, see you don't judge. It's in human nature to trust, you don't really...Even if I have to take a taxi, it wouldn't be my father's brother, he would again be a stranger. So we *have* to trust. At a work place we don't know the people we are working with. You see we have to trust. I don't know if my boss is a murderer or rapist...but he could turn out to be like that, when he gets me at a vulnerable moment. Because of my boss I might shut my mouth and not say anything. So I want that women should, you know, even if their boss does this, she can just slap him and walk away and fight for it because no one has the right to do that.

Even if she is a prostitute you know, nobody has the right to rape her…what's the word that everybody uses…you abuse her…you can't do that…you are not allowed to treat another human being as an animal, okay? On the basis of humanity you should not, you cannot do that. You should not do that. Then you don't belong to the class of humans. You belong to a different class. You don't even belong to a class of animals. It is beyond anyone's comprehension why a person would subject another human being to rape and torture. I don't get this.

So I would like the people to know, I am fighting my case. I have not yet got justice for it. I still have to go through that, through eyes that look at me with, you know, with doubt and many questions and many people ask…'but she took a lift', 'she was at a night club', in fact more than a night club. But I never committed a social crime. I didn't commit *any* crime. Night clubs are everywhere throughout the world. Yes, I drank…Just because I drank that doesn't mean the whole of Kolkata can rape me! I like drinking, I paid for my own drinks, I used my debit card. I am a working woman…the names people called me, you know, the indignities…they referred to me as a prostitute, referred to me as lady with a client and a deal gone bad…so you know all these things. They should have thought of the repercussions, because what you are saying is that a prostitute can be raped and she has no fundamental rights to work…you know I have been raped please help me. She has no rights because people think you have committed such a thing where the deal went wrong…get out!

People should think before they speak because words matter, maybe not to them, but they matter to the people in question. Other perverts lurking around, others you know, psychopathic criminals have pervert ways of brutality like the one at Kamduni, like the one of Nirbhaya [Jyoti Singh Pandey, Delhi gang-rape case], like the one with Guria [mentally challenged woman raped and murdered in a home for the mentally challenged], these rapes are rape and like...inconceivable. You can't even think about the way they have been brutalized. Although you cannot define a rape, rape is a rape at the end of the day BUT the brutality with which these girls were raped is unthought of.

So when you make comments like this actually it is encouraging these people. Like you know, go ahead, do what you are doing because we are here to justify you, to condemn the woman, to say the woman is characterless, we are here to put the woman at different levels, to say the woman was a prostitute and at a night club... [they think] no woman is going to come forward and say she was.

Much to their surprise, I actually came out and said, yes I was at the night club, yes I *had* been drinking from 9:30 [pm] onwards and I had three beers there and I had a pint of beer there and I had two pints of beer in Tantra and I paid for it. And I didn't take it from anybody. So why would you condemn me? And I did it openly. I am not lying about it. If I am coming here and am telling you that I had beer, I went to the night club and I am telling you I was raped. I am not lying about anything, I am not mad that I am going to lie and I am going to put myself in a position where all eyes are on me and I will be humiliated and am going to be tortured not only by the police, but *after* the police, you know, by society, by the people I live with, the people around you, by family people.

Thankfully, in my children's school I never had to face that. I never ever had to face that because the children, they have been loved; they were loved always they are loved more now. My children's principal and I have had a difference of opinion on many occasions before my incident. As I said before, I am not a person to keep quiet, so when there is any problem with any teacher in the school, anyone saying anything to my daughter, I would go there and I would fight. So he and I never got along. Ever. You know...I even threatened one day to take him to the police, my daughter's school principal (laughs), because he caught the kid's phone and that phone was my office phone that I got from the call centre I was working with, and she took it to school without asking me. She was caught with it and he confiscated it, gave it back to me after two years. I threatened him with the police (laughs)...so I always *fought*, I didn't care. I fought.

But after my incident the *same* principal...I can do anything, in his eye I am a lady...that's the way he looks at me. And treats me with so much dignity you know, he makes me feel special. So now, today I know that that man genuinely is a nice man and just that I am such a fighter inside and you know when you fight you don't want to reason out like I never have to reason out for arguing. I have always argued and then reasoned out. So this incident actually taught me a lot.

You know as the months went on I came to know different people, what people were about, I came to know how mean and selfish people are, I came to know that people can condemn you to such an extent just to cover their tracks, you know...they will characterize you and they will make your situation so bad that you don't want to fight any more. And when you do that then thousands of other women who are already suffering in silence don't get a chance to come out, and as the years go by things just get worse than they already are.

See, our women in the villages in India, we are very conservative... in the papers [there was a story of a] six-year old girl being raped by her grandfather. The mother comes out and says no, the girl is lying. Why? Family values! We live in a hypocritical society. How can you say you have family values when your own daughter is going through hell, her own grandfather has been doing it and now she is 14 so he has been doing it since she was six years old. Can you know the psychological effect on her? She can't even be normal any more. She never will be normal. So when we say we live in India or we have family values...it's a whole lot of shit. You pray to Ma and you are doing it to your own daughters and granddaughters; you are holding your daughters-in-law… you are feeding her poison so the girl baby in the stomach dies; or you are taking her to a clinic and aborting the baby when she is seven months pregnant because you have found out that it is a girl. Why? And then you come to a big statue of Durga Ma or Kali Ma and you pray and you offer her fruit. I call that hypocritical. I will say from my own experience that we live in a society where people are blind, or people are not blind but they choose to be blind.

I will come to these questions later. I am glad you talked about them.

Like I said, when you start talking.

You have answered so many of my questions.

Because when the car started, the person driving turned the (music) volume up so it had to be planned. I think, after gathering information from so many people, talking to so many survivors and other counsellors on the other sites, rape sites, I think that seeing me alone they probably thought that you know, 'Oh she is too gutsy, let's break her down' or maybe he saw bitterness in my face, you know? [He has probably] seen violence from his father on his mother and he probably feels that every woman is a piece of shit. And he can dominate the person or he can bully the person and the person has to believe that. That person has to be subjected to his violence. This is what I feel.

Because when I sat forward and when the car started moving, he grabbed me by my breast…I sat forward he grabbed me by my breast…and I said that I have to get off [and] go to the taxi. So I was preparing myself and I was stopped brutally, when he grabbed me by my breast. So I turned around and I slapped him and I shouted at him and I leaned over him to open the door and the door was auto-locked. That's when he grabbed my hand and started to beat me. He caught me, and because I screamed he put my head down and of course the music was loud, nobody is going to hear me. So he started to beat me. He beat me and beat me like he had an age-old vendetta against me so rape is all about violence. Apparently, it was all about violence of being in this world, maybe that gave him pleasure...Ruman guy was sitting on the right hand side, the guy who I befriended. The guy absconding is Kader.

The guy [Ruman] who asked you to come?

The other guy sitting on the left.

The other guy...not the guy who asked you to come, he was absconding.

Yeah, like you know, he held my head ... he was viciously hitting me. By that time I was semi-conscious, the car took off but I... when he took up the revolver, then the guy on the left of him, who is caught now, his brother Naser, on the left of him, he held one hand, then Ruman caught this hand [the other]. He was like hitting me, and frightening me and he yanked off my nose pin you know, just torturing, sheer brutality. And he could do it. Because I was not ... you know...and what made it worse was because I slapped him, that probably made him feel like his manhood is gone...'[you] slapped me! [Do] [y]ou know who I am?'...So then he took out the gun and then he held my mouth and he put it into my mouth, the butt of the gun, held my mouth and had it in. And I was like, 'Oh god...', you know. I couldn't swallow, I couldn't swallow my spit, I couldn't breathe...I didn't know, I didn't *know*... I thought I am gone, I am dead now. Forget about seeing anything, you are gone.

He took it out and he gave it to somebody in the front. He said, if she moves, kill her... Of course, he said it in Hindi in that crass language they use, used that language as well when he started to unzip my jacket and then he pulled my blouse down and then he started to sodomise me. I bit him on his hand. Because I bit him, he had my neck like this (gestures), you know, and then of course, he started to rape. He couldn't, I was struggling so much with me being in that semi-conscious state. I struggled…I was feeling that if I was going down I might as well get down with a fight although I was crammed, I was screaming but at that point I'm not able to tell you whether the car was moving or stationary. I wouldn't, I wouldn't know. I did get into the car when everything started and the car was moving. When he was raping me, if the car was stationary or moving, I can't tell you because I don't know. I was fighting to save myself. You think I was going to keep an eye on all that? Definitely not.

When everything was done … after raping me, he got up suddenly, he told his friends, 'Aaahh! There is nothing in her, you know? Come on rape her, rape her, rape her!' Forcing rape, kind of. The guy sitting, Naser, he was like cheering his brother on. In Hindi, I could hear screaming and his brother cheering on you know, screaming and I could hear their laughter and Ruman, he was quiet. He kept saying stop, you know, stop. I heard him on two, three occasions but that's all. Though he held my hand. He was still holding my hand. So much of my body was on him, was resting on him you know, so I couldn't understand…I mean if he wanted to help, or the driver…he could have just driven off to the police station if he wanted to help me so much. So it was all a planned thing.

And then when he got off [of] me and nobody was coming…he threw my legs off onto the car floor and then he pushed the rest of my body also. So I fell in a crouching position, face-down, onto the floor. My head was on the right hand side of the door. So he caught my head and he banged it on the door, it was not enough for him and he socked me in the centre of my back.

How long I was gone for, I don't know. Who did what to me during that time, I don't know…yeah I was still in the car. I don't know, during that span of time when I wasn't conscious, what happened to me. I have no clue.

But when I came around my position had been altered. My head was not on the right-hand side, my head was [on a] different side. My legs were on the right-hand side and he has his foot on my face…neck… and he was trying to wake me up. Yes…he was trying to wake me up like [shouting], '*Ooth Saali!*' [Get up, bitch!] you know, with his foot. And then he lifted me up, my entire body with the weight of my hair. Held my hair and lifted my whole body because when you faint you are dead weight. He lifted my entire body with the weight of my hair till I was on my knees, but not entirely on my knees, on my knees, bent, you know, crouching. Then I vomited. Then again he raped me. It was not enough for him that I had just come out of [unconsciousness]…I was unconscious…so he, you know, he slapped me again, and then Ruman screamed, 'You leave her. You are going to kill her. Leave her.'

The car didn't stop, it slowed down a bit, but it didn't stop… Nandan [theatre in Kolkata]. Just next to Nandan…he opened the door, and he threw me out. The right side of my jeans were on till here [gestures]…the left was off. My bra, my blouse were torn off, my jacket he had unzipped, the sleeves came here [gestures], so it's hanging. I got up, put my jeans on, I couldn't do anything with my blouse because my bra was torn off…you know those plastic strap[s]…so the blouse was also torn off. It was winter so I just zipped my jacket up…not a single soul was on the road. Not a single soul, it was 3:30. Nobody was on the road.

At first when I put my clothes on, I screamed, you know. Then I thought, you know, like they will again come back… another one of his dreams replaying to turn around and run me over. So I said, let's just run. I ran straight down towards Haldiram, Exide and then I took the left. Trust me, in that state I didn't even realize that there was a police *chowki* [station] there. And even if I did I would never go. I would never go. At least not looking like that.

I don't know what they would have done. I have no clue if they would have done the same seeing me half naked and I don't know, I just turned left and then I was running and then I realized that my phone [was on me]...why my phone didn't fall off because it was in my right side pocket and it's like this[gestures]. So you see, when he pulled my jeans off, my jeans rolled. So the phone didn't fall out.

You know, I called my dad. But my phone was turned off and I never keep my phone off especially if I am out at night, my phone is always on because my daughters need to get in touch with me, so I don't keep my phone off. But my phone was off so I don't know whether they turned it off and then they switched it on. Yesterday, I asked my daughter, 'Baby, did you call me that night?' She said, 'Ma, I can't remember.' I said, 'You called me.' She said, 'I can't remember. But I think your phone was off.' But I think they did.

I called my Baba, but he didn't pick up because it was 3:30 [am] and he was sleeping. So I called my friend Farooq [Halim]. I called him, normally when I don't get sleep I always talk to him, I always call and talk to him, you know. He has been my friend for almost fourteen years. So I called him and he didn't answer. I kept running and he was not answering. Then he called me back... 'Yes Sue, tell me what happened'...and all I did was scream and he said, 'Where are you?' and I wasn't able to tell him where I was. He said, 'Can you see a taxi?' Can I see a taxi? Trust me Rajashri, where would I see a taxi, it's hardly likely [that] I would see a taxi...At 3:30 in the morning? No chance. But there was a taxi. He said, 'Get into the taxi, come! I am waiting on the road'. Asiatic Society. I took the taxi, I went straight there.

He was standing in Holy House of Animals ... a little ahead where he was standing on the road. He got in and asked,

'*What happened*?' and I was screaming and was telling him, 'They raped me. Help me.' You know, I was like, screaming and when he got in, I started beating him. I didn't know what to do. He said, 'Come on to the hospital and let me take you'…I said, no I need to get to home. I was screaming, you know. I get at that point so frustrated, best I should go home, you know. So he took me straight home.

He's a close friend?

Very, very close friend. Yeah, very very close friend. See, even he has a wife and a family but he didn't think what they think, to come out at 3:30 [am] to help another lady, you know. I mean I think that was a very honourable thing for him to do for me.

I had met him at the Grill Club, he used to come to the club, I see him talking to my father and uncles and we became very friendly. He is a minister`s son [his father Hashim Abdul Halim, was the longest serving Speaker of West Bengal Assembly during Left Front rule]. He has come a lot to the club, he and his partner or friend or whatever and that way we got friendly. Since my youngest daughter was two years old I have known Mr Halim and whenever I needed any advice I have called him up. We talk about it and I kind of looked up to him actually.

I called Farooq Halim because at Chowringee the only person I thought closest to me, to help me, pick me up would be him. So I called him and he came.

I relied on him and always looked up to him. I always respected him because he has always advised me. He has *always* advised me throughout my life, he has always come forward and helped me whether be it financial, be it as a friend be it as an adviser, be it as a mentor – everything. Even religion, I can talk to him on any topic. So why do people destroy that relationship? 'Oh she was having sex with him'… 'Ohh it's a political scam'. Why? That does not say anything about me or Mr Halim, that says a lot about what people actually think what others can do or can't do. You people don't deserve to govern a state. Sorry.

Anyway, I came back home and I wouldn't let my mom touch me. He told my mom what happened. 'Get her cleaned and take her to the doctors and to the police'. And he left because he couldn't do much. I was just screaming. I was sitting on the ground in my home, you have been to my flat, *na*? Sitting in the centre of the hall room and only crying and screaming and was telling Mamma, 'They raped me, they raped me, they raped me' and it took 40 minutes for her to calm me down, it was my eldest daughter who calmed me down.

She doesn't sleep until I come home.

She is seventeen, she will complete seventeen on 21st June. She won't sleep until I come home. I go out maybe twice in a month but not all the time. It's her time to watch TV. Saturday night she watches TV till late if I am out. They even couldn't touch me. My hair was falling out in bunches, my mother was doing this (gestures) and it was falling such a lot, bunches of hair where he had pulled my hair.

My daughter was crying with me, Rhea she took me to the bathroom, she gave me a bath, not my mom, my daughter. And she said, 'Don't worry mamma, I am cleaning you I am taking all the difficulties from you', you know, and I can't explain to you. It's like funny enough if I am tense she is always the one who comforts me, always. The most darling child, my younger one is also sweet but she is still naïve and immature, she got up and saw me, and went back to sleep. She is timid. Rhea is like me, you know, she is very bold and very compassionate also, *extremely* compassionate. She is a *beautiful* child.

She cleaned me. I sat on the toilet pot for I don't know how long, over an hour, finally I could urinate it was painful, what I couldn't understand was why it was so painful. One guy … painful yes but *that* painful, I couldn't understand it. And then the next day also when I decided to go to the toilet to do potty, I couldn't, as if somebody put a thousand chillies or something you know, that was the feeling. So I knew something more had happened but I don't know what happened. I had no clue. I know he tried to sodomise me, it hurt so I bit him. So he started to do it in my vagina. I don't know when I became unconscious whether he tried again. So I don't know. So after that, my mom came to me and she started to do this [gestures petting] and I started to feel little at ease but was still crying, she couldn't stop too, from crying. Then she called my father, my grandmother and the rest of my family people. My father came...My mom and dad were divorced now, for many years, I just cleared my boards when they got divorced.

Yeah, that night I reached by 4:30 [am]. So by then they consoled me and got me cleaned and it's 6.30. My father came within fifteen minutes of the call because he lives five minutes from my house. So he came immediately. My father was the first person to come. My grandmother lives on S.N Banerjee Road. So by the time she got up, she is an old lady she is 78 years old, she is a *fighter*...she was the headmistress of St. Paul Mission school, you know. Everyone used to call her Hitler. Students were afraid of her. Even I was afraid of her as a child. Everybody says that I am like her. In every way, you know when I get old I will start to look like her. I love her too and I am her pet since I was the first grandchild. So she came, with my uncle and my aunt. Of course when my dad got in first, when he saw me he shouted, 'Aaaaaahhh! I don't understand, you are not a guy you are a girl!' Then he came around me and seeing me alive he was relieved and then saw that all my body parts were intact. And then my grandmother did the same thing. She walked in, she first shouted then she came, loved me and...[trails off into silence.]

On that day I felt like a little baby. Just born, everybody came to visit me in the hospital, something like that. A different kind of a baby or a different kind of a story to go with it, you know.

Anyway, she [her grandmother] took me to her house and then it followed after that you know.

My dad didn't want me to go to the police station, because he said eleven years since you have been a single mom, they will bring that up. What has that to do with my rape? He said, you don't understand and everything he warned me of, I have been through. I fought with him. I said I am not taking this lying down, Dad…he carried me to the bathroom, even in my grandma's house when he came to see me he had to hold me to the bathroom …I said, 'Do you feel proud doing this? Are you happy to see me like this?' 'No I am not', he said. 'But I also won't feel happy when people start calling you names.' I said, 'Let them. I am going to fight. I want to go with the complaint'. My grandmother is like, 'Don't stop her from going. Let her go.'

My grandmother and my younger uncle, my father's younger brother. He left for Indonesia…He accompanied me to Park Street.

After how many days?

The 9th, after two days. I couldn't walk, Rajashri. I couldn't get out of bed. I was in a very bad way. Here I knew I wanted to go but because the family, you know, part of the family they were discussing it in front of me, then part of my family hears, but my grandmother, as head of the family said, 'Yes you go!' But my dad was like, 'No you don't!' Mamma, because of my grandmother, brought me back to her house. She didn't want my kids to see me like that everyday, you know and I was constantly crying, she didn't want that, so she brought me back with her. And then my mother is also an asthma patient. So she was, she was having a lot of paranoid attacks, kind of.

What does your mother do?

I call her [her grandmother] Rock of Gibraltar, she is 78. My mother is a very quiet lady. She is a total housewife. She worked as a teacher in St. Paul Mission for kindergarten kids and then she worked as a matron in Darjeeling.

My mother has nothing to do. Ma goes with whatever I do. My children are like, 'Ma go to the police!' It was my daughter who cleaned me, she was the one who took off my torn panties. Wanted to throw them in the bin… they're all with the forensic [department].

On the 9th, I walked in to the Park Street police station. They made me feel like a slut. I walked in. They were like, 'So? Rape *hua*? Okay.' [You were raped? Okay] Another officer [said], '*Kya rape?*' [What rape?] No lady constable was there. I went at 8.30 at night to the Park Street police station. My uncle is a teacher in St. Thomas school, he gives tuition and so I had to wait. I didn't want to go with grandma, I wanted to go with a male figure. My dad was against it and didn't even come with me; and he didn't want me to hear things I was hearing. My uncle was stronger. One by one the male cops kept coming and asking. My IO, the investigating officer, he took my papers. I told him what had happened and he went in to the OC's [the officer in charge] room.

I had gone that day to NRS [Nil Ratan Sircar] Medical College… so he took the hospital thing. On the outdoor ticket was written: 'Sexual assault and physical torture.' So he took that and he went into the room of the OC and they were talking, they were talking for some time there.

When he comes out from there, then he sits down and [asks], 'Are you sure you were raped?' My uncle stood up, 'What do you mean, she is telling every other officer that she has been raped, she has of course been raped at gunpoint into her mouth. Tell them Suzie…'

No, not a single woman was there. And he says, 'Oooh…what did you take that day?' 'I had beer.' The officer [said], 'Oh beer is your favourite drink? Hmmm.' Trying to make conversation, he was writing down in the diary. Then this Mr Niyogi came and discussed the case, 'Section 354? If someone is raped then 354?' Another is saying, '336?' They are discussing among themselves in front of me.

My uncle said, 'What are you saying? She has been telling everybody that she has been raped. My niece has been raped. Can't you see her state?'

The officer says, 'Don't worry, don't worry, I will catch these guys and beat them...Go to the corner and write your complaint.'

The Investigating officer, when I was writing this, he said' Come now, the OC wants to talk to you'. I went to the OCs room and he asks me to sit down. From behind his glass spectacles he asks, 'Rape? Position *kya tha*? I mean in the car?'

I know he has to know, but the *way* he was asking you know, I know that I am supposed to say, but there is a way to ask me like...don't worry, I am here, tell me, start from the beginning... then the person will feel comfortable. You look me up and down and you scrutinize me through your eyes around my breast and then you ask me, you know with that attitude. So you have already humiliated me. I have already been humiliated outside by a bunch of other officers. Now I am in front of you, you are doing the same thing and then you will insist that I write a rape complaint. With that mental trauma I have already been going through for the last three days of discussion in my house about coming and not coming and exactly what my father told me, I still want to go ahead but this attitude...I was going crazy. So anyway, I wrote down my complaint and finally he took the complaint at 10:40 [pm].

I think they wanted me to feel that they didn't want to take me seriously, they thought probably I was telling them lies or maybe [because] I am a woman they wanted to make me feel like you know dirty, they wanted to make me feel like it was all my fault for coming to the limelight...aahh they kept stressing on the night club, 'Tantra? You are regular at Tantra?' You know like, I said, not regular but for days I go a lot with my friends.

By that time I was absolutely quiet and I wanted to scream… but there was no outlet there. There is no way you can share this with anyone else, at that time because you are facing it yourself. My uncle is there and I am feeling bad for him, actually. Because he was angry about the way they were treating me. I can see he is angry because when he is angry his hands begin to shake. I know that he is right, I know. I know that the guy in front of me is not treating me right, I know it. At the end of it all, he says, 'Don't worry, Suzette, keep your phone on. Call me tomorrow. Medical tests, your medical tests we can't understand the hand writing. So be at Court tomorrow. I will call you in the morning and let you know. You can go now.' 8:30 pm I was there [at the police station], 1:15 in the morning I left the Park Street police station. So I went home to my grandmom's house

I would suggest that we should have more women there and they need to keep a counsellor there, a lady counsellor. A kind of a person who will relate to a woman who comes complaining of rape or domestic violence, you know? Any kind of violence against her, a counsellor who will comfort her and treat her with compassion. To get out the facts of the incident, how is the person going to relate to these? How are you going to say your problems? You can't talk to this man and especially if he looks at you the way he does. And why should you be treated the way you are by this man when he is sitting there and his job is to protect you?

Tell me about Damayanti Sen, the police officer who investigated your case.

I was very scared of her [laughs] because she was pretty stern but again I tell you, with kindness, I can't define it really. She was stern but with kindness. You know very matronly but with compassion. And she can…and for her it was her job to keep her city safe. That is her job and she carried it out. She made sure, she got to the bottom of it, she got to the bottom of impersonation and got these guys arrested.

Ahhh, she is a very nice lady, she has never made me feel bad, never uncomfortable at all. In fact, I look at her and feel frightened; you know what I am saying…the women who are working for the law, they need to be strong figures who can relate and handle issues like this… Because that doesn't work there. If the woman sees her so quiet she may not be able to relate to her.

The victim, again is scared, and she will not be able to relate to her. She sees the officer who is so quiet, how will she tell her story? How will she relate her incident? She can't do that. Our society does not relate with the word compassion, it does not even *exist*! Counselling is a very long involvement.

You said the police were callous when they questioned you. You also mentioned that it was important for them to question you. What is it that angered you at that time? What were you expecting?

I was expecting compassion. I was expecting…like, I am not only my father`s daughter, you know, it doesn't have to be that you have to be my own blood for me to stand up and fight and protect you.

When you take your vows, you are a person of the law. So you have taken your vows to protect not only your own child but every other child and person within your limit, within your jurisdiction. Now, some heinous crime has taken place, that's the crime against me – I was brutally raped, I was beaten, I was thrown out of a car, left to be run over again or die or be raped again by the next slum dweller or the next man walking who wakes up at 3:30 in the morning…you know…the state I was in. I was in a vulnerable state so at that point anything could have taken place but I just picked myself up and out of fright, out of anger, out of frustration, and mixture of all these emotions I ran…

So what I am saying is with all these, when you muster the strength and courage to go and to speak about it and to lodge a complaint to tell the officer in charge, you know…within your jurisdiction, there are some…there are some people, there are some men who are doing this, this is what they have done to me.

So instead of intimidating me, or any other victim in my place they have to…they have to…come out with compassion, with love. Okay, people say, you know, women are taking advantage of this, in many cases women are lying. Again, I am saying the only thing, the only way to get through is with love.

You cannot achieve anything with anger because when you are angry you just give rise to more [anger]. Or when you are trying to humiliate the person because you feel in your head you know, 'Awwh, it's a lie and I am not going to take it seriously and how *dare* she come up and say that she was raped and she was in a night club!'

Did they humiliate you?

Oh yes! I felt totally humiliated. I felt humiliated, I could hear them laughing. I could hear them, ahh.. you know I could hear the word 'rape' coming from the room inside Park Street *thana* as you walk straight in, on the left hand side there is staff men's room, there is a curtain drawn and each officer kept questioning me, I heard them talking among themselves, you know, like the word 'rape' and they were laughing and then then the word 'beer' and then they were laughing, and I was sitting outside. I know they were talking about me. So instead of coming forward and, you know, talking to me with compassion, I would have…that day itself I would have said everything in details or as much as I could remember, I would have said it…but if they had talked to me with compassion, if they had talked to me without intimidating me if they had talked to me without…you know, those eyes that can see through your body.

They were trying to look through me. Oh it's a possible thing. And no woman should be allowed to feel that way especially when you come out, survived, you have *survived* the entire thing you know…you are not…you are there and your intestines have not been touched, your hands and legs are intact your face is intact, no one has thrown acid on you, no one has cut off your tongue no one has cut off your legs, your feet, if your body has been traumatized, you have gone through the entire episode of being raped and beaten and frightened and violently mistreated...you have gone through that...you, you are already traumatized, your mind is already traumatized, you mustered up all that strength all that courage to fight back.

So instead of standing by your side, they want to stand behind you and give you a push, like in the sense, *push* you in the direction you know, *push* you into a corner...where they will try to humiliate you and make fun of you where you feel like, you know, let's not give them any edge because I feel some of the people who work for the law are very... Because had they been more efficient in their jobs and had they been more compassionate in their jobs, this would not have happened.

What was your experience later with the police?

It's very laid back, very laid back. No. When I came across some senior officers, those who took my case seriously because see I had gone to the media with it, I demanded justice, but there was a section that said a lot of things because the names those people [the accused] had used with me were false. Now that wasn't a fault of mine. I went with whatever I knew, with whatever I remembered. Instead of, you know, finding out what the real story was, everyone again said, there were discrepancies in her statement, she is lying, she is making it up, she is concocting it. I am not concocting anything, this is what happened to me! If I had to lie from the very beginning I wouldn't even have told the officer that I have been drinking and he wouldn't have known that I have been drinking. But why would I lie? I have nothing to *hide*.

From the very beginning, I know that my father had warned me against all these and whatever he warned me against I had gone through and more, I had gone through the entire thing and more. I am still going through it, even in the court.

So you see after my case, after all the rape cases are coming up, the brutal way in which these girls and these women have been raped has not created any compassion in the minds of the law enforcement, in the minds of people in power, nor have they you know, moved a bone in their body towards awakening. One should think that…this can't happen within our limits, within our state and our women are not safe anymore.

So you are talking about their attitude…what kind of change, what kind of questioning did you face, when they questioned you, when you say questioning is important.

Definitely. They questioned me with, with you know like, aaaah! With a tone in their voice that stated, 'You are a liar anyway,' and that itself intimidates the victim because she comes to you with all that energy she has left to fight. She wants help, she is seeking help. She is telling you that they are dangerous people. Today, I have survived, tomorrow somebody won't. And it could be even more brutal.

You said you met some police officers…what change or difference did you see in them?

That happened only after I went to the media. The change I saw was they were very…okay…the difference was that because they, being senior officers and efficient officers and you know honest officers, they carried out their job honestly. They made sure I was also questioned by some for a while, not that I wasn't, but it was done with patience, it was done with compassion and it was not done to make me feel like I was out to get somebody for money. Because it was never about money. It's never about money. It's always…you need to know how to fight back, you need to know how to fight back.

I was watching some TV yesterday, where a man tells a short story that a rabbi and a priest went for a boxing match. And just from the boxing ring before the priest could start his bout before he could fight, he made the sign of the cross. The rabbi asked him what does it mean? He says, doesn't mean a damn thing if you do not have a fight in you…you know, so we all pray and we go to church and we go to mosque and we go to the *masjid*, don't mean a damn thing if you don't have the reason to fight, if you don't believe in yourself…so when a woman believes that I dare and I go up there and I stand up and I fight, I will get justice.

Yes there will be people in fact from the very onset in all walks of life, there will be people to tell you even if you do something wrong they will say, it's right. But it all depends on you to stand up and say: it's wrong. You have that choice. So, I had the choice too. But because of intimidating me so much I had no choice left. But I didn't allow them to make me feel that way. I didn't allow them to, they did get away, they did intimidate me on the first day in Park Street. I felt like running away and hiding…

What pushed you back?

Because… I went back and I sat and I went home and in fact I thought about it, I asked my grandmother. I said, 'Nan, do you think they are going to help me?' Then she said, with a long shot. 'No. We are here, you go on, you have taken the first step, so let's see, let's wait.' Again my grandmother, because my parents honestly speaking they were very… my mom is a very simple lady, so basically she will stand by me no matter what. My dad being a worldly man, he is a man of the world and he knows people and he knows you know the reactions of many. He told me that it would be a bad idea because I have been single mother for the past eleven years since my younger daughter was two years old. Today, my youngest daughter is fifteen years old and I am still a single mother.

So just because I go out to the disco or to a night club doesn't make me…you don't know me. You haven't even met my children. When you see a person's children and you will know their upbringing, then you judge me. Then you tell me what you want to tell me. I think I won the right to spend money at a nightclub with my friends if I want to. If I can be a mother and a father for eleven years for my children, I have the right to drink, the whole liquor shop on Park Street and nobody has the right to rape me. That does not give a right to anybody to rape another woman just because she is standing at the night club and having a drink. She has earned the right to do it. She has empowered herself whether she is class 10 pass or class 12 pass, she has empowered herself with jobs, with coming up to the way she is, and with taking herself out and moving in a society and treating herself. When she is going through depression, you don't steal that right away from her by calling her a prostitute because you don't want to do your job. You need to go out there and do your job.

Even if I were a prostitute which not only me but many of the women who have been raped have been called in the past, and now taking my case as well, how does that matter? They always characterize you. Why do they do that? Because if a woman is a prostitute she can be raped? How dare you? A prostitute is prostituting. Today, you call her a prostitute and when did you give her and many other prostitute jobs and homes? You will not do that, so who gives you the right to throw stones on them because she is a prostitute? You need to introspect and speak to yourself. Nobody is flawless in this world. Everyone has done something they have to be ashamed of in their life. From the poorest to the richest. No one is flawless.

Nobody has the right to be judgmental. You cannot judge somebody just because you feel that you are right. And… you have to damn well get off your high horse and set things straight. You need to get off there and set things straight. Not only for the person in question at that point but for many women who could be in a problem because of your stupid comments and that laid back attitude that you have when you are people of the law. Because remember one thing, it's our taxes that give your salary, so you are by far a servant as well. Nothing makes you so important in uniform unless you earn the right of actually working straight heads up in the very uniform that you wear and that you mock everyday in and out.

You were in a bad shape, how did you get out of that? And your family?

Yes, I was in a very bad state. Most of the day I was medicated. Most of the day I mean throughout the day I was…of course my grandmother didn't know but whenever she was not looking I was taking another sleeping tablet just if I could deep sleep , you know.

You were with your grandmother?

Yea, I was with my grandmother, she took me back on the very day. I am her pet. I am her pet (laughs) because I am the…my father is the eldest son and of course I am the first grandchild. [She was a] very strong support because last year most of the time, most of the month there was no food in my home to eat. And my grandmother herself is not a working person. Her sister helps her from London, my aunty Suzan, in London. My uncle, my aunty who lives close by, they were all coming together and helping her and with that she was helping me. So I would take a bus every day go to her, she would cook I would wait there bring back the food in the night then my kids would eat. This happened throughout last year.

There was no money because I didn't have a job. Nobody was willing to give me a job. I had lost my business in January, so whatever savings I had left carried me on for February, March, April, May. From the month of May I started to look for a job.

Because I didn't have the courage to go out, I needed time before I could start working. I didn't even get enough time to heal myself, because I was too busy thinking of what I am going to do now, you know. Now what…not to forget about my kids, now I need money to work, I need to travel, if I get a job I need money to travel, because you don't get a salary as you join, you get the salary after a month. And not only my travelling, my kid`s school travelling. Which is why my kids hardly went to school, if you check the school records you will know. In a month maybe two or four days, five days they went and rest of the days they never went because I didn't have the money to give them to go up and down. I didn't have the money to pay their bus fare. In fact, till this month I have not paid their bus fare from last year. Because I just got a job three months back which is again 10,000 [rupees], which pays, you know, for my living, my rent, the electricity, my travelling – what I make all goes on that. The debt from last year that I owe is still very much there. I have cleared it up till January but there are friends I still have to pay up. So when I think why we live in a misogynist society where people will characterize a woman, they will not give a woman a chance to work, the guys are locked up, he is eating well, he is doing fine, he is doing fit, his name is not being published, nobody knows about him but what about the victim? Everybody gets to know. Her neighbours, society, the people around her where she lives and she is looked down on, she is cast away as if she has plague, or some disease.

That's a question which I am trying to find an answer to. I seriously don't understand this. How dare they even think the way they think? For a woman to go through all the pain, of someone beating you and brutalizing your body and then raping you… How can you cast away the person instead of coming together and standing together in solidarity and helping the person to get back on her feet? It takes the person years and years before you can actually do that…I am still trying to do that.

I am not superhuman, you know, behind my mask of strength lie all my weaknesses. There lies somebody who is also frightened. But, I am not a person who is going to give up. At least not so easily.

I thought of that last year. I was suicidal last year, tried to hurt myself last year. I tried to take my life on many occasions last year. Not because of society but because of the frustration that I had to repeatedly make it known to people – yes, this was it and that I had to *convince* people I was raped. Why does a girl have to go through that?

But there were people who passed remarks that oh, you are ruining his life! That I had ruined their lives! Really? You can actually stand in front of me and tell me that?

If they are young and if they have decided to ruin every one's life because they don't respect women, they don't deserve a life.

People who know you said this or strangers?

No, strangers, you know who said it to friends and friends came and told me. You know they didn't tell me to my face, strangers that might have been talking and this topic came up because of the disco timings were cut down. Some people are grumbling that because of her, you know the timings are changed…ahh she didn't have to complain…this was the problem then – disco timings. People were selfishly thinking of themselves and their fun and their access, while in all parts of the world where there are women and children they were suffering day in and day out. Either it's being bombed and their children are lying in hospitals, or suffering in the floods and children and women have been lost …misery is all over and the world is one big cruel hell hole and we need to fight to find ourselves

You went for a medical examination?

That's even worse, the medical…when I had gone to NRS (Nil Ratan Sircar hospital), for medical examination.

How did you know that you had to go to NRS Hospital?

Because my grandmother's house is five minutes' walk to NRS and my aunt took me. My grandmother told me that the police would do it. It is their duty to do it for me. But I just thought that maybe I should just go and, you know, go to the hospital for treatment.

Yeah, so I went on 9th of Feb at about 1:30 [pm] to the hospital and when I walked in there, it was of course very, very crowded, because I had gone to the emergency ward and I couldn't speak… I…out of shame again, I couldn't relate to the person at the outdoor ticket counter. So my aunt told him that, you know, what had happened to me. And he noted in the outdoor ticket and gave it to my aunt, there was a sticker inside.

What did he write?

Sexual assault and physical torture. So I went in and the doctor made me sit in front of him and he starts to, with his stethoscope, touch me in wrong places like you know…I didn't know what to expect. I thought it was part of the procedure because he has seen what I have gone through. I looked at my aunt you know and she also gave me a certain look and then he sort of looked at me, he wasn't paying attention to what I was saying…It was like, aaaah, okay, you know very, very funnily, very lazily, very creepily like you know he had that creepy look, creepy touch…I wanted to… wanted to run away from there. He just checked my hands and legs and asked me to go in to the next room. There were two nurses there and he comes and says you know, '*Buke phuke ki keteche*?' 'Did they bite you in your breast?' …so I said yes and he lifted up my t-shirt and two ladies were there but he had a good look of my breast before he put my t-shirt down and said, '*Baire jaan, baaire jaan*' (go out, go out) ...So again I got taken, or made to feel like an idiot all over again.

So I think with all the education, even if a woman is well educated it's not going to help. It's not going to help. So what do we need? It's to educate them on situations like this, so nobody gets into such a similar situation you know...this does not happen.

This happened during the medical examination?

At NRS yes, then I went out he wrote on a form, he took the names of the people who had done this to me, then he said, '*Haa haa tumi jao, police station e jao aar ei oshudh khabe*' (yes, yes you – using the familiar term 'tum' – go to the police station and take this medicine) while he was doing that another little boy, six or seven years old came in gagging on his PT [Physical Training] teacher's sperm. Six, seven-year-old...so the doctor got up...I thought that the little boy has broken his arms the way his father was carrying him like a listless body and my aunt, of course, she ran to find out what had happened. And then she came back telling me you know this boy was abused by his PT teacher and he is carrying his sperm. He got choked. So you can imagine the nature of some of these men you know and the way they carry out their deeds. I mean it is sick if you think about it...I mean a seven-year-old kid...four-year-old kid...three-year-old kid...it just never stops. Because every time there is a rape there is always somebody to justify it. There is always somebody in the hospital to overpower that, and once again they are justified. There is always somebody in the law again to justify that. To justify the act...

Looking back, how should a medical examination be conducted? How to make it more humane?

Again, you make it dignified by, you know...firstly, it should only be carried out by women. I know there are male gynaecologists as well, male doctors as well, but the woman has already gone through a rape. She does not want another man touching her private parts, touching her body, checking… even if the doctor is a good man. He will come across as bad at that point. Even if the doctor is honestly carrying out his duty, to the victim it's not going to be felt that way. In all honesty, it's not going to *ever* be felt that way. So definitely if a victim is being checked it should be done by a lady doctor. Not a lady doctor standing and watching. Because that makes it uncomfortable, I have been through that. I was standing naked and four of them were standing there watching me. This was in Medical College on the 14th of Feb.

What happened there?

You know they were kind to me, I am not saying that they were bad. But I had to stand naked with everything off my body and three doctors and a maid servant were standing there. The maid servant was the one bringing in the swab and the cotton and whatever was required for the testing.

They were male doctors?

No, no, all female, all female…no one was male in the medical college. What I am saying is it becomes uncomfortable and my test was done in a big laboratory with windows all open. If you've been to Medical College…it was not in a closed room. So you see there is no facility for cases like rape. They need to have a room with that sense of comfort…there was no counsellor as well. There was a doctor who took a statement from me. She wasn't a counsellor, she was a doctor. She asked me about you know my sexual history like in the past if I had any boyfriend and all…I said of course I had. My husband left me or I left my husband, we are not together. That doesn't mean I am dead. You know I am young. And I think I may meet somebody and if I think I may have a chance of a good marriage with that person I am going to try it. And if it doesn't work, it doesn't work. But my life doesn't stop there you know because my husband and I are not together. So why is a woman always a target for everything negative?

They just wanted to know because of my age or because of the fact that I was a mother of two...whether I had a previous history of sexual interaction. So I was on that as well and that also bla bla bla bla everywhere... Oh she has previous issues then she is used to sex...yes, it has come up, it has come up.

Sexual history is immaterial.

But all the people were talking about it. She had sex before...of course I had sex before, I am not, I am not saying I am a virgin, no way. I am not saying that. And to somebody`s answer, I have not lied over anything so why would I lie about this...yes of course I had sex. But I have not had sex-sex. I was in a relationship so for me it was more than sex. How do I explain this to people? So I just stopped talking. I thought if I don't mention anything it ends there, it ends there. But again that was made like a taboo. She had sex *before*, you know. And that's bad! She is used to having *sex* and they made that sound like that...

The pain and everything you go through and then this...I don't know what all they did to me...honestly Rajashri, I have from last year struggled, fought with my mind, fought with myself to think about this. But I cannot, you know, come to the point where I can let go...and I have spoken to my aunt about it whether I can go for hypnosis, you know. I have shouted at my father because he refused...are you seriously crazy, he said? You want to get into it? You need to move on...I said, no I need to know, it's important for me to know...and they told me, no.

They don't want me to go through with it ...they...they could see that it has affected me.

Why do you want to undergo hypnosis?

Because I *want* to know what they did to me. I know the moment, but I can't remember…not knowing what they did to me… knowing what they did to me is bad. Not knowing what they did to me is even worse. For me, I don't know about any other victim, I cannot speak for others like that but I can speak for myself and this is what I feel. And you know every time I think of it, it makes me sick to my stomach. Every time I hear people comment and when they say, especially when they say it was a deal gone bad between a lady and a client, it actually makes me want to throw up, to think how *cheap* these people are, how cheap their thinking is. It does not show who I am, it definitely shows what they are made up of. And that is absolutely nothing. Gas, in the head.

You brought this up earlier also, both the chief minister and another minister went to town commenting on the rape…

One minister said that I was thirty-seven and it was time that I was raped.

Oh, he said that?

Yes…Madan Mitra [the then transport minister]. That was the first comment he made…when she is married and separated from her husband what was she doing in a nightclub? How *dare* you question me like that? I am not sitting in a ministry post and begging money from everybody. I am working hard for it. You have no right to talk about me like that.

I don't know why they did that. They took my rape so personally. I am clueless why they would do that because at a meeting after my rape, I begged and pleaded with the chief minister, 'Ma'am if you can hear me, please help me'…I am a daughter, you are the mother of the state…*Ma Mati Manush*…(Mother, Land, People, the slogan of the Trinamul Congress) I am your daughter. One of your daughters is pleading, please help me. Please come forward. Please help me. With all that I was still commented on and I was cast aside, I was cast away like a piece of wood, just a thing thrown away. My case was politicized.

Why would they do this?

I don't know why it was politicized. Because maybe a part of my family…you know when the Left were ruling, some of my family members were CPI (M)…I think, and because of Mr Farooq Halim being a CPI (M) ex-minister`s son, I have a feeling, because I can see how everything is politicized. He was the one I called that night. And he came out of his house at 3:30 [am] to help me and he had to face the flak …why something happened then…that's why my case was politicized, I think.

My case was politicized and after Damayanti Sen [Joint Police Commissioner] was transferred [after she told the media that there was evidence that Suzette had been gang-raped, contradicting the chief minister who had commented the rape was a 'concocted' incident] my case is hanging on a string.

What is the status of your case?

Well it's…in trial and sub-judice so…and it's held *in camera* so… No, no, I don't go everyday to court because till the time they needed me to give my statement

I went with the complaint of rape, after she (Damayanti Sen) interrogated them, she confirmed rape and she confirmed gang-rape. So definitely she knows much more. You know…then whatever happened…so all the more I want to know from the *inside* what she knows. Or what anyone knows [laughs] when they were being interrogated, what does it mean…my witnesses are made hostile.

The girl [who was with Suzette the night of the incident] had to give witness, she was made hostile. She was told that I was a liar, she was told that those guys will not leave me, they will not leave her, and they will not leave me. She was told a lot of things…

Yeah, so I said to her one thing, do you believe in God? If you believe in God you will do the right thing. If you see I am a liar, then go ahead and say what you have to say. But remember you have eight sisters and God is watching. That's all. Don't listen to me, don't listen to them, don't listen to anybody. You believe in God, you are a god-fearing person, you will do what is right. I am also frightened. I live alone you can see. It's very easy to come into my house.

How many have got charge-sheeted?

Three. All five have got charge-sheeted but three are arrested and the other two are absconding. So the case is going on with the three who are arrested. Two of them were the main people.

So I say this, when you haven't committed a crime why the hell do you run so far and why would you go through the trouble of running…come out, face the law.

Have they been questioned in court?

Where? That's over. You mean cross-questioning? No, no, not yet. Even in the court room, Rajashri they make you…there is no compassion. They really have no compassion. No, I go with my dad.

Your dad is allowed?

But my dad is not allowed inside. Nobody… I am alone. There's the judge, my lawyers, their lawyers and the three accused.

The accused are present when you are giving your statement?

Yes, they are standing in the dock. Just two feet away from me, not even two feet. It's scary, very scary and they stare at me a lot when I am giving my statement and I just say a prayer and ask God to speak through me.

The public prosecutor?

Yes, she is there, she is also there. She is an elderly lady and she has a very soft tone. I have to kind of come very close to her, but she is also there and she is doing a good job. They have taken my statement and one of my witnesses…

The main witnesses. After the incident it was Mr Halim who saw me and I was relating the incident to him and the other main witness is one of my friends who, when she was leaving she saw me talking to the guy and she saw the other guy was there and she was able to identify them.

The restaurant watchman?

The watchman was outside, I didn't know that they were witnesses because Park Street police told me that there was no proof that I was even there.

Your card …you used your [credit] card?

I told them, sir…but I paid in both the places with my card. I told my dad, why don't the police just check my card…that's a salaried account card. When I was working for the IT Company in New Alipur they pay you through the bank, so they make you a salaried account…so I said all the three cards I have lost are all salaried account. So I said, ask them to go and check. You know they will get to know. Why don't they do a background check before they start to use that term…

There is no police protection for witnesses, police protection has to be there. Today, I was watching the news and a girl in UP…a minor in UP was raped on 22nd of January and she had to give a statement on 24th of this month. Her tongue was cut off. Just now on the news. So there is no protection for the girl. So protection is a very important thing, especially until her entire statement and cross questioning are not over. A witness protection programme is a must. She needs to be kept in a secure place. They need to have… they need to open an entire school because the number of rapes coming in, they need an entire school to shelter victims because if you can't do anything outside, make sure that you have a shelter home where the witness can come and be safe, and where you have a counsellor present to counsel them, to help them relate whatever happened and to come to terms with what happened and to start to get back to normalcy. Whatever the normal way, try to help them to empower themselves. After that…if there are very poor people, help them with small things.

What was the reaction of your neighbours?

My neighbours, oh my god…atrociously vicious, very, very bad considering their age, old people…an old aunty, kaku (uncle)… the year before I was raped during Christmas and New Year, I had a party where my landlord was there till 4 in the morning…but after my incident, I wasn't even allowed to come back home at 10:00 [pm] and their gates were closed. And they passed remarks like, '*Kothai theke asche, dekho dekho, dekho.*' (Where has she come from? Look, look at her.) I was being scrutinized by the building people, each guest who came to my house had remarks passed on them, remarks are passed at my daughters, my mother constantly. They picked fights with us on the smallest of things. They laugh when I pass by, they joke about it…there were about three, four complaints in Parnashree police station that I made because of the building and because I didn't have a job and couldn't afford to pay the rent, it was a very high rent, I always brought my kids up in a very good way, the best way I can, so they always used to have their own room you know, because I worked hard.

I worked in many call centres. Plus, I worked for Taj Bengal, plus I worked for Samilton Hotel and I worked for a leather company as a secretary…when I was in Delhi I was in a hair clinic for a year, Dr Sarin's Hair Clinic…then I worked as a sales girl, then when I was pregnant I used to sell T-shirts door to door, so I have gone through it all. I have given tuition, during my pregnancy when I was at home, I have taught in spoken English classes, so it's not that you know, I sat at home and did nothing…11 years!

The relationships changed? Did you try to talk to them?

They just *changed*, and no, I don't think that was necessary. Me trying to talk to them, I never talked to them before that day. They used to talk to *me*. So why would I after my incident go out to make friends? Wherever I have lived, not from now, from years back, I don't mix, I don't mix with anybody. I am very quiet by myself. We listen to music, we watch TV, in my own home but I don't have the habit of interacting like that.

It was very bad. For me it was bad but it was worse because of my daughter[s]. Then because of the fact that they knew that I lived alone, even the *darwan* [guard] used to turn around and back chat, not only to me, also to my mother. The same one in 2011, when the call centre business was running good, I used to tip him in the night because we had night duty so we came over at 1:30 [am], so he had to get up to open the gate and we would give him fifty rupees, sometimes a hundred. Christmas day, two hundred or three hundred for his little daughter, I gave all my daughter`s *baccha baccha* [children's] clothes and toys and… that same guy, Rajashri, after my incident, the way he spoke to me and my daughters…they took away our right to go up to the terrace also. Because I live on the fourth floor that is the highest, so sometimes in the evening, you know, to feel better you go out and get fresh air, so I used to go to the terrace. I go to him and ask him, '*Chaabi do.*' (Give me the key.) He'd say go here, go there and ultimately I would never get the key. My landlord [would also say,] '*Haan* you take it from the *darwan*, this is between you and the *darwan*'. When I first shifted in, when guests from the call centre, my colleagues, when they came, it was one of their birthdays so we wanted to have a small party at my place. So the party was over and they were leaving at 12:30 [am], before my incident the *darwan* wouldn't open the gate. My landlord came and he made a big *hallagulla* [scene]...how dare you talk to my tenants like this, bla bla bla...and he made a big scene. After my incident, the *same* landlord went against all he had fought for, for me, why? Coward. That's all I can say.

Friends?

A lot of friends kept away and a lot of my friends have stood by me. In fact most of those friends have come, have helped me with groceries, with money. I owe a lot to my friends. I have to pay back a lot as well. But you know what touched me the most was that they were there for me you know. They are not just friends because of friends and a friend who was with me that night has let me down even till today. She is one of the witnesses and she is hiding. And she was my childhood friend.

Is she frightened?

She is frightened. I know she is frightened. You think I am not frightened, Rajashri? I am frightened everyday I am out on the road that somebody might run me over or shoot me down. Of course I am frightened. But is fright going to help me or anyone else because either way people get injured?

No. She [this friend] did come on two occasions to this house in the month of March because since last year nothing was happening. So she thought it was all over. This was before my trial began but I didn't tell her that my trial is going to begin on the 14th of March because I didn't know myself, I was not sure of the date. The beginning of March or in the end of February, she came here. Since then I have not heard from her.

She was also one of the witnesses. She was with me from the Grill Club. She came to Tantra for five minutes and left. But she basically doesn't know anything. She didn't even know the guys over there. She just walked in, found it boring, she said I am going. Even till that part she can't... Last year I told her when she had to give a statement to the police, I explained to her. She said but why? I said you just have to say the truth, you were there with me in Grill Club, Someplace and you walked in to Someplace and in five minutes you left. You are not even part, your statement does not help me, trust me. It's not going to be any help. The fact that you corroborate my story, you were with me because other people have seen us. CCTV footage will also show that you were with me. I was trying to get her to be brave and she was very upset. Oh don't involve me in all this.... and that really hurt me, you know. That somebody I knew from the time we were young, from my school days.

And later day friends?

The other friend, also a witness, is *her* friend. So I met them that day. They both were present in court, now you can see the difference. The two people I met that day, *her* friends, they were present in court. But you are my childhood friend, you are not present. So that says a lot. I know that you are a woman, what do you think I am? Or what do you think the other witnesses? She is a girl too. She comes from a family of eight sisters. The youngest sister I think is ten or eleven, the oldest is twenty-seven. So they all are very young. She herself is twenty.

Right now you are just a witness for the prosecution?

Yes. Actually, I didn't know this but was told about it by the cop, '*Ekhon tomar case ta state lorche*' (the state is now fighting your case.) '*Sheta mane ki*?' (what does that mean?), I asked and the response was, '*Ekhon shudhu tumi witness, tomar case e*' (you are only a witness in your case). I couldn't understand, I said, 'Sir?' He said...he was laughing because he couldn't get me to understand

and then my grandmother said, 'No, the state is fighting your case, you are a witness in your *own* incident but you are a witness and the state is fighting for you.' So I said, 'But it's *my* case.' You know, tomorrow if I don't want to fight my case they can't force me. Can they? They can't.

And you have no control now?

Now I don't…there was a point last year when I…in the month of October, when I saw nothing, no news, the charge-sheet was being filed, it was not filed yet…I couldn't understand. Charges were not framed, the charge-sheet was filed, the charges were not framed. This difference I also didn't understand last year. What is the meaning of framed and charge-sheet was filed means it was filed. There is no need to be framed. Filed and not framed, you know … so these are the things that women and common people will never understand. That's why I want to come forward and say you know there are a lot of things I want to…[I want to] have a workshop where you go on telling women, making them aware, this is what is going to happen, these are the things you go through and I want to be there and in every part of the city there should be women who can assist other women. So that they don't get exploited. Groups of women, like you have your NGOs, like you have your health centres for women, like you have your *mahila samitis* [women's committees]. But you actually work, not just that they are behind the *mahila samiti* name and say, '*ami mahila samitir kaj kori*' (I work for a women's centre).

What is your experience of women's organizations?

Everybody called to offer me their support and comfort and say you know how sorry they were. There was one NGO, the name was Swayam that stuck by me…this lady, Anuradha Kapoor who I trust implicitly. From the time my case went to the media and after the arrest of the three, she gave it sometime to settle down and then she contacted me. She said I need to come and talk to you and I want to explain few things that you are going through and that you will feel and but I want to tell you that we are always there together and ever since ...when I have been down, I have cried to her, every time there is a problem in the building I called her, I called late night and she always had time for me, no matter what.

It's through her that I went for all these [job] interviews. She was shocked that you know the same response everywhere, and she said, don't worry, we will figure some way out and she always sort of...I am talking about a couple of interviews someone sent me to, I had lost my confidence completely because more, more than you know...before my interview it was the body language that spoke. So by the body language having known that I was the 'Park Street girl' [gestures], they won't keep me. So it was that bad that my confidence level went down.

I said, I am not going to any more interviews. She says, 'Why? Don't do this to yourself, you need to stop blaming yourself, Suzette. You need to ask yourself who am I and what do I want to do...', and she chalked out a whole list of these questions for me and said, 'Get up in the morning and give me these answers, you need to see a counsellor.' Till today still she says, 'Do you know how badly you need a counsellor?'

Did you?

No, I did not because I need to connect. For me, that is very important. Connect in a way where I know that the person will be able, like you, and I found that...I have been able to talk very easily with Anu (Anuradha Kapoor) and she has actually always been there. In fact, when I saw, when I went to the protest rally and I went up to her and she hugged me, she was shocked to see me but very happy to see me there. Because she has been trying to drill into my mind, you know, 'Get out there...not your fault...you are fighting it, you are a survivor...'she used to keep on telling me this and I thought, yes, yes...you know she would...and I cried to her and she is always on the phone with me, you know. Then I joined this lady, Santushree Chowdhury, and she was also kind, helped me a lot. You know, like explaining to me how important it is for a person to stand up and what they believe in. I agreed with her on most of that and she actually dragged me to the protest. So when I got to the protest and I was not wearing a veil or a dupatta, I was actually open to people who knew me, who saw me immediately that I was she, the 'Park Street victim', you know.

What can the role of women's organizations be? What help can they extend? You had a good experience with Anuradha.

She offered to help me get a job, she offered her time, she was compassionate, she was ever-ready to listen whenever I called, she made me feel she was not judging me. Every time I felt weak she was there to tell me, 'No this is not right, don't feel this way, Suzette. That you have to stop hurting yourself, you have to stop blaming yourself you *have* to stop blaming yourself, most importantly you need to get out of that, you need to move on.' So when I see women's organizations I actually come out. They should have a home for witness protection. This is very important. The witness can get hostile, the witness gets murdered, the witness gets killed, their family gets threatened you know.

So that's what they need to make it feel like a home. Not like you are going to a school and you are sitting and somebody is watching over you...that's not the way. That is not the way at all. They need to feel it is their own home, some of them need to be home, to be given shelter. That should be one of the ways to help them. Maybe to start their lives, help them with basic amenities to start their life. You know with a small amount of money, a small job to start your life; when it is required they can bring you for the procedures in the court. I think that's important. I think that's very important. Because we are unsafe, normal women are unsafe.

So you can imagine a girl who is fighting for justice. Definitely she is going to be intimidated by the party that has done this to her.

Were you ever threatened?

Many times. I was threatened, not directly but through my father. A man stopped him on the road and said we know who you are, we know who your daughter is in Bengali '*Amra jani apni kothai thaken ar apnake to khub bhalo korei chini, apni apnar meyeke ektu bolun ki paglami charge chere boshte. Ekhon khub paglami korche.*'(We know where you live and we also know you very well. Tell your daughter that she should stop behaving in such a mad manner. She is behaving very foolishly) when I revealed my identity. It was two days after I revealed my identity.[1]

How dare they? Who are they? Who gives them that *right*? Who gives them the authority to come up to my father and speak that way? They have authority from somebody. They have the power. If you don't have the power and authority you won't come to a person, you don't have the guts to say that. You can't do good, just don't do anything. '*Nijer barite boshe thako*' (Sit in your own home) like a coward. Like the coward everybody is. You can't do anything, don't even think of doing anything.

When I joined this job, you know, working for Santushree Chowdhury, she had taken me to Kamduni, a village on the outskirts of our city, where this girl was brutally raped and murdered. When I went there, this is my first experience going… I had read about Nirbhaya's [Jyoti Singh Pandey's] case. I watched the news on TV. But this was actually going to the place where the girl was raped and murdered and the body was thrown. I was speaking with the locals and my blood boiled, you know, I was like…I started to hyperventilate I started to perspire from the palms of my hands and my heart started hyperventilating fast and you know, I was saying, 'Ma'am, just let's go from there.' I couldn't imagine what that girl…seeing the place where she was raped

I couldn't get it out of my head you know, and then I got mad when I actually went to her house and saw her mother who was completely delusional and I wanted to hug her badly, Rajashri, but I didn't have the guts to do it. Ma'am of course extended a hug but then the lady moved her hand away. She was totally delusional. I don't know what she was saying, she kept repeating, *'Asche, asche, ora asche'* (they are coming, they are coming…she is coming) So I was supposed to see…and I thought, 'Oh my god, you know? It's terrible, what can I do here? What have we come to do here? We cannot give her daughter back, she saw her daughter in that state, raped open and beaten and brutalized and…'.The very thought was upsetting me so much, you know and then we left for the day. And then I went there for the second time and this was after I revealed myself. She was told I was also…

She didn't know?

No. Nobody knew. The second time I went was after I revealed my identity. Yes, and somebody told her that I was also fighting for the past fourteen months. She hadn't spoken to anyone. She first spoke to me. She asked me, 'Are you fighting as well?' in Bengali. Of course I couldn't understand that so somebody there had to translate it for me and then I spoke to her. I was telling her, 'Yes I am', and I told her how painful it is and I couldn't do anything to undo what had happened. But right now all she needed was strength. If she wanted to see or she wanted to get any justice for her daughter`s soul. I asked her husband to be with her, to help her in this because it's hard, I could see how hard it was for them both. That was all I could do. In fact, what angered me was that you can't do more than that. Nobody wants money. Nobody wants land, property or a job. They want their daughter back, can we give them back their daughter? So how do we make that up to them? We give them back justice. We give them back those people who were the cause of her daughter`s death. We punish the people.

Only on the basis of humanity, so that her soul can rest in peace. So that mother earth can stop crying out, the ground, the land [can] stop crying out. Nobody understands that. Nobody understands that and I can't make people understand.

Three or four days after the murder I first went to Kamduni, there was a protest rally for the Kamduni girl and women in general you know and the lady, Ms Chowdhury and I was like, okay fine, I will go and maybe it's my calling maybe I am supposed to do that. When I got there and I saw the solidarity not only women, but men, girls....And there was an old lady walking near me she was seventy-four years old. She was also a woman and she came with a walking stick and we walked for four hours and she walked four hours. That should count for something.

I could feel my hair standing on edge in that walk. And Anu was there, and she was shouting and she was making me shout, '*Halla bol halla bol halla bol*', ['Raise your voice!' a common rallying cry] you know, I never shouted in the beginning. I thought, no, you know I won't shout and when she came up and she kept saying, come on shout, *halla bol* and I was shouting...it made me feel so good and I was like hell with this veil and this mark...today I am going to come out as a woman. I am not here for my case. I am not here for my case at all, I am here just as a woman, like any other woman and I am going to fight. This has to end. But if we don't do it together or work in peace together this can never end. We will still be fighting to make amendments still trying to put some law in place so that it gets enforced and that you know we get help and we have been talking about this for so many years. You are an activist, you have been fighting for these clauses for how many years now? How many of these clauses have actually been amended? How many of these clauses have been enforced? We shouted, 'Law, law, law, stringent law, stricter punishment!'. What happened? We shouted shelter for women, what happened? Because it stops and dies down, dies a natural death. So we have to be consistent enough to fight for justice. We can't just fight one month and give up for six months.

When I went the second time [to Kamduni] I was more open, mainly because I had been there the first time. So the second time was bad but I was able to talk and you know I was able to…and it was couple of days after so the mother was more…I can't say… she was absolutely you know stable because she had a blank look in her eyes. There were reporters, they were clicking, clicking and clicking and she didn't bat an eyelid, she just had her eyes wide open. When I click you and use the flash you blink, she never ever blinked. So there was a blank look, and I thought that she couldn't see us…It…made me feel guilty.

Why?

Because I am *alive*. This poor girl is dead you know and she can't even fight back. She can't even tell them who raped her and there is a big controversy over that now. Because [they] don't even have the shame… to do this to that girl. She is dead, brutally, in such a brutal manner and they are fighting about it, they are lying about it and…I mean come on, where is humanity? These are acts against humanity. And then you people, instead of being sorry, instead of making, you know, giving justice to the parents so that they can get some closure, you don't allow their daughter's soul to rest in peace. You don't even allow them to rest in peace. You are torturing them, you are terrorizing them with all the comments with all the accusations for them being whatever politically… they have politicized her death can you believe it? I am alive, am fighting, am surviving, am fighting. If they politicized me I can understand that is allowed, she is dead. The least you can do give that girl justice if nothing else.

The media…it's because they…they are coming out with these [stories] you know, so…they are creating awareness…because if the media won't, then all these cases would have been hushed up and then again you see women are put [inside]....you belong in the kitchen to cook, you stay there. You are not to leave the house. That's a wrong way. For years women have showed that they are much more than what you think they are. For years down the line. So how dare you tell a woman that she is only meant for the kitchen or she is only meant for sex? I wish that they get news of many more cases so that we can extend that help.

The media coverage your case got...

That is the saddest part. Because I am educated I was able to have the opportunity to voice my feelings. There are women who want to do it but don't know how. You know, that's where women's organizations should come in. You asked me before. This is when women's organizations should come in: for the people, for the women who cannot voice their pain, to stick with them, to be for them, to stand up for them, to be there for them, to articulate in words for them because they can't do for themselves. You need to see the pain, you need to feel the pain, before you can actually talk for that person. You can't just go bla bla bla.

I grew up in a boarding school in Kolkata. It's called Pratt Memorial, in Acharya Jagadish Chandra Bose...I know my school is my heart and I was very independent as a child. Being in a boarding school they teach you how to be strong, they teach you how to be independent, so you see that was instilled in me as a child. I was always independent. I was always a fighter. I was a total rebel and not without a cause, for a cause. If any student in school had problem they came to me because boarders are known to be strong, bold, cheeky you know, so they would come to me. My classmates from the senior classes (I was in the lower classes)... Suzette you know this has happened. Can I go there....I wouldn't allow anyone to be bullied. I hated that. I hate liars. I hate, hate, hate liars. I can't deal with liars. You know we all still lie. I also lie, but I lie about if I use my sister's deodorant I will say, no I did not. Stupid things, things that don't hurt another person, you know. But I am talking about *lying* as in where you cause another person pain.

I studied till Class X and my mom and dad, they were fighting for a divorce and I didn't know that they were. So when I came home for one of my holidays my father sat me down. I am very close to my father as well. So he sat me down and he explained to me you know how he loves my mom but he needed a divorce as they were not compatible. And I couldn't understand why because I never saw them fight. I never heard them fighting or saw them fight. I knew when my mom was upset as that was the day when she stopped eating her food. Then I know, you know, my mom and dad, there is something on. But it was never verbal it was... never anything like that, it was always, you know, love and fun in my house. Music was always on and always there was fun and laughter. So I didn't understand why they needed to be separated.

How did it affect you?

Very badly because I didn't go back to school. I rebelled. Again, I became so rebellious like you know you can't tell me what to do and I just didn't go back to school.

What did you do?

I joined an evening school, I didn't go back to Pratt. I joined the evening school and when I joined the evening school it was during that time I met my husband, and when I met him I was only seventeen. I just started to live with him. I left home. I waited till I was eighteen and when I completed eighteen, I walked out. Just to show them you know, you don't have control over me, if you people are not together. I was very hurt because I had the most beautiful mother. Since that day till today she has been single. When I was 17, now I am 38, she has been single. She does not leave the house, she is what I call a 'serial killer', serial as in TV serial! She watches TV from morning to night, she works her butt off to make good meals for us too, takes care, she does everything for me and for my daughters. So I couldn't understand...

My brother was in Lucknow, La Marteniere in Lucknow in a boarding school. When he came back he stayed with my grandmother but my mother moved out and I moved out with her. My sister was in Pratt. Then three years after I left Pratt, she left too and she was put into Kalimpong, Dr Grahams. So she studied there. She studied there and came back and joined the Open School here because Dr Graham was not ...the food was not good, they were not treated well, it was not what it is supposed to be, not what they make people think it to be and now it's even worse. So you know given all that she came back.

I had my eldest daughter when I was twenty-one. I never had an abortion, never, thank God. I am a Roman Catholic. But when my mom got a divorce, I stopped going to church because I stopped believing in God. I felt he is very selfish and mean. Then I met my husband and when we separated all the more I hated God, not hated God but I felt he didn't love me enough. Why was I going through all these problems? Why me? Why do I have to face everything? I felt this way.

How old were your daughters when you divorced?

My younger daughter was two years old, my elder was three. Since then I have been on my own. On weekends, during holidays, they go to their father. They are supposed to go for the whole week but as soon as they reach, they call me that night...mamma make an excuse and take us back home tomorrow. Say *nani* [grandmother] has fever.

Does your ex-husband help at all?

No, he doesn't help me like that...sometimes he gives the children when he has money, when he doesn't, then he doesn't. But sometimes he does, he asks me now and again if I require anything and I can ask him, but he doesn't make it a point to put it in my hand you know like this is monthly *kharcha* [expense]...no. If I need, then I ask him, if he has it, he gives it. Most of the time he doesn't.

Nobody stood by me, though in church everybody respects me and I go to church. I started going to church after my incident.

Yeah, Mr Gomes (headmaster of her daughters' school), we had a difference of opinion and I always fought with him. One day, I threatened to take him to the cops, and so you know we never got along but after the incident he is like so sweet and so kind and so so supportive, it's unbelievable. In fact, Mr Brouten, the owner of the school, Mr Chicky Brouten. They've all been very, very supportive. So I must say that you know there are people, I can't remember all their names, but there are people who have been supportive of me and most importantly my lawyers who are fighting my case pro bono, I think all credit goes to them. Because it's in their hands that my life lies, it's in their hands whether or not I get justice. Yes I have a very good team of lawyers and yes, they are going to fight.

You are an Anglo-Indian... Is your community standing by you?

No, not a single person. Not a single person. And I have no regrets on that. I have no regret for that. Because I feel if nobody comes forward to help you in solidarity then they have got a lot to hide. People are afraid...you are hiding something. You might just get caught. In case you come out and somebody asks you, what do you do?

Why do you think people didn't come forward?

Scared or frightened. The very fact that police intimidate you, the very fact of the word courtroom, fighting a rape case you know? It's a shame because I never knew Anglo-Indians are looked down on because our culture is different in so many ways. When I say we are open with our children I don't mean we start drinking with our children at fourteen or thirteen. We are open with our children like I am open…I am a very strict mother, at the same time, my children can talk to me about anything. About boys, about who passed a remark to them after them, who they think is cute, who they think is not cute, they can talk to me about everything and yet I am also strict. You need to have an open relationship with your child.

I have definitely felt [this discrimination] because that's how I was looked at in the police station and they kept repeating my name: Suzette Jordan, Suzette Jordan. Why? Do I need to be a Das or Banerjee or Mukherjee for you to take me seriously? Why? I am Suzette Jordan that is what my parents named me. Right?

Definitely. I have felt this 100 per cent. 100 per cent. Anglo-Indian, nightclub, drinking – *'thik hoeche'* [serves her right]. You get me? I have felt that. Why? Anglo-Indians just because of Anglo-Indians…so? *'Bicchiri kapor poreche!'* [what shameful clothes she wore] what *bicchiri kapo*r? [bad clothes?] I had on jeans. I had on a spaghetti top and a jacket. It was winter. I am not going to roam around naked! I am not going to walk into a disco with a sari on am I? I am not going to walk into a nightclub with a *salwar* on. I am going to wear jeans. So how do you say I was dressed badly? And we are in the 21st century, everything has evolved. A rickshaw-*wala* is carrying a mobile phone. And when I wear jeans to walk into a nightclub you say that I was badly dressed! What about the four year old who got raped? How was she dressed? Or the eighteen-month-old baby after two weeks of my case who was raped in Park Street by a slum dweller? How was she dressed? What are you saying? You need to stop instead of passing comments because when they do that they give rise to much more brutality. There are so many kinds of rapists, the psychopathic ones, the friendly ones to make you feel, 'Oh my God! you are my soul mate!', who makes friends with you, like with me. Like the man who sees a girl and says, 'Hi baby, have a chocolate, have a chocolate', and takes her to the room and rapes her! Like that friendly one. Or like the Nirbhaya one, the psychopath, the perverted one. He was seventeen and so while he was committing the crime he doesn't show seventeen at all! You know this seventeen-year-old-boy shoving [an iron rod], doing whatever he did to that girl? That means he needs to be put into mental hospital, not a reformatory home, he is beyond comprehension, he is beyond reforming. He needs to be in the mental hospital and behind bars for the rest of his life.

There is nothing sane about those kinds of people, there is no sanity in them, how can you say about these people that you don't want to give them capital punishment? ...capital punishment, even I don't agree with it because they need to feel the pain they inflict on others. They need to *feel* what they made that person *feel.* Confined. You can't get out. Try doing it to somebody when you are on your own. Alone. Single-handedly and see what that woman will do to you. She will beat you to a pulp. You get her in a gang and you call yourself a man! Shame on you, then shame on society for justifying your act!

Suzette when you went to Kamduni, the family was was...completely destroyed, the young girl was dead...and people were talking about rape being the worst thing in life. What do you think? Is it the worst thing or is life much more important?

So here lies the thing, that rape is the *worst* thing. Rape is the worst thing...

Worse than death?

Well, if you die being raped, nothing could be worse. If you die because you are raped nothing could be worse. But if you live through it and you are a survivor, then God has given you a chance to fight back. Fighting…you should just know how frightful and painful it is and it's going to be right till you live and there is no cure….Until we see that the people who have done this to us are convicted. Until we don't see changes, until we don't get *respect.*

There is no such thing as going to see a counsellor. Get us all these. Justice for what these men have put us through *then* we will see a counsellor. Then there is a reason to be counselled. You see, what they have done to you, now they are punished! Then you start counselling the girl and you see the change it makes.

Why should it take so many years? Why? Why should anybody kick their life? Why should anybody not fight in the first place? The only way you can heal yourself is when you fight your fight and you get justice for it. So why should justice be delayed *all* the time? A person in Bombay, he gets a death sentence within six months to a year. And if you rape a girl, have you not ruined her for life? I am sorry I was thirty-seven when this happened to me but has this not changed my life in many ways? Definitely. It has changed my life drastically but I am not going to give them the upper hand because I am not the one to go down without a fight. I have never been. God knows that I might get killed doing it and I don't fear this you know.

Because I am too fed up. *Everyday*, there is news, there is rape of another baby, there is rape of another child, there is rape of another girl that some young girl is humiliated because she was raped. Why are we going through this? Why are our women suffering the way they are? Girls are very scared. My eldest daughter, she said, 'Mamma now I get frightened to go in the bus. I get frightened to walk down the street.' I am frightened myself. But I tell them you know…whoever comes near you, it is your right to stand and scream as loud as you can, attract as many people as you can. It's important for these people around you to know. Don't feel frightened and I think it's important that mobile phones should be allowed. Children should be allowed to take mobile phones to school and keep the mobile phone at the desk as they enter and take it back when they are leaving. I think this is important because without communication... since the mobile phone is allowed and children do carry them to school but they are not allowed to take them in, they are confiscated, but they should be allowed to. Yes they are not going to, they should not be allowed to take it to their classroom, they should put it in the desk there, and when the children are leaving they should be handed over. So from school to home you can communicate to your child because nobody gives you a guarantee that your child is safe in school or in a college or on the way to school or on the way back from the school. I think that these are the small things that need to be looked into. I may sound, you know, like I am trying to say, you know, break the law, but no, going with the present situation this is what we need to do.

One and half years have passed and you have come a long way... thousands of people are supporting you...they read about you, they have heard about you...

Yeah, that I know, I know that's what I am saying, you know.... Always, always, we looked to those people for support because those are the people who know compassion. It's a word that they used as well. They have acted on that word... I want to open a shelter now. Just like I was talking about.

I want to open a shelter especially for witness protection where the women can come to me. I want to see them, I want to bring back that smile in their life again. I know it's wishful thinking [smiles], it is a shot in the dark but that's what I want to do. I think this was my calling, I want to do it so much. Not only for women, *especially* for children.

I feel more healed after I revealed myself. Yes, after I told the world, this is me. Stop calling me the Park Street rape victim.

I was victimized, true, but I am fighting. I have a life. I have a family. I have kids, I have a mother and a father. I have an identity, you know. If this incident hadn't happened to me then I would have introduced myself to you as Suzette Jordan, very proudly. So yes, I have an identity. I am not ashamed of something somebody else did to me, to entertain themselves you know. Why should I go through life with the tag of 'Park Street rape victim' while these guys get to run around the whole world enjoying themselves and those three guys were there in jail leading a cushy life? Why should I go through all this pain everyday with that tag? I am not going to do that, no girl should be subjected to that. [I have not met many survivors] but on social networks such as 'Don't rape us', 'Stop rapes', 'Sexual Abuse: My Body Uncontrolled', 'Weight Is No Joke', all the different sites that I am on, I chat with survivors every day and most of them are my friends.

One girl just had a baby, she is a very nice girl… she has a son. The other one also had another baby, a girl…so we have been chatting you know about how life has to carry on and how you should never give up. That's what I want to show others like, you know, even if you lose, even if I lose my case, at least I did it with dignity, with respect but don't you be sad because I have lost, because the fight never ends, it continues. It's just you have to be consistent in fighting.

It angers me, you know, when we think about it, you put your whole life in this fight and then you don't see any changes and people comment, two political parties fighting childishly, contradicting each other and using women to do this. I think that's very, very naïve and that's so cheap. I mean somebody gets raped and you say, …it's a political game to malign your government. How can a person be raped to malign your government? For Christ's sake! Why would a woman do that? A woman gets brutally raped and murdered and again it becomes political.

Why would the rape and murder have anything to do with the government? You should be ashamed that this is happening under your government. You should come out. You are…she is a woman, she [Mamata Banerjee, the Chief Minister of West Bengal] herself is an emblem of woman's empowerment. As a woman among all those men, she is still fighting. So when women in your own state are fighters why do you put them down? You are a model, you are an idol, if you have the strength of what you did why can't we have the strength? We learn from you…so we are learning from you. So why do you chastise us then? Why did you criticize her? You taught her. When we voted for you to fight because you are a woman we thought we voted you for a change for the fight that we have been fighting for years. But again you swept it off under the carpet as politicizing. Why? Why does this happen? Women in power become different. When they get power, women act like men, don't you think so? Where is that woman inside? You have to make things right sometime. Otherwise nothing is right, and everything starts to fall apart, everything will crumble. Believe me it will all crumble. There are too many souls fighting, there are too many souls crying in pain. Do you think there is going to be happiness? I doubt that. I doubt that. People in pain, women in pain, children in pain…how do we know when in the outskirts one girl is raped and murdered? You think people are going to rest in peace? Not in this situation. Yes, when it's cleared, when it happens, when it's enforced, then there will be smiling faces and there will be peace and joy. I feel that. I felt like that. Otherwise things just will get worse. Nothing is going to change. I think I have spoken a lot about the government but I am so annoyed, really I mean, I don't know why they do that. It's so hurtful, no? No…they will never be happy. They can never be happy, at least not here. They can pretend, but they will always feel insecure. Do you know why? Because thousands of souls that have died will never allow you to feel secure. How can you feel secure? Women have died, lost their lives, they are being raped, murdered, tortured, having acid thrown at them, and you want to rule and be happy? You think that this is going to work?

And at the same time you worship Ma Durga? Ma Kali? How can you be such a hypocrite? You want favours from Ma, you need to respect Ma, your theme is *Ma Mati Manush*. Then where is the meaning of *Ma Mati Manush*? Lost! It got lost long ago in the scream, in the shout for help, in the souls burning, for some justice, for one conviction.

You think after Nirbhaya [the 2012 Delhi Gang-rape Case] there would have been some change…I have a problem sleeping, so I was watching news till three in the morning and I saw, it kept flashing on News Now: four-year-old girl brutally raped, her genital parts were totally mutilated, she was murdered. Can you imagine that? What man would look at this child and have a sexual desire? What man can do something to a child? Baby doesn't even know how to say A B C D…at that age, they don't know the difference between right and wrong, and you take the child and you rape the child! You need to be flogged till you die. Seriously. The situation doesn't change and my heart aches, honest to God, it aches when I think about it. When I was watching it last time also I was so upset and asked myself, God can anybody do that? Just a baby! Guria, they did the same thing to her, she could not use the toilet again. How can they do that to children? An 18-month-old baby. What do they feel? I can't understand. My brother`s daughter, she is three years old, and I look at her and I say…my God my brother`s wife is a Bengali, Mou please don't let anyone come near her. My brother`s son is twelve years old, I get worried about him because men are pigs. They are killers, please don't let him go when I see him talking too much to the boys around, looking at any elderly man…why are they talking to that old man for so long? And then he said, Suzie he is my friend. I say he is an old man, he is not your friend…go up…because I don't know what anybody has in their mind. You see I have become protective over everybody after my one incident. Protective over my daughters I have been since the day they were born. My children never sat on the train till last year when they had to go to boarding school when I tried to put them into Dr Grahams, but I brought them back after 14 days because I missed them. Then they were missing me and they were crying and I was crying and it was a very bad thing. I brought them back. I never lived without my children, not for a day! Yes, I go to the night club in a month twice, so what? I never lived without my babies ever. Not for a second. So you know those 14 days were like, I felt like years. My daughters were like, Mama, I want to smell you …it was so bad.

I am sorry this has upset you.

No, no I was thinking of that four-year-old girl, so sad. I had a bad dream, yesterday my mom woke me up. She came to me and she woke me up in the morning and I was dreaming that my younger daughter was four years old and she was lost. I can't find her. Some guys have taken her away and my mom woke me up, and I got up from sleep and said what a shitty dream I had.

They mutilated her, there is nothing I mean they…her genital parts are so badly hurt, I mean I saw in the news they mutilated her. How could they? A year old…must have been that…I mean think about it…I…I can't, it hurts…[cries] No, I don't do this often, just that nothing changes, you know.

It will change. Has to change. You have to open your eyes to see the change.

People are ready to exploit and they are ready to use you, that's more upsetting, you know. They let you think, women's organizations. Women's organizations also kind of want to get chances like this so, instead of helping they want to grab names for themselves, or for their NGOs. This is the worst part. We women also do not have compassion, we are as bad as the rapists. Because after the entire ordeal it's the healing part. Where you and I, women like us, come forward to help and we should actually help not by just words and not by just gaining fame, but by actually coming forward to help, you know. Being there for the person, this four-year-old girl…you can't give up on her mom…that's what I felt in Kamduni, you know. She didn't even, her eyelids didn't even blink and I am sitting in front of her and I am looking at her face. She got a blank look on her face and I don't want to talk to her also, I just gave up and ran away. Even the second time. But I spoke to her because I was there. I spoke to her but it's so difficult, and I didn't know how to talk in Bengali when I…I can talk in Bengali but when I stay in such a situation words don't come to my mind you know, so I had to take the help of Moushumi from Akash Bangla, asking for a word like soul and patience… I forgot the Bengali word…*dhoirjo* (patience)…so things are like that, you know. So they don't know…you can't return their daughter back. You really can't. And it's sad that it becomes such a political thing, they were termed Maoist. They were termed CPM [Communist Party of India-Marxist]…these are terms I don't get… it means if you are a CPM person then don't get in. If you are TMC [Trinamool Congress] then you get raped. So this again you know, I don't understand. She doesn't deserve to be where she is. This lady doesn't deserve to govern our state.

All of us want to see a change. But damn it, we have been fighting for so many years, you have been fighting as a woman activist so you know. I am fighting on my own because of my case. So now we should think the situation has got so bad, our fight should be stronger. I mean it should carry on and we should make sure that the change comes, and not sit back. That's the thing, you know, be consistent in our fight.

Interviewed by Rajashri Dasgupta
in Kolkata
Transcribed by Debolina Chakraborty

NOTE

1. On June 19, 2013, one year and four months after she had been gang-raped, Suzette Jordan revealed her identity.

12

Understanding Consent

Interview with Christine Marrewa Karwoski

URVASHI BUTALIA

There has been a great deal of talk about sexual violence in the media recently. Often, the spotlight is shone on a particular case when it happens; sometimes, if the case goes to court, the legal proceedings are followed through to their conclusion. But what happens to the survivor of sexual violence? Whether or not the law provides justice, what are the demons survivors live with, how do they put their lives back together again, how do they begin the process of healing themselves? What do they have to say when they feel justice has not been served? These are questions that are seldom asked or addressed.

On July 30, 2016, a Special Fast Track Court in Delhi convicted theatre personality Mahmood Farooqui of rape. He was sentenced to rigorous imprisonment for seven years and ordered to pay a fine of Rs 50,000. The complaint of rape by a US Fulbright scholar doing doctoral research in India had been registered in a First Information Report (FIR) in June 2015. Farooqui went on appeal and in September 2017, the Delhi High Court overturned the judgment of the trial court and acquitted him. The High Court judgement[1] stated, 'It remains in doubt as to whether such an incident, as has been narrated by the prosecutrix, took place and if at all it had taken place, it was without the will/consent of the prosecutrix, and if it was without the consent of the prosecutrix, whether the appellant could discern/understand the same.'

The court stated, 'Instances of woman behaviour are not unknown that a feeble "no" may mean a "yes". If the parties are strangers, the same theory may not be applied... But same would not be the situation when parties are known to each other, are persons of letters and are intellectually/academically proficient, and if, in the past, there have been physical contacts. In such cases, it would be really difficult to decipher whether little or no resistance and a feeble "no", was actually a denial of consent.'

In January 2018, the Supreme Court dismissed the plea against Farooqui's acquittal. 'We will not interfere with the High Court verdict,' the bench said, 'It is a well-decided judgment.'

In the interview below, Urvashi Butalia speaks to the survivor in the case, Christine Marrewa Karwoski, who has chosen to make her identity public. 'I do not want to feel like I am in hiding because of what someone else did to me. I am proud of what I did to regain control of my life again, no matter how difficult it was. To keep my name hidden makes me feel like *I* have something to be ashamed of and if I am certain of anything it is that none of the shame is mine.' (This interview first appeared in Scroll and is reproduced here with permission.)

It's been some time now since you took a decision to file a case against someone who was a friend and a sort of mentor to you. It could not have been easy to take that decision – there is so much that is involved there. Could you talk a little about what it was that led to your coming back to India and taking a step which must have also made you so vulnerable. I am trying to understand, for the many women who go through the sort of experience you've had, what it takes in terms of courage, what the costs are, what the person has to deal with.

The decision to press charges against a person is never a onetime event. For me, it was a decision that I had to make repeatedly day after day as pressure to drop the charges surrounded me – some of it even coming from well-meaning people attempting to protect me from further pain. It was a decision that I questioned daily because I was never quite sure if I would have the strength to survive the process. Reliving your trauma time and again to strangers, a necessary requirement of partaking in the judicial system, is – in a way – beyond explanation. It is hard and it is heart-breaking. But in the way in which it breaks you apart, the act of being heard, of having a voice also made me grateful. It allowed me to have hope that I could put myself back together again. It reminded me that I am still alive and able to fight for myself. Of course, I hadn't anticipated being socially ostracized by groups of people I had considered friends, both in India and America, that was perhaps the most difficult. What led me to return to India to press charges against Mahmood Farooqui in the beginning was, I suppose, desperation. I was desperate to find my old self again. I had become a ghost of the person I was before my assault, atrophied in both body and mind, and no matter how much my family tried to love me into wellbeing, it wasn't enough. I needed to tell the truth. I needed to be heard. I needed to regain a feeling of control again in my life. What had been done to me was wrong in so many ways and it had broken me. When I finally came to the realization that I had to have an active role in my recovery, the only way I ever envisioned that, for myself, was through the courts. I couldn't look at the faces of my nieces anymore and see how I had deteriorated in their eyes. I wasn't the brave aunt they once knew, but a depressed child that they felt the need to comfort, and that wasn't right. I was supposed to be the adult. I was supposed to be the one who was strong and fixed things. In my mind I had no choice but to return to India and press charges. For me it was not only the responsible thing to do, but the only thing that could possibly heal me.

What are the consequences for you, now, of having to live with the results of the judgment? You must be having to deal with so much, the sense of hurt and betrayal, not only by a man you liked and had affection for, but by a system in which you put your faith, and also a country that you chose to come to, worked in and clearly empathized with. So, the betrayal is on many fronts. How do women deal with such complex emotions, how did you deal with it?

In retrospect, I was obviously naive about the potential fallout of coming forward. I really didn't consider the power dynamics involved in my filing charges. I only saw it as something that needed to be done. Before I had filed, I had full support from many people that I considered friends in India and America who tried to help me through my trauma, but after I filed the FIR reality set in. No one wanted to be associated with a case in which I had accused such a highly regarded and professionally accomplished man of raping me. I understand now how many people were concerned about their own careers or their family name, but at that time, to me, it didn't matter, I felt completely betrayed. I am still struck by the selective silences of people who I had considered friends and years later, I am still crushed by just how much I lost in the past three years. Here were people that I had known, been friends with, and worked with for years suddenly turning away from me at a time when I needed support more than anything else. I oscillated between extreme anger and depression. At times I still do. During that time – and at this time as well – I've found solace in the few people who surrounded me with their protection, love, and truthfulness. These people spoke up for me in both the courts and otherwise. They picked me up when I didn't want to live anymore. I am fiercely protective of the women and men in India who took me in and ensured my survival. These days I continue to focus on the people who supported me. They were not the people I had planned on leaning on, but they are the gorgeous souls that I got. Today I focus on the fact that Mahmood Farooqui was indeed found guilty in the lower court and when I had testified I was found to be a sterling witness. The truth was heard and I was believed. Of course, the intellectual gymnastics it took for the High Court to find him innocent, disgusts me. The idea of a 'feeble no' enrages me and I am deeply concerned about how this will impact people in the future. But for now, I am focused on returning to my academic work, learning how to trust again, and on forgiveness. Most importantly I try to remember – both in my own healing and in the courts – that the battle for justice is a marathon not a sprint.

A sort of extended question coming up from the first one. What was it that decided you to take recourse to the law? I ask this because it's a difficult system to put your faith in, especially in another country. And it can have serious and long-term consequences. Could there have been any other way of dealing with this? Once again by this I am not questioning your decision at all, but for a lot of women, the law is not an option they are willing to consider, it needs both courage and strength.

I never considered anything but the law. Of course, I didn't realise exactly what I was getting involved in, but even today I would still make the same decision. The legal system is far from perfect and it has at this point failed me, but this, I suppose, is also part of the process. For attitudes to change, for laws to be refined, people need to keep standing up for justice. Unfortunately, that means that someone has to do the heavy lifting. For me, this brought both incredible pain as well as a return of my inner strength. I envision it something like the way we build muscle. In order to grow, first our muscles must tear from lifting the things that weigh us down. It is not something that I recommend for everyone, but for me, it healed me and allowed me to feel my own power again. At times it also came dangerously close to completely destroying me. There has never been a time when I haven't wished that more people would have lent a helping hand. God knows, it does not take a person of 'letters' to understand why many people do not want to come forward or trust the legal system to protect their rights.

For many people court is not a viable option and I support them finding a way to heal themselves outside of the legal system as well. Survivors of sexual assault have already had their power taken away from them. They deserve the right to make critical choices and be supported in the ways in which they choose to heal from atrocities committed against them.

I'd like to ask you about more current developments where you sometimes find yourself a spectator in a different sort of discourse, where your violation becomes a kind of route to political point scoring, and often an occasion for attacks on women who stood by you. What do you feel about this? It's one thing to be betrayed by an indifferent and patriarchal system, but when the discomfort stretches to people on the same side of the fence as you, it must be even more difficult.

As I come out more publicly, something I hadn't done over the past three years, I have found it both interesting, and at times infuriating, the manner in which the news of my violation is invoked for political purposes. While I respect a person's right to come forward and find justice in any way that they can, I do have serious concerns about crowdsourcing shame. It is not that I think that everyone must go through due process –we know how difficult and flawed that is – but I take issue with accusations made against individuals where no details are given to the accused concerning the allegations made against them. I feel that that is not only irresponsible, but ethically wrong. I realize my opinion will not be popular with a large group of women who will perhaps call me old fashioned, women who are looking for other ways to achieve the justice they deserve. However, I don't think there is anything fashionable about ethics. This, to me, is not a passing fad. As far as the verbal attacks that have been made against the women who stood by me, as I have already said I am fiercely protective of these women. I know first-hand the love and dedication they have for their work and the people they support. I find it both enraging and laughable when people have said to me that not everyone can afford a lawyer like I have had. This is true, except for the fact that Vrinda Grover has been working on my case pro-bono for over two years. I am frankly amazed and devastated that women who I think would be supportive of me and my experiences would shut me down and tell me to stop talking when I speak out in support of people like [activist] Kavita Krishnan. To be silenced by people who I would imagine would be sympathetic to my story is traumatizing. I cannot comprehend how my story can be invoked in the third person to prove a political point while my first person narrative can be shut down by the same groups of women.

One of the things I have been wanting to ask you is this: right from the start you spoke the truth, you offered the police information, truthful information, about that day that need not have been told. In its acquittal of Mahmood Farooqui, the court rejected his defence that nothing had happened that day for various reasons. But at the same time, the court used information that they had access to because it was information you gave, information that was truthful and that was more than you needed to say, and this very information was used to make conclusions that went against you. I want to go to the deeper question of truth-telling. It can't have been easy for you to tell the police what you did, did you at any time think it may turn against you? Why were you so truthful? Is this a question that has troubled you since? I mean many women would have instinctively filtered out this kind of information, but you did not.

Yes, some of the things I said that happened that night were used against me, but I do not regret telling the truth. What I mourn for is India's judicial system which has callously thrown women's bodily autonomy into the fire with its acquittal of Mahmood Farooqui. Of course, I feel let down that the court used information that I had disclosed against me, to undermine my statement, disbelieve my refusal. Clearly the court lacks the ability to grapple with the truth, the *whole* truth about being raped by a "friend". The message the Court has sent out not only to me, but to all women is that the lived experience of rape by a man known to them cannot fit into their imagination of rape. This is not only tragic but ironic. It is striking that the narrative often spun around rape cases is that women lie and exaggerate. It is shameful.

Yes, it was incredibly difficult to tell the police, and the Court but I knew what had happened wasn't consensual. I knew it wasn't my fault. I also narrated to the police and the Court that I repeatedly said no to Mahmood Farooqui's advances, but somehow that was omitted in the High Court judgment. I had no reason to lie or omit anything, because I had never consented to any type of sexual relations with him. He, against my protestations, had crossed a boundary that I had firmly articulated. I will in no way own the violations of this man or the misogynistic judicial opinion which acquitted him.

You must have thought a great deal about choosing to go to the law, I know you have worried about how this case may negatively impact Indian women – you said that on the phone. I am wondering if you can speak about how, in light of what is happening across the world, the #MeToo revelations [about sexual violence in the US academia], the [Harvey] Weinstein revelations [about sexual assault in the American film industry] and so on, do you now feel about the path you took.

I go back and forth on this daily. It's difficult to not feel like my case may have hurt other women. Had I known that such a troubling and absurd judgement (the 'feeble no') was even possible, I may have been deterred from taking the judicial route. Then again, I may not have. I don't know. At that time, I was focused on survival. I was focused on my own healing. I wanted justice. Although the #MeToo movement has helped many women begin a conversation about sexual violence and harassment, the circumstances surrounding my case were historically and emotionally different. I still want to believe in the Indian judicial system and I think it was the best route for me to take in order to regain my sense of self. At this point though all I can do is look forward and keep fighting against the High Court's judgement, keep rallying around and listening to other survivors, and continuing to speak out so that maybe my voice will help other women raise their own.

NOTE

1. *Mahmood Farooqui v. State (Government of NCT of Delhi)*, Crl.A.944/2016, delivered on September 25, 2017.

About the Editors and Contributors

Temsula Ao is a poet, short story writer and ethnographer. She is a retired Professor of English in North-Eastern Hill University. She was awarded the Padma Shri in 2007 and the Sahitya Akademi award in 2013. Her books include *These Hills Called Home* and *Once Upon a Life* (both published by Zubaan).

Divya Arya is an award-winning correspondent with the BBC, based in India, reporting for its TV, radio and websites in English and Hindi. She has focused her journalism on exploring human rights issues with specific attention to gender. Divya won the Laadli Media and Advertising Award for Gender Sensitivity 2014-15 for her radio feature on 'Why motherhood makes Indian women quit their jobs'. She was part of the Indian government's National Consultation on Women and Media, an exercise aimed at formulating the government's National Policy for Women, released in 2016. Divya was a Knight Wallace Fellow at the University of Michigan (2014-15).

Urvashi Butalia is the director and founder of Zubaan, and the author and editor of numerous books, including *The Other Side of Silence: Voices from the Partition of India* (1998) and *Partition: The Long Shadow* (2015). She has co-edited *Women and the Hindu Right: A Collection of Essays* and *In Other Words: New Writing by Women in India*. She has been active in the women's and civil rights movements in India, and writes on issues relating to women, media, and communalism. She is the recipient of the French Chevalier des Artes et des Lettres, the Nikkei Asia Prize, the Goethe Medal, and the Padma Shri from the Indian government.

Uma Chakravarti is a feminist historian who taught at Miranda House College for Women, University of Delhi from 1966 to 1998. She writes on Buddhism, early Indian history, the nineteenth century and on contemporary issues. Among her many publications are: *Social Dimensions of Early Buddhism* (1987); *Rewriting History: The Life and Times of Pandita Ramabai* (Zubaan, 1998) and *Gendering Caste Through a Feminist Lens* (2002). She is co-author of *Delhi Riots: Three Days in the Life of a Nation* (1987) and has edited *Shadow Lives: Writings on Widowhood* (Zubaan, 2006); *From Myths to Markets: Essays on Gender* (1999) and *Faultlines of History: The India Papers Volume II* (Zubaan, 2016). She has a close involvement with the women's movement in India as well as the movement for democratic rights and has been part of many fact-finding teams to investigate human rights violations, communal riots and state repression. She was a member of the International Tribunal on Justice for Gujarat in 2002 which reported on the experiences of survivors of the Gujarat riots. She has also visited and reported on Kashmir and on a range of other political conflicts in India. As part of the Women Against Sexual Violence and State Repression (WSS) she has been involved in a number of investigations in other theatres of conflict in India.

Rajashri Dasgupta is an independent journalist based in Kolkata, specialising in issues related to gender, health, human rights and social movements. She has been working as a journalist for more than 25 years and started her career in *Business Standard* before she moved to political and social issues as a senior editor at *The Telegraph*. She was awarded the Panos Fellowship and exposed the unethical drug trials with quinacrine to sterilise women in West Bengal. She has contributed articles in edited volumes on health, women and violence, and co-authored a book, *Our Pictures, Our Words: A Visual Journey Through the Women's Movement* (Zubaan 2011). She is on the editorial board of *Himal Southasian.* She is involved in peace and women's rights movements, and is on the board of several organizations working for social change.

Padma Bhate-Deosthali is an independent researcher and trainer working on gender, health and human rights. Her research interests lie at the intersection of health services and gender. She has worked on the standards of care in the private health sector and its unregulated growth; the integration of gender in medical education; women's work and health; and violence and women's health. Padma was a member of the World Health Organization's Guideline Development Group for policy and clinical practice guidelines for responding to violence against women. She was also a part of the committee for drafting the 'Guidelines and Protocols for Medico-legal Care for Victims/Survivors of Sexual Violence', 2014 under the Ministry of Health and Family Welfare. She coordinated the setting up of Dilaasa, the first public hospital-based crisis centre in India. Her doctoral work looks at gendered patterns of burn injuries and responses of hospitals to the same. She has co-authored two essays, 'Responding to Sexual Violence', and 'Addressing Domestic Violence within Healthcare Settings', that have been published in the *Economic and Political Weekly.*

Neha Dixit is an independent journalist based in New Delhi. She covers politics, gender and social justice in South Asia. She has worked with multiple mediums and reported for *Al Jazeera, The New York Times, Smithsonian, Caravan, Outlook* and others. The Press Institute of India (PII), Chennai and the International

Committee of the Red Cross (ICRC) have awarded her the PII-ICRC Award for Best Article on a Humanitarian Subject 2015. Neha has also won the Kurt Schork Award in International Journalism 2014, the Trust Women Honorary Journalist Award given by the Thomson Reuters Foundation, and the second prize, Lorenzo Natali Prize for Journalism, 2011, Asia-Pacific Region among others. She is a contributor to the UNESCO Casebook of Investigative Journalism 2011.

Bani Gill is a PhD Fellow at the Department of Cross-Cultural and Regional Studies, University of Copenhagen, Denmark. Her doctoral work explores contemporary migration from the African continent to India for purposes for business, education, medical tourism, as also for refuge and asylum. Bani holds a master's degree in Modern History from Jawaharlal Nehru University, Delhi and is also a graduate of the Erasmus Mundus European Master in Migration and Intercultural Relations. She is currently on the Executive Committee of the Emerging Scholars and Practitioners on Migration Issues (ESPMI) Network, and has previously worked as Research Associate with the South Asia Forum for Human Rights, India and with the Refugee Law Project, Uganda.

Vrinda Grover is a human rights lawyer and former Executive Director of MARG, New Delhi. She handles cases related to human rights issues across the country. Focused on the impunity of the state in relation to human rights violations, her research and writing inquires into the role of law in the subordination of women; the failure of the criminal justice system during communal and targeted violence; the effect of 'security' laws on human rights; rights of undocumented workers; and the challenges confronting internally displaced persons. She examines impunity for enforced disappearances and torture in conflict situations.

In her book, *Kandhamal: Introspection of Initiative for Justice 2007–2015*, published in 2017, she documented the reaction of the state to victims of communal violence in the small town of Kandhamal, Odisha, with her co-author Saumya Uma. Vrinda was on TIME's 2013 list of the 100 most influential people in the world.

Suzette Jordan was a prominent women's rights activist and rape survivor from Kolkata, who was reductively labelled as the 'Park Street rape victim' in the media coverage of her case. She waived her right to anonymity in 2013 to further her work as an anti-rape campaigner and embraced the public image of a rape survivor who refused to give in to the discourse of rape being 'a fate worse than death'. She briefly worked as a counsellor for a helpline for victims of sexual and domestic violence and spoke up against the humiliation and discrimination that rape survivors face. Her work as an activist contributed significantly to the reconstruction of the image of the 'pure' victim. Suzette passed away in 2015, mere months before her years of activism and campaigning led to the conviction of three of her rapists in the June of 2016.

Christine Marrewa Karwoski, a graduate of Columbia University in the city of New York, is a cultural and religious historian of South Asia who focuses on the confluence of language, print, and politics in North Indian religions over the longue durée. Her current research focuses on communal identity formation and the literature of the Nath yogis of Northern India from the 17th through the 20th centuries. Currently she holds the position of ASIANetwork-Luce Postdoctoral Teaching Fellow in South and Southeast Asian Studies at Bowdoin College and is a doting aunt to seven amazing children.

Laxmi Murthy is Contributing Editor with *Himal Southasian*, the region's only political review magazine. She also heads the

Hri Institute for Southasian Research and Exchange, a unit of the South Asia Trust, Kathmandu. She is deputy coordinator of the Sexual Violence and Impunity Project at Zubaan. She has authored *Four Years of the Ceasefire Agreement between the Government of India and the National Socialist Council of Nagalim: Promises and Pitfalls*, with Ram Narayan Kumar. She is co-author, with Rajashri Dasgupta, of *Our Pictures, Our Words: A Visual Journey Through the Women's Movement* (Zubaan, 2011). She has co-edited, with Meena Seshu, *The Business of Sex* (Zubaan, 2013) and with Mitu Varma, *Garrisoned Minds: Women and Armed Conflict in South Asia* (2016).

Farah Naqvi is a feminist activist and author of two books: *Waves in the Hinterland: The Journey of a Newspaper*, published by Zubaan in 2009, that follows the tale of small-town journalism done by the dedicated reporters of *Khabar Lahariya*, an eight-page newspaper published every fortnight since 2002 from Uttar Pradesh's Chitrakoot district; and *Working with Muslims: Beyond Burqa and Triple Talaq: Stories of Development and Everyday Citizenship in India*, published in 2017. Her articles and essays for publications like *Scroll*, *Outlook* and many others, focus on the intersection of gender, religion, and caste in rural India. Her work for nearly three decades—from villages to public policy spaces—has focused on justice, development and freedom from violence, for India's perpetual un-equals: women, Muslims, and dalits.

Kavita Panjabi is Professor of Comparative Literature and Co-ordinator of the Centre for Studies in Latin American Literatures and Cultures at Jadavpur University, Kolkata. She has been an activist in the Indian women's movement and the Pakistan-India People's Forum for Peace and Democracy for over two decades. Concerns relating to violence against women, the continuing impact of the Partition, and the violence of political borders underline her work. Her book *Unclaimed Harvest: An Oral History of the Tebhaga Women's Movement* was published by Zubaan in 2017. She has edited *Women Contesting Culture: Changing Frames of Gender Politics in India*, 2012 (jointly); *Poetics and Politics of Sufism and Bhakti in South Asia: Love, Loss and Liberation*, 2011; and *Cartographies of Affect: Across Borders in South Asia and the Americas*, 2011 (jointly). She is also currently editor of the *Jadavpur Journal of Comparative Literature.* Her 'partition diary' *Old Maps and New: Legacies of the Partition,* 2005, evolved in the context of academic interactions, peace activism and family history across the borders. In 2002 she jointly compiled *The Next Generation: In the Wake of the Genocide: A Report on the Impact of the Gujarat Pogrom on Children and the Young.*

Jagadeesh Narayan Reddy is a Professor of Forensic Medicine at the Vydehi Institute of Medical Sciences, Bangalore. He is a member of the World Health Organization's Guideline Development Group that is responsible for developing policy and clinical practice guidelines for responding to violence against women. With an interest in approaching the medico-legal field through a gendered lens, his work has been focused on developing policy for clinical practise in the context of violence against women. He is regularly invited as guest faculty at various conferences and workshops across India. His research work has been published in the *Indian Journal of Medical Ethics*, the *Indian Journal of Forensic Medicine & Toxicology*, *Journal of Karnataka Medico-Legal Society*, and in the *Economic and Political Weekly.* Dr. Reddy is also a consultant at Centre for Enquiry into Health and Allied Themes (CEHAT).

Sangeeta Rege is currently the Coordinator of Centre for Enquiry into Health and Allied Themes (CEHAT). Focusing on training, research and advocacy on issues that lie at the intersection of violence against women and healthcare, her work involves leading initiatives that reform the response that the healthcare system has to survivors of violence; and the integration of gender in medical education. She was at the forefront of CEHAT's public interest lititgation on advocating for gender-sensitive healthcare for survivors of sexual assault. Sangeeta has written papers and manuals pertaining to violence against women and healthcare, and has co-authored, 'Responding to Sexual Violence' with Padma Deosthali and Jagadeesh Reddy that was published in the *Economic and Political Weekly*.

Meena Saraswathi Seshu is the General Secretary of SANGRAM (Sampada Gramin Mahila Sanstha), an organization that works on the rights of sex workers and people living with HIV/AIDS, based in Sangli, Maharashtra. In 1996, this work broadened into the organization of a collective of women in sex work, VAMP (Veshya Anyay Mukti Parishad). SANGRAM's Centre for Advocacy on Stigma and Marginalisation (CASAM) advocates for the reduction of stigma, violence and harassment of marginalized communities, especially those who have challenged dominant norms. She has more than a decade's experience with global movements addressing violence against women and sex workers' rights. She has co-edited, with Laxmi Murthy, *The Business of Sex* (Zubaan, 2013). In 2002, Meena was awarded the Human Rights Defender Award from Human Rights Watch.

Navsharan Singh is a feminist researcher and is associated with democratic rights and women's movements in India. With Patrick Hoenig, she has co-edited *Landscapes of Fear: Understanding Impunity in India* (Zubaan, 2014). She also shares a close association with the people's theatre movement in Punjab. She is currently with the International Development Research Center, based in their New Delhi office.

Shobna Sonpar is a clinical psychologist and psychotherapist in private practice in New Delhi. She has a Doctorat in Clinical Psychology from the National Institute of Mental Health and Neurosciences in Bangalore, and has worked as Student Counsellor at IIT Delhi and as a lecturer in clinical psychology in Nepal. Apart from clinical and professional work, she engages in research and consultancy that brings insights from the discipline of psychology to bear on topics that are of contemporary social relevance. These have included gender, psychosocial development indicators, psychosocial support and trauma in the context of armed conflict, and social and political violence. Shobna's book on the mental health of Kashmiri millitants, *Violent Activism: A Psychological Study of Ex-Militants in Jammu and Kashmir*, was published by the Aman Public Charitable Trust in 2007.

People Involved in the Project

Advisors

Amena Mohsin
Hameeda Hossain
Kishali Pinto Jayawardena
Kumari Jayawardena
Mandira Sharma
Nighat Said Khan
Saba Gul Khattak
Sahba Husain
Sharmila Rege
Uma Chakravarti

Country Groups and Coordinators

Bangladesh: Ain o Salish Kendra
Amena Mohsin
Hameeda Hossain

India: Zubaan
Ishani Butalia
Laxmi Murthy
Meghna Singh
Satish Sharma
Shweta Vachani
Urvashi Butalia

Nepal: Advocacy Forum
Mandira Sharma

Pakistan: Simorgh
Hira Azmat
Neelam Hussain
Zahaid Rehman

Sri Lanka
Priya Thangarajah
S. Sumathy

Researchers and Writers

Afiya Zia
Amena Mohsin
Anar
Bani Gill
Bina D'Costa
Bishnu Maya Bhusal
Chulani Kodikara
Dhiraj Pokhrel
Dina Siddiqi
Divya Arya
Dolly Kikon
Essar Batool
Farzana Haniffa
Faustina Pereira
Gazala Peer
Guneet Ahuja
Hameeda Hossain
Hooria Hayat Khan
Huma Qurban Fouladi

Iftikhar Firdous
Ishita Dutta
Ifrah Butt
Jayshree P. Mangubhai
Jagadeesh Narayan Reddy
Jeannine Guthrie
Kabita Chakma
Kavita Panjabi
Kirsty Anantharajah
Kishali Pinto Jayawardena
Laxmi Murthy
Maliha Zia Lari
Mallika Aryal
Mandira Sharma
Meena Saraswathi Seshu
Meghna Guhathakurta
Munaza Rashid
Natasha Rather
Nazish Brohi
Neelam Hussain
Neha Dixit
Noreen Naseer
Padma-Bhate Deosthali
Parijata Bhardwaj
Pranika Koyu
Pratiksha Baxi
Priya Thangarajah
Rajashri Dasgupta
Reshma Thapa
Rohini Mohan
Roshmi Goswami
Rubina Saigol
S. Sumathy

Sahar Bandial
Sahba Husain
Samreena Mushtaq
Sanjay Barbora
Sarah Zaman
Sarala Emmanuel
Seira Tamang
Shahidul Alam
Shobna Sonpar
Surabhi Pudasaini
Temsula Ao
Uma Chakravarti
Uzma Falak
V. Geetha
Zainab Z. Malik

Zubaan Team

Ishani Butalia
Laxmi Murthy
Meghna Singh
Satish Sharma
Shweta Vachani
Urvashi Butalia

IDRC

Navsharan Singh